Between the Pen and the Rifle

Dilemmas of the Revolutionary Intellectual in Latin America

Claudia Gilman

Translated by **Rebecca Wolpin**

Foreword by **Gonzalo Aguilar**

Latin American Intellectual History Series
LASA Press and Prismas Ediciones
www.lasapress.org / www.historiaintelectual.com.ar
lasa@lasaweb.org / centrohistoriaintelectual@gmail.com

Original version in Spanish published by Siglo XXI (Argentina) in 2003 and reedited in 2012.

Centro de Historia Intelectual has received support for this initiative from the Open Society Foundations.

Cover design: Estudio Entre
Cover image: © Asela Pérez, 1970
Print version typesetting: Lara Melamet
Digital versions typesetting: Estudio Ebook
Copy editor: Melina Kervandjian
Bibliographic editing: Eleonora Centelles

ISBN (Paperback b&w version): 978-1-951634-58-2
ISBN (PDF): 978-1-951634-59-9
ISBN (EPUB): 978-1-951634-60-5
ISBN (Kindle): 978-1-951634-61-2
DOI: https://doi.org/10.25154/book17

Suggested citation:
Gilman, Claudia. 2025. *Between the Pen and the Rifle: Dilemmas of the Revolutionary Intellectual in Latin America.* Pittsburgh/Buenos Aires: LASA Press and Prismas Ediciones. DOI: https://doi.org/10.25154/book17. License: CC BY-NC 4.0.

To read the free, open-access version of this book online, visit https://doi.org/10.25154/book17 or scan this QR code with your mobile device:

About the Latin American Intellectual History Series

The Latin American Intellectual History Series is a joint initiative of LASA Press and Prismas Ediciones (Centro de Historia Intelectual, Universidad Nacional de Quilmes). The series is part of the existing LASA Press collection, In Translation: Key Books in Latin American Studies, with a more specific objective: the translation into English of works that are significant to the field of Latin American intellectual history.

In alignment with the long-standing tradition of the Centro de Historia Intelectual, the series defines this field in a very broad way, as the historical study of the symbolic dimension of social life. This is an inclusive definition of various traditions, welcoming diverse perspectives, from conceptual history to the history of ideas, from the sociology of intellectuals to cultural history, among many others. The scope includes ideas viewed as acts of discourse, ideological languages, and works of thought and of artistic expression, examining how these elements are woven into the social fabric, tracking the trajectories of intellectuals and the institutions they both inhabit and create. The approach balances the intrinsic meaning of a work with its materiality—the textual or physical formats through which ideas are produced and circulated. It may also include the study of more diffuse cultural dimensions, such as social imaginaries, collective representations, and urban cultures.

The series selects books already regarded as foundational for their contributions to understanding the cultural life of the continent, alongside innovative new works that challenge and renew the methodologies of intellectual history.

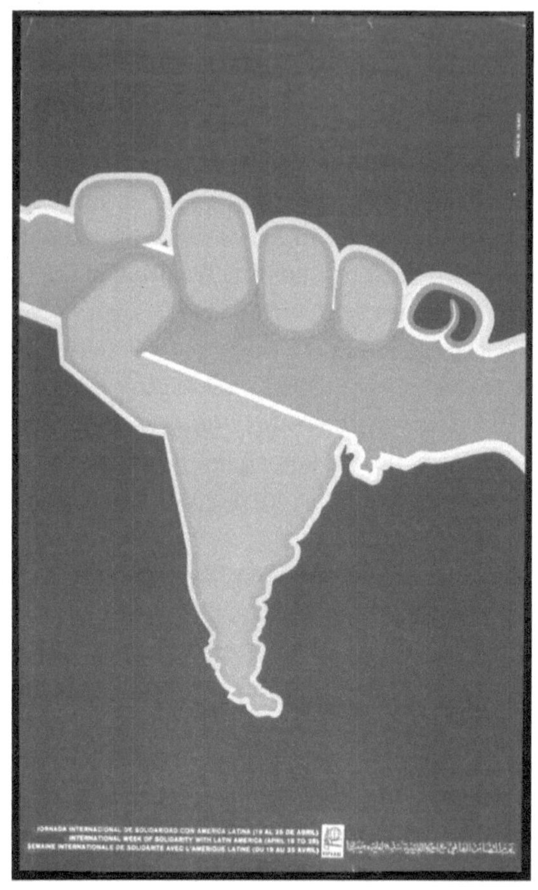

Asela Pérez (Cuban, born 1934), *International Week of Solidarity with Latin America*, poster, 21 x 13 in. (53 x 33 cm), published by the Organization of Solidarity with the Peoples of Asia, Africa, and Latin America (OSPAAL), Havana, 1970.

This book is based on a doctoral thesis defended in 1999. The 2001 crisis in Argentina postponed its publication until 2003. It was republished with minimal changes and a postface in 2012. The French translation of that edition was printed in 2018. This English-language edition, except for a few paragraphs, retains the 2012 postface. But beyond these details, it remains the same book.

Table of Contents

Foreword to the English Edition

Gonzalo Aguilar

No period in Latin American history has been studied as extensively as the 1960s. Essays, exhibitions, academic papers, conferences, books, and films attest to this. I would even venture to say that in everyday life and café conversations, the 1960s are the decade that most often comes up when speaking about the past, even though the period is perceived as increasingly distant and the generations that lived through it are dwindling. Amid this proliferation of discourse—by no means free of mythmaking—*Between the Pen and the Rifle* by Claudia Gilman emerges as a singular work: panoramic yet exhaustive, intelligent while also engaging, and as accessible as it is sophisticated. The author takes the bull by the horns and traverses the period through the "dilemmas" (as specified in the subtitle) faced by intellectuals during the 1960s.

Even with the anachronistic irony of the title (pen instead of typewriter, rifle instead of weapons), which invokes a dilemma dating back to antiquity and alludes to one of the most famous moments in *Don Quixote* (chapter XXXVIII), Gilman carves out a theme that allows her to dissect the "fourteen prodigious years" stretching from the Cuban Revolution of 1959 to the fall of Allende's government in 1973 (as a coda, the book extends to 1976, but those three years are no longer prodigious, but rather an extension of the agony). Central debates of the period are woven throughout the volume, such as the Padilla affair or the controversy between Cortázar and Collazos, alongside analyses of the workings of the cultural market, the relationship between literary genres and social change, and, with special emphasis, on the vicissitudes of journals such as *Marcha*, *Mundo Nuevo*, *Casa de las Américas*, and *Libre*, which reveal different facets of literary and cultural life.

It is surprising that a book that has already become a classic of Latin American criticism and is inevitably cited whenever the 1960s are addressed took so long to be translated into English. I do not know whether there is a specific reason, but its approach may perhaps seem unusual to readers accustomed to academic texts in that language. Gilman does not confine herself to a specific topic, nor does she offer original or arcane ideas; rather, she works with an arsenal of fairly standard concepts from which she extracts remarkable heuristic operability. "Period," "intellectual," "family ties," "writer-intellectual" are some of these concepts. In chapter 1, she approaches those years "considered as a period" and explains the reason that led her to include dissimilar and heterogeneous phenomena occurring across the continent but responding to a shared logic: the imprint left by the Cuban Revolution. The parabola of that period is narrated with style and grace: the chapter opens and closes with quotations from Dante Alighieri, but while the epigraph belongs to *Paradiso*, the final words come from *Inferno*. "From euphoria to depression," the author notes, situating the period within a longue durée history and interpreting it as "the swan song of lettered culture in Latin America."

The delay in translation, however, allows for a more distanced view of the book's context of production, the result of postgraduate studies the author completed at the École des Hautes Études en Sciences Sociales in Paris and a doctoral dissertation submitted at the Universidad de Buenos Aires, where she pursued her studies and teaches. The research was carried out during the 1990s, and the book—no longer bearing traces of the "thesis" genre, as evidenced by the healthy scarcity of footnotes—was published in 2003. It forms part of a series of investigations produced at that time that share several common traits: the assessment of extended periods; a panoramic survey organized chronologically; the theoretical presence of Raymond Williams, Beatriz Sarlo, and Pierre Bourdieu (marking a shift from the poststructuralist textualism of the 1980s to a more sociohistorical perspective); the central weight of archives in the argumentation; and a mode of writing that abandons the essay of ideas in favor of an argument closer to the social sciences. In different fields, books were produced that returned to narrating history by establishing a critical-theoretical break with previous studies: *Los primeros modernos* (2001) by Laura Malosetti Costa for nineteenth-century art; *Vanguardia, internacionalismo y política: arte argentino en los años sesenta* (*Avant-Garde, Internationalism, and Politics: Argentine Art in the Sixties*, 2001) by Andrea Giunta for the twentieth century; *La grilla y el parque* (*The Grid and the Park*, 1998) by Adrián Gorelik for urban studies; *Del Di Tella a Tucumán Arde: Vanguardia artística y política en el 68 argentino* (2000) by Ana Longoni and Mariano Mestman, also for the 1960s. These titles may be understood both as the products of the return of long-term research enabled by doctoral studies (which had no strong tradition in Argentine academia) and as the result of a period of democratic consolidation (which had been in doubt during the 1980s), favoring retrospective views and the need to narrate once again—especially in areas where academic criticism had been weak (art history, urban culture, film studies), as opposed to other fields with a very strong tradition, such as literary criticism. Even there, however, studies emerged that, for various affinities, could be added to this list, though the existence of that tradition allowed for greater thematic specificity (I am thinking of *Regueros de tinta: El diario crítica en la década de 1920* [1998] by Sylvia Saítta or *El tiempo vacío de la ficción: Las novelas argentinas de Eduardo Gutiérrez y Eugenio Cambaceres* [2004] by Alejandra Laera). Undoubtedly, the book by Beatriz Sarlo and Carlos Altamirano, *Literatura/Sociedad* (1983), left a strong imprint on these investigations, as did *Intelectuales y poder en la década del sesenta* (1991) by Silvia Sigal and *Nuestros años sesenta* (1991) by Oscar Terán, or the meetings of the Seminar on the History of Ideas, Intellectuals, and Culture founded by Terán himself in 1988 at the Instituto de Historia Argentina y Americana Emilio Ravignani. These are not history books, but the presence of history was fundamental to the narrative organization of the material and to the underlying idea that this was a cycle already concluded (definable through the concept of modernity) and one that allowed for—and even demanded—critical assessments.

Within this panorama, the distinctive feature of Claudia Gilman's book lies in its Latin Americanist ambition, and it could hardly be otherwise, given that the 1960s were not national but continental. Four capitals—Buenos Aires, Havana, Barcelona, and Mexico City—functioned as the nerve centers of the period, but with the advantage, from Gilman's vantage point, that the Argentine city was not as isolated as the Cuban capital nor as external as the Spanish city, while at the same time being less endogenous than Mexico City. In the book's trajectory, another capital acquires particular relevance: Montevideo. Not only because it embodied the most complex and rigorous articulations of the two critical positions that marked the 1960s (the textual imprint of Rodríguez Monegal and the sociocriticism of Ángel Rama), but also because Gilman's lucid reading of the weekly *Marcha* (1939–74) allows her to explore both the antechamber and the genealogy of that period.

One concept acquires multifaceted power in the book: it defines the central dilemma, makes conflicts visible, and lends narrative rhythm to the analyses. I am referring to the concept of "imminence." It is as if all the protagonists of the period wrote and acted according to urgency and a daily rhythm subordinated to a historical teleology: that of Revolution just around the corner. Thinking this imminence leads the writer to become, as Gilman proposes, a "writer-intellectual," referring to the fact that even novelists, short-story writers, and playwrights needed to define "their actions and ideas according to the rules of the culture of critical discourse." She sees this not only through Alvin Gouldner (to whom the previous quotation belongs) but also through Pierre Bourdieu and Norberto Bobbio, who proposes that "definitions of intellectual identity are basically self-definitions." To this approach, which continues the existing bibliography on the subject, Gilman adds a term that becomes fundamental to the development of her argument: "anti-intellectualism." The following passage not only demonstrates the operability of the concept in the Latin American context of those years but also the author's precise, rigorous, and ingenious prose:

> Anti-intellectualism had an aspect of self-flagellation, with a rhetorical character that may even overshadow the sincerity of its discourses. An attribute of subordinates? The voice of a guilty conscience? Masochism? A necessary prolegomenon to initiate non-figurative combat against the bourgeoisie and its armies? Although the question of abandoning literature in order to politicize the role of the intellectual was raised, it should be noted that most of the discourses collected here belong to writers who, in very few cases, actually stopped writing, although they fervently devoted themselves to the anti-intellectualist ritual.

For Gilman, the 1960s witnessed a collision between the "revolutionary ideal" and the "critical ideal." Opposed to the "critical ideal," which from the anti-intellectual position ends up being seen as indebted to conformism or a bourgeois attitude, is the "revolutionary ideal." From this opposition, Gilman delves into the debates shaped by the Cuban Revolution and the promise of generalized change. For anti-intellectuals, "politics was considered more important than the relationship with Truth," a stance that became particularly intense with the Padilla affair, which marks an irreversible rupture in those "prodigious years."

These elaborations are strikingly current, not only because of the place that the concept of truth occupies in contemporary social discourses but also because the general climate of that period is the opposite of the one we live in today. Gilman quotes Ambrosio Fornet, who said that everyone, "even reformists and the right," speaks "the language of the left." *Between the Pen and the Rifle* offers several keys for thinking about the rightward turn of language and the ways in which we can position ourselves in relation to it—and, eventually, weaken or undo it.

I do not know whether the notion of a spoiler applies to academic books, but I believe it is important to anticipate the ending, because Gilman's stance endows her book with a polemical character that has not diminished over the years but has rather intensified and taken on new contours. It is the survival of the "critical ideal" (against the subordination of truth to politics) that makes it possible to narrate history and unfold it before our eyes. Ultimately, *Between the Pen and the Rifle* is a genealogy of how critical independence and the affirmation of the autonomy of intellectual labor have their own specificity in Latin America for historical and political reasons. It is not a retreat, nor a plea for neutrality, but a way of positioning oneself in relation to the times we live in and their diverse demands.

Acknowledgments

I was born in the sixties, to which I owe my very "epochal" name. My parents were atheists, modern, progressive, psychoanalyzed, psychedelic, educated, divorced, anti-bourgeois transgressors. I grew up in a library of revolutionary, feminist children's books, which grew with the first editions of David Viñas, Ernesto Sabato, Julio Cortázar, Beatriz Guido, Gabriel García Márquez, Mario Vargas Llosa, José María Arguedas, Juan Carlos Onetti, Herbert Marcuse, Paulo Freire, Frantz Fanon, Jean-Paul Sartre, Simone de Beauvoir, and so many other authors of the sixties and seventies, the period I explore in this book. As a child, I had the privilege of attending María Elena Walsh's concerts and of being brought up listening to her records. In the café at the San Martín theater, she once gave me an imaginary flea, placing it in my hands for safekeeping; I still have it. Her paideia is quite possibly one of the best and most evident outcomes of the political-cultural agenda of the "long sixties."

In 1971 or 1972, I reserved my Mother's Day gift at a record store on Pedro Goyena and Puan, just around the corner from my house: it was the *Cantata de Santa María de Iquique* by the Chilean group Quilapayún. Months before, my mother had pointed out a balcony in Barrio Norte saying "this is where they kidnapped that son of a bitch Aramburu." I learned the details from *El Descamisado* magazine, a must-read at home. I attended clandestine screenings of *La hora de los hornos* [*The Hour of the Furnaces*] as well as its premiere in theaters. I went into the streets to celebrate the release of political prisoners when Héctor Cámpora took office.

While the epoch I analyze in this book was taking place, I found I was insufficiently prepared to understand the urgent issues and debates that it was assumed everyone was aware of: the path to socialism, the positions of Juan Lechín Oquendo and the Bolivian Workers' Confederation, the differences between Guevarism, Marxism-Leninism,

Maoism, revolutionary Peronism, the essential characteristics of the national and popular movement, reformism, deviationisms, the secrets of tactics and strategy, and everything else that the times demanded. I made a decision that, when I was older, I would do whatever it took to truly grasp all that information that was difficult to process in such a short time and without having done the reading. As a researcher, I dedicated myself to filling in some of the gaps that I considered the most unforgivable. I tried to compensate my past ignorance with the utmost rigor and thoroughness in consulting documentary sources.

It took me a very long time to finish this book. Some came to believe it would simply be another of Godot's promises. I came to believe this as well as I played all the characters in turn: Vladimir, Estragon, Pozzo, Lucky, and, especially, the absent Godot. As in Beckett's work, the difference between yesterday, today, and tomorrow eluded me. This ambiguity was masterfully exploited by shopkeepers who used to hang signs in their stores: "No credit today; tomorrow, okay." Eventually, I trusted the conventions of the calendar and managed to bring this project to an end.

During that time, I came to know the pleasure of a luminous idea, a *trouvaille*, in the innumerable libraries and archives consulted, the anxiety of any long-term project, the misadventures of the bibliographic Third World, and the strange sensation of traveling in a time machine that transported me to an immediate past that is both definitively over and still in living memory.

Beatriz Sarlo, Oscar Terán, Silvia Sigal, Carlos Altamirano, Raúl Antelo, Daniel Link, Ana Longoni, Mariano Mestman, Susana Zanetti, David Viñas, Ricardo Piglia, Julio Schvartzman, Jorge Ruffinelli, Saúl Sosnowski, Isabel Stratta, Adriana Rodríguez Pérsico, Nora Domínguez, Renata Rocco Cuzzi, Enrique Oteiza, Andrea Giunta, Jorge Cernadas, Mariano Plotkin, Claudia Kozak, Claude Fell, Adrián Gorelik, Hugo Vezzetti, Carlos Díaz, Ezequiel Gatto, Luciana del Gizzo, Ximena Espeche, Jacques Leenhardt, Horacio Tarcus, Luz Rodríguez Carranza, Gonzalo Aguilar, Renata Cardarelli, Francis Simón, Noé Jitrik: friends, teachers, conversation partners, and colleagues who helped me to think and to live. I am forever indebted to you. Along with their intellectual contributions, I must also acknowledge the efforts they made, unanimously, though without prior agreement, to "keep me bound to the mast." In writing this book, I understood why Odysseus demanded that his crew tie him to the mast of his ship so he could hear the sirens without losing his mind or straying from his goal. This particular expression has stuck with me since reading an editorial by Carlos Quijano in the weekly tabloid *Marcha* entitled "Atados al mástil" [Bound to the Mast] in which he referred to the need, the obligation, and even the fatality of resisting. Luckily, I was destined to become a mermaid, as I later discovered. There was no need to tie me down.

Juan Camilo Lorca, of the National Library of Chile, went to the trouble of copying articles from the magazine *Casa de las Américas* and sending them to me by mail. Blanca Busto, of the National Library of Uruguay, microfilmed almost the entire collection of *Marcha* in 1988 onto more than twenty rolls and also sent me the huge package by mail. The words "thank you" are not nearly enough to do justice to their selfless efforts. They are an honor to their profession and to humankind. Whether grumpy, indifferent, or solicitous, other librarians were indispensable collaborators who contributed to the incalculable archival treasure I was able to draw on for the research that led to this book.

I would also like to thank the students of the various courses and seminars I have taught since 1986, perhaps with more audacity than wisdom.

Some of their questions, final papers, and dialogues fed my enthusiasm and stimulated my curiosity for learning. Colleagues I have never met from a range of backgrounds and traditions, from a surprising variety of disciplines, have found in this book inspiration to corroborate hypotheses and indeed expand the horizon of questions, objects, and problems that were only hinted at or developed in my work. In many cases, I would never have imagined the possible outcomes that I have discovered in reading them. I have benefited from the privilege of current technologies: seeing the potential of one's own ideas encourages rethinking, teaches unknown aspects of what we presume to know, and broadens the boundaries of understanding and thought. It is an extraordinary synergy that I owe to other researchers and to the present itself.

Obviously, despite the valuable contributions of others, I take full responsibility for what I have written in these pages, for any imperfection, error, or omission and, I hope, for what I have gotten right as well.

Buenos Aires, December 2024

Introduction

Over the course of many years of work on the sixties and seventies in Latin America, I have approached a number of different objects: literary texts, magazines, letters, documents, declarations, polemics, aesthetic and intellectual trajectories, *idées-forces*, social imaginaries, institutions, reception of literary texts, critical studies, and journalistic and scholarly criticism.

The difficulty in defining my own object of study was directly proportional to the proliferation of the material being studied and to the conviction that none of these materials could be considered a complete source of information in themselves: not a magazine, nor a national intellectual field, nor an intellectual trajectory, nor a particular author or text, nor literary market data; not even the exclusive analysis of the relationship between intellectuals and the Cuban Revolution (an issue, on the other hand, that is crucial in understanding the Latin American literary and intellectual history of the period).

Like the writers who sought to tie their specific work to the revolutionary task, it seemed to me that lived experience (the work) could only be formulated in negative terms.

Why was this material so resistant to organization? In part due to its constant reformulation of assumptions about the relationship between literature and politics, which projected an effect of closure and termination that made those assumptions conceptually elusive. The difficulty also reflected a need for new ways of thinking about a *new* object and, therefore, *new* perspectives of analysis, with the idea that the existing ones were insufficient to open up new spaces of understanding and, moreover, because it was crucial to give the object of study a continental scope. Not only that: there was a need to rethink the period within an *international* framework, as a response to the "internationalism" that had been one of its particular features.

The greatest challenge was not only conceptual, terminological, or categorical (although it was all that as well), but the need to establish a connection between objects that had already been analyzed and described, but that were unable to dialogue with each other. I had to find a way to relate objects such as literary texts, manifestos, declarations, magazines, critical and theoretical bodies of works, political ideas, experiences, expectations, and social actors. With what categories? How could this be done without crystallizing a period that resists crystallization, which continues to be perceived as something inaugural?

A study like this can only be done by bringing into play subjects and perspectives that have been previously considered separately. A unified field of analysis will require the exploration of the interdependence between the period under study, the writers-intellectuals, the political-cultural magazines, criticism, and the programmatic debates on the role of art and intellectuals in society.

All the works that have explored this period describe it as one of rapid modernization and great revolutionary expectations, characterized by cultural modernization, the consolidation of a public interest in artistic productions, and the emergence of new market and consumer conditions.

The overall and canonical hypotheses, no doubt relevant, emphasize the appearance of new national publishing houses and cultural magazines and the importance of the Cuban Revolution—a phenomenon that has generally been considered the undisputed source of attraction and repulsion of the decade—without, however, any in-depth analysis of what this centrality consisted of and how the emergence of a debate on the nature of a "popular" and "revolutionary" culture and the role of literature and intellectuals in the revolutionary processes affected writers throughout the period.

The studies devoted to this period—their generalization of "the sixties" should be explained and analyzed—have considered various types of objects relevant, most notably intellectuals, literary production, and magazines. Although it is no doubt difficult to classify them as studies with a single focus, the distinct approaches employed by specialists overlap and draw on each other, and in general terms, thematic differences are resolved in a significant consensus, which will be described later on, over the uniqueness of the period. Undoubtedly reducing the complexity of these works, I will discuss the fundamental objects that have constituted the focus of their interest.

The Intellectuals

The works that Beatriz Sarlo (1985), José Aricó (1988), Silvia Sigal (1991), and Oscar Terán (1991)—all members of what the latter terms the "critical fraction" and most of them intellectuals of the sixties themselves—have devoted themselves to the intellectual history of the period, emphasizing the importance of politics as a foundational and legitimizing value of intellectual practices (of their practices and convictions at the time). Their hypotheses and the relevance of an analysis from the perspective of the "intellectual" object or figure are inevitable starting points in analyzing, in this context, the literary production of the period and the search for an aesthetic-ideological program consistent with these values.

The figure of the *intellectual* is unavoidable in connecting *politics* with *culture* since it implies a position with respect to culture and also with respect to power. Intellectual history is particularly significant since intellectuals are the object of a de facto, global, and tacit delegation for producing representations of the social world. These representations, which constitute a fundamental aspect of the political struggle, are practically the exclusive domain of intellectuals.

Within the abundant literature on intellectuals, several of Pierre Bourdieu's tools and concepts have been particularly useful, especially his definition of the *intellectual field* as the first horizon of aesthetic-political conflicts. What Bourdieu terms the intellectual field is a differentiated social space with its own logic and systems of internal relations. The intellectual field is linked to society as a whole through an initial mode of organization in which the cultural products, artistic trajectories, and decisions of the producers acquire meaning. This field constitutes a space of struggle and competition, in which each member sees their individual actions restricted, to the extent that they are part of an organization that has its own particular legality. The notion of field allows us to establish a sociology of intellectuals that can account for the diverse alternatives of each of its members, according to the historical, political, economic, and social situations in which the field functions at any given moment. It is thus possible to formulate overall hypotheses and establish the field of alternatives of each of its members without resorting to explanations that are valid only for each individual and each work since they are integrated into a structure in which reciprocal relations, sociability, and the recognition or indifference of peers are fundamental, an inescapable aspect of artistic practice in modern societies. Of all the concepts tied to the notion of the intellectual field, those that enable the analysis of the relations within that intellectual field involving the groups competing for the defense of their cultural capital have been especially useful (Bourdieu 1966, 1984, 1992).

In this book, the notion of the intellectual field will be particularly helpful in interpreting the anti-intellectualist discourses and positions of a significant fraction of intellectuals. Nevertheless, we do not feel a need to sustain, as Bourdieu would seem to suggest, the "blindness of the producers," whose aesthetic positions would be strongly limited to the relations of force within the intellectual field. In this sense, we diverge from Bourdieu, as well as in our use of the category beyond the limits of the nation-state in which it was conceived. What is important about Bourdieu's contribution, however, is that, by desacralizing intellectual practices, he provides tools that allow us to relate the acts of intellectuals to the profane rules of a social game (Sarlo 1993).

I have also found the hypotheses of Alvin Gouldner (1980) very useful, particularly the characterization of intellectual culture as a linguistic community, whose members argue and position themselves according to what Gouldner calls the culture of critical discourse. Gouldner's work includes a provocative invitation to consider the cultural capital that characterizes the type of possession of intellectuals in a non-metaphorical sense, and his analysis of the relations between intellectuals and revolutionary avant-gardes is extremely interesting.

According to Gouldner, one of the characteristics of intellectuals is that they all seek to justify their actions and ideas according to the rules of the culture of critical discourse, which prohibit relying on the person, authority, or social status of the speaker to justify their claims.

As a result, the culture of critical discourse disavows all language based on the traditional authority of society.[1]

Gouldner wrote *The Future of Intellectuals and the Rise of the New Class* in 1979. It is a brief text, but one that nevertheless proposes and formulates a remarkable number of hypotheses on how intellectuals have constituted themselves in the process of the secularization of society. One of the criticisms his work has received (which in my opinion leaves out the most interesting aspects in the development of his ideas) is related to his hypothesis that intellectuals constitute a new social class.[2]

What strikes me as valuable in Gouldner's thesis lies in the historicization of the process whereby the secularization of society engenders a new socio-professional stratum, which—based on the separation of the spheres of social life—ceases to accept criteria of authority that are not based on rationality and embraces the culture of critical discourse as its own. This new culture of discourse places intellectuals in a slightly separate position with respect to the rest of society, which allows it to function according to "its own" supposedly "rational" standards of validity. On the basis of this certainty, intellectuals have taken for granted their ability to transcend their historical determinism, imagining themselves as the most universal and generic type of humanity.

The fact that intellectuals tend to consider their particular interests as universal is a hypothesis that was already present in the formulations of George Konrád and Ivan Szelényi when they wrote that intellectuals of every age:

---

1 See "Thesis Six" (28–42) or the assertion that "Most importantly, the culture of critical speech forbids reliance upon the speaker's person, authority, or status in society to justify his claims. As a result, CCD (the culture of critical discourse) de-authorizes all speech grounded in traditional societal authority" (29). For the relationship between intellectuals and political avant-gardes, see "Thesis Ten: Revolutionary Intellectuals" (53–56) and "Thesis Thirteen: Dilemmas of Marxism and the Vanguard Organization" (75–82).

2 See Stanley Aronowitz 1990, 41–52. One might fault him for rendering Gouldner as overly "bound" to Merton's influence. Even though Aronowitz is right in emphasizing the *lacunae* in Gouldner's essay, he fails to refute Gouldner's proposals as a whole.

> have described themselves ideologically, in accordance with their particular interests, and if those interests have differed from age to age it has still been the common aspiration of the intellectuals of every age to represent their particular interests in each context as the general interests of mankind (14).

It is interesting to note that when they wrote their book *The Intellectuals on the Road to Class Power* in 1974, Konrád and Szelényi, two Hungarian dissidents, presented hypotheses similar to those of Gouldner, but valid for Eastern Europe, according to which—under state socialism in that region and for the first time in the history of humankind—the intelligentsia was in the process of forming a class. Norberto Bobbio makes a similar claim when he stresses that definitions of intellectual identity are basically self-definitions (1998, 13–23). And, of course, he is not alone in insisting that the question regarding the "being of the intellectual" is the most typically intellectual of all questions.

Whatever the case may be, we will explore to what point, for intellectuals, forming part of the culture of critical discourse is tied to the dilemmas that confronted the Latin American intellectual family in the sixties and seventies.

Indeed, intellectual history is particularly relevant for analyzing literary debates during a period in which the transformation of the writer into an intellectual was a key aspect of the literary field. The notion of the writer-intellectual in analytical and historical terms and from the perspective of those authors as well as that of authors who, without focusing specifically on the period of the sixties/seventies, centered their analysis on the category of the intellectual, has allowed me to establish a bridge between the various objects. The possibility of linking them is correlative to the notion of *epoch* as the field of possibility of the existence of a system of beliefs, of the circulation of discourses and interventions.

The Literature

The notable interest in studying Latin American literature of the sixties underscores the importance of this production, its institutionalization and emergence as a continental production, and its recognition on a global scale. It was precisely during this period that this literature reached its peak of visibility and contributed to reestablishing a new Latin American tradition. Without a doubt, the phenomenon of the boom—in all the various ways in which it was defined—served as a catalyst in questioning the ways in which the acclaimed texts were qualitatively different within the context of Latin American literary production and served to propose the category of a new Latin American narrative. An example of this concern is the collective volume *Latin America in Its Literature*, compiled by César Fernández Moreno (1972), which revealed some of the attributes that characterized the new canon (in the most programmatic sense of this term). Its general emphasis on aspects that are more aesthetic than ideological illustrates one of the typical visions of Latin American literary production toward the end of the period. Haroldo de Campos's contribution to that volume is a perfect example of this turning point and explains the modernizing extreme of the question ("Superación de los lenguajes exclusivos" 1972, 279–300).

Latin America in Its Literature could no doubt have represented a definitive overview of the question if it had not remained trapped in the dynamics of intellectual history, in which the issue of politicization also played a strong role. José Miguel Oviedo's article in the same volume illustrates this perspective of being immersed in a reality that was still unfolding, when it refers to the fact that Cuba, origin and stimulus for the Latin American literary discussion, would have the last word in the debate to the degree that his contribution ends with a key question, still unanswered when formulated: "What new theories and interpretations of literary phenomenon will come out of this tense exchange of opinions?" (1980, 318).

The closed or conclusive nature of the characteristics of the culture of the sixties/seventies inspired the publication of critical assessments of those years in the period that immediately followed. The collective volume edited by Ángel Rama, *Más allá del boom: Literatura y mercado*

[Beyond the Boom: Literature and Market] (that brings together the papers and the discussions they inspired at a conference organized by the Latin American Program of the Woodrow Wilson International Center for Scholars, held between October 18 and 20, 1979, in order to discuss the "emergence of the new Latin American narrative" during the period 1950–1975), constitutes in itself a state of the question closely tied to my work: the aim of the papers collected in said volume is, as Rama comments in his "Introductory Note":

> to proceed to elaborate a critical assessment, using an interdisciplinary approach, of the development and diffusion achieved by Latin American narrative . . . considering not only its artistic and ideological aspects but also the economic, sociological, and political aspects that served as a framework (1984, 9–10).[3]

This institutional approach is a methodological and thematic starting point for my research. Given the rather heterogeneous set of diverse voices it includes, *Más allá del boom* enables the identification of complex institutional issues, underscores the tension between modernization and politics, and emphasizes the need to reflect on the triangle formed by literature, the market, and the revolution. As a symptom of this emphasis, it is worth citing the words Cuban writer Edmundo Desnoes used in his contribution to the book—provocatively entitled "A falta de otras palabras" [For Lack of Other Words]—to challenge his audience: "Where you speak of the market and Latin American narrative, I would have to speak of politics and Latin American narrative" (1984, 251).

Despite the chronological period selected for the conference that inspired this volume, the articles and papers are strongly focused, as Elizabeth Garrels admits when she summarizes the discussion, "on the artistic production of the sixties and seventies" (289). This kind of reduction of the original theme established for the conference reflects

3 All translations into English of sources in other languages are by Rebecca Wolpin, unless otherwise noted.

the problematic nucleus that those years configure on their own, for reasons that I will explore below.

Ángel Rama in "La tecnificación narrativa" [Narrative Technification] (1981) and Jean Franco in "Modernización, resistencia y revolución: La producción literaria de los años sesenta" [Modernization, Resistance, and Revolution: Literary Production in the Sixties] (1977) attempt to address the relationship between art and society. In both cases, the desire to explore the political-ideological assumptions of the incorporation of new literary techniques into the literature of the continent implies a critical rereading of the ideological foundations of this technification, inevitable in any approach to the literary production of the most representative authors of the so-called boom in Latin American literature. Jean Franco attempts to explain the relationship between this technological zeal and the political efficacy of the artistic production by drawing an analogy between literary renewal and political change. Her keen observations on the problematic nature of the expectations of a revolutionary literature in Cuba are weakened by the allegorical interpretation of the texts she analyzes, which hinders the ability to analyze how poetics were constituted on the basis of particular moments in intellectual history. In a general sense, the works mentioned, as well as the issue of the *Bulletin of Latin American Research* (no. 2, 1984) dedicated to the topic, establish the perspectives that help define the specific characteristics of the culture of the sixties.

The Magazines

Analyses of magazines of the period carried out in recent years highlight the fact that the cultural-political magazine was, at the time, an essential tool for the constitution of writers as intellectuals since it meant the dissemination of their work to a broader public. They also support the hypothesis that controversy was a constitutive discourse given the number of polemics in magazines and the fact that they became privileged actors that helped ensure that their echoes were disseminated across the continent.

These studies help us understand to what extent analyzing magazines from the sixties/seventies involves the need to navigate the vast network of Latin American magazines of the period. This is undoubtedly where the limits of the study of a particular magazine to determine the logic of the constitution of fields of actors emerges, confronted with a context that exceeds the limits of the magazine itself. Work on magazines is forced to adhere to partial periodizations, imposed by the evolution of the magazine itself and its changes. In other words, magazines are always incomplete actors and are unable to offer the possibility of addressing the institutional analysis of literature.

This assertion is made with full knowledge of the facts: the origins of my research date back to the attempt to study several Latin American magazines of the period, an attempt that demonstrated the limitations of this type of approach. In 1987, I received an initiation grant from the National Council for Scientific and Technical Research (CONICET) to carry out work on the Uruguayan magazine *Marcha* during the period of 1959–1974. Along with the reports submitted to the research council, I published several papers on this important Uruguayan weekly that ran from 1939 to 1974, when it was definitively shut down by censorship. However, I found it necessary to cover the period of study more extensively and to open up the field of research to the various textualities of the period (including magazines, of course) in order to fully grasp the issues involved. This gave rise to a new work focused on one of the main ideological-intellectual debates, which examined the confrontation between two antagonistic notions about the role of the intellectual, based on the study of the magazines *Casa de las Américas* and *Libre*. The present book develops many of the hypotheses contained in that and other works (Gilman 1993a, 1996a, 1996b, 1997).

The fact is that, due to their methodological choices, studies of magazines cannot affect an analytical approach to literary production, since, in addition to covering various genres of discourse, magazines tend to close in on themselves in a series of understandings and contracts with the reader that require a comparison outside their own space (Gilman 1999). Hence, this work has required a broad survey of the most important Latin American magazines of the period: the numerous years of archives back the hypothesis that navigating through the dense network of magazines—one of the most defining products of the period—was necessary. It is also true that, despite the many years of archival work, the result is far from being as exhaustive as I would have liked.

However, I have tried not to lose sight of the warp of very diverse threads that weave the distinctive colorations of the relationship between literature and politics in the sixties and seventies in Latin America. Multiple approaches, intellectual history, the history of ideas, literary history, history in itself, literary criticism, and theory: I have drawn on all of them in an attempt to avoid being an overly clumsy or lethal Fate, weaving something that suits only my own purposes. For this reason, rather than starting from preexisting institutional spaces or specific professional disciplines, I have chosen to start from *idées-forces* or a "structure of feeling" as Raymond Williams puts it: a concept that seeks to express meanings and values as they are actively lived and experienced (1977, 150–58).

In part, the continental scope of the study has made it necessary to erase data in order to re-establish only that which is strictly relevant; in part, this initial erasure seems to better fit the idea of the void of Latin American culture and literature that writers and critics lamented so much at the beginning of the period. Writers and critics whose voices I have followed: from the jeremiads to the jubilees (from the Latin Americanist *horror vacui* to the cornucopian "plenty" of that culture that in its apogee seemed to displace that of the rest of the world), from the attempts to give a "function" back to culture (and especially to literature), establishing starting points and/or renouncing preexisting institutions and the norms inherited from them to the bitter realizations that perhaps culture was not as political as previously imagined.

Although these critics and writers pieced together traditions with available ancestors and existing models of thought, as Fidel Castro did with José Martí, whom he repeatedly deemed the "intellectual author" and "Apostle" of the Cuban Revolution (Castro 1983a, 31, 63–64; 1983b, 71; 1983c, 72), at that time particular emphasis was placed on the idea of the beginning.

As this work emerges from a general concern to establish various questions related to the relationship between politics and culture, or, formulated in other terms, between literature and society, I am indebted to all those analyses that reveal the historicity of these relationships and the need to explain them according to the historical, political, and social processes that define, at any given moment, the uses and norms, forms of institutional organization, and textual reception. In contemplating the ties between politics and literature in our century, it is crucial to consider the process of the secularization and autonomization of the spheres of social life, particularly the process of the autonomization of literature, recognizing that the autonomization of art is not a unilinear process of emancipation leading to the institutionalization of a sphere of value that coexists with other spheres, but instead a highly contradictory process characterized not only by the acquisition of new potentials but also by the loss of others (Bürger 1983, 419–33). The literary institution has a special function in the social system as a whole; it develops an aesthetic code as well as a system of limits with respect to other literary practices; it claims unlimited validity since it determines, in a given period, what is considered literature and what is not. If the normative aspect is at the core of this concept of institution, this concept must include organizational aspects (Hohendahl 1989, 1–43). In any case, it is clear that literary debates—as struggles to establish the norms of the literary institution—must be accorded a central place.

My intention is not to find a single thread to orient this work but, first and foremost, to present the relationship between culture and politics during the period as an inextricable composition of continuities, ruptures, and permanencies where chance also plays a role. The greatest difficulty for the researcher lies in the language itself: a word can remain intact, but its semantic field can expand or shrink, become contaminated, or designate very different things. Thus, when avant-garde or revolution are mentioned in discourses of the period (and in current ones as well, of course), we must establish to what extent the words and the concepts they denote slip, migrate, and name according to each particular intersection between a moment in history and specific speakers. The touchstone of this history, *the* word, has undoubtedly been *revolution*, the reality of revolution, the concept of revolution, and the attributes of revolution as a necessary guarantee of legitimacy for writers, critics, works, ideas, and behaviors. Raymond Aron recalled this, with displeasure, when he acknowledged in *The Opium of the Intellectuals* that intellectuals agreed on the essentials and that even the most virulent polemics did not pit them against each other since they all concurred that the end goal was revolution while they were busy debating the various interpretations of the "sacred word," *revolution* (62).

Latin America: Intellectuals, Literature, and Politics

The decision to consider Latin America as the object of reflection strikes me as conceptually and methodologically relevant. Broadening national frameworks, eliminating abstract frontiers in cultural analysis, is essential. Although it is true that as an entity *Latin America*, in terms of cultural homogeneity, is more a problematic horizon than an actual reality, it is no less true that during the period in question an idea (or the need for an idea) of Latin America takes shape, perhaps with the same force and the same voluntarism as during the period of emancipation or the modernist whirlwind, which was also influenced by certain historic political circumstances, ideological matrices, and the weight of certain institutions, such as parties, governments, cultural institutions, and even market forces.

The deliberate foundation of a new framework of geopolitical relevance meant that the continental reference became a space of belonging for Latin American intellectuals. This Latin Americanism also became embedded within a current of Third World solidarity. This perspective sought to unite culture and politics in a concept that transcended national borders, the "wretched of the earth" as a whole, according to the formula that Frantz Fanon made famous at the time in his no less famous book of the same name. The protagonists of the period made an effort to detect and disseminate the progressive contributions that the writers of the continent were making in order to produce a new literature in a new world, notions that were both based on nebulous foundations and hazy references, characteristic of those years. The regular, periodic, and voluntary dissemination of the state of Latin American literature through the contributions of various authors, year after year, was a task promoted by practically all the political-cultural publications of the period. The shared patrimony emerged as a product of the collective accumulation from the most distant corners of the continent. This broadening of what was *ours* did not imply, however, a blatant denial of nationalist components, but instead sought to overcome them at the cultural level.

A study that extends beyond national perspectives makes it possible to verify the similarities and simultaneities of certain apparent historical and ideological idiosyncrasies in the process of discussing and developing a new revolutionary Latin American culture. To perhaps establish, over time—blind and insensitive to meaning—the outlines of an *epoch*. First, because the period that begins in the sixties had a strong internationalist dimension and an interest in public affairs that transcended national horizons. Second, because working from national perspectives makes it difficult to evaluate the impact that the Cuban Revolution (and its various vicissitudes) had on the process of revamping literature and creating a new paideia for Latin American intellectuals over a period of approximately fifteen years.

The relationship of Cuban intellectuals in particular, and Latin American intellectuals in general, with the Cuban state generated important changes in the positioning of key issues discussed during the period, such as the function of literature and artistic experimentation, the role of the writer in relation to society, the normative criteria of art, and the relationship between intellectuals and power. The influence of the Cuban Revolution on the literary and intellectual history of the continent merits further study through a chronology that takes into account the various Cuban cultural policies. Halperin Donghi observes in *The Contemporary History of Latin America* that, as the Cuban experience tended to lose immediate relevance in terms of the potential for emulation, support for the Cuban cause, far from declining, became more intense (1997, 498). This explains why the Cuban Revolution produced its most poignant effects on the written word and interventions—the real and symbolic places where the potential for meaning and understanding and the presumption of truth in the discourses were developed—almost ten years after Fidel Castro's triumphant entry into Havana on January 1, 1959, as a result, among other acts, interventions, and situations, of Cuban support for the Soviet invasion of Czechoslovakia in 1968.

Even though many of these questions emerged in response to the specific situation and within the particular framework of Cuban politics, they were unique in that they expanded until they became a general problem for Latin American intellectuals, to the point of generating specific divisions and solidarities.

Throughout the sixties and seventies, politics became the parameter for the legitimacy of textual production, and public space was the privileged setting in which the voice of the writer—thereby becoming an intellectual—was authorized. This conversion from writer to intellectual is the result of several processes: the dominance of political progressivism in the field of cultural elites; the generalized hypothesis concerning the imminence of world revolution; the debate on "new revolutionary subjects" that considered which social actors would carry out the radical transformation of society—such as, for instance, intellectuals, students, young people, Black people, and, according to the various regions of Latin America, other diverse figures of the "revolutionary class" (the urban proletariat, rural proletariat, peasantry, etc.)—; the desire for cultural politicization; and the interest in public affairs.

The political importance accorded to the intellectual and their specific output (especially literature) was accompanied by a constant examination of their social value or shortcomings and by the intense programmatic will to create a political and revolutionary art. From this perpetual questioning came transitory and antagonistic responses. The growing metastasis of the instrumental logic of politics had important effects on literary production and the justification of that production in political-ideological terms and on the vicissitudes of the intellectual field.

Anti-intellectualism is one of the fundamental strands of the periodization of Latin American intellectual history. It was the position adopted by a fraction of intellectuals who defined themselves as revolutionary, based on their ideological radicalism and the increasing value of politics and its logics of efficacy and instrumentality. Anti-intellectualism was one of the responses of the intellectual field to the dilemma of reconciling the traditions of the intellectual as a critic of society and a new definition of the revolutionary intellectual that established a type of subordinate relationship with respect to the revolutionary political leadership: especially that of the Cuban state and the guerrilla movements. It also intensified with the establishment of Latin American literature in the publishing market. This process led to a confrontation between intellectuals who defended the critical ideal and those who defended the revolutionary one (Gilman 1993b).

Two observations opening this period seem at the very least paradoxical: on the one hand, the assumption that intellectuals are called upon to become the spokespersons of a vague but widespread urgency for social transformation; on the other, the acceptance that the continent's artistic output, due to its erratic and restricted circulation, falls short of constituting a true Latin American literature. Criticism then tried to make up for the lack of reciprocal knowledge and established channels of communication within the continent.

Two events at the beginning of this period that appeared to respond to very different desires converged to bring together writers and their output and confirm their expectations of transformation, in the dual sense of cultural modernization and social change. The Cuban Revolution and the emergence of an incipient publishing market suggested that expectations of participation in a process of transformation were possible and that culture and politics on the continent were finally reaching that inaugural stage. The encounter of writers with an audience was widely celebrated and, in particular, the fact that it was the new proposals for aesthetic modernization that seemed to gain general acceptance. However, in the long run, the market reorganized the authors' space with its own dynamics that did not correspond to the criteria of quality that were initially invoked. The space of commercial success generated conflicting positions in the literary field, and 1967 (the year the successful *Cien años de soledad* [*One Hundred Years of Solitude*] was published) marked the peak and the end of the prospects for new acclaim in the market. This phenomenon of the climax and almost immediate exhaustion of the possibilities of the publishing market was crucial in the constitution of ideologies or "writer figures" and marked a boundary between writers considered "revolutionary" and those who were "acclaimed" that led to a pejorative rereading of success according to political criteria that regarded writers who achieved acclaim in the market as traitors to their revolutionary duties.

The period was characterized by the emergence of a strong normative spirit, so disciplining that its rigidity led to the abandonment or failure of the attempt to develop an aesthetic-ideological program that would satisfy those involved. I do not use the word failure here in the same sense in which it appears in some critical analyses, where projects and programs that critics define as non-explicit programs of texts, movements, or poetics are considered "failures." My aim is simply to reflect on the conditions in which the explicit and widespread attempt to politically define the world of forms encountered its ideological, aesthetic, and historical limits. It proved impossible to establish a common program, and the initial euphoric cohesion of a bloc of writers ended with the realization that they disagreed on more than they agreed on. I consider this result a failure in that these were the most important projects that united the Latin American intellectual field (and constituted it as such) at the time.

Debates, commentaries, reviews, polemics, and pronouncements gave rise to a (sometimes Byzantine) search for content, forms, and genres that would fully capture the perfect (revolutionary) definition of literature and politics and induce participants to act accordingly.

The will to politicize art was expressed in a strongly programmatic way that saw significant changes in a relatively short period. It was highly reactive to transformations in the situation at the time; it responded to mixed logics, specifically cultural and specifically political (which also competed with each other); it was permeable to subtle variations of nuance; it reflected the intense struggle of interests at stake and of power relations between agents competing for the distribution of cultural capital; and it gradually defined alignments, discourses, and practices.

The bibliography devoted to analyzing those decades ventured the hypothesis that at the time "everything was politics." But it would be more appropriate to state that the characteristic grammar of the discourses was more exclusive than cumulative. From thinking that "everything was politics" there was a shift to questioning that belief and trying to clarify what was being talked about when talking about politics.

Therefore, this process resulted in statements along the lines of "nothing is (sufficiently worthy of being considered) politics, except. . . ." Or, in other words, as Michel de Certeau put it to capture the challenge of conceptualizing the events of May '68: "What was *positively* experienced could only be expressed *negatively*..." (1997, 14).

Ellipses came to express increasingly antagonistic positions within an intellectual field initially constituted by broad consensus, discarding (increasingly ephemeral) provisional agreements and leading to more violent polemics. These years that focused so much on reconciling the demands of modernity, action, and the expansion of justice defined the field of notation as a notably acrimonious space.[4]

Throughout this period, literary production was formulated within the dual horizon of modernization and politicization. The rejection of realism (particularly in the normative Soviet variant) was unanimous. However, the notion of realism (often conceived as critical realism) served to describe much of the textual production. Thus, Carpentier, advocating for "the marvelous real," or Abelardo Castillo, defining the genre of fantasy as a means of grasping "deeper zones of reality," recognized that aesthetic production required some mention of objectivity in order to be thought of in political terms. The attempt to reposition literature within the horizon of the avant-garde introduced the question (acknowledged by both writers and critics) of the tension between communicability and legibility, between democratization and personal taste as a problem for writer-intellectuals.

The period of the sixties/seventies constitutes an *epoch* that was characterized by a shared perception of the inevitable and desired transformation of the universe of institutions, subjectivity, art, and culture, a perception through which truly groundbreaking events, such as the Cuban Revolution, were interpreted, not only for Latin America but for the entire world.

---

4 I find it fortuitous to be able to put it as follows: "The history of a concept is not wholly and entirely that of its progressive refinement, its continuously increasing rationality, its abstraction gradient, but that of its various fields of constitution and validity, that of its successive rules of use..." (Foucault 1972, 4).

1

The Sixties/Seventies as an Epoch

"...among / those who shall call this time the ancient time."

DANTE, *The Divine Comedy* (*Paradiso* XVII, 119–20)

1. Epoch: The Search for a Meaningful Nomenclature

There are fourteen prodigious years between the arrival of the victorious guerrillas of the Sierra Maestra in Havana and the overthrow of Salvador Allende followed by an avalanche of dictatorial regimes in Latin America. A period in which everything seemed about to change. Some speak of these years as "the sixties" and "the seventies," attempting to outline irreducible differences in that short span of time.

However, I would like to "denaturalize" these nomenclatures and decline to simply bestow on them the significance attributed to calendar cycles as if they naturally had them. How can we understand a beginning or an end that is removed from the cosmic order—since "unlike the cosmic order, in history there exist days that do not dawn" (de Certeau, 1997, 31) —, avoid encouraging mass suicide at the appearance of Halley's Comet, resist the temptation to conceive of the present in terms of the theoretically empty category of "the end of the century," or "the nineties," in the same way as the immediate past, like "the sixties" or "the seventies," without giving this economy of language such undeserved categorical weight?

The attempt requires problematizing the question of scope and boundaries. With respect to this question, which is central to history (in the case of both short and long cycles), what facilitates the contemplation of discontinuities, thresholds, ruptures, cutoffs, and transformations? Michel Foucault, in *The Archaeology of Knowledge*, asked himself: What is *a* science? What is *an* oeuvre? What is *a* theory? What is *a* text? We could add to this list: What is *an* epoch?

Undoubtedly, the notion of *epoch* shares certain traits of a caesura and can be thought of as the conditions for the emergence of an object of discourse; that is, the historical conditions that imply that one cannot simply talk in any *epoch* about anything. How is it that this utterance has appeared rather than another in its place? It could be said that, in terms of a history of ideas, an epoch is defined as the field of what is publicly sayable and acceptable—and enjoys broad legitimacy and attention—at a particular moment in history, rather than a time lapse dated by simple events, established as a mere resource *ad eventa*.

Thus, the period of the sixties/seventies, without quotation marks, constitutes an epoch with its own historical density and more or less precise limits, which separate it from the constellations immediately preceding and immediately following it, surrounded in turn by boundaries that allow it to be identified as a temporal and conceptual entity in its own right.

It is a relatively short period of time, with a focus on its *extremely short duration*, which therefore determines the need for a powerful magnifying glass to develop a meaningful periodization of this temporal segment in which the convergence of political situations, intellectual mandates, aesthetic programs, and social expectations changed the institutional parameters and ways of reading and producing literature and discourses on literature. The Cuban Revolution, African decolonization, the Vietnam War, the antiracist revolt in the United States, and the various outbreaks of youth rebellion point to a web of institutional, political, social, and economic relations that help explain the perception that the world was about to change and that intellectuals had a role in that transformation, either as its spokespersons or as an inseparable part of the revolutionary energy itself.

When speaking of epoch to refer to the period of the sixties and seventies, I wish to refer to the emergence and overshadowing of these notions. During that epoch, according to the manifestos and declarations that emerged, the logic of history was seemingly unavoidable and its temporality was expressed through the emergence of *fast times*, best reflected through the metaphor of the *speeding chariot of history*, which trampled the hesitant in its inevitable course.

The notion of *epoch* seems to be an appropriate heuristic concept to conceptualize the years from the late fifties to the mid-seventies, given that current forms of naming them, based on the periodicity of years ending in zero, do not constitute satisfactory explanatory frameworks and do not allow us to understand the internal continuity of the period of the sixties/seventies. That period (1959 to *around* 1973 or 1976) is what North Americans and Europeans generally refer to as the sixties; the differences in nomenclature are related to the fact that the early years of the seventies were crucial to the process of revolutionary politicization in Latin America and the decline of that process in the rest of the world. It is likely that in Europe and the United States, the so-called oil crisis had a decisive influence in prompting the countries involved to seek solutions not only to their economic predicament, but also to the new area of conflict that was opening up with respect to the Arab countries in the Organization of Petroleum Exporting Countries (OPEC). What is clear is that the distinction between the sixties and seventies is meaningless if we recognize that the whole period is affected by the same problem: the increasingly important role of politics and revolutionary expectations. Naturally, this process of radicalization shifts, in both temporal and geographic terms, throughout the period, but the difference is one of intensity. Visualized on a map in constant diachrony, it can be seen as concentrated in one place, weakened in another, but always active somewhere in the world.

Inevitably, for many European and North American scholars, the year 1968, marked by rebellion, appears as a condensation of this period. An example of this perspective can be found in Aronowitz's statement: "In 1968, students and other intellectuals presented themselves as new agents—not only in Paris, Berlin, and other Western capitals, *but also* in Mexico, Buenos Aires, and Prague" (129–30; emphasis added). One might be tempted to ask, why *but also*?

Many—though not all—of the analyses presented by scholars from the European or North American perspective lose sight of the fact that the origins of the revolutionary groundswell came from the Third World, from the Cuban and Vietnamese Revolutions and, before that, from the processes of decolonization in Africa, and as a result, they often push back the "sixties" to date its origins in 1968. This is sometimes even done by some in the Third World who attribute the iconography of their discontent to the student protests of 1968: their posters of Che, Ho Chi Min, Mao, and other leaders of the rebellion.

However, there is no real need to delay the revolutionary period by that much, at least not in Latin America, Asia, or Africa. And possibly not in other locations either. As Serge July, editor of the daily *Libération*, acknowledges: "The defining characteristic of my generation is Algeria. Leftism did not emerge from '68, it emerged from the generation of the 1960s" (Cohn-Bendit 111).

Despite emphasis on concrete situations that are shaped by the perspective of the analyst and differences in designation, the period is characterized in the same way: an intense interest in politics and the conviction that a radical transformation, on all levels, was imminent. To settle this discussion, one might consider the "long sixties" as a potential designation, were it not that the category of epoch is conceptually more descriptive for this period.

Although the sixties/seventies time period constitutes an *epoch*, this does not imply discarding, within the internal coherence that this designation suggests, turning points, contrasts, and moments of rupture that, while finding their place within the dominant discursive formation, mark internal periodizations that must be revealed bearing in mind some key *conceptual* criteria.

2. Uniqueness: Impending Revolutionary Transformations

Practically all the disciplinary approaches that have explored the question suggest more or less implicitly that ideas, concepts, events, practices, discourses, etc., served to configure the particular historical profile of the period in terms of the notion of radical change (customs, mentalities, sexuality, experiences, political regimes). It is important to emphasize the extent to which the overwhelming similarities among scholars on this period (beyond their positive or negative assessment of it) come from the most diverse voices, fields, disciplines, and perspectives.

This descriptive consensus and the emphasis on attributing a strikingly unique historical quality to the sixties and seventies are common both in academic essays[5] as well as in texts for the broader public, testimonies, journalistic essays, and in social memory, none of which hesitate to view the sixties (as they are commonly dubbed) as a period characterized by a unique density of experience of the world, of temporality, of subjectivity, and of institutional life, separated from historical continuity by its own significance.

Collective volumes, dossiers in university journals, course topics, doctoral theses, popular books: the sixties appear to be an inexhaustible quarry of questions and issues. Undoubtedly because in that past, at once so close and so distant (the distance with which the present observes a bygone era), there is a persistent desire to understand how what happened only thirty years ago can be so far removed from the present. An immediate past that awakens our interest and never ceases to challenge us to think, especially those of us who, in the course of a lifetime, have lived through at least two epochs.

Oscar Terán sums up in a single sentence the most distinctive aspect of those years as that of a growing but problematic conviction: that politics had begun to define the meaning of various practices in the region, including, of course, theoretical ones (15). All scholars of the period coincide in characterizing it by the widespread perception of an inevitable and desired transformation of the universe of institutions, subjectivity, art, and culture, a perception through which truly groundbreaking events, such as the Cuban Revolution, have been interpreted. Following the model proposed by Albert Hirschman in *Shifting Involvements: Private Interest and Public Action*, the period could be included in a theory

---

5 See, in addition to sources already mentioned: Jameson 1984, Hobsbawm 1995, Bell 1988, 121–42, Hohendahl 1982, 126–58, Bürger 1984, Marcuse 1968a, Prieto 1983, Hollander 1981, and Jitrik 1984.

of cycles of collective behavior, as a particularly notable example of the kind of cycle defined by a sudden and intense interest in public affairs.

The heuristic nature of the notion of *epoch* is underscored by the way in which, from cultures of affluence and cultures of poverty, and from extremely diverse political-economic contexts (the welfare states of Europe, the postwar prosperity of the United States, the turmoil of the African continent, and the awakening of revolutionary ideals in Latin America), a predominantly progressive discourse of the international intellectual field was formulated.[6]

Conservative sociologist Daniel Bell also stresses these aspects, describing the period as one of political (decidedly revolutionary in nature) and cultural radicalism (merely rebellious), of turbulent sensibility, and harsh distinctions. It is interesting that Bell refers to the cultural production of the sixties in terms that are similar to the way Peter Bürger characterizes the main features of the historical avant-gardes: "An effort once and for all to erase the boundary between 'art' and 'life'; and a fusion of art and politics" (Bell 121).

There is a notable convergence in defining the epoch as a historical moment that attracts, in a very significant way, a common denominator of discourses, in which a nucleus (politics) is constituted, around which all actors position themselves, either to reject the firmness of that bond (Raymond Aron in Europe, Emir Rodríguez Monegal in Latin America, to give two emblematic examples) or to tighten that bond, as in two equally emblematic positions, which can be represented by Mario Benedetti and Jean-Paul Sartre. It was a structure of sentiments that crossed the globe. As the French intelligentsia said at the time, it was better "to be wrong with Sartre than right with Aron" (*avoir tort avec Sartre qu'avoir raison avec Aron*), which is a conceptual encapsulation that in itself strongly suggests that the relationship with Politics was considered more important than the relationship with Truth, without implying that

---

6 Given the rapprochement between the political and artistic avant-gardes, that period has been associated with the feverish twenties, since both cases gave way to the same interesting confusion between a type of formalist radicalism and a socialist radicalism that for historical reasons were thoroughly intertwined.

Politics and Truth are necessarily antagonistic, but merely that they can be and that, in part, they indeed were at some point during that period.

Left-wing affiliation became such a crucial element of legitimacy in intellectual practice that, as the Cuban Ambrosio Fornet rightly argued:

> even reformists and the right dramatically demand an "agrarian reform" and if the social revolution makes their hair stand on end, the semantic revolution intoxicates them: they all speak, or try to speak, the language of the left (1967, 106).

Raymond Aron expressed a similar view when he noted that the overwhelming superiority of the prestige of the left forced moderate or conservative parties to borrow the vocabulary of their adversaries,[7] and American student leader Jerry Rubin said as much when he recalled:

> In the sixties, the left had all the ideas. The debate was centered within the left. All the important issues were debated: family, marriage, sex, creativity, politics. The right had no ideas. It only mumbled a few platitudes about God, the Mother, the Fatherland, and Militarism (Cohn-Bendit 47).

The belief in the inevitability of socialism went hand in hand with the idea that it (not capitalism) embodied true historical rationality: the domination of majorities by minorities was, for a good part of the intelligentsia, a reality that offended not only their ethics but also their intelligence.

As Régis Debray, an undisputed protagonist of the time, recalls in a 1996 interview, in the early sixties the world was swept by the sense that a global victory that would change the face of the world and of humanity was imminent ("Un contrapunto entre Régis Debray y Daniel Bensaid" 10). After all, the belief that change was imminent was even reflected in hyperboles such as those that foreshadowed messianism and prophetism and that could be expressed in the idea—mentioned in the first editorial of the Peruvian magazine *Amaru*—that "a potential

7 "The left has such superior prestige that moderate or conservative parties strive to adopt certain terms borrowed from their opponents' vocabulary."

mutation of the species" may be taking place ("Una revista de artes y ciencias" 1).

Even in the United States, in a televised speech on May 9, 1966, Senator Robert Kennedy publicly acknowledged what seemed obvious to the left at the time: "A revolution is coming . . . a revolution which is coming whether we will it or not. We can affect its character; we cannot alter its inevitability." After this categorical prediction, how could the conviction that Latin America's stormy history had entered a decisive stage not become widespread? (Halperin Donghi 1984, 153).

In December 1962, the Chilean (and Catholic) magazine *Mensaje* echoed this inevitable imminence of the revolution:

> faced with the "revolution underway," it is impossible to remain neutral. Either one opposes it and fights it openly or covertly, or one supports it; there is simply no other alternative ("Revolución en América Latina").

In short, these were "years of historical fever," as David Viñas defined them, an epoch quintessentially characterized by the appearance of a new revolutionary desire that moved people toward socialism (Castillo 9).

Even the discourse of the Catholic Church was transformed by the climate of the times. Beginning with Pope John XXIII's papacy, in which the encyclicals "Mater et Magistra" (May 15, 1961) and "Pacem in terris" (April 11, 1963) were proclaimed, the Church introduced what came to be known as the *aggiornamento.* As a result, official ecclesiastical discourses were suffused with reinterpretations of the commitment to charity. During this modernization, which became increasingly pronounced following the Vatican Council, Paul VI defined the moment as a *new era* of history, characterized by the gradual global expansion of rapid and profound changes. Of course, when it came to matters of faith, not everyone in the hierarchy agreed with the guerrilla priest Camilo Torres, fallen in combat in 1966, for whom to be a revolutionary was a commandment and not to be one, a moral sin.

Under the banner of guerrilla mystique, an alliance was sealed between the Christian faith and revolution that created and preserved a Christian symbology embodied by the mythical figure of Che Guevara (de Certeau 114). The ties between Christianity and revolution became the subject of sophisticated conceptual formulations.

Without any major theological innovations, the Catholic Church revisited the Christian message, devoted itself to the "social question," and promoted a Christian revolution and the vision of the "new man." If it wanted to be faithful to the values it was founded on, it had to identify itself with the causes of the continent's poor and promote a more just world on earth. The Second Episcopal Conference of Latin America held in Medellin (1968) represented a culminating moment in this process. Among the revolutionary activists there were many Christians who entered politics through faith. The fact that the millenarian and conservative Catholic institution found it necessary to update itself would suffice as proof of the unique orientation toward the future that began during that period.

3. Third World and Revolution

Germany's defeat in 1945 did not guarantee world "peace" or the end of war, despite agreements to that effect, which in many cases led to other wars. Several European armies also continued to occupy Africa, following a colonial push to partition it in the late nineteenth century. The confrontation between the two major world powers that consolidated after 1945 led to wars on other battlefields in areas that, although they have not succeeded in modifying the narrow concept of "world," are nevertheless included in "globalization."

In the mid-fifties, a group of intellectuals who were highly critical of state intervention in the economy and who would later become advisers to neoliberal governments announced that ideologies, that is, the ideas of others, were dead. The others—in this case the leader of the Soviet bloc at the time, Nikita Khrushchev—proposed "peaceful coexistence" which was intended to restrict competition between communists and capitalists to emulation. The contest that would identify the winners was not limited to the conquest of space, which provided televised entertainment. The arms race in pursuit of the longest-range nuclear missiles was undoubtedly one of the contenders' most ambitious projects.

Meanwhile, Africa, Asia, and Latin America were the scene of a wave of revolutions that many saw as the driving force toward world revolution. In 1959, according to Frantz Fanon, two-thirds of the world's population were ready to commit as many machine guns as necessary to the revolution, and the other third gave their moral support to the cause of the wretched of the earth (1969, 10).

Political boundaries have always been movable, but the acceleration of their reconfiguration did not appear to generate widespread vertigo until that period. In the bipolar political context of the processes of decolonization in Asia and Africa, the idea of a Third World capable of political intervention without allying itself with either the United States or the Soviet Union gradually began taking shape. Frantz Fanon, Patrice Lumumba, Amílcar Cabral, Antonio Agostino Neto, Kwame Nkrumah, Abdel Nasser, Gandhi, and Nehru, among others, sparked interest and sympathy among the ranks of progressives.

Through a regular series of encounters, an alliance between nations was forged, culminating in the creation of the Non-Aligned Movement in Belgrade (1961), joined by Cuba, which promoted a broader alliance that materialized in 1966 with the Organization of Solidarity with the People of Asia, Africa, and Latin America at the Tricontinental Conference in Havana. Undoubtedly, African decolonization, the Cuban Revolution, and the Vietnamese resistance radically disproved the predictions of those who only a short time earlier had anticipated the end of revolutionary ideologies.

The resulting political and intellectual agenda proposed repudiating all colonial powers and postulated an anti-imperialism which, without renouncing the idea of sovereignty and national liberation, coexisted with the expectation that the world revolution had been set in motion. It also strengthened the conviction that history was changing location and that from then on it would be taking place in the Third World. These expectations concerning the revolutionary potential of the Third World were periodically reiterated in speeches that were almost tirades: it is no coincidence that Fredric Jameson situates the origins of what he calls "the sixties" precisely in the Third World, specifically the Cuban Revolution, and that Herbert Marcuse, considered the ideologue of the French revolt of May 1968, emphasized that little could be expected of the European and North American proletariat on the eve of the revolution.[8] Arguably, the period saw a shift from a Eurocentric, pro-Western, or North Atlantic perspective to a polycentric outlook, although in the case of Marcuse's theses it is above all a reflection on capitalism rather than an abandonment of the Eurocentric perspective *per se*.

Frantz Fanon and Albert Memmi developed new hypotheses of social conflict, such as the colonizer versus the colonized, which went beyond the notion of class struggle and identified other actors, such as the proletarian nation and the Third World. Third World leaders were outlining a new revolutionary theory for new actors and new battle scenarios. Thus, in Sartre's view, it was not true that the time had come for the Third World to choose between capitalism and socialism. Rather, underdeveloped countries should refuse to take part in this contest since the Third World could not merely define itself in relation to previous values.

The perception of new antagonisms, while it did not eliminate class struggle, did underscore other elements in conflict.[9] Oppositions

---

8 It is surprising, however, that Jameson analyzes the student revolt of May 1968 in France as a question of "domestic politics." As for Marcuse, in his 1967 lectures at the Freie Universität of Berlin, he argued that while student protests could not generate a revolution in themselves, they represented spontaneous and disorganized social tendencies that presaged a complete break with the prevailing needs of the repressive society. In *The End of Utopia*, Marcuse alluded to the level of the integration of the proletariat into the welfare society of the developed world: "We are not fighting against a terrorist society. We are not fighting against a society that has already shown that it cannot function. We are fighting against a society that works, on the contrary, extraordinarily well and, what is more, we are fighting against a society that has succeeded in eliminating poverty and misery to a degree that previous stages of capitalism have not achieved." Marcuse is one of the few who recognized what would become blindingly obvious in later literature on the period: the flawless functioning of a machine that, as Eric Hobsbawm argues, allowed the vast majority of the world's population to live as aristocrats and potentates had lived a century earlier.

9 "The colonial situation is based on the relationship between one group of people and another. The leftist colonizer is part of the oppressing group" (Memmi 2003, 82). The first fragments of *The Colonizer and the Colonized* were published in 1957 in the French magazines *Les Temps Modernes* and *Esprit*, and

expressed in terms of oppressor and oppressed nations or developed versus underdeveloped nations implied new or different views of domination and exploitation and posited that the rebellion of the substratum of the outcast and the alien, the exploited and the persecuted of other races and colors, the unemployed and the unemployable was revolutionary, even if their consciousness was not (Marcuse 1968a, 271). Che Guevara, in his *foco* theory, affirmed something similar: the military vanguard could trigger the conditions for a revolution even if the subjective conditions were not in place.

Certain intellectuals in advanced capitalist societies concluded that their countries were experiencing a sort of "Iron Age" of the planetary era, as opposed to the revolutionary ferment they were witnessing in other places (Morin 1969, 1–10). From this assessment came an urgent need to renew the political program in favor of a revolutionary leftism—one that was independent of the leadership of the traditional Communist parties—that Third-Worldism appeared to inaugurate. In the developed and prosperous world, those who had adopted the hypotheses of Marxism were perplexed by their own reality: social democracy, the economism of the proletariat, proved to be not only incapable but also unwilling to radically transform society.

The explanatory category of "imperialism"—formulated by Lenin in *Imperialism: The Highest Stage of Capitalism*—was called upon with new force to explain why the revolution had not begun in advanced capitalist societies as Marx had predicted. According to this explanation, the absence of proletarian revolutions in developed countries was due to the material well-being that even the less favored classes enjoyed thanks to the exploitation of the colonies and neo-colonies. In the words of Mexico's Enrique González Pedrero, capitalist countries had mitigated revolution and social conflict within their societies because they had raised the standard of living of their proletarians at the expense of the exploitation of the impoverished masses of Africa, Asia, and Latin America. But he also claimed in *El gran viraje* [The Great Turning Point] that this situation was about to come to an end. Enslaved countries had

---

it was later published in book form by Pauvert Editions, Paris, 1966. See also Ramos 1973, 51; and Fernández Retamar 1968.

become aware of the struggle they had to carry out to liberate themselves and once again generate the conditions in the exploiting countries that would make the proletarian revolution inevitable; only then

> will colonization return to its place of origin: living standards will once again fall in the capitalist countries; the paralyzed social conflict will regain its natural dynamism, and the Marxist premises will once again enter into effect. The parenthesis that has sustained the capitalist world will disappear thanks to this human, national, and democratic Revolution that is the Revolution of the underdeveloped countries, the Revolution of the slaves of which Hegel spoke.

In terms of conceptual development, the formulation of what later became known as dependency theory by Latin American sociologists and economists was of crucial importance. The origins of these analyses were twofold; they were based on the interpretation of the United Nations Economic Commission for Latin America and the Caribbean (ECLAC)—inspired by Raúl Prebisch—of the increasing deterioration of the *terms of trade* between underdeveloped countries, which produced raw materials with little value added, and industrialized countries.

In this sense, the proponents of dependency theory (including Fernando Henrique Cardoso and Enzo Faletto, whose book on the topic is emblematic) believed that as a key starting point it was important to refute the hypothesis that, in order for periphery countries to develop, they must repeat the developmental phase of the economies of core countries.

In response, they proposed an integrated model of development, in which development and underdevelopment were seen as two (mutually necessary) sides of the same coin rather than successive stages in a universal model of development. Dependency theory was also based on a Marxist framework, in a rereading of Lenin and his concept of imperialism. In this sense, there is a crucial need to revisit the political categories suggested by this theory, which maintained the absence of a metaphysical relationship between states and posited that these relationships are possible through a network of interests and coercion that bind some social groups to others, some classes to others, all of which made it necessary to show in each case how state, class, and production are related (31 and 162).

This crisis in political thinking also affected confidence in the revolutionary role of the Soviet Union, the leader of the socialist camp, though at the time it was disputing that leadership with China. In fact, anti-communists who believed that the weakening of the Cold War would finally put an end to a long dispute for hegemony between the two major world powers, thanks to what had come to be called "peaceful coexistence," had not perceived that there were new sources of revolutionary energy and that these no longer came from Communist parties.

None of the existing Communist parties or states appeared to be suitable spaces for promoting the revolution in the Third World. Despite the fact that more than half the world had been won over to socialism, as the French communist publication *La Nouvelle Critique* affirmed in early 1963 (Haroche 50), the party of professional revolutionaries created by Lenin was paradoxically focused on the defense of the thesis of socialism in a single country.

Although it focuses on the specific case of Argentina and the particular difficulties that Peronism posed for leftist thought in the country, José Aricó's diagnosis holds validity in Latin America as a whole with regard to the relationship of intellectuals with the Communist parties. Comparing the achievements of European communism with those of the Latin American variant, Aricó affirms that in Europe communist mediation had succeeded in bringing intellectuals and the working class closer together, while elsewhere, especially in Latin America, party support did not solve this problem (1988, 47). The nationalist component of the new Latin American left, along with the characteristics of the continent's Communist parties, which were always subservient to the positions established by the Communist Party of the Soviet Union (CPSU), revealed the need for a new progressive path (Aricó 1964, 241–65). If the party members themselves considered the struggle against party dogma to be crucial, for those who had never been part of the party's directives this theoretical struggle was even less traumatic. Mexican Víctor Flores Olea, for example, believed that his generation did not experience Stalinism as a conflict of conscience and that, although the 22nd Congress of the CPSU had been welcomed as a kind of liberation, they were not traumatized by the revelation of crimes, torture, and forced labor (1962, 80).

The accusation of neo-leftism launched by Communist Party leaders was emphatically rejected by a critical intelligentsia that no longer accepted criteria of unquestionable authority nor perceived its social importance as diminished.

For the members of the new revolutionary causes in Asia, Africa, and Latin America, and also for their intellectual fellow travelers, the generalized discrediting of the bourgeois-democratic political systems and the traditional Communist parties led to the conviction that only a violent revolution could lead to authentic socialism.

Violence took on a key role in the political life of left-wing activists and intelligentsia. In the prologue to *The Wretched of the Earth*, Sartre once again alluded to violence as the midwife of history.

The perception and understanding that the social order was founded on violence made it possible to contrast the violence of the oppressors with revolutionary counter-violence. The topic of violence even permeated the discourse of the Church. During the papacy of Paul VI, the encyclical "Populorum Progressio" (promulgated on March 26, 1967) went so far as to justify violence in cases of evident and prolonged "tyranny." For the left, the notion of revolution was to gradually occupy the entire semantic range of the word "politics"; revolution would become a synonym for armed struggle and revolutionary violence.

It was not only that the general resolution of the Cultural Congress of Havana stipulated that the highest form of culture was the people's war in defense of the future of humanity. If we trust an important body of testimonies, there was a relatively vast social consensus in favor of armed violence. A substantial part of left-wing intelligentsia and political activism naturally supported armed struggle and revolutionary counter-violence, but they were also supported by large sectors of the general population. On one occasion, a group of journalists covering the Tricontinental Conference held in Havana in 1966 had the opportunity to speak with Fidel Castro and asked him about the Cuban delegation's report that claimed that to speak of guerrilla struggle in Chile or Uruguay was as senseless and absurd as denying this possibility in Venezuela, Colombia, Brazil, Guatemala, or Peru. The journalist Carlos María Gutiérrez commented in the article "Conversación con Fidel" [Conversation with Fidel] (*Marcha*, no. 1366, August 18, 1966) that both the Chileans and Uruguayans present were "intrigued by a statement in the

Cuban delegation's report to the Latin American Solidarity Organization that said that to speak of armed struggle in Chile or Uruguay" was "as absurd as denying this possibility in Venezuela, Colombia, Brazil, Guatemala, or Peru," and that, as a result, "the Chileans and Uruguayans among us felt insulted by such a blunt statement."

For his part, political scientist Guillermo O'Donnell estimated that in Argentina there was a high degree of sympathy for the guerrillas among a significant part of the population. And, most strikingly, several of those kidnapped by the Tupamaros, subsequently interviewed by María Esther Gilio and Guillermo Chifflet for *Marcha*, recounted curious conversions during their captivity: they acknowledged their role as "exploiters," stating that they had gained an "awareness" of the situation and argued that there was a need to consider the real causes of the violence rather than its effects. And last, an Argentine military government even stated in a speech that it understood there were social and political causes behind the emergence of the guerrillas, whose ranks, according to that document, consisted of "well-meaning young people" (cited in Ollier).

4. Questions of Closure

While determining the beginning of the period of the sixties/seventies may be relatively simple, determining the moment in which it came to an end is not.

When (once again) reviewing his own life and political history, Debray called left-wing political activism a spectral community, as if to imply that it had coalesced around a completely mistaken, ideological, or blind vision of the world. For Debray, the period covered in this study represents the last wave of Marxism, which, whether reformist or orthodox, had been the period's main theoretical guide (1996, 40–42, 120–25).

This is a period of frustrated expectations, the swan song of lettered culture in Latin America and in the world. We know the facts: the world revolution did not take place. That leftist community—so powerful in its production of discourses and so convincing with respect to the changes it announced—and that period—in which great masses were mobilized as never before—, were they the result of an unfounded illusion?[10]

If, in Debray's view, the left was mistaken, is it not conceivable, on the other hand, that the succession of military coups and the brutal repression were a response inspired by the same conviction that the revolution was coming (and that there was therefore a need to fight against it)? Was the assessment wrong, or were the relations of force changed in order to stifle the existing revolutionary drive?

We are unable to answer these questions even though we feel compelled to ask them. Many protagonists and witnesses of those years are still reassessing the beliefs and convictions they held at that time. This can be seen in the growing number of books and studies on the period, revealing more or less sympathy for the revolution that never was and suggesting that the interpretation of those years has not yet come to an end.

Yet if an epoch is defined by the field of objects that can be said at a given moment, the end of that period is tied to a strong redistribution of discourses and a transformation of the field of objects that may or may not be discussed. In 1971, the Bolivian general Hugo Banzer overthrew his colleague Juan José Torres, whose national populist government was supported by a significant portion of the left. Between 1971 and 1974, Banzer consolidated a repressive regime that was remarkably similar to that of other Latin American dictators. In 1973, a truly dark year for Latin America, one of the experiences that bolstered the expectations of transformation came to an end (I am referring to the overthrow of Salvador Allende's socialist government in Chile). In Uruguay, President Juan María Bordaberry, who had come to power in 1971, defeating the leftist Frente Amplio in the elections, had violated civil rights in a process that intensified when Aparicio Méndez was installed as the de facto ruler in 1976. In August 1975, Peruvian General Francisco Morales Bermúdez overthrew General Juan Velasco Alvarado, who had been supported by important leftist intellectuals and even former guerrillas and who had carried out an agrarian reform to the detriment of owners of large estates.

10 See Jameson 1984, 82.

In March 1976, a new military regime was established in Argentina, ushering in an unprecedented level of repression in that country. The coercion of the dictators imposed the objects of discourse by force and led the objects of silence to an extreme, silencing them through censorship and worse.

Returning to the topic of the Church, it should be noted that it also yielded to the effects of the end of the epoch. Many of the words that had once had a particularly important significance were reinterpreted. The encyclical "Evangelii nuntiandi," promulgated by Paul VI, "the pope of Medellin," redefined in far less political terms the uncomfortable connotations of the word "liberation," which had been emblematic of the Colombian conference.

In several respects, the epoch can be thought of as a crisis of hegemony in the Gramscian sense; Antonio Gramsci defines the crisis of hegemony (a crisis in the usual pact between the dominant and the dominated, a standoff of antagonistic forces) with an emblematic metaphor: *the old dies before the new can be born.* "It is a crisis of confidence that affects the parties, extends to all organs of public opinion—especially the press—and throughout civil society, and implies that the ruling class ceases to fulfill its economic, political, and cultural function; that is, it ceases to push society as a whole forward." As a result, the ideological bloc that lends it cohesion and hegemony tends to split apart. It is important to remember that, for Gramsci, the construction of hegemony is the condition for a dominant class to become a ruling class, leading to the disintegration of the ideological bloc that gave it cohesion and hegemony. The plausibility of this hypothesis would appear to be supported by the idea at the time of a paradox in which the governments in power and the sectors ideologically linked to them held political, military, religious, and economic power, but did not exercise any dominion, not even a moderately powerful influence, over intellectual activity, especially with respect to writers and artists.

Gramsci makes it clear that crisis is not necessarily a prelude to revolution—as the history of capitalism and its capacity for rebirth demonstrate, that not every crisis leads to revolution and the formation of a new historical bloc. Moreover, Gramsci warned that the collective consciousness of the subaltern classes does not necessarily become revolutionary consciousness, and he warned that the politicization of the subaltern classes and their intellectuals had fewer possibilities of success, given that these classes did not possess the same capacity to orient themselves rapidly and reorganize themselves with the same rhythm as the ruling classes. Gramsci recognized that in the modern world the most frequent examples in which crises like this were resolved were regressive; in other words, they ended with the reconstitution of the old historical bloc. The ruling class always had better alternatives: the rearrangement of civil society; the utilization of political society through the use of the state apparatus to crush the reaction of the subordinate classes and separate them from their intellectuals by force or political attraction; and Caesarist-type solutions in which providential or charismatic figures appear, when the two sides are on equal footing and neither has an absolute chance of winning.

Regardless of whether there was indeed a crisis of hegemony at the time, what is undeniable is that in one way or another the international left read the generalized process of politicization, along with other signs, as though they were really facing a crisis of this type, especially in Latin America. In fact, through their press organs, critical intelligentsia and political activism announced the impending end of capitalism, the agony of which was *read* as much in the events of Vietnam as in the replacement of the dollar standard, in the rejection of American policies by significant groups of "liberal" intellectuals in the United States, and in the emergence of Black Power and other movements, considered evidence of the decay within the very entrails of the monster, as Martí once put it.

One scene that shocked the world, given the eloquence of the image, took place in July 1968. At the Olympic Games in Mexico, two American athletes won first and second place in the two-hundred-meter dash. John Carlos and Tommy Smith took their places on the podium. They were Americans, but above all they were Black; and instead of looking at their country's flag as it was raised and the national anthem of the winners played, they raised their clenched fists, gloved in black.

For the left-wing activists and intellectuals, it was hardly insignificant that the American army, with all its paraphernalia and professional training, lost a war in which all its prestige as a world power was at stake against a poorly armed nation of amateur fighters.

Therefore, if we consider the epoch in the Gramscian terms of a crisis of hegemony, its end would coincide with the reconstitution of the old mode of hegemonic domination, which put an end to the revolutionary expectations that had characterized its inception. This hypothesis allows us to suggest another: its conclusion as the moment that the crisis was considered over.

The process of the death of the old before the new can be born thus implies the demise of a potential future, a future that had been meticulously outlined by the progressive sectors of society. In that sense, the epoch came to an end when that future was called utopia, when, in Dante's words, "*del futuro fia chiusa la porta*" [the door of the future has been shut] (*Inferno* X, 108).

2

The Role of Intellectuals and the Cultural Agenda

Usurers, bandits, moneylenders,
farewell. You have been erased
by the fire of the Revolution.

Heberto Padilla (1962, 119)

God: I suspect you're a left-wing intellectual.

Graffiti at the Lycée Condorcet,
May 1968

1. The Left and Legitimacy: The Role of the Intellectual

In her work on Jean-Paul Sartre, Anna Boschetti comments on the close relationship between literary legitimacy and support for the cause of the Resistance during the German occupation of France in the Second World War. Neither clerics, nor intelligentsia, nor scholars, nor elites: the word "intellectuals" remained on the side of the left and of the just cause. Of course, there were clergymen, poets, writers, and artists, who, through the complex ideological arc of the right, indifference, or individual affirmation, had absolutely no affinity with the left and no desire for (and even had a fear of) revolutionary prophecies. They rarely competed for the semantic title with new intellectuals, who instead used the word as a badge of honor, reserved for the progressive dictionary.

As Carlos Fuentes stated in *La nueva novela hispanoamericana* [The New Spanish American Novel]: "In recent decades, and particularly after the triumph and example of the Cuban Revolution, the intelligentsia of our countries is mainly on the left" (29). Right-wing intellectuals remained in a marginal position, as John King proves in his work on *Sur* magazine. There were also cases of writers who did not occupy the position of intellectual, though it may seem debatable: this is the case of García Márquez throughout the period and, even more clearly, that of Bioy Casares, Manuel Puig, and Lezama Lima, to give a few very diverse examples of writers who were reluctant to be considered intellectuals.

Belonging to the left became a crucial element of legitimacy in intellectual practice. Although not all writers adopted left-wing positions, the general trend in that direction was very strong. One example, which is almost fit for a collection of disgraceful anecdotes or malicious gossip, is the strange maneuver carried out by the Argentine writer Marta Lynch and denounced by her more "radical" colleagues.

Lynch had published the story "El cruce del río" [The River Crossing] in the Cuban magazine *Casa de las Américas*. In it she recounted the last days of the guerrilla Tania, assassinated in the Bolivian jungle along with Che Guevara. The story published in Cuba was set in Bolivia, and its characters bore the real names of the historical protagonists. In the edition published in Buenos Aires in the volume *Cuentos de colores* [Colorful Tales], the story had been changed, with all of the changes made along the same lines. Tania was no longer Tania; a Coya named María was no longer Coya but simply "Indian"; the Commander of the first version had been demoted to Lieutenant in the second, and the Frenchman (Régis Debray) of the Cuban version became Argentine in the new version. Lynch dedicated the Cuban edition of the story "To Tania, Argentine citizen and guerrilla fighter, killed by the soldiers of the Barrientos regime. Bolivia, August 1967," while the second version was dedicated to "María Estela Ocampo." This strategy reveals that if one did not necessarily belong to the left, it was still convenient to appear to do so. The magazine *Nuevos Aires* published an unsigned condemnation:

> Indignation is futile: everything fits with the odd duality of this author; a duality that allows her to express support for Chile's new government and—a few days earlier or later—deliver a talk in the Golden Hall of La Plata's Jockey Club ("Las malas traducciones de Marta Lynch" 73–74).

In a progressive movement that achieved its *quantitative* culmination in the sixties, artists and writers used public space as a tribune to address society. In other words, they became intellectuals. In addition to their shared progressivism, Latin American intellectuals shared a new conviction: that the intellectual could and indeed should become one of the main agents of the radical transformation of society, especially in the Third World.

This conviction, which helped shape the intellectual field at the time and can be found in all the documents of the period, is retrospectively described by Beatriz Sarlo as "the certainty that intellectual discourse must be important for society and especially for the popular sectors" (2004, 254).

The intellectuals developed the theory that they must take responsibility for a mission or social mandate that saw them as representatives of humanity, understood at the time to transcend audience, nation, class, town or continent, Third World or other possible and conceivable collectives.

The influential American sociologist Charles Wright Mills put this mandate into words in a lecture delivered at the Colegio de México attended by Carlos Fuentes and some of Mexico's intellectual elite: there he defined the intellectual as the key social actor and the only factor for change in the poor and illiterate societies of the Third World, adding that if no revolutionary transformations took place, the blame would fall primarily on intellectuals.

The conviction expressed by Wright Mills and shared by a large group of the Latin American intelligentsia was that the peripheral zones of the world offered favorable conditions for the rebellion of intellectuals against the ruling classes and thus supported the belief of the importance of intellectuals in revolutionary transformations.

For Wright Mills, artists and independent intellectuals were the only ones capable of offering resistance, which was why "it is in politics that intellectual solidarity and effort must be centered. If the thinker does not relate himself to the value of truth in political struggle, he cannot responsibly cope with the whole of live experience" (2008, 19). Many members of the left-wing intelligentsia quoted extensively from Wright Mills[11] and other thinkers, such as Sartre and the American left-wing economist Paul Baran, to argue that the role of the intellectual in the historical process underway had never before been so widely acknowledged or so important. The intellectual can contribute "to the spiritual palingenesis of a society" and be the "structurer of the new social order" (Rama 1964a).

> They all had the Second Declaration of Havana in mind:
> The current global correlation of forces and the universal movement for the liberation of the colonial and dependent peoples indicate to the working class and the revolutionary intellectuals of Latin America their true function, which is to place themselves resolutely in the vanguard of the struggle against imperialism and feudalism (Fidel Castro 2008, 115).

---

11 At the time, Wright Mills was at the height of his celebrity. He had gained local and international prestige with his study of the American political system, *The Power Elite* (1957), in which he shattered the idyllic image of the "great democracy" of the United States. The work was not well received by US elites and intelligentsia who felt attacked by it. Martin Seymour Lipset declared that Mills lacked any relevance in contemporary American sociology. Nevertheless, Wright Mills enjoyed massive public acclaim: *The Causes of World War Three* and *Listen Yankee* were huge publishing successes, with more than half a million copies sold in the United States and close to a hundred thousand in Latin America. Wright Mills was one of the first intellectuals who in those years began a series of "initiatory" journeys to Cuba, and Fidel Castro confessed to him that *The Power Elite* had been the book of choice of the guerrillas in the Sierra Maestra (Karol 28). Mills's support for the Cuban cause earned him greater prestige among the leftist intelligentsia. *Listen Yankee* (published in Britain under the title *Castro's Cuba*) was the most famous of the early defenses of the revolution (Thomas 1657n54). György Lukács held him up as a model intellectual (Liehm). Herbert Marcuse recognized the importance of his sociological works (1968a, 19).

As Baran asserted, in a speech that was widely disseminated in Latin America and the rest of the world, the intellectual was a figure capable of interconnecting the totality, and his function was to remind us that "the seemingly autonomous, disparate, and disjointed morsels of social existence under capitalism—literature, art, politics, the economic order, science, the cultural and psychic condition of people—can all be understood (and influenced) only if they are clearly visualized as parts of the comprehensive totality of the historical process" (1965, 5). According to Baran, the task of intellectuals consisted in eliminating obstacles to a more humane and rational social order. Their capacity to rebel against the system could be proven by the fact that they were considered by the ruling classes to be troublemakers, utopians, and subversives. Because of their historical education and tradition, intellectuals were seen as people who could apply a more rational outlook to their choices.

As these theoretical formulations show, the *epoch* represented a new perspective in terms of the politicization of intellectuals. Just as in the twenties (as Alejo Carpentier stated in his speech at the First National Congress of Writers and Artists of Cuba), political concerns helped re-establish the ties between Latin American intellectuals, but this time on a firmer basis since neither "the scientific foundations of socialism," nor the constitutive principles of continental unity, nor the identification of the United States as the common enemy were ignored (1967, 88).

With the above in mind, there is little need to stress the importance of the Cuban Revolution of 1959 as a catalyst in the desire for intellectual politicization. The Cuban Revolution showed that the conditions for a successful revolution were not tied to the predictions established by the classical tradition. The Cuban Revolution "made it possible to presage the recovery of the revolutionary impulse," exclaimed José Aricó enthusiastically in the pages of the journal *Pasado y Presente* (1964, 248).

The Cuban experience, theorized in *La guerra de guerrillas* [*Guerrilla Warfare*] by Che Guevara and then by Debray, established an even greater role for the political vanguard by suggesting that it was not always necessary to wait for all of the conditions for revolution to be in place: the fire of the insurrection could generate them. As Guevara affirmed, the guerrilla *foco* ignites the flame and spreads it. Intellectuals, not necessarily with arms at the ready, regarded their collaboration in the expansion of the subjective conditions of the revolution as part of their role.

The importance attributed to progressive intellectuals capable of expressing the core ideas of opposition to the system also emerged from the conviction that in order to achieve profound transformations, such as those desired, there was a genuine need for *superstructural* reform.

In the advanced capitalist countries of the second postwar period, the importance of the intellectual was linked to a rethinking of the notion of the historical agent of change in societies in which the working classes had lost interest or the potential to engage in revolutionary activity and where the welfare state had integrated them into a relatively pacified equilibrium. In Latin America, on the other hand, it focused on the insufficient constitution of the classic actors. In both contexts, faced with the difficulty of conceptualizing social and political dynamics in the class terms of classical Marxism, an appeal was made to concepts borrowed from other political and theoretical universes.

Eric Hobsbawm notes the shared interest and convergence of various disciplinary fields (sociology, history, anthropology, literature) in studying the problem of social transformations in general and revolutionary transformations in particular, and especially the issue of such transformations among the subaltern classes or (in the case of underdeveloped or colonial countries) among the subaltern peoples, and claims that "the political and social movements of our time are those of the peoples who live in underdeveloped (i.e., pre-capitalist or very incompletely capitalist) countries or areas" (1960). With the same concern for the question of agency and change, in 1960 Zygmunt Bauman and Julian Hochfeld recovered the notion of social formation. Interest in the topic was renewed with the publication of essays by Romano Luperini and Nicos Poulantzas and would continue throughout the period, as can be seen in the extensive debate carried out in the journals *La Pensée* and *Crítica Marxista* between 1970 and 1972. The term "pueblos en disponibilidad" or "available peoples," according to the Argentine Marxist journal *Pasado y Presente*, has no standard definition, but its "Third World" nomenclature implies a relationship with colonialism through direct domination or through the formal subtlety of neocolonialism. In different terms, but still related to the question of agency, it is important to note the influential work of Régis Debray, who theorized (*ex post*, no doubt)—based on the model of the triumphant Cuban Revolution—the inefficiency of the indispensability of the Marxist-Leninist vanguard party of the working class, at least while seizing power. His hypothesis becomes stronger when he points out the framework in which that vanguard party loses its usefulness: colonial or semi-colonial countries, in which the "de facto aristocratization of a numerically small working class and the national character of the anti-imperialist struggle" require other actors and modes of action, as he argued in "El castrismo, la larga marcha de América Latina" [Castroism: Latin America's Long March], another of the texts widely disseminated during that period in Latin American publications. Although, in many cases, the desire to take part in an inevitable process of revolutionary transformation was also enough.

The radicalization of intellectuals was also inscribed in the generalized crisis of the traditional values and institutions of politics: parliamentary democracy, the parties, the politicians themselves, and even the traditional modes of political representation that constitute some of the characteristics of the epoch.

Even from the most orthodox communist positions, Rodney Arismendi, the most important leader of the Uruguayan Communist Party underscored the significant participation of students and middle-class intellectuals in the Cuban victory and postulated the revolutionary potential of these social sectors in "our" revolution (274).

Antonio Gramsci's thinking, which was just beginning to be discussed during this period (for the role he assigned the revolutionary initiative and subject and for the way in which he postulated the relationship between intellectuals and the masses, or intellectuals and the people-nation), helped convince numerous intellectuals that they had a vital role to play in the social fabric.

Many intellectuals attempted to adapt the terms of the new challenge to a Leninist vocabulary. Ricardo Piglia proclaimed that the task of the intellectual was to work on the ideological struggle (1964, 4–6), and Abelardo Castillo defined it as the task of "awakening revolutionary awareness" (9).

Many (almost all) of the writers whose paths are analyzed here repeatedly confessed the lack of theoretical-political education. Even a theorist of the revolution as extensively quoted as Régis Debray retrospectively affirmed having started out in revolutionary theory with merely a schoolboy knowledge of Rosa Luxemburg, the Spartacist movement, and October 17, although he strongly defended his "more in-depth, affective, and genuine knowledge of the Algerian war, the Vietnam movement, the Cuban Revolution, and Guatemala" ("Un contrapunto..." 10). For this reason, it is not my intention to reconstruct the universe of theoretical readings that supplied the arguments for this widespread politicization of intellectuals: it can even be thought that this politicization *preceded the interest in revolutionary theory.*

Max Horkheimer, Theodor Adorno (1987, 146–47), and Herbert Marcuse (1968a, 17) argued that conditions in Western societies of advanced capitalism lessened the nineteenth-century contradictions between proletariat and capital, the individual and society, high culture and low culture, presenting the image of a homogenized whole, a seamless web of interconnected parts.

In these societies, the last negative and partially autonomous spaces would have been eliminated through the culture industry, and with them, any nucleus of resistance capable of creating works of art endowed with a critical spirit.

However, it is not impossible to imagine that the Latin American societies of the sixties—in some respects premodern, or at least modern sui generis—where the culture industry was in its infancy, with exceptions such as Mexico and Argentina, and where inequalities were far from being lessened, constituted a scenario in which it was possible to find the conditions for the critical impulse and revolutionary energy when, in other parts of the world, the conditions of existence had disappeared. Much of the belief in the leading role intellectuals were to play in society's transformation can be explained by the institutional conditions under which the actors' capacity to act in society was developed and perceived. We need only compare Peter Uwe Hohendahl's analysis of the situation of German artistic production in the sixties with the situation prevailing in Latin America during the same period to highlight that, although certain cultural traits of the sixties are present on a world scale, there are significant differences in terms of the consolidation of the cultural industry, cultural consumption, the role of the media, differentiation within artistic criticism, and access to symbolic goods.

In Latin America, the importance of intellectual tasks was directly proportional to the inadequate configuration of the market as a legislator of culture and a vehicle of its own criteria for the evaluation of its products. On the other hand, situations in which artists and intellectuals in Latin America were persecuted or censored (by governments such as those of Fulgencio Batista, Marcos Pérez Jiménez, Alfredo Stroessner, Miguel Ydígoras Fuentes, Juan Carlos Onganía, and many others) merely confirmed assumptions regarding their own importance.

This conviction was only reinforced through repeated attempts by the United States at intellectual co-optation and its preoccupation with neutralizing the revolutionary impetus of rebellious intellectuals by way of the cultural policies of the Alliance for Progress, outlined by the United States.

2. Artistic Modernization and the Cold War

The vast majority of Latin American artists defended cultural modernization and were open to contact with international cultures. If there was a specter or trauma among the critical left-wing intelligentsia, that trauma was largely due to the forms of official Soviet art and Stalinism and the poetics of realism and sentimentality. For the Latin American intelligentsia, rejecting subordination to Communist Party directives was perhaps more important in aesthetic than in political terms given that they saw the party's cultural policy as unsustainable and indefensible.

Cuban artists, immersed in a revolution that was seen as completely unique and groundbreaking, were especially susceptible to the Stalinist trauma and were the most insistent in their repudiation of official Soviet art. They declared, through all means at their disposal, the need to revisit Marxist aesthetic theory and accused the official Marxist aesthetics, as defined by Zhanovism, of being anti-dialectic. It was not enough that in 1959 the Third Congress of Soviet Writers showed indications that it was rejecting subordination to the aesthetics of socialist realism, nor was it enough that the 22nd Congress of the CPSU, in 1961, renewed its criticism of Stalinism, giving the impression that the liberals were gaining ground.

On that occasion the poet Yevgeny Yevtushenko read his denunciatory poem "The Heirs of Stalin." That same year Aleksandr Solzhenitsyn's novel *One Day in the Life of Ivan Denisovich*, about the life of a man condemned to forced labor by Stalin, was published with Khrushchev's personal blessing. Nor were Yevtushenko's tours propagandizing the so-called Soviet thaw enough, although his presence in global media made him a worldwide celebrity at the time. Between 1961 and 1963 he was a frequent guest in the pages of journals such as *Spiegel*, *Marcha*, and *La Nouvelle Critique*. In Latin America his book *A Precocious Autobiography* was published, and several of the most prominent poets of the continent wrote Spanish versions of his most famous anti-Stalinist poems. José Emilio Pacheco tackled "Babi Yar" and Heberto Padilla translated "The Heirs of Stalin."

However, the opinions of the leader of the Soviet Union, Nikita Khrushchev, revealed that there should be no great expectations of artistic liberalization in the USSR. On December 1, 1962, when visiting an exhibit at the Moscow Manege, he violently disqualified abstract art, stating that the paintings had not been created by human hands but rather by donkey's tails. He also asked those present whether the artists were "pedophiles or normal people" and declared that he would not spend a single kopeck on that kind of art, which he called "dog excrement" (stenographic version published in *Encounter,* no. 116, London, May 1963).

The alternating phases of restriction and liberalization that followed in the USSR did little to dispel suspicions regarding its ability to culturally spearhead the new demands of modernization of artistic means. Yevtushenko's tours were quickly juxtaposed with the trial against Iosif Brodsky, a twenty-four-year-old poet condemned to five years of forced labor for antisocial parasitism. Many left-wing publications transcribed that trial, as well as the one against Andrei Sinyavsky and Yuli Daniel that followed it.[12]

For reasons related to politics and the dynamics of the artistic field, Latin Americans had lost interest in Moscow's artistic directives. It was easy to see this simply by comparing the submissions from behind the

---

12 The transcript of the trial was printed in several publications of the "critical" or "non-aligned" left. See, for example, "Juicio a un joven poeta" [Trial of a Young Poet], *Marcha* and *Temps Modernes*: "Writing about Iosif Brodsky, the young Russian poet tried on February 18, 1964, for social parasitism and vagrancy, requires a commitment that goes beyond the purely literary" (Varela 89).

Iron Curtain at the São Paulo Biennial in 1961 with those from the rest of the world.

The emergence of Pop art (first in England, then in the United States, where it went through an impressive development) and the beatnik literary movement reestablished North American modern art on new foundations. The group consisting of Allen Ginsberg, Williams Burroughs, Jack Kerouac, and Lawrence Ferlinghetti was considered the seed of rebellion in the United States. The truth was that US artists were able to offer new aesthetics and, with them, inspire artists worldwide.

Although they adhered to socialism, Latin American artists were aesthetically closer to the United States and Europe. For that reason, US efforts to attract them were not unrealistic. Their co-optation strategies focused primarily on the field of visual arts in Latin America. In the early sixties, many US institutions sponsored visual artists from Latin America, promising them international visibility through traveling exhibits, scholarships, grants, biennials, and awards (Giunta 1995, 277–84).

There was a second wave of US efforts to capture the goodwill of artists and intellectuals on the continent. This time it was aimed at seducing writers and the emerging group of professional sociologists. This included the seminar on elites and development led by Seymour Martin Lipset in Montevideo as well as the conference organized in April 1965 by the University of Texas; and the creation of intellectual centers in Latin America (such as the Latin American Institute of International Relations), the financing of journals (such as *Mundo Nuevo*), the establishment of funds for sociologists, the projects Camelot, Job, Simpático, and Marginality, and others.

In the case of writers, the strategy of the US foundations was not as well received given the highly active and militant resistance of the intellectual groups involved in the new co-opting crusade. It is enough to recall the Latin American campaign against the journal *Mundo Nuevo* or Haroldo Conti's rejection of the Guggenheim Fellowship.

3. Writers/Intellectuals: A Field of Action and a Strong Associative Ideal

> The "engaged" writer knows that
> words are action.
> He knows that to reveal is to change and
> that one can reveal only by planning to change.
>
> JEAN-PAUL SARTRE, "What is Writing?" (1949, 23)

> Words are actions.
>
> RESOLUTION OF THE COLUMBIANUM OF GENOA

"The writer who writes a novel is a writer, but if he speaks of torture in Algeria, he is an intellectual" (Morin 1960, 35). This definition gives forcefulness to a shifting of terms between the categories of writer and intellectual that, although already part of an extensive tradition dating back to when Zola became the prototype of society's scholar-prosecutor near the end of the nineteenth century, was never more fluid than in the Latin American literary field of the epoch. Within the context of the politicization of letters, it was natural that both terms circulated as synonyms.

It is certainly a synonymy with a history. Although the label of *intellectual* has been applied to a wide range of categories ranging from *philosophe* to scientist, successively or simultaneously throughout its history, the written word appears (in all cases) as the characteristic means of intervention or identity of the intellectual. In his etiology on the constitution of intellectuals, Zygmunt Bauman points out:

> The word was addressed to a motley collection of novelists, poets, artists, journalists, scientists and other public figures who felt it their moral responsibility, and their *collective* right, to interfere directly with the political process through influencing the minds

> of the nation and molding the actions of its political leaders (1987, 1; emphasis added).

The mention of novelists and poets at the top of the list can hardly be considered random. Literary texts were a repository of enigmas for political power. Perhaps this was because some literary procedures serve to mask, through the use of point of view for example, the political opinions of the authors and the ideological "truth" of the texts. The emblematic question is the one the prosecutor puts to Yuli Daniel in 1966 (in the trial that began in February 1966): "Where is your positive hero?" It is the uncertainty of knowing where the author himself stands in terms of what has been said, what has been written. The distance between the narrator and the writer, coldly analyzed using the methods of literary theory, is a source of confusion for those in positions of power. The truth of the literary text may be indifferent to the critic; it is not, however, for those who consider the "effects" of that truth circulating in a universe of readers. The enigmatic status of fiction: document, propaganda, lie, invention, imaginary creation, etc., explains the remarkable interest of politicians and their continuous, though not always systematic, reflections on literature. Not surprisingly, many political theorists have reflected, with more or less abstract, more or less pragmatic criteria, on the nature of literature and how it can serve—or not—political causes.

From the trials against Gustave Flaubert, Charles Baudelaire, D. H. Lawrence, and Allen Ginsberg to the death sentence imposed on Salman Rushdie and the disappearance of Haroldo Conti and Rodolfo Walsh at the hands of the Argentine dictatorship, the censorship and control of literary discourses are proof of the influence that political power attributes to literature.

The fact is that in a characteristically dated definition of the *epoch*, the *Diccionario de política* [Dictionary of Politics] edited by Norberto Bobbio distinguishes two meanings of the word intellectual: a broad one that includes the social stratum that engages in non-manual activities, and a more restrictive one (and "more widespread," according to Carlo Marletti, author of the entry) whereby intellectuals are "committed writers." The latter, according to the same text, "is related to the controversial problem of the political behavior of intellectuals and their critical and questioning attitude that predisposes them to left-wing opposition and, not infrequently, to militant support of revolutionary movements" (819–20).

The willingness of Latin American writers of the time to take on political responsibility emerges as a topic at a writers' congress held in Chile in 1960. In their final declaration, the participants stated that "writers cannot and must not forget" the "urgent reality" marked by "the unfortunate and in many cases miserable exploitation of dominated and exploited countries" (Sabato). As Rama used to say, this reinscription of the literary figure as an intellectual was essential if the writer was to lose "that deleterious sensation of the gratuitousness of his work."

What is more, intervening in public affairs was also an obligation. Based on their confidence in their own discursive potential, writers deduced the importance of their practical intervention in society. In the hypotheses on the role of the intellectual, it is almost impossible not to see the traces of the effect of these ideas on those who entrusted them with such lofty missions.

The past shapes the future while in the present other technologies, other messages, other voices without a program compete for a monopoly on representations of the social. At the same time, other powers are also preparing, enemies who seek not to persuade, but to take control.

Additionally, the social, cultural, and economic context of the continent reinforced the idea that engaging in politics was inevitable for a writer, because, as Carlos Fuentes acknowledged, "When writers do not deal with politics, politics ends up dealing with writers" (1967, VII–IX).

At the beginning of the *epoch*, an extensive set of tasks emerged as the field of action for intellectual writers or, as they were called at the time, "committed intellectuals." The notion of *committed intellectual* preserved the idea of professional membership and referred to intellectuals as a group of subjects partially specialized in a particular type of knowledge. Paradoxically, however, it also made them the spokespersons of a humanist and universal conscience that transcended borders and nationalities. The doctrine of commitment assured intellectuals a participation in politics without abandoning their own field, by defining the intellectual task as always, and inherently, political labor.

In the construction of this space for artistic and intellectual activity, one cannot overlook the powerful presence of Jean-Paul Sartre, whose books and attitudes have served as a reference point since at least the mid-fifties. Sartreism provided all kinds of theoretical assurances to the transformative role of the writer-intellectual: in particular, the Sartre of *What is Literature?* brought the political aspirations of intellectuals and their professional concerns closer together. It was Sartre who forged the notion of commitment (*engagement*), which served as a foundation for the conversion of the writer into an intellectual. Furthermore, his powerful influence on Latin American leftist intellectual groups was reinforced when he embraced, early on, the Cuban cause and promoted it in Europe, as he had previously done with the liberation movements of the African colonies.

His preface to *The Wretched of the Earth* connects his arguments and his style: he writes as if he were out of breath, each sentence intensifying the urgency to put an end to a state of affairs that threatens to destroy the world. At the same time, it should also be noted that when asked by a number of his compatriots about how to become engaged, Sartre replied on his return from Cuba: "Become Cubans!" to all those who wanted the French intellectual to teach them how to support just causes. With his rejection of the Nobel Prize, which he was awarded in 1964, Sartre also established a new path with respect to the traditional institutions of distinction, while carrying out the ultimate gesture of independence with respect to the Nobel Foundation in response to the policies of confrontation between institutions at the time.

Commitment implied an alternative to concrete party affiliation; it maintained its universalist nature and made it possible to preserve the definition of the intellectual as the position from which critical thought could be formulated. Out of this symbolic place of the intellectual as a critical conscience, many of the writers of the period founded their legitimacy.

Another intellectual model was found in Bertrand Russell. Russell, who in the forties had been a victim of McCarthyism, was also very active at the time. In 1958 he published *Why I Am Not a Christian*; the following year he published *Common Sense and Nuclear Warfare*. He was emblematic of the culture of critical discourse combined with commitment. In 1966, a trial was held in Europe against US imperialism for the crimes committed in Vietnam. The so-called Russell Tribunal was presided over by Bertrand Russell, accompanied by Sartre, Josué de Castro, Stokely Carmichael, and Danilo Dolci.

The way that Ángel Rama describes Russell was fully in keeping with the theory of commitment when he mentions both specialization and universal conscience: "Philosopher, logician, mathematician, winner of the Nobel Prize in Literature, and man of our century, concerned with moral, social, political, and religious problems" (1959). The second part of this commendation is constructed on the basis of the first: specific activity in the area of culture and knowledge is the conceptual basis for the consideration of someone as an intellectual. And complementarily, his position as a "concerned" intellectual ensures that he will seek to relate scientific knowledge to human progress.

In order for the tasks of the writer-intellectuals to acquire the necessary predominantly progressive political dimension, there was a need to argue that the writer made the powers that be *uncomfortable*. Carlos Fuentes justified this ideology of writing ("every word is dangerous") by postulating that every word that announced "a real act" that broke "the new charm of consumption" (1967) would be an enemy word. By claiming that the potential word of the writer demonstrated the impossibility of the words of power, Fuentes made literature's ideological legitimacy pass for its independence from any outside interference or authority. It is this particular relationship with a political power considered illegitimate that helped consolidate the belief in the *oppositional* nature of art. The outlook that was wary of literature was that of the political enemy itself. The state was the writer's natural *Other.* Of course, as we will see below, a definitive turning point came from the existence of a revolutionary model of the state that became "real" and demanded affirmative positions from its intellectuals and from those who aligned themselves with it, thus unsettling the main hypothesis that had shaped the ideology of the progressive writer up to that point.

These "dangerous" words made their way into manifestos, conferences, and journals and sought out (or shaped) their addressees. Novels and poems were undoubtedly important, but they acted—if it can be said—on a secondary level, in a sort of historical accumulation and an accumulation of readings that was different from the dazzling and circumstantial (but no less powerful) intervention of the words published in journals or uttered in occasional speeches.

This confidence in the value of literature was most emblematically expressed in the speech that Vargas Llosa gave when he received the Rómulo Gallegos Prize. In that speech (which several Latin American journals published under eloquent titles: "Literature Is Fire" and "The Writer as Spoilsport") Vargas Llosa affirmed that the bourgeoisie would want to integrate the writer, make him official, conjure up his dangerousness, because literature meant nonconformity and rebellion given that the writer's raison d'être was protest, contradiction, and criticism, and that literature was a form of permanent insurrection that stimulated a desire for change. Perhaps inspired by Sartre, whom he admired, he offered a passionate defense of Cuba, imbuing the prize with political implications, in a context in which Venezuela—the host country—had broken off political contacts with the island and following Fidel Castro's polemics with the Venezuelan Communist Party, which provoked fierce criticism in official circles (Vargas Llosa 1967a). Needless to say, Cuban magazines were delighted with this provocation. *Unión* partially reproduced the speech under the title "Vargas Llosa, aguafiestas en Caracas" [Vargas Llosa, Spoilsport in Caracas], and the article commented that at the end of his splendid speech Vargas Llosa pointed out that he accepted the Venezuelan award because he felt that it did not require even the slightest shadow of ideological, political, or aesthetic commitment from him. No doubt, the outstanding Peruvian novelist spoiled the party for the generous officials of the National Institute of Culture and Fine Arts of the Leoni administration. Vargas Llosa had delivered his acceptance speech "in the midst of a ferocious press campaign against him" ("Una vez más"). For his part, Emir Rodríguez Monegal declared:

> I think Mario has perhaps unintentionally breached a taboo that had to be breached: the mention of Cuba in an official Venezuelan act. Though the operation was risky, the need for it in this case was obvious. Because he could not let his acceptance of the prize be interpreted as acceptance of the regime (1967a, 17).

One of the most significant spaces for intervention at the time was undoubtedly magazines (generally referred to as *political-cultural) as a whole.* The networks constituted by the various publications and their echoes were key in encouraging confidence in the discursive power of intellectuals. The first editorial in the Argentine magazine *Pasado y Presente* postulated a shared conviction when it stated that

> all journals are invariably the expression of a group of people who tend to voice a shared will, a similar process of maturation, a common position vis-à-vis reality. In other words, they express the vehement desire to critically explore what one is, what one has become, through the long and difficult historical process that characterizes the development of all intellectuals (1963, 1).

Pasado y Presente was explicitly inspired by the work of Antonio Gramsci. Although this was not the case with other magazines, they all seemed to be imbued with the conviction that they played a role in society similar to that of the state or political parties and that they constituted an unavoidable hub of ideological development.

The establishment of the Latin American network of magazines confirmed the extent to which political subjects are constituted at the discursive level: they were one of the scenarios in which writers confirmed themselves as intellectuals, in addition to disseminating Latin American authors and texts of the epoch. The number of journals that emerged at the time (short or long-lived, depending on the vicissitudes of politics and the availability of funding) is not insignificant. As the journals appeared, the task of remaining up-to-date on the state of literary production on the continent was one of their constant concerns.

Through dossiers dedicated to specific authors and countries, emphasizing their "newness" ("new" writers from Venezuela, Colombia, Uruguay, Argentina, El Salvador, Cuba, etc.), bibliographical reviews that appeared almost as soon as the works were published, interviews and mentions, and the creation of literary prizes, the mechanisms of recognition sought to renew the Latin American canon among the authors of the time. Through the magazines, we can trace the constant re-evaluation of existing production and the attempt to build a tradition based on aesthetically modern criteria, moving closer to the perspective of modernism and the avant-garde and rejecting the tellurisms, folklorisms, and nativisms demanded from Latin America by a sort of international division of artistic labor that was rejected at the time.

Writers found that their discourses had a powerful resonance in the magazines and at the same time they felt compelled to speak out and take positions on contemporary issues. Thus, the political-cultural magazine was the material platform for a privileged circulation of names and shared ideas, as well as the stage for the main polemics, which gradually became more violent as the years went by and whose main point of divergence was their positioning with respect to the Cuban Revolution from 1968 onward and with a major turning point in 1971, with the eruption of the Padilla affair. At the very least, these specific episodes can be seen as a symptom of a process in which the criteria of intellectual legitimacy and prestige varied.

The political-cultural magazine represented a form of intervention that was particularly suited to the profiles of the time and the programmatically sought relationship between culture and politics as a way of thinking about political activism at the cultural level.

Beatriz Sarlo, who founded and participated in several magazines, recalls all the connotations implicit in the phrase "let's publish a magazine" (undoubtedly repeated many times throughout the period in question). Sarlo notes in that phrase an impulse toward the public marked by the willful tension to intervene in the present (almost "urgent") situation given that their desire is to intervene in order affect change (1992, 2).

As Claude Fell states, the Cuban Revolution played the role of a true "cultural engine" (164). In March 1959 it created an institution, Casa de las Américas, which became the revolutionary center of Latin American culture. The magazine of the same name, the first issue of which was published in May–June 1960, brought together several of the writers who would become the center of the future boom: Fuentes, Cortázar, Vargas Llosa. The Latin American newsweeklies *Siempre!* (Mexico), *Primera Plana* (Buenos Aires), and *Marcha* (Montevideo) expanded their literary supplements and opened their pages up to new authors. Certainly, of all the magazines, *Casa de las Américas* occupied the most visible and central place. The Casa de las Américas institution, directed by Haydeé Santamaría—one of the women who participated in the attack on the Moncada Barracks—up until her death by suicide in July 1980, defined itself as a cultural institution aimed at serving all the peoples of the continent in their struggle for freedom (back cover of no. 4, December–January 1961–62). These objectives were clarified and expanded, becoming more overtly political following the blockade imposed on Cuba and the country's expulsion from the Organization of American States in 1962.

The map of the epoch that the magazines enable us to construct is also characterized by its own cartographic tendency; in those years, the discourses of the magazines systematically invented an object by talking about it: Latin America, the Patria Grande, and its literature. Many of them locate this creation, which goes beyond geography, in the very choice of their names themselves: *Casa de las Américas*, *Latinoamericana*, *Hispamérica*.

The magazines were a site of convergence for, on the one hand, the recovery of the horizon of aesthetic modernism and, on the other, a space of recognition that served as an alternative to traditional institutions and government bodies. And, finally, the creation of a place for the enunciation and practice of the committed intellectual. In a sense, a place that provides an object, a symbolic space, a context, or a purpose. That object or purpose was called Latin America.

Marcha, a pioneer in its field, demonstrated this will to create over the course of twenty-five years, tirelessly sustained by Carlos Quijano and later endorsed, in its cultural aspects, by Ángel Rama. If, from the historical point of view, the Cuban Revolution encapsulated this aspiration in the country dubbed "the first free territory of the Americas," from the point of view of the magazines, the legendary Uruguayan weekly was one of the first to recognize this object and make it the slogan of a struggle. In its first issue in 1939, *Marcha* had already declared its Latin Americanist vocation through the contributions of its director, Carlos Quijano, in which identity was defined in anti-imperialist and Third-Way terms: "The most shocking and decisive reality of the continent is its subjection to the economic imperialism of the great powers."

In its last issue of 1961, the cultural section of *Marcha* was organized in response to the slogan "Panorama of Latin America." "Nuestra America" [Our America], the title of the literary supplement, directed by Rama, could not be more explicit; a tradition and a history were being retrieved for this object:

> The subtropical siesta seems to have ended. New forces are shaking it up. Latin America is entering the scene. The social, political, and economic transformations that are threatening Our America are simultaneous to those taking place in the cultural sphere.

Undoubtedly, this awakening from the subtropical siesta has much to do with the Cuban Revolution and the liberation movements of the African colonies.

Historical unity? Unity of struggle? Unity of culture? What are we talking about when we talk about Latin America? To answer this question, they turned to a series of essayists who, starting late last century, had been concerned with exploring the cultural unity of the continent and its various denominations: Hispanoamerica, Latin America, Iberoamerica, Indoamerica.

In addition to *Marcha*'s continued insistence, there were magazines, both long-lasting and short-lived, that in every city of the continent explicitly ratified their belief in belonging to a greater unity called Latin America. For example, *La Bufanda del Sol* from Ecuador that claimed in its editorial to be involved "in the process toward an authentic national and Latin American culture," or the Peruvian *Amaru*, whose avowed program was to create a nucleus for Peru that would concentrate and radiate intellectual and civic concerns without limiting itself to national problems but instead would address all of the problems, traditions, and circumstances shared by the countries of "our language."

The impulse that characterizes the emblematic name of the Cuban institution Casa de las Américas is also the motivation for the Chilean University of Concepción to hold its international summer schools with the leitmotif "knowledge of the Americas" ("Discurso de inauguración del Primer Encuentro de Escritores Americanos," January 18, 1960).

For many years, Casa de las Américas centralized, co-opted, redistributed, and legitimized names and discourses in a system of loans and echoes with other magazines on the continent. In good part because the vast majority of the writers whose names began to circulate on a continental scale were like unaccredited diplomats for the Cuban Revolution in Latin America and the rest of the world. Havana was the unifying capital, the real and in other cases symbolic headquarters of many of the encounters that made the "rallying call" resonate, bringing together writers-intellectuals. In reality, it is also because the word "intellectual" is used in the plural, i.e., intellectuals. As Bauman argues, the word itself constitutes a "rallying call" that resonates across the carefully guarded frontiers of professions and artistic genres; in short, intellectuals exist to the extent that they are connected by some sort of associative ideal. That ideal was Cuba, which turned dozens of magazines into echoes, correspondences, bastions of its politics. A considerable number of the Latin American magazines of the time served as "embassies" of the island. Latin American intellectuals could have said of Cuba what André Gide said of the Soviet Union prior to disenchantment in his book *Return from the USSR*:

> Who shall say what the Soviet Union has been to us? More than a chosen land—an example, a guide. What we have dreamt of, what we have hardly dared to hope, but toward which we were straining all our will and all our strength, was coming into being over there. A land existed where Utopia was in the process of becoming reality. Tremendous achievements had already made us exacting. The greatest difficulties appeared to have been overcome, and we entered joyfully and boldly into the sort of engagement this land had contracted in the name of all suffering peoples (xiv–xv).

The Latin Americanist vocation of *Casa de las Américas* was established from its inception, and it is easy to confirm the cohesive success of its proposal by tracing the way in which its list of collaborators from the region expanded. A bimonthly magazine, its first issue came out in 1960. Haydeé Santamaría and Alberto Robaina were listed as director and deputy director respectively, although neither wrote in the magazine. Its chief editors were Fausto Masó (former contributor to *Lunes de Revolución* and later to *Mundo Nuevo*) and Antón Arrufat. The issue included texts by Argentine Ezequiel Martínez Estrada, Cubans Antón Arrufat and Virgilio Piñera, Guatemalan Miguel Ángel Asturias, Colombian Luis Enrique Valencia, and Mexican Carlos Fuentes. Starting with the fifth issue, an editorial board was established, including Martínez Estrada (who remained on staff until his death), the Mexican Juan José Arreola (Cortázar's first editor in Mexico and sponsor of Carlos Fuentes, whose first work, *Los días enmascarados* [The Masked

Days], he published) and the Paraguayan Elvio Romero. In the following issue, the position of managing editor disappeared, and Antón Arrufat became part of the editorial board (without Arreola.) The position reappeared in the ninth issue and was held by Pablo Armando Fernández until he left for London as cultural attaché. Later on, Manuel Galich, a Guatemalan exiled in Cuba, joined the editorial board, and the ties with writers and critics of the continent continued to deepen through the presence of Roque Dalton, Manuel Pedro González, Ernesto Sabato,[13] Julio Cortázar, José María Arguedas, and Rodolfo Hinostroza; a member of the young generation of poets, [Hinostroza] was living in Cuba at the time. In issue 13–14, July–October 1962, Antón Arrufat returned as editor in chief, and Cortázar and the Mexican Emmanuel Carballo, key figure of "La cultura en México" [Culture in Mexico], a supplement of the weekly *Siempre!*, were added to the board. The group that owned the weekly also published the *Revista de la Universidad* and the *Revista Mexicana de Literatura* and would take over the intellectual milieu as representative of the intellectual and artistic vanguard. Derisively, the group was dubbed "the most advanced of the country" (Agustín 205).

In mid 1963, Santamaría ceased to appear as director and became a member of the editorial board. The board was once again expanded in issue 24 with the incorporation of Ángel Rama and in issue 26 with that of Salazar Bondy (until his death). From issue 30 onward, the magazine was directed by Roberto Fernández Retamar. There are several different accounts regarding the replacement of Arrufat with Retamar. One is Retamar's own version. Another, much more controversial, is the one told by Guillermo Cabrera Infante, where he refers to Retamar as an "envious poetaster," who in his desire to take over, reminded the authorities that his predecessor was a homosexual, among other things (1992a, 89).[14] Whatever the case, the magazine continued to rapidly attract Latin American contributors. Haitian René Depestre, Cuban writers Lisandro

---

13 For those who may not be aware, Sabato was also a prominent figure at the time. His prestige would later be eclipsed by that of Julio Cortázar, especially after the publication of *Hopscotch*.

14 As the reader might imagine, Fernández Retamar is not the only one to have fallen under Cabrera Infante's crosshairs.

Otero and Edmundo Desnoes, and art critic Graziella Pogolotti joined the editorial board. Later on, Mario Vargas Llosa, Roque Dalton, Jorge Zalamea, David Viñas, and Mario Benedetti also became members, at the peak of its popularity.[15]

It would be tedious to note, magazine by magazine, the persistent appearance of an article or a name, but it is worth tracing at least part of the system of relationships and echoes that was established at the time. In particular, a system of loans or mutual sharing that lasted for years. One of the most fruitful collaborations took place between *Casa de las Américas* and *Marcha*, and also included "La cultura en México" (cultural supplement of the weekly *Siempre!*) and the Argentine magazines *El Escarabajo de Oro*, its continuation, *El Grillo de Papel*, as well as *La Rosa Blindada*, and even later ones that republished old material, showing that, even after years had passed, the themes and authors could still maintain their relevance and prestige, as in the case of the Argentine magazine *Nuevos Aires*. In many cases, it could be said that crucial texts, authors, and issues were at stake and that the repetition of names, articles, and themes, in contrast with the logic of exclusivity that generally guides each publication's quest for identity, was inspired by the need to ensure that all Latin American readers were aware of the shared program of the continent's progressive intelligentsia. The confluence between *Marcha* and *Casa de las Américas* even allowed for the publication of articles drawn from the same foreign medium, and permits us to see how the magazines formed a network through a system of reciprocal loans: a particularly significant article by Juan Goytisolo on the commitment of the writer ("Buenas y malas relaciones entre literatura y política" [Good and Bad Relationships Between Literature and Politics]) was published in both *Marcha* and *Casa de las Américas* in 1964.

A survey by the Uruguayan Carlos Núñez on the role of the intellectual was published simultaneously in both magazines in 1966. The same happened with a long series of interviews with writers Roque Dalton and Ernesto Cardenal conducted by Mario Benedetti or the one Ernesto González Bermejo did with García Márquez, which were published in

---

15 See Campuzano 1992, 62; and the testimonies of Jaime Quezada and José Ángel Cuevas (Bianchi 76 and 105).

Marcha and *Casa de las Américas*. Relationships were also established between *Casa de las Américas* and the Argentine magazines *El Grillo de Papel* and *El Escarabajo de Oro*. The letters that Retamar and Monegal exchanged concerning *Mundo Nuevo* magazine were published in a number of the continent's magazines. *Marcha* was one of the first, but they also circulated in *Casa de las Américas*, *La Rosa Blindada*, and *Siempre!* Régis Debray was a key author of the period, so his texts were systematically published and commented on. The extensive system of loans also benefited from the collaboration of the Mexican weekly *Siempre!*. The first declaration of the *Casa de las Américas* Collaboration Committee was published in *Casa de las Américas*, *Marcha*, *Siempre!*, and *Margen*. The examples are endless, and reviewing them all would be extremely tedious.

The system of loans and echoes between publications developed naturally out of the community of shared interests and strategies. Soviet policies toward writers (the trials of Iosif Brodsky, Andrei Sinyavsky, and Yuli Daniel) connected *Marcha* with *Siempre!* and *Tiempos Modernos* given that their leftist positions strongly defended cultural autonomy. Both *Marcha* and *Tiempos Modernos*, edited in Buenos Aires by Arnoldo Liberman, reproduced Brodsky's trial in 1964 and echoed Sartre's positions regarding the discussion of artistic decadence, which was the basis on which Soviet culture rejected the work of authors such as Marcel Proust, Franz Kafka, James Joyce, and Samuel Beckett.

David Viñas, Pedro Orgambide, and Noé Jitrik often wrote for *Marcha* throughout the period of the Onganía dictatorship in Argentina at a time when censorship prevented them from expressing their opinions freely. Benedetti contributed to *Tiempos Modernos*, while *El Grillo de Papel* reported on Rama or published his articles. The Chinese Cultural Revolution, as seen by K. S. Karol, was of interest in Mexico, Argentina, Uruguay, and Cuba.

Loans between magazines are useful in revealing the frequency of names and themes as indicators of both importance and authority. Those with a strong and unquestionable presence include Mario Benedetti, whose texts are published in all the continent's magazines, Julio Cortázar, Ángel Rama, Mario Vargas Llosa (contributor to *Marcha* and *Amaru*, and member of the committee of *Casa de las Américas*), Carlos Fuentes, and, most notably, the Cuban Roberto Fernández Retamar, director of *Casa de las Américas* starting in 1965, visible face of Cuban literary culture and author of some of the key texts of the period, such as the poems "Ud. tenía razón Tallet, somos hombres de transición" [You Were Right, Tallet, We Are Men of the Transition] and "Explico al lector por qué no terminé aquel poema sobre la Comuna" [Explanation for the Reader as to Why I Did Not Finish That Poem on the Commune] and the articles "Hacia una intelectualidad revolucionaria en Cuba" [Toward a Revolutionary Intelligentsia in Cuba] and "Calibán."

The task of the Latin Americanization of culture and the creation of Latin America as a space of belonging was so successful that it made the opposition between "national" and "Latin American" plausible to the benefit of the second term. A writer could be asked whether they felt they were a national writer or a Latin American writer. In fact, Leopoldo Marechal, Marta Traba, Salvador Garmendia, and Jorge Adoum answered a questionnaire that included precisely that question. Their answers are unanimous: faced with the choice between "national" and "Latin American," they all opted for the latter. Garmendia also stated: "What is understood by national writer is a form of provincial canonization, which in the end will serve to enrich *costumbrista* satire" ("Sobre la penetración imperialista").

4. The Search for (and Encounter with) an Audience

One of the main tasks in the circulation of intellectual discourse was the search for an audience. The most significant challenge was to find a public. On the one hand, because intellectuals were faced with a political task in the cultural domain in that they needed not only to engage an audience but, more importantly, *to create one*. The issue of the lack of an audience was repeatedly raised as a challenge, and one cannot underestimate the extent to which writers, critics, cultural journalists, and professors (a population that grew as social and economic modernization expanded its membership to the point of creating a new socio-professional sector) contributed to generating this audience over the course of those years. For many intellectuals, one way of analyzing the question of the writer and the public was formulated by Sartre in

What is Literature?, which not only posited the political nature of prose, but also set out a coherent project of literary production and analysis in terms of practical efficacy. This model not only considered literary content and form, but also how to adapt them to an audience, fundamental for the politicization and aesthetic representation of the society into which the artist must fit in order to fulfill their specific role. Sartre's emphasis is synthesized precisely in his call *to find a reader* (1990, 80–157).

In the late fifties and early sixties, efforts to examine the relationship between literature and politics focused on the issue of communication in an essentially pragmatic sense. It was based on the observation that readers and writers within the same country were not finding each other, coupled with the existence of a widespread lack of knowledge of the respective literatures and contemporary national authors at the continental level. In this context, it was logical that the very existence of a national or continental literature could only be validated by the existence of readers, a fact that did not appear to be obvious, as reflected in the early observation made by Ángel Rama (quoting Antonio Candido) and Carlos Real de Azúa in the pages of *Marcha* that there was neither Hispano-American literature (and this would have been relatively logical at the time) nor even a national literature ("La construcción de una literatura" 1960). As Real de Azúa argued:

> The only certainty is the presence of a constellation of national novels, of a novel, of novelists embedded in their respective literatures. At most, one could assume that on the surface there would be, if anything, a dozen novels, a dozen Hispanic American authors ("La novela hispanoamericana" 1960).

This assessment was valid for the entire continent. What was lacking was a canon that was both contemporary and alive, endorsed by a reading public. And therefore the question: "For whom do we write?" It was an essential condition for the functional concern of making literary practice ideologically effective, but even before that, it was an inescapable requirement of the simple fact of being aware of the possibility of putting the works themselves into circulation. For this reason, the public that was openly called for was, in these early conceptions, a set of readers defined as readers, a first step in thinking of them in terms of social relevance: a class, a group, a stratum.

In his groundbreaking book *Sociología del público argentino* [Sociology of the Argentine Public], Adolfo Prieto argued that the moment represented an excellent opportunity to find this desired public:

> The Argentine [and, I might add, Latin American] writer has a magnificent opportunity to win over an audience, . . . to hasten the crystallization of that amorphous, expectant, unknown collective soul. His [the writer's] salvation will lie in turning to the anonymous mass of presumed readers, questioning it, getting to know it, interpreting it, assuming for it the duty of becoming aware of situations, changing it in any of its dimensions (1956, 145).

One way of connecting literature and politics was to posit the literary work as the reflection of a social and political experience. The emphasis on experience inevitably pointed to the writer, *less to their biography than to their conscience*, assigning significance to the formula of the committed author, as a problem confined to the limits of intentionality. From this perspective, the call for new forms of realism and the defense of the intrinsic criticality and oppositionality of literature supported the idea of literature as a potential tool for transformation, with a privileged position in ideological terrain. In those terms, literature retained the legitimacy of its own rules and proposed a specific type of action, suited to the objectives of the desire for politicization.

The initial assessment was that of a lacuna affecting all aspects of Latin American culture: a lack of reciprocal knowledge of the various national literatures (neither authors nor audiences were connected to each other), aesthetic stagnation, and a lack of readers for the literary output. The nonexistence of a Latin American literature, the lack of mutual familiarity among the authors of the continent, the disconnection between writers and readers were recurrent topics of critical commentary. In late 1959, Julio Moncada commented on the lack of knowledge about art in the rest of the Latin American continent, and Gonzalo de Freitas argued that the Hispano-American reality still eluded literature. However, some signs of new interest were already in the air, as Adolfo Prieto announced.

The year 1960 also marked the beginning of the love affair between Latin American writers and the continent's reading public. Two words were key that year: "publishing" and "commitment." Across the continent there was talk of an explosion in publishing: in the bestsellers section of *Primera Plana* there were always books by the Jorge Álvarez publishing house, which released some ten books a month. The same was happening in Peru, Venezuela, and Ecuador, where book festivals were organized and cheap paperback editions were published with a concrete objective: to get books out into the streets.

The phenomenon was on the rise. 1964 was the year of recognition for the new narrative: Rama organized issue no. 26 of *Casa de las Américas* with the participation of Julio Cortázar, Carlos Fuentes, and Mario Vargas Llosa, whose names, from that point on, as well as those of José Donoso and Gabriel García Márquez, began to appear frequently alongside the already strong presence of Augusto Roa Bastos, Juan Rulfo, Juan Carlos Onetti, and Alejo Carpentier. In that year, both *Marcha* and *Casa de las Américas* confirmed the fact, announced by Ambrosio Fornet, that the age of imitations and that of goodwill that produced bad literature were over for the Latin American novel.

The Latin Americanist shift was consolidated by the international recognition of the continent's literature. Europe became less and less a provider of aesthetic parameters, and the focus was increasingly placed on Latin America's *own* productions. From the stagnation of Latin American literature, which had been a grievance only a short time earlier, there was now euphoria: literature was ablaze, literature was on fire.

News coming out of Mexico reported on the statistical fever that dominated Mexican cultural journalism, elated with the movement in publishing and the number of copies per edition. 1964 surpassed 1963 in the number of novels, with print runs of three to five thousand copies each. The novel with the largest circulation was *Los relámpagos de agosto* [*The Lightning of August*], by Jorge Ibargüengoitía (published in Cuba rather than Mexico), which won the Casa de las Américas Prize and sold some ten thousand copies. There was talk of a "new wave" in Mexican literature. The phenomenon was perceived from the perspective of writers as well as by publishers and readers. The new writers, it was argued, worked with more universal themes, were influenced by the big city, were more "up-to-date" in the use of narrative techniques, and were less localist; and the public celebrated this renewal (Segovia 1965).

And 1965 surpassed the previous year: twenty-seven novels were published in Mexico, compared to nineteen the previous year. The best-selling novel in 1965 was *Estudio Q.* [Studio Q.], by Vicente Leñero (who had won the Biblioteca Breve Prize in 1963). The following year, the Siglo XXI publishing house inaugurated its "Literary Creation" series with *José Trigo* (six thousand copies). José Agustín's first novel, *La tumba* [The Tomb], published when he was twenty years old, was rewritten and republished. Sales were so exorbitant that the publisher, Joaquín Mortiz, received orders for Agustín's new book, *De perfil* [Profile View], before it was even finished (Sainz 1967). A survey conducted by *Mundo Nuevo* in Bogotá showed that the most widely read authors were Vargas Llosa, Carlos Fuentes, and Truman Capote ("Lo que se lee en Colombia" 95).

According to *Primera Plana*, the sales figures of books by national and Latin American authors reflected the appetite of readers, whose hunger for these morsels had been piqued between 1964 and 1965. Seix Barral's advertisements presented the novel *La ciudad y los perros* [*The Time of the Hero*] as "a literary hit," and Cortázar was already described as "the notable Argentine writer." The Uruguayan publishing house Alfa advertised "the books that matter": Vargas Llosa's *Los jefes* [*The Leaders*] and *The Time of the Hero*; Carlos Fuentes's *La Región más transparente* [*Where the Air Is Clear*]; and Juan Rulfo's *El llano en llamas* [*The Burning Plain and Other Stories*].

In the mid-sixties, Latin American literature had found its present: the new poetics were constructed on the body of new texts that seemed to have heeded the proclamations of the modernizing critics; there were no signs of *indigenismo* or respect for the international division of repertoires and literary procedures.

The empirical evidence of the emergence of a public interested in reading works published on the continent (initially on a national scale) and the growth of national publishing houses were the subject of various aesthetic and ideological interpretations during the period and were greeted with satisfaction. With the publication of *One Hundred Years of Solitude* in 1967, a kind of hyperbolic climax was reached. The first "greatly anticipated novel," judging by the avalanche of previews and comments it generated before its appearance, this unprecedented publishing success helped mark the beginning of a new period within the epoch, although not only from the perspective of changes in the market.

With international recognition came, unintentionally, the decline of the last European experiment: the *nouveau roman*, which—although it produced some great successors in Latin America (José Emilio Pacheco, *Morirás lejos* [*You Will Die in a Distant Land*])—was considered a sterile experience, in which the priority given to form was not accompanied by vital or imaginative impulses. In June 1967, the Di Tella Institute in Argentina received the thirty-four first editions from the Mexican publishing house Siglo XXI. An article in the Argentine magazine *Confirmado* commented:

> Fernando del Paso has just justified the suspicion of many Europeans; Latin America has already left behind its uncomfortable dependence; it has its own novel that is mature enough to identify and discard influences on its own. While sterile objectivism is spreading like oil over European capitals, the great intellectual novelty of the last five years is the Latin American novel (cited in "Mexicanos en Sudamérica").

And Cortázar, Vargas Llosa, and Fuentes appeared as the triptych in which the contributions of a homegrown intelligence could be seen.

Finally, there was talk of "the maturity of Hispanic American literature," a title chosen by *Siempre!* to republish an article published in *The Times* on Latin American narrative. It declared that "until the current decade, the Hispanic American novel was, at best, provincial." But following *Pedro Páramo* and the impetus of works by Julio Cortázar, "the greatest of the Latin American writers to emerge in the last decade and the author of *Hopscotch*, the first great novel of Latin America," an "anti-realist" movement took place in Cuba and the rest of Latin America ("Cómo juzga el exigente *Times* de Londres la novela hispanoamericana").

But there is more: two years later, *The Times* literary supplement (November 14, 1968) was already claiming that the most significant contribution to *world literature* came from Latin America. One of the Europeans who celebrated Latin American literature *in statu nascendi* was also of the opinion that those years were marked by the emergence of Latin American literature on the world stage, the most obvious signs being the Nobel Prize awarded to Miguel Ángel Asturias, the proliferation of translations of Latin American works in Europe and the United States, the prizes awarded to Latin American authors, and the impressive print runs that a number of novels achieved (Fell 164).

Not only did Latin American literature find an audience, but there was also a phenomenon of institutional recognition, backed by the incredible string of prizes awarded to its authors. Beyond the prestigious Casa de las Américas awards, the Seix Barral publishing house's Biblioteca Breve was added to the list, rapidly enhancing the value of literature on the continent. In 1962 it was awarded to *The Time of the Hero*, by Mario Vargas Llosa; in 1963, Vicente Leñero, for *Los albañiles* [The Bricklayers]; in 1964, *Tres tristes tigres* [*Three Trapped Tigers*], by Cabrera Infante;[16] in 1967, *Cambio de piel* [*A Change of Skin*], by Carlos Fuentes; and in 1968, *País portátil* [Portable Country], by Venezuelan Adriano González León. That same year, Jorge Onetti, with *Contramutis*, and David Viñas, with *Cosas concretas* [Concrete Things], were finalists. Although in 1969 the prize was awarded to the Spaniard Juan Benet for *Una meditación* [*A Meditation*], many of the finalists came from Latin America (such as the Peruvian Bryce Echenique, the Chilean José Donoso, the Colombian Alberto Duque López, and the Argentine Eros Fernán Bortolato), and the jury itself consisted of prominent members of the group of recently acclaimed writers, such as García Márquez and Vargas Llosa.

The award was important enough to back the claim that the most important event in recent Venezuelan literary life had been the granting of the Biblioteca Breve award to the Venezuelan novelist Adriano González León (*Papeles*, no. 6). And *Primera Plana* covered this news, announcing that the honor given to González León could earn him a

---

16 The history of this book and its author's trajectory merit a comment of their own. The novel's original title was *Vista de un amanecer en el trópico* [*A View of Dawn in the Tropics*], which Cabrera later used for another text. It took three years for the novel to be published, and several sections were cut. During this time, it went through significant changes, in part due to Cabrera's statements against Cuba. It is one of the few cases in which a book was almost entirely rewritten after being awarded a prize. The complete version was not released until 1991. See Miranda 1991, 132–34, and González Echevarría 1985, 137–68.

place in the "Parnassus of Latin American literature" ("Otro pariente para la familia" 1968, 55).

In 1970 there was no specific winner, as a dispute between Seix and Barral forced them to suspend the prize. But José Donoso won a moral victory since, had the prize been awarded, it would have gone to him for *El obsceno pájaro de la noche* [*The Obscene Bird of Night*]. Donoso was one of the strongest and most anticipated candidates for that year's Biblioteca Breve Prize created by Seix Barral. The jury's decision to not intervene in the contest given the litigation between the Seix and Barral companies made Donoso a temporary and involuntary victim of the editorial conflict (Martí Gómez 15).

In 1967, as mentioned, Vargas Llosa won the Rómulo Gallegos Prize (which would be awarded to García Márquez next for *One Hundred Years of Solitude* in 1972), and that year the Nobel Prize for Literature was awarded to Miguel Ángel Asturias, the second Latin American to receive this distinction after Gabriela Mistral. A short time later, in 1971, another author from the continent would be recognized with the Nobel Prize: Pablo Neruda.

In 1967, the market data and figures were truly impressive. In a series of articles dedicated to the phenomenon, Rama declared that the boom was the most striking feature of cultural life that year. This was not surprising since the production of books had *doubled* compared to the previous year. It is true that 1960 could have been characterized as a year of publishing and commitment. But the first editions, which were soon sold out, were no more than a thousand copies. If there was no talk of a boom until 1967, it was because of a specific aspect of publishing behavior: the books published later reached print runs of fifteen thousand copies.

And there was the new public. A public that asked questions and wanted answers; a public that was national and Latin American, progeny of the great upheaval of 1959 that had thrown into debate both the continent's sociopolitical reality as well as its culture, as Rama put it (1967a).

At the time, the phenomenon was perceived as *transcendental*. That is how Cortázar described it in a letter to Retamar where he spoke of a reading public that for the first time "celebrated its own authors instead of demoting them and letting itself be carried away by the obsession with translations and the snobbery of the European or Yankee writer in vogue" (1984, 18).

As a critic at the time, Noé Jitrik pointed out that the writers themselves were astonished by the explosive emergence of the public. Since 1962, domestically published books had been selling in previously unimaginable quantities:

> Books by Argentine authors are at the top of the charts in Buenos Aires. We are witnessing the death of a myth—the myth of mental colonization, and the birth of a new one—that of the writer who can been seen and touched, that highly gifted person who can reflect us all (1967, 81).

It was as if Latin American writers as a whole had come together and earnestly expressed the same desire. That these desires came to fruition at the beginning of the epoch seemed to confirm the success of the interventions and the belief in the social role of the writer-intellectual. Although much has already been said about the process of professionalization of Latin American writers between the end of the nineteenth century and the beginning of the twentieth, when the role of the writer became detached from state patronage and from the close but indirect relationship with political power, never before were the signs of a professionalization that also involved *making a living* as a writer more evident than in the period we are describing. The profession of the writer has perhaps never achieved such social prestige as it did at that time.

There is no doubt that the public's interest was also awakened by the shared project of authors who had spoken and written in terms of a new literature. The commitment to a modernization of current aesthetics and what today would be referred to as a "revision of the canon" and the construction of a new tradition, was part of the task that led to that recognition. Because it was not only a matter of awakening an already indifferent public, but of offering it something new. Rama had clearly proposed this when he asserted that the cultural responsibility of intellectuals was to *construct a literature* (1960). The question of the public was not, in fact, unrelated to the quality of the literary products on offer. As Oscar Masotta wondered, was the public's indifference real or was it that the myth of the solitary and somber writer hid the poor quality of their works? This first stone in the form of a question mark thrown by Masotta into the literary scene was likely shared by many: "Could it be that some Argentine writers do not reach the public simply because they are not good writers?" His conclusion coincided with that of Rama when he stated: "Before speaking of national literature (we should) take stock of the national works that are literature" (1959).

The provocation was aimed at a long list of avowedly leftist authors whose literature was limited to serving as a vehicle for delivering *messages*. The great discovery, as Pedro Orgambide put it in "Libertad y compromiso" [Freedom and Commitment], was that writers of the left were discovering that they could write *as well as* those of the right, and younger writers were no longer astonished that Cortázar was writing his stories of *cronopios* and defending the Cuban Revolution at the same time.

In 1967 Mario Benedetti had declared that the great Latin American narrative had already been written: "What literature today can offer a collection of similar quality to *Los pasos perdidos* [*The Lost Steps*], *Pedro Páramo*, *El astillero* [*The Shipyard*], *La muerte de Artemio Cruz* [*The Death of Artemio Cruz*], *Hijo de hombre* [*Son of Man*], *Hopscotch*, *La casa verde* [*The Green House*], and *One Hundred Years of Solitude*?" (1967a). Emir Rodríguez Monegal expressed similar pride a short time later:

> With its novel, Latin American literature is now sweeping the world. Translations in Europe and the United States are proliferating, foreign critics are beginning to consider books coming from countries that were previously known only for their revolutions or their picturesque landscapes. . . . The ordinary reader is no longer so surprised that Latin America has a literature worthy of consideration. . . . Latin American literature is already functioning as literature not only on the Hispanic continent but throughout the world (1976, 36).

The cultural agenda offered the possibility of future action that, even if it were measured, could prepare the ideological terrain for society's transformation. This appeal to literature and art as a space for intellectual commitment, that is, the recognition of an *effectiveness* in the specific field of the formation of the committed intellectual, characterized the leftist culture of the sixties as a potential space for consensus and political negotiation. To this could be added the reflection on revolutionary theory as an intellectual activity: as Régis Debray put it, "the armed struggle conceived of as an art (in the dual sense of technique and invention) is meaningless if it is not within the framework of a politics conceived of as science" (1967a).

In short, whether as a critic, an ideologue, a good writer, or a political activist, in the early sixties the writer could try on any of these hats and look in the mirror to discover in their reflection the profile of the committed intellectual.

3

Family Histories

1. The Constitution of a Field or "Intellectual Party": The Rallying Call

The acclaim that *One Hundred Years of Solitude* received was a sign of the existence of a professional market capable of offering unprecedented recognition to Latin American authors. Even more significant, however, is that this unprecedented recognition of a work that was published only a short time after *Hopscotch*, *The Time of the Hero*, and *The Death of Artemio Cruz*, reflected the effectiveness of the Latin American community in positioning a work in the highest echelons of consideration. *One Hundred Years of Solitude* is certainly a novel worthy of all accolades and remains a landmark of world literature. What is interesting to note here, however, is the extent to which its impressive success was due to one of the most important phenomena of horizontal recognition ever documented in Latin America. The irruption of *One Hundred Years of Solitude* in Latin American literature is the clearest indication of the strength of the intellectual field constituted between 1959 and 1967. While no other novel of the period achieved such renown, this phenomenon can also be explained from the point of view of the intellectual field, which began to propose a new agenda and new concerns shortly after the appearance of that novel. As Rama later noted, no work or author appearing in the seventies had managed to make such an impact on the international consumer market (1984, 97).

There is a whole myth about the unexpected success of García Márquez's novel, the first eight thousand copies of which (in Sudamericana's first print run) sold out in a few days and, in November 1967 (five months after its release), was still at the top of the bestsellers list. Apparently, Paco Porrúa, then literary director of the publishing house, had received the finished manuscript in April 1967 with a note from García

Márquez in which he asked him to read it and forget it if he disliked it. Could Paco Porrúa or any other reader have been disinclined to read it? Not likely: we can even establish the chronicle of an anticipated success.

In Mexico around 1964, Rama met with García Márquez who at the time felt he was the unfortunate author of a work that lacked continental dissemination. The two agreed they would launch a campaign to gain recognition for García Márquez's work in the continent's south. Through Arca, Rama published the third edition of *La hojarasca* [*Leaf Storm*], which "was destined to be stubbornly defended by the critics" (1995, 47). And, undoubtedly, it was also defended by Rama himself in his dual role as editor and critic of *Marcha*, one of the publications with the broadest continental scope.

In 1964, Rama introduced García Márquez to his compatriots and to the rest of the Latin American readers of *Marcha*. At the time, he argued, García Márquez's work was "completely unknown in these latitudes," despite the fact that he was "one of the leading narrators of the current generation of Latin Americans" (1964b). And he would continue to praise the Colombian writer in subsequent articles. In addition to highlighting—in the titles of both articles—the profound "Latin Americanness" (*americanidad*) of García Márquez, an adjective that up to that point had not often been associated with new writers, Rama presented him as the main reformer of Latin American narrative, the inventor of the new artistic expression *of the continent* (1964c). Apparently at the suggestion of Carlos Fuentes, Luis Harss dedicated a chapter of his book *Into the Mainstream* (published in Spanish in 1966 under the title *Los nuestros*) to García Márquez. The inclusion of García Márquez in an anthology of celebrated writers, in which he is the only one whose participation has more to do with his future projects than his past accomplishments, is interesting. In fact, in the interview, García Márquez gives a preview of the plot of *One Hundred Years of Solitude*, which he was writing at the time, and that of *El otoño del patriarca* [*The Autumn of the Patriarch*] (Harss 1969, 381–419).[17]

---

17 García Márquez's own statements make his inclusion in Harss's report even more unusual: "Sometime in 1963, Luis Harss went to Pátzcuaro, where I was with director Arturo Ripstein shooting *Tiempo de morir* [*Time to Die*]. It was

Drafts of *One Hundred Years of Solitude* had been seen by many of the most influential writers and critics of the time, and excerpts of the novel were published as previews in leading Latin American magazines, which was not a common practice. *Amaru* published fragments of the unpublished novel ("Subida al cielo en cuerpo y alma de la bella Remedios Buendía" 24–29) along with a review stating: "Fame already shines down on this remarkable young writer and senses in him one of the greatest Latin American novelists to have emerged in the last ten years" (Oviedo 1967, 87, 89). *Mundo Nuevo* also published an excerpt with the title "El insomnio en Macondo" [Insomnia in Macondo] (no. 9, March 1967), and so did *Marcha* in May of that year ("Diluvio en Macondo" [Flood in Macondo]), referring to the novel as the most anticipated book of all those announced that year. *Primera Plana* gave the same impression when it published a fragment that month ("La muerte de Buendía" [The Death of Buendía]) and put the author's face on the cover next to the caption "the novel of the Americas." In August of that year Miguel Otero Silva presented García Márquez, at the 13th Congress of Hispano-American Literature in Caracas, as the author of a marvel (the originals of which had been *shown to the whole world*) that would *definitively* position him at the leading edge of Latin American novels ("Los novelistas y sus críticos" 1968, 66–67).

Surprised by this presentation of the novel as still unpublished, Tomás Eloy Martínez suggested to me that it was likely that, since the novel had not yet arrived in Venezuela and Otero Silva was at the time quite a powerful figure in Latin American literature, no one (not even García Márquez) would have wanted to correct him in public, so the inaccurate and confusing information was left circulating. Furthermore, at the time García Márquez had not yet seen his book. Tomás Eloy Martínez adds that the confusion that existed for years over the publication dates of *One Hundred Years of Solitude* stems from the fact that the author was in Caracas, where the book was still unknown, and

---

then that he conducted the interview with me that appears in *Into the Mainstream*. I was not thinking about *One Hundred Years of Solitude* yet, and I told him about the novel much later, in a letter, announcing that it would be ready by March or April 1967" (García Márquez 1994).

that he himself inadvertently contributed to the confusion for some time because, in his recollection, the appearance of the book and the presence of García Márquez in Buenos Aires had been simultaneous.

Thus, the novel *shown to the whole world and approved by the whole world* was practically a guaranteed success. *One Hundred Years of Solitude* was read as the ultimate model of Latin American fiction, as evidenced by the title of one of the multiple commentaries devoted to it in *Siempre!*: "*One Hundred Years of Solitude*. The great novel of the Americas, already unexpected, still timely" (Batís) or Rama's assessment of it, in which he described the novel as possessing "the entire joy of novelistic storytelling full of adventures and unusual characters" and that it corrected, "in a severe and sudden manner," the course of the modern novel by taking "a path that although it has illustrious ancestors is very audacious with respect to its contemporaries and itself" (1967b).

The novel came out the third week of June 1967 (three weeks later, it already topped the bestsellers list). In August, García Márquez traveled to Buenos Aires and spent six weeks savoring his success. The most anticipated (and *world-renowned*) novel continued its successful path via an avalanche of definitively appreciative reviews in all publications. The hyperbole of the novel was reproduced in the hyperbole of its reviews: García Márquez was the "Amadís of America" in Vargas Llosa's view, and *One Hundred Years of Solitude* was read as the ultimate model of Latin American fiction. From whatever angle one looked at it, the novel had arrived to fill a void that had been tailored to suit it: the most important and "definitive" novel of the continent had found the "ontological intuition of the Hispanic American being," as one critic said (García Ascot). The text was considered the *summa* and metaphor of the Latin American totality and of all possible totalizations: it was the model fiction of the truly universal literature produced on the continent:

> It is always Macondo, of course, and that mythical town, even in previous books, was perhaps an image of Colombia as a whole; but now Macondo is more or less Latin America; it is tentatively the world (Benedetti 1968a, IV).

The joy with which it was incorporated into one of the most powerful aesthetic reflections on Latin American narrative art (the marvelous real, Carpentier's portent and program) and the unique opportunity at the time of its appearance, with a consolidated intellectual field capable of producing an accolade of such magnitude, made *One Hundred Years of Solitude* a textual prototype. Before that, however, the unanimity of its acclaim affirmed the absolute existence of a system of personal relationships in Latin American literature. In his novel, García Márquez referenced some members of the family through subtle allusions: a line from Rulfo, the incorporation of Rocamadour, the Victor Hughes of *Explosion in a Cathedral*, Artemio Cruz, while at the same time tracing ties between himself and Borges and also Carpentier. On the other hand, unlike Fuentes or Cortázar, García Márquez "hid" his erudition and his readings by producing a communicatively perfect apparatus, unaffected by the symptom of cultural exhibition that could disturb the "female-reader" of *Hopscotch* or *A Change of Skin*.

Thus, the novel represented a major milestone in the history of literature and Latin American intellectual history, as was noted in the long lede listing the significant events of 1967 in *Siempre!* (January 3, 1968):

> Truman Capote watched the filming of *In Cold Blood*; the CIA's cultural support was liquidating its beneficiaries; American writers were confronting genocide and Johnson; Buñuel triumphed in Venice and Antonioni in Cannes; Margot Fonteyn and Nureyev were experimenting; Miguel Ángel Asturias accepted the Nobel Prize; Cuba was preparing its cultural congress; Andy Warhol was eternalizing Pop; John Cage and Xenakis continued to represent the musical avant-garde; Duchamp and Bonnard were being honored; Witold Gombrowicz received the international publishers' prize; García Márquez became a classic with *One Hundred Years of Solitude*.

How was such a powerful front formed? As a result of the numerous overlaps with respect to aesthetic and ideological issues, one of the most important phenomena of the period was the establishment of a Latin American intellectual field that transcended the boundaries of nationality and found in the Cuban Revolution the prospect of openness and a sense of belonging. Below, I will focus on analyzing how, when, and around what the Latin American lettered city of this period was constituted, focusing on analyzing what Zygmunt Bauman calls, in *Legislators and Interpreters*, the "rallying call": the deliberate, complex, and voluntary constitution of a corporation or intellectual front—in this case Latin American—in the early sixties. The belief in a shared Latin American identity corresponded to the establishment of an empirical field of intervention based on sociability, conceived as an active part of the desire to transform the world.

In the process of creating a nucleus of intellectuals who responded to the "rallying call," a dialectic took place whereby, as gaps were noted, they were filled, given that part of the cultural agenda involved overcoming a mutual lack of knowledge among Latin American intellectuals and, thus, the creation and institutionalization of an intellectual community.

Benedict Anderson defines what unites the members of a nation as an "imagined community" (23–24). The members of this community do not know each other, yet the image of their communion is present in each of them. Given that it is a question of developing the grounds on which the group cohesion of individuals is generated when due to their number, they exceed the possibility for personal acquaintance and ties (of course not to the same degree as the imagined community that forms the basis for nationality); the concept of "imagined community" seems to approach the image of the Latin American intellectual community of the sixties and seventies. But it should also be noted that the dynamics established between the Latin American cultural magazines and the personal encounters between the critics and writers who contributed to them make it possible to postulate both the existence of an intellectual community that functioned as an "imagined" community, creating a sense of belonging and affinity, and the importance of a more limited community based on personal contacts that reinforced and objectified the nature of community.

One could even speak of a Latin American intellectual family. In fact, the term "family" is quite suitable. Consider the title that *Primera Plana* used for its article on the prize received by Venezuelan novelist González León: not only did it use the word family, but it exaggerated the characteristics of the associated field of words (to avoid repeating "family of words" here): "Another relative for the family."

This suggests, in the same terms in which I am going to present it, the creation of a community connected through practically filial ties among writers. It is true that there was also talk of cronyism and mafia, adding a critical and negative emphasis in describing the power of the network of personal relationships to generate inclusions and exclusions in the literary field. The Venezuelan critic Manuel Pedro González complained that editors, narrators, and critics formed a sort of "mafia" or tacit alliance to promote a certain type of aesthetics (36). What interests me, however, is the significant decision of all members in the field to establish institutional relationships throughout the period.

From 1960 onward, there were several attempts to organize and institutionalize a Latin American intellectual community, in the sense of both a union and in political terms. This ranged from the 1960 encounter of writers of the Americas in Concepción, Chile, to the 1965 gathering in Genoa, the project of a Latin American Community of Writers launched at the First Latin American Congress of Writers in Arica, Chile, in 1966, to the Second Latin American Congress of Writers in Mexico in 1967, the Thirteenth Inter-American Congress of Literature in Caracas in 1967, and the many meetings and gatherings in Havana.

The intellectual community was characterized by a strong network of personal relationships between writers and critics of the continent, a network powerful enough to generate an impact both on the forms of professional criticism and on alliances and divergences and even literary successes. Rodríguez Monegal commented at the time, without drawing very substantial conclusions: "The two stars of the novel, García Márquez and Vargas Llosa, have not met yet, but they have exchanged letters. Mario has been one of the most constant promoters of *One Hundred Years*" (1967, 36).

Carlos Fuentes recalled in a report that "something extraordinary had happened in the life of Hispano-American literature: all the prominent figures of the boom were friends with each other" (Macadam and Ruas 134). María Pilar, José Donoso's wife, emphasizes the family profile even further when she refers to her recollection as "domestic": "Yes, we were all very close friends, like cousins, even the children" (1983, 106).

These were new solidarities and rejections based, moreover, on a position where the logic of friendship or intimacy blends with the growing institutional importance of the figure of the writer.

The magazines underscored circuits that were already present in the books and rooted in personal acquaintance: Carlos Fuentes dedicated

The Death of Artemio Cruz to Wright Mills, *A Change of Skin* to Cortázar and Aurora Bernárdez, and his short story "Fortuna lo que ha querido" [Fate's Fickle Hand], which appeared in the *Revista de la Universidad de México*, to García Márquez. The latter no doubt expressed his gratitude for the many favors received through references to colleagues and his colleagues' characters in *One Hundred Years of Solitude*. Benedetti dedicated his poem "Habanera" to Retamar; Donoso, *Hell Has No Limits* to Rita and Carlos Fuentes; René Depestre, his "Memorias del geolibertinaje" [Memories of Geolibertinage]—a chapter of his *Autobiografía en el Caribe* [Autobiography in the Caribbean]—to Debray; David Viñas dedicated his *Hombres de a caballo* [Men on Horseback] to Vargas Llosa, Walsh, and Del Peral; Gregorio Selser dedicated his book on the Alliance for Progress to Carlos Fuentes as a tribute to one of the first promoters of the "Cuban party," who at the time was denied a visa to enter the United States.[18] A deeply emblematic meeting took place in Paris in 1960, when Carlos Quijano and Roberto Fernández Retamar met. The by then sixty-year-old director of *Marcha* was passing on something akin to an Olympic torch to the young Cuban professor who was soon to become one of the main spokespersons of the intellectual family. Recalling that meeting, Retamar underlines the fact that it was Quijano and his magazine who received Che's letter known as "El socialismo y el hombre en Cuba" [Socialism and Man in Cuba] (Sarusky 140).

The fact that the rallying call (with the Cuban Revolution and others to follow as an indisputable beacon) was a major concern for US policy is revealed in the concern expressed at the time by the Congress for Cultural Freedom, a Cold War institution founded in 1950 as a clearly and definitively anti-communist intellectual front to support US policy. The representatives of the Ibero-American Associations of that congress met in Paris on December 14, 15, and 16, 1960, to evaluate the potential dangers of the politicization of the continent's intellectuals. They also discussed the Cuban "problem," presented as a new "totalitarian" threat by the magazine *Cuadernos*, the congress's organ for Latin America.

---

18 Fuentes finally did manage to cross the border, as he attended the PEN Club meetings in 1966.

The Paris conference "was essentially devoted to the examination of the various national situations and the study of the general evolution of the continent with respect to civil rights and basic freedoms" ("Supplement," *Cuadernos*, no. 47, March–April 1961). Efforts were quickly made to convince intellectuals and "ensure objective information was available to all sectors of opinion" that would counter the enthusiasm that the revolution had generated among intellectuals.

Of the various deliberations and declarations, the choice of the document published as an addendum to the above-mentioned issue of *Cuadernos* fell, not surprisingly, to the text produced on Cuba, the only document that the editorial board of *Cuadernos* published in that supplement. In general terms, the "Declaration on Cuba" lamented that a year and a half after the victory against Batista, the Cuban people's desire to establish the rule of law and bring about the creation of a free and democratic society had not been fulfilled. Naturally, it was reported that Cuba had become a satellite of Soviet Russia and Red China and, what was even more concerning, that it intended to achieve the same goals in the rest of Latin America, where it seemed many still clung "to the belief that the Castro regime is merely a more or less radical nationalism that is heading toward an eventual democratic restoration through deep economic and social reforms."

In the name of free intellectuals, the members of the Ibero-American associations of the Congress for Cultural Freedom addressed the free people of the world and in particular intellectuals so that they would mobilize all their critical faculties for a serious and objective examination of the Cuban reality, which at no time was called a revolution. That the pro-US policy promoting what was then called dialogue or peaceful coexistence was not to the liking of most of the members of the new Latin American intellectual family is demonstrated by the fact that *Cuadernos* died out in June 1965 with little fanfare. One need only look at the names in *Cuadernos* to find a family album of ghosts: none of the names of its collaborators were or would be seen again in the following years in any important position. The magazine belonged to the old liberal guard and had neither a public nor a good reputation (Mudrovcic 21). Julián Gorkin, editor of *Cuadernos* from 1953 to 1963, explained the reasons the venture had become impossible and argued that the only way to produce a credible intellectual magazine would be to constantly attack the United States and sing the endless praises of Sartre or Pablo Neruda (Coleman 85). Along with appreciating the irony, we can add that the "credible" Latin American journals did indeed devote significant space to the figure and thought of Jean-Paul Sartre (although this does not imply that they sang his endless praises). On the other hand, Neruda's presence was neither so frequent nor so adored. Gorkin could not have anticipated the questioning that Neruda would have to endure from members of his own "family" in 1966 as a result of his visit to Peru under Belaúnde Terry and his presence in the United States. On January 17, 1960, the First Encounter of Writers of the Americas was held in Concepción, where the university brought together the new Chilean left.

In an article published in the literary supplement of the newspaper *Clarín* on February 14, 1960, Ernesto Sabato, who had attended the conference, commented on the generalized politicization that was stirring up Latin Americans: "The great majority of Latin Americans were speaking out in theoretical analyses for a committed literature, and, in almost all cases, for a committed literature in the most strictly social and political sense." The few who defended what was then called pure art (including Enrique Anderson Imbert) found themselves violently refuted by the great majority. What was unusual about the conference was its Latin American tone and the "intense passion that clearly demonstrated that this immense continent of brotherly countries now has an urgent reality that writers cannot and must not forget." The visit of the writers in attendance to the Lota mines appeared to constitute a symbol of that "pathetic unity of the continent, in those beings that emerged from the bowels of the earth of the Americas, in those men smeared in black as if wearing tragic disguises, before the saddened eyes of the Latin American writers, one could see the witnesses—that is, the martyrs—of this continent dominated by miserable exploitation." This vision of the social panorama of the continent prompted the participants in the encounter to insistently propose the theory that nothing important could be written if it were not from the standpoint of the scorned and neglected, as Sabato wrote. The Peruvian writer Sebastián Salazar Bondy even wondered whether it would not be more worthy to stop writing poems and novels and simply join the struggle for the liberation of Latin America through political activism. It should be noted that these doubts precede the polemic between Sartre and Claude Simon on the same question and echo, throughout the history of intellectuals, the rhythms of a pendular movement that either defends or strongly questions the specific craft of writing (or any other) in which the practitioner of this craft is placed in the position of intellectual. Sartre's autobiography, *The Words*, reveals a crisis on the part of the author that calls literature itself into question. In various interviews he had affirmed that the writer should take the side of the starving and either write for them or stop writing altogether. Sartre's positions were attacked by Jacques Houbart, Yves Berger, and Claude Simon in *L'Express*.

In Latin America, Lucien Mercier provided an astute analysis of the debate for *Marcha*'s readership: he saw that Sartre was questioning not only literature in general but also committed literature and concluded that a literary work could not—and should not—be asked to "contribute to the progress of the revolutionary cause on a practical level." This did not detract from the moral imperative for the writer, whose task was to fight for the liberation of consciences, to commit themselves to their work ("Ser Mallarmé o Lenin" 1964).

For his part, Vargas Llosa also expressed his opinion on the topic, stating that Sartre's opinions revealed his strong sense of historical responsibility, although the Peruvian did not think he was right since he believed that, in the end, even if he were not convinced of the usefulness of literature, Sartre would continue to write ("Los otros contra Sartre").

A regional episode of a similar nature pitted David Viñas against Noé Jitrik. The former, in line with Sartre, had proclaimed the need to abandon literature if the goal was to translate into action projects inspired by literary works oriented in a certain direction. Noé Jitrik expressed his disagreement with these positions by affirming that:

> a writer's revolutionary nature consists in their critical illumination of the world through words rather than the system of declarations they invent to protect themselves from isolation or their lack of faith in the revolution. A leftist writer who projects a task marked by these imperatives, a writer who trusts in their specific power of action, will be able to resist the present (1966).

Uruguayan writer Carlos Martínez Moreno, who was also present at the Chilean conference attended by Ernesto Sabato, commented that the event had been dominated by the insistent complaints of the attendees regarding the lack of mutual knowledge among Latin American writers, a situation that encounters like this one were attempting to remedy. Martínez Moreno agreed with Sabato in stating that the encounter had been dominated by discussions of the relationship between art and the social, commitment in literature, and the responsibilities of the writer as a member of society ("Escritores de América en Concepción" 1960).

At the end of that same year, a colloquium on the Hispano-American novel was held in Buenos Aires, with the participation of Ángel Rama, Carlos Real de Azúa, Miguel Ángel Asturias, Ciro Alegría, Augusto Roa Bastos, Bernardo Verbitsky, and Ernesto Sabato. The disconnect between Latin American authors was once again discussed. However, despite some degree of pessimism, there was hope for a different future in which a large and enthusiastic public attended the colloquium, foreshadowing the emergence of a new reading public, which that year, 1960, had responded with interest to the growth of the national publishing industry in almost all of the continent's countries.

The complaint about the mutual lack of knowledge of authors and artistic productions on the continent acted as an appeal to remedy the situation. It acted as a trigger for the rallying call that channeled the desire for an associative ideal. The magazines as well as the project to create a Latin American society of writers helped the reasons behind this complaint vanish.

The frequency of writers' gatherings through countless colloquiums, congresses, conferences, and seminars reveals the importance given to discussion, dissemination, and the potential for achieving consensus on the issues raised regarding the responsibilities of writers to society. The effectiveness of the rallying call was affirmed by Chilean writer and diplomat Jorge Edwards only a few years later: "We writers, especially in Latin America, form a kind of family that recognizes each other from one country to another" (1982, 349).

While the cliché of the mutual lack of knowledge persisted in numerous complaints, the family constellation that the encounters fostered helped capture it in writing but also to make it less true. Little by little, they began to get to know each other. Between January 15 and 27, 1962, the University of Concepción in Chile organized the Congress of Intellectuals, which formed part of the cycle "The Image of Man in Latin

America," held as part of the Seventh International Summer School, directed by Gonzalo Rojas. Participants included Pablo Neruda, José María Arguedas, Carlos Fuentes, Claribel Alegría, Alejo Carpentier, José Miguel Oviedo, José Bianco, Emir Rodríguez Monegal, Roberto Fernández Retamar, Thiago de Mello, Gerardo Molina, Mario Benedetti, Héctor P. Agosti, and Augusto Roa Bastos. José Donoso remembers it as "very international and modern—simultaneous interpreters and all—, a sort of grand carnival of intellectuals, with picnics, swimming in the ocean, exhibits, flirting, and food" (1989, 35).[19]

In his presentation, Carlos Fuentes defended the right of writers to intervene in politics, publicly presented a principle of Third World faith, citing the shared interests of Asia, the Americas, and Africa, and ratified the principle of the self-determination of nations, in a clear reference to Cuba (1962, 4–8). Roa Bastos asked that the speech delivered by Fuentes be sent to Punta del Este (where the conference of the Organization of American States—OAS—, from which Cuba had been expelled, was being held) as a manifesto of the intellectuals of the Americas. Strong personal friendships and relationships of mutual literary admiration emerged at that conference. It was there that Fuentes and the Uruguayan critic Emir Rodríguez Monegal met each other for the first time, as both would later recall in the first issue of the controversial magazine *Mundo Nuevo.*

Of the potential lapses and deceptions of memory, one statement by Donoso seems to run through all the archival sources unscathed. It is the reference to the relationship between the intellectual community and the Cuban cause. Donoso states that it was Pablo Neruda and Carlos Fuentes who gave the conference its historical tone because of the fervent way in which they raised awareness among those present and won them over to the Cuban Revolution (46). What is clear is that at that conference—a "major tournament," as Ariel Dorfman described it—"the need to repeat this type of meeting became clear" (201).

---

19 To get a sense of the presentations, see "Antología de las intervenciones: Imagen del hombre en América Latina en la VII Escuela Internacional de la Universidad de Concepción," *Alerce,* no. 4 (June 1962), and Alex Tarnopolsky, "Imagen de América Latina," *El Escarabajo de Oro,* no. 14 (August 1962).

It did not take long for a new encounter to materialize. Between January 21 and 30, 1965, a colloquium was held in Genoa under the auspices of the Columbianum, a cultural organization based in that city, which, in its concern for Latin American issues and as the product of ecclesiastical *aggiornamento*, combined Christianity with social issues. Rama described the encounter as a pluri-ideological dialogue between Marxists, Catholics, conservatives, and left-wing independents (with the absence of representatives of the liberal right). The "Declaration of Genoa"—published in *Casa de las Américas*, no. 30—proclaimed the existence of Latin America as a unity beyond diversity and considered the Cuban Revolution to be the central event of that period. The manifesto "Nuestra América" [Our America], emanating from the event, affirmed that the Latin American intellectual had made the anti-imperialist position their own, as a "moral conscience" (Rama 1965a).

The Genoa agreements, which created the Latin American Writers Association (presided over by Mexican poet Carlos Pellicer), launched a more ambitious project of unity: the Latin American Community of Writers, the statutes of which would be promulgated at a subsequent meeting to be held in Mexico. Referring to the Genoa meeting, Dorfman stated:

> what emerged in Genoa was not the Latin American conscience or the vision or knowledge of our own reality. That existed before and will continue to exist with or without writers' congresses. The novelty consists in having given a *lasting and institutional shape* to the desire of the continent's authors to act together (210).

It no longer mattered that the intention of creating a Latin American Community of Writers was being declaimed. In effect, it was already functioning as such. And one of its main hubs was Havana.

Cuba, the "Antillean Rome," as Halperin Donghi called it, was the epicenter of the establishment of the Latin American intellectual family of the sixties, which gave the intellectual family a sense of unity: the island was the great host of the literary world. Cuba also served as an obligatory reference in the contributions of many intellectuals. Additionally, it is important to remember that it became the gathering place (both real and imaginary) for a large number of intellectuals who lived there, following Guevara's example. These included, among many others, the Uruguayan Mario Benedetti, the Haitian René Depestre, the Salvadoran Roque Dalton, the Peruvian Javier Heraud, and the Chilean Enrique Lihn.

One political-cultural reason behind the ritual of traveling to Havana, a symbolic trip at the time, was to participate as jurors in the Casa de las Américas awards, the continent's most prestigious prize. Both the participation as jurors and the receipt of the award (which generally also served as a prerequisite to becoming a juror in the following edition) strengthened the visitors' ties with Cuban cultural institutions and with the political defense of the revolution.[20]

The intense sociability of which Havana served as headquarters yielded friendships and texts. Roberto Fernández Retamar, a figure of incalculable importance in the intellectual history of the period, certainly contributed to forging this sociability. The future director of *Casa de las Américas* had welcomed Miguel Ángel Asturias to Havana in 1959. In 1960, he met Octavio Paz and Pablo Neruda in Paris. In Havana, in late 1960 and early 1962, he saw them again and met new "relatives" in

20 Between 1962 and 1969, the members of the jury included Raúl Larra, Leónidas Barletta, Gerardo Pisarello, René Depestre, Juan Goytisolo, Julio Cortázar, Emmanuel Carballo, Raúl González Tuñón, Aurora Bernárdez, Ángel Rama, Blas de Otero, Italo Calvino, Juan Gelman, Ida Vitale, Fernando Benítez, María Rosa Oliver, Atilio del Cioppo, Bernardo Verbitsky, Ezequiel Martínez Estrada, Carlos Fuentes, Miguel Ángel Asturias, Sebastián Salazar Bondy, Allen Ginsberg, Camilo José Cela, Mario Vargas Llosa, David Viñas, Bernardo Canal Feijóo, Antonio Larreta, José Pedro Díaz, Mario Benedetti, Leopoldo Marechal, Juan Marsé, Mario Monteforte Toledo, José Lezama Lima, Emilio Adolfo Westphalen, Claude Couffon, Jorge Edwards, Rodolfo Walsh, Federico Álvarez, José María Arguedas, Jorge Semprún, José Revueltas, Carlos Heitor Cony, Edmundo Desnoes, Salvador Garmendia, Noé Jitrik, Julio Bareiro Saguier, Hans Magnus Enzensberger, and Carlos María Gutiérrez. Prizes or mentions were won by Víctor García Robles, Noé Jitrik, Alberto Szpunberg, Antonio Dal Masetto, Marta Traba, Jorge Onetti, Jorge Zalamea, Enrique Lihn, Hernán Loyola, Antonio Benítez, David Viñas, Félix Grande, Dalmiro Sáenz, Federico Brito Figueroa, Virgilio Piñera, Norberto Fuentes, Pablo Armando Fernández, Renato Prada Oropeza, Héctor Béjar, Antonio Skármeta, Carlos María Gutiérrez, and María Ester Gilio.

Genoa. Before taking charge of the magazine, he had already forged ties (again in Paris, in 1965) with Cortázar and Debray. Retamar dates three poem-letters or letter-poems (which he personally refers to as "letters," in direct reference to the intimate genre facilitated by personal relationships of affection) in Havana, in March–April 1962. One of them is dedicated to Juan Gelman "in Buenos Aires" and bears an epigraph from a poem by Gelman dedicated to Retamar: "Is anyone called juan? who is still called roberto?" Another letter-poem is dedicated to his compatriot Fayad Jamís and yet another to Salvadoran Roque Dalton, a great admirer of Cuban life in those years and a frequent contributor to *Casa de las Américas.* Gelman, for his part, also writes a poem-letter dedicated to Fernández Retamar and published in the same issue along with "Habana revisited" [Havana Revisited] (27–30).

During his visit to Havana, Ángel Rama organized practically the entire twenty-sixth issue of *Casa de las Américas* magazine, devoted to the new Latin American novel. Emmanuel Carballo (one of the most prestigious critics in Mexico, who wrote in the *Siempre!* supplement) dated his text "Del costumbrismo al realismo crítico" [From *Costumbrismo* to Critical Realism] as written in Havana-Mexico in February and March 1963, and it was published in *Casa de las Américas* issue 19, July–August 1963. That same year, Julio Cortázar was also in Cuba and delivered a talk. The Chilean Jorge Edwards, friend of the Peruvian Emilio Adolfo Westphalen, director of *Amaru*, was in charge of taking copies of the Peruvian magazine to Cuba, and through him, Enrique Lihn sent greetings to Retamar, Padilla, and Pablo Armando Fernández. *El Corno Emplumado*, the bilingual magazine edited in Mexico by Margaret Randall, Sergio Mondragón, and Harvey Wolin, was particularly concerned with its reception on the island. Along with the practically compulsory anthology of Cuban poetry that all the magazines of the continent published, *El Corno Emplumado,* in its July 1963 issue, included a fragment of Fidel Castro's speech "Palabras a los intelectuales" [Words to the Intellectuals], and in its section "Cartas letters cartas letters," it published one from Marco Antonio Flores, dated "La Habana, Free Territory of the Americas, International Workers' Day," in which he wrote: "Regarding *El Corno*, don't worry, everything is going smoothly, it has been received with enthusiasm. There are more and more people every day who ask and want to collaborate, I have stories and poems they have given me" (169).[21]

On the other hand, in addition to the intense literary life emerging in Cuba, a series of important Third World encounters were held on the island. During his last official trip to Africa, Che Guevara had garnered support to expand the organization of solidarity of the Afro-Asian peoples and to integrate Latin America. As a result of these efforts, the Tricontinental Conference was held for the first time in January 1966 in Havana. It was attended by representatives of socialist states, liberation movements—such as those of the Portuguese colonies in Africa, members of the guerrilla groups of Venezuela and Guatemala, and leaders of the Vietnamese National Liberation Front. The conference led to the creation of the Organization of Solidarity with the People of Asia, Africa and Latin America (OSPAAAL), with its headquarters in Havana, and a bimonthly publication, *Tricontinental*. But it was not only attended by political delegations, as reflected in the coverage of the conference published simultaneously in *Casa de las Américas* and *Marcha*. One of the main lines of discussion that transcended questions of tactics and strategy and was more closely related to the issue of writers was the definition of the social role of intellectuals; more specifically, their role in the struggles for national liberation (Núñez 1966).[22]

The first meeting of the *Casa de las Américas* Collaboration Committee was held between January 5 and 8, 1967, with the participation of Emmanuel Carballo, Cortázar, Roque Dalton, Depestre, Desnoes, Fernández Retamar, Manuel Galich, Lisandro Otero, Ambrosio Fornet,

---

21 Months later, he would write in another letter: "Without exaggerating, *ECE* is currently the most popular literary journal in Havana. It gets stolen from libraries, and I have to replace it every time (once in the *Casa de las Américas* and twice in the Unión de Escritores); young and old writers alike ask me for it. Please send me more packages of CORNOS ASAP." *El Corno Emplumado*, no. 9 (January 1964): 145.

22 Those who responded include Vargas Llosa, Alberto Moravia, Manuel Rojas, Alfredo Varela, Régis Debray (presented as a sociologist, essayist, and specialist in "guerrilla psychology"), Manuel Galich, Fernández Retamar, and Gonzalo Rojas.

Graziela Pogolotti, Vargas Llosa, Rama, Viñas, and Jorge Zalamea. This led to the committee's first declaration, which was published by *Casa de las Américas*, *Marcha*, and *Siempre!*: "Los escritores asumen su responsabilidad" [The Writers Assume Their Responsibility].

A few days later, between January 16 and 22, 1967, an "Encounter with Rubén Darío" was held as a tribute to the centennial of his birth, attended by Jean Cassou, Lumir Cvirny, Carlos Pellicer, Jaime Torres Bodet, Enrique Lihn, Ángel Rama, Manuel Pedro González, Ernesto Mejía Sánchez, José Portuondo, René Depestre, Mario Benedetti, and Eliseo Diego. In *Casa de las Américas* issue 42, May–June 1967, poems dedicated to the Nicaraguan modernist were published by Nicolás Guillén, Pita Rodríguez, José Lezama Lima, Blas de Otero, Gonzalo Rojas, César Fernández Moreno, Mario Benedetti, Eliseo Diego, Idea Vilariño, Ida Vitale, René Depestre, Pablo Armando Fernández, Roberto Fernández Retamar, Fayad Jamís, Paco Urondo, Heberto Padilla,[23] Roque Dalton, Víctor García Robles, Noé Jitrik, and Margaret Randall, many of whom also attended the gathering. It was then suggested that those present sign the declaration of the *Casa de las Américas* Collaboration Committee, which focused on the question of the intellectual and their role in society, following a concern that had already been outlined in the survey conducted among the intellectuals present at the Tricontinental. The idea that it was necessary and urgent to redefine the task of intellectuals also formed part of the conclusions of the encounter in tribute to Darío held in Cuba since one of the decisions made there was to convene a conference of all of the continent's intellectuals.[24]

---

23 As an interesting side note, this was the issue in which his polemic poem "En tiempos difíciles" [In Hard Times], which was to cause him so many problems, was published.

24 As a result of the agreements ratified by those present, a resolution was made: "1) For those willing to undersign the document issued by the *Casa de las Américas* Collaboration Committee to sign it, committing themselves to discussing this document and disseminating it in all the Latin American countries of the participants. 2) To prepare a conference of the intellectuals of our continent. 3) To create the Institute of Latin American Literature. 4) To create the Martí Room in the National Library of Cuba" ("Sesión final del encuentro con Rubén Darío").

On the other hand, the Tricontinental Conference also led to the idea of forming, with the twenty-seven Latin American delegations, an organization of their own, the Latin American Solidarity Organization (OLAS, for its acronym in Spanish). The Cubans were disappointed by the long-term practical results of this attempt at multi-continental cooperation and in fact gave up on a second conference of this type. They preferred to concentrate on Latin American issues and thus attributed incomparably greater importance to the OLAS conference (Karol, 397–98, and Tuttino 1968a, 385, 388).

The meeting of the Latin American Solidarity Organization, chaired by Haydeé Santamaría, was held from July 31 to August 10, 1967. President Dorticós formally opened the conference with a speech. As an emblem of the conference, the phrase "What is the history of Cuba if not the history of Latin America?" was written in bright letters on a huge poster with the portraits of Bolívar, Máximo Gómez, Martí, and Guevara. The public documents of the controversial meeting established two key points of the agenda: first, that the armed struggle was the only path to revolution and, second, that Cuba should be considered the vanguard of the Latin American revolution. This was expressed in point 14 of the general declaration, stating that "the Cuban Revolution, as a symbol of the triumph of the armed revolutionary movement, constitutes the vanguard of the Latin American anti-imperialist movement" (Karol 399–423, Tuttino 1968a, 403–8).

The OLAS conference was held at the same time as another major event organized in Cuba. To commemorate the July 26 anniversary (of the attack on the Moncada Barracks), lavish parties were held in 1967 in which the Salón de Mayo was transferred from Paris to Havana and attended by one hundred and fifty European painters, sculptors, intellectuals, writers, and journalists. An encounter of Cuban and European painters was also organized, as well as a gathering related to protest songs in Varadero. Ninety artists and writers painted a giant mural entitled *Collective Cuba*. The sheer intensity of cultural life led to the conclusion that, in spite of the blockade and isolation, Cuba was at that moment one of the most vibrant and unique cultural centers in the world ("Cultura y revolución en Cuba"). All this political and cultural effervescence was reflected in the creation, in December 1967, of the Center for Literary Research, with Mario Benedetti, living in Cuba at the time, as its first director.

In short, following these encounters and as a result of new situations that will be analyzed below, a good part of the Latin American intellectual family, by then quite well established, with the Cubans at the head, decided to organize an international congress of intellectuals. The call for the congress was approved and signed by the European political activists, artists, and intellectuals who attended the July 26 celebrations in Havana and the OLAS congress. With the participation of almost five hundred intellectuals from Latin America, Asia, and Africa, the Havana Cultural Congress was held between January 5 and 12, 1968. The aim was to overcome the isolation to which Cuban intellectuals had been condemned and put them in contact with the most radical currents of thought in the world and with the main cultural currents of the avant-garde. From an ideological point of view, it was a question of forging relations between foreign intellectuals (particularly European ones) and the extraordinary radicalism of the Cuban Revolution, and for them to inform their respective countries of its existence. From a political perspective, the idea was to bring together, for the first time since 1936, a world congress of intellectuals, appealing to all possible forms of struggle against imperialism, colonialism, and neocolonialism. After the Tricontinental and OLAS, the Cultural Congress marked the third stage in long-term actions to constitute a "world front against imperialism." The conference's agenda underlined the question implicit in the Núñez survey regarding the role of intellectuals, but also included issues related to aesthetic traditions, the avant-garde, and revolutionary art. In his closing speech, Fidel Castro shared with the intellectuals present his confidence in the potential of revolutionary action that they, as a vanguard, could carry out, also tacitly expressing his disappointment following discussions with the Marxist parties and organizations of the continent that did not support the armed struggle enthusiastically enough. The Congress also coincided with the ninth edition of the Casa de las Américas award. All these events resulted in an exceptional influx of intellectuals from Latin America and around the world.

To take advantage of this convergence, a lecture series on Latin American literature was held between January 16 and February 18, 1968, in which twenty-four critics and writers from seventeen countries presented their views on the state of literary production in each of their countries. The participants were Jorge Enrique Adoum (Ecuador);

Edmundo Aray (Venezuela); José María Arguedas and Alejandro Romualdo (Peru); Max Aub—who, though born in Paris, had lived in Mexico since 1942, José Revueltas, and Emmanuel Carballo (Mexico); Carlos Wong Broce (Panama); Manuel Galich and Arqueles Morales (Guatemala); Jorge Zalamea (Colombia); Álvaro Menéndez Leal (El Salvador); Rodolfo Walsh, Juan Carlos Portantiero, and Francisco Urondo (Argentina); Mario Benedetti (Uruguay); Jorge Edwards and Enrique Lihn (Chile); Edelberto Torres (Nicaragua); Carlos Heitor Cony (Brazil); Roberto Fernández Retamar (Cuba); and René Depestre (Haiti). Talks were also given by Spanish critic José María Castellet and Frenchman Claude Couffon, great promoters of Latin American literature. The lectures were compiled in the volume *Panorama de la actual literatura latinoamericana* [Panorama of Current Latin American Literature], published by the Centro de Investigaciones Literarias Casa de las Américas, Havana, 1968.

In short, in less than a decade, the island became a space for the reception and massive recruitment of artists and intellectuals, strengthening community ties regarding the defense of the revolution and the discussion of the appropriate intellectual and aesthetic means of intervention to expand the revolutionary possibilities throughout the continent.

2. The First Disruptions: The Case of *Mundo Nuevo*

> In our times, history moves at a dizzying pace, and in the two brief years since the Genoa meeting, *the events that have shaken the world have been so numerous and so explosive* that many of those who attended the previous meetings may not hold the same views today as those that were acceptable in January 1965.
>
> "Declaración" (1967, 99)

The year 1966 was key for the Latin American intellectual family. The debates on the role of the intellectual and the institutionalization of the Latin American intellectual community cannot be separated: in fact, they are interdependent. The only possible separation is methodological. Below I will focus on the analysis of the configuration of the Latin American lettered city, taking into account that the debate did not take place in an abstract space and that the structure of the intellectual field was decisive in imposing the objects of discourse. From the point of view of Latin American intellectual history, the configuration of the intellectual field around 1966 also marks a milestone that deserves careful analysis.[25]

The fact that the rallying call, established on the basis of new personal and professional relations between writers outside their national borders, had a tremendous capacity for achieving consensus is demonstrated both in the success of *One Hundred Years of Solitude* as well as in the chapter of Latin American history represented by the episode of the *Mundo Nuevo* magazine.

There was a long-standing enmity—based mainly on ideological differences but also including disagreements over differences in literary tastes as well as some degree of competition or intellectual jealousy—between Emir Rodríguez Monegal and Ángel Rama, who succeeded each other in the role of director of the literary section of *Marcha*. Rama warned the "family" of the relationship between *Cuadernos* and its projected successor, *Mundo Nuevo*, run by Emir Rodríguez Monegal until 1968, when it changed director and headquarters (from Paris to Buenos Aires). Rama took the lead in the polemic against *Mundo Nuevo* and even named his crusade, which he dubbed "against cultural facades," going so far as to turn the cultural section of *Marcha* into a platform for that campaign.[26]

---

25 From a methodological perspective, the analysis of the magazine as an object finds in this type of rupture precise and powerful limits.

26 "It was Ángel . . . who first warned Cintio and me during the congress in Genoa, and then sent me a letter, about the magazine project that Emir would be in charge of, and which, with the backing of the CIA, would eventually be recognized by the Anglo-American press" (Retamar in Sarusky 144–45). See from 1966: "El mecenazgo de la CIA," *Marcha*, no. 1302, May 6; "El amo y el servidor (Cultura y CIA)," *Marcha*, no. 1304, May 20; "Los intelectuales en la

In order for the strength of one of the contenders to cross borders and win the battle, the family had to have existed beforehand. And that was indeed the case. The polemic correspondence that marked the beginning of the controversial existence of *Mundo Nuevo* underscored both the impact of personal acquaintance and the importance of the Cuban *nihil obstat.* In the first of the letters written to announce the intentions of the new magazine to Cubans, Retamar sent Monegal "Genoese greetings," referring to the 1965 congress in Genoa where they had met.

Monegal sent copies of the letter he wrote to Retamar about *Mundo Nuevo*'s objectives to several publications and asked that it be published with the clarification that the Cuban Embassy in Paris had not yet given him a visa to go to Cuba (to gain key support for any project in which the Latin American family could participate). In his letter, Monegal declared that *Mundo Nuevo* was not willing to exhume Cold War rhetoric, that he would not answer rudeness with rudeness, and that he would not accept the role of "enemy of Cuba" that they were projecting on him ("Correspondencia Retamar–Monegal").

The dynamics of the network of magazines in solidarity worked perfectly: *Marcha*, *Siempre!*, *La Rosa Blindada*, and *Bohemia*, among others, published the polemic correspondence between Retamar and

---

época desarrollista," *Marcha,* no. 1305, May 27; "Las fachadas culturales (Cultura y CIA), " and *Marcha,* no. 1306, June 3, 1967; "Más vale tarde que nunca," *Marcha,* no. 1345, March 22 [1967]: Rama had written the title of the article, but the content was the letter announcing the suspension of activities of the Centro Uruguayo de Promoción Cultural, headed by Benito Milla and sponsored by the Latin American Institute of International Relations (ILARI, for its acronym in Spanish). Rama included a sidebar in which he declared: "An empire not only incorporates marginal zones into its economic structure but also intellectual activities" ("El tigre en el flotante camalote"). Vargas Llosa contributed by sending reports on the denunciations of the financing of publications tied to congress, sending articles on the scandal to *Marcha* and *Casa de las Américas.* On the resignations of Frank Kermode and Stephen Spender, the directors of *Encounter,* see "Epitafio para un imperio cultural," *Marcha,* May 27, 1967, reprinted in fragments in the section "Al pie de la letra," *Casa de las Américas,* no. 44 (September–October 1967). In its June 2, 1967, issue, *Marcha* published an extensive chronology of the controversy and the articles published up to that point.

Monegal, clarifying their support for the Cuban position of a complete rejection of *Mundo Nuevo*. Ambrosio Fornet announced the presence of *Mundo Nuevo* with an allusion to *The Communist Manifesto*: "A new literary specter haunts Latin America." For the Cubans and their allies, the purpose of this specter was to work in favor of cultural "neutrality" and encourage the gradual depoliticization of the Latin American intellectual, sedating intellectuals. As a tribute to the times, *Mundo Nuevo* formulated its objectives, according to Fornet, in "leftist" language. Also, as a tribute to the times, Fornet claims that *Mundo Nuevo* wanted to appear to be paid for through gold from Moscow in order to hide its dubious financing by US foundations linked to the CIA (1967).

Fornet's position was endorsed by the first declaration of the *Casa de las Américas* editorial board, which warned against the US cultural offensive aimed at neutralizing, dividing, and winning over intellectuals. The list of US plans included Camelot, the financing of sociological research throughout the continent, the commissioning of academic studies through universities and foundations, the acquisition of publishing houses and magazines, and the activities of the Latin American Institute of International Relations (ILARI).[27]

ILARI members (in their first—and last—declaration, as indicated in the section "Sextante" [Sextant] of *Mundo Nuevo,* no. 13, July 1967) defended themselves by appealing to objectivity as a guide in their search for knowledge, to the need for cultural exchange, and accused their opponents and critics of being "cultural oligarchs," or "purity lunatics," comparable to "inquisitors on the right and the left."

A new declaration by the *Casa de las Américas*, dated October 5, 1967, in Havana, stressed the importance of the role of intellectuals in the revolution, thereby justifying US interests in co-opting them:

> By trying to neutralize intellectuals, distancing them from the continent's urgent political tasks, imperialism seeks to stifle the

---

27 Those in charge were Luis Mercier Vega (Paris); Vicente Barretto (Rio de Janeiro); Benito Milla (Montevideo); Horacio D. Rodríguez (Buenos Aires); Enrique Chase (Asunción); Eduardo Mac Lean (La Paz); Martín Cerda (Santiago de Chile); and Jorge Luis Recabarren (Lima).

> development of intellectual cadres who will be the Ches or Fidels of tomorrow. . . . High-level dialogue and peaceful coexistence are the refined instruments of capitalism. . . . A few years ago, it might have been the crude anticommunism of the Congress for Cultural Freedom and its magazine *Cuadernos*; today it is the mellifluous and coexistential tone of ILARI and the magazine *Mundo Nuevo* ("La intervención de los Estados Unidos en la vida latinoamericana").

By then, the scandal over the financing of *Mundo Nuevo* (and the rest of the magazines associated with the Congress for Cultural Freedom), supported by Rama's incessant denunciations, was already making things difficult for the members of the Parisian magazine. Emir Rodríguez Monegal insisted, however, on pursuing the *Mundo Nuevo* enterprise, arguing that he had had absolute freedom to disseminate his ideas and those of his collaborators. There were some writers and critics who considered *Mundo Nuevo*'s proposal acceptable, especially in view of the winds of aesthetic modernity it sought to unleash. Although the replacement of publications was clearly a strategy of the Congress for Cultural Freedom, which placed *Mundo Nuevo* in an ambiguous position, some members of the intelligentsia did not feel that there was enough evidence to establish a direct relationship between *Mundo Nuevo* and *Cuadernos*. A contributor to *Amaru* maintained that *Mundo Nuevo* had presented itself up to that point with a Latin American flavor that "no magazine possessed to such a high degree," and in spite of the Cubans' refusal to participate in the magazine, the good faith of the director, Emir Rodríguez Monegal, had prevented *Mundo Nuevo* from being reduced to having nothing but right-wing contributors. He concluded by stating: "Progressive intellectuals who feel that no forum . . . should be overlooked have helped prevent this" (Oquendo 92).

The defense was either blind to or deliberately ignoring one aspect: *Mundo Nuevo* did not take a sympathetic view of Cuba, and this rendered the umbilical cord that associated it with *Cuadernos* visible. And, like it, despite Oquendo's opinion, it shared the same proclivity to publicly denouncing any hint of communism. Cuba was clearly the bête noire of *Mundo Nuevo*.

The *Mundo Nuevo* case introduced a wedge between existing agreements. The tension between recognition and revolution, between the use of the intellectual autonomy acquired in the specific task of writing versus fidelity to the positions of the anti-imperialist ideological program, permeated the decisions of the members of the community. *Mundo Nuevo* burst onto the scene emphasizing the modernizing scaffolding of culture and supporting the rhetoric of dialogue and coexistence denounced by Cuba and its Latin American allies as the new and refined instruments of capitalism.

The new combativeness of the intellectual family was also evident on the occasion of the thirty-fourth edition of the PEN Club Congress, held in New York from July 11 to 18, 1966. If the most visible place on the map, the radiant promontory, was unquestionably Cuba—the privileged focus of the articles that endlessly propagated from center to periphery—, the United States, in contrast, was the boundary that marked the limits of political activism, an absolute otherness that not even bodies could penetrate.

The thirty-fourth edition of the PEN Club Congress had its immediate antecedent in Dubrovnik (Yugoslavia), presided over by Arthur Miller and held in Eastern Europe for the first time following the Second World War. The idea of a meeting of writers from throughout the world in the zone behind the Iron Curtain, followed by a meeting in the United States, was part of an effort to strengthen East/West ties, in the long-awaited thaw that a good part of the world intelligentsia supported.

The institution of the PEN Club itself was not held in the highest regard on either side of the world ideological dispute. The gathering in New York was therefore to be something of a litmus test. As an unsigned article in *Primera Plana* stated: "If the Soviets send a notorious representation and the State Department collaborates by extending visas to East Germans and Cubans, we will have achieved a genuine international meeting of intellectuals." But uncertainty prevailed: "In twelve months we will discover whether hopes will continue to grow or whether the PEN Club will remain an elegant pensioner" ("¿Puede el PEN Club rejuvenecer?").

The New York meeting of PEN was attended by Mario Vargas Llosa, Carlos Fuentes, Nicanor Parra, Emir Rodríguez Monegal, Pablo Neruda, Carlos Martínez Moreno, Juan Carlos Onetti, Victoria Ocampo, Homero Aridjis, Juan Liscano, Haroldo de Campos, and João Guimarães Rosa (Rodríguez Monegal 1966a, 66–67). The presence of Neruda, who had also attended the congress in Yugoslavia, caused extraordinary commotion and discontent, further reinforced by his visit to Peru, where he had accepted an award from Peruvian president Belaúnde Terry. Following this, Cuban artists wrote a furious letter to the Chilean poet. The letter, dated July 25, 1966, in Havana, and addressed to "comrade Pablo," warns him of the "uneasiness caused in Cuba by the use our enemies have made of your recent activities." Included in the complaints was the clarification that neither his participation in the PEN Club Congress nor his visit to the United States was the cause of the rupture. What the signatories found puzzling were the reasons that the United States had allowed him access after twenty years of steadfast refusal to grant him an entry visa. What was most disturbing, it was suggested, was the endorsement of the claim that the Cold War was over: "No one with decency can sustain that criterion," when a socialist country "has been receiving the systematic physical aggression that Vietnam is currently experiencing," "when the United States has actively participated in coups d'état in Indonesia, Ghana, Nigeria, Brazil, and Argentina." And if the United States granted visas to certain leftists, the reasons for this could be one of two options: either the authorized visitors had ceased to be leftists or, as in Neruda's case, the host country expected to benefit from their presence. How was it possible, the signatories continued, that Carlos Fuentes, in collusion with the "imperialist propaganda organ" *Life en Español*, could publish a note (Fuentes 1966) in which he held up Neruda as an example of those who were open to dialogue? Even more interesting is its criticism of Neruda for having spent his time in New York with Emir Rodríguez Monegal, who had been commissioned to direct a new magazine in Spanish (following the demise of *Cuadernos*) by the Congress for Cultural Freedom, an organization financed by the CIA, as reported by *The New York Times* itself. The open letter, signed by hundreds of artists and critics, was published on Sunday, July 31, 1966, in *Granma*, and over time it received more endorsements ("Carta abierta a Pablo Neruda").[28]

28 *Casa de las Américas* later republished the letter and incorporated the endorsements received following its original publication (no. 38, September–October 1966, 131–35). Subsequently, there were even more endorsements,

Similar arguments were presented at the round table broadcast on August 10, 1966, by Radio Havana, which included Fernández Retamar, Lisandro Otero, Edmundo Desnoes, and Ambrosio Fornet. They were convened to discuss the topic of the "intellectual penetration of Yankee imperialism" in Latin America. At the core of the discussion was the trip several Latin American intellectuals took to the United States (precisely during the PEN Club Congress), although it was not the trip itself that was being questioned. In short, the claim was that the Cuban Revolution had brought about a change in US policy toward intellectuals capable of "alienating themselves."[29] As a result of the support for the revolution by the majority of the world's intellectuals, the United States, concerned about the danger of the radicalization of the continent's intellectuals, began to implement subtle methods of co-optation in order to, according to Desnoes, "undermine resistance, flatter the vanity of the writer, and lead him to silence abuses and humiliations in order to maintain those advantages." That policy, launched by Kennedy, "the first enlightened president of the United States after Roosevelt," as Lisandro Otero put it, resulted in greater attention being paid to intellectuals as well as offers of training, major translations, and other means of flattery, as a "subtle form of perks, assimilation, attraction" (Retamar et al. 133–38). Given the strained relations between Neruda and his natural allies, *Mundo Nuevo* took advantage of the opportunity to emphasize the incantatory effect of Neruda's verses as he recited them before an audience transfixed by the spell of his poetry (Rodríguez Monegal 1966a, 43–44). And the magazine quickly "captured" the questioned poet as one of its own, dedicating several articles to him and publishing fragments of his works (Rodríguez Monegal 1966b, 70–74, and Neruda 1966, 19–22, in *Mundo Nuevo*).

With respect to Neruda's presence in the United States, it should be noted that it also caused concern among the weak ranks of the right, which wondered how it was possible for an avowed communist to recite

---

including those of young Peruvian writers, who decided to send their support during their first convention, held between September 28 and 30. The letter was also published in *La Rosa Blindada* 2, no. 9 (September 1966).

29 In the words of Gouldner 82–100 and Hollander 40–73.

his verses before such a large audience. Carlos Fuentes commented that Murena had told him that the PEN Club meeting in the United States had been a communist maneuver. The rumor was denied by Juan Liscano, director of *Zona Franca*. Murena's actual commentary regarding Neruda's reading was apparently the following: "On leaving, it was not we, the Latin Americans—already immunized—, who were indignant. Was it the other attendees, especially those from beyond the Curtain? A Stalinist!' they exclaimed. 'Who organized this? We are offended and humiliated. We are here too, and we have very important writers in our delegations.' We tried to calm them down: Neruda is not to blame. He was invited and accepted. That's it. He is not the one planning the event" (Liscano 1967a, X).

Another target of the attacks was Carlos Fuentes, who not only participated in the PEN Club but also contributed to *Mundo Nuevo*: Edmundo Desnoes had accused him of being an accomplice for contributing to the pro-US magazine *Life*. Ambrosio Fornet, in whose view *Mundo Nuevo* proposed "consolation through literature" for those who resolved to "depoliticize themselves," accused Fuentes, "whose sophisticated image appears on the covers of the great North American magazines destined for Latin America and whose frivolous articles are proudly published by *Life en Español*," of being the "Boethius" of that resolve. Annoyed by Fuentes's statements in an interview with Monegal (1966c), Fornet compares him to a guerrilla fighter "who has picked up a rifle not to fight against the fetishism of the market, mass culture, and the alienation of the modern world, but to turn society upside down" (Fornet 109). Following these remarks by Desnoes and Fornet, Fernando Benítez published an open letter in *Siempre!* addressed to Fernández Retamar in defense of his compatriot Fuentes (Benítez x). In the response that *Casa de las Américas* addressed to Benítez, Fuentes was presented as a friend with whom they wished to have an open dialogue and whom they in no way intended to insult. It is true that in that same issue of the Cuban magazine they published a letter from Carlos Fuentes to Retamar, dated February 22, 1967, in which, in a very friendly tone, Fuentes clarified:

> Through a letter from Vargas Llosa and conversations with Julio Cortázar, I have learned of the success of the meetings that were

> recently held in Havana, in reference to the first meeting of the Collaboration Committee and its declaration. He also expressed his desire to see a chapter of *A Change of Skin*, published in *Casa de las Américas*, and to visit Cuba to discuss, in a friendly tone, many problems they shared, the solutions to which require a variety of approaches (1967b, 134).

The pragmatics of discourse, the limits of the sayable, objects that can or cannot be discussed, and places where one can or cannot speak: Augusto Roa Bastos also sent a letter to Retamar (universal recipient), dated September 1966, which was published alongside Fuentes's letter. Roa Bastos requested an intensification of the dialogue on what he called "an episode of *Mundo Nuevo*," a magazine in which, when he promised Emir in 1965 that he would collaborate; "the enlightening polemic that you initiated" (in reference to Retamar) had not yet unfolded. Roa Bastos reiterated his loyalty to Cuba, the "guiding light of the Revolution of the Americas." The Paraguayan novelist knew why the minor and intimate genre of the letter was appropriate for speaking of *sins* committed:

> I am not asking for a bill of indemnity or prerogatives of tolerance and privilege for those who, like me, have incurred through no bad faith in some of the oversights or blunders excoriated in the letter to Pablo; my collaboration with *Mundo Nuevo*, for example (1967, 135–40).

The appearance of *Mundo Nuevo*, framed within US policies of intellectual co-optation, produced the first of the strong tremors that shook "our own," as they had been dubbed in 1966 when the Spanish version of Luis Harss's book *Into the Mainstream* was published under the title *Los nuestros* [Our Own]. It is no coincidence that it was at precisely that time that the discussion of the "intellectual as a problem" emerged. In the first place, intellectuals could allow themselves to be seduced by US policies aimed at co-opting them; second, literary success could lead them to believe that the legitimacy of their discourse, sanctioned by anonymous readers in a kind of plebiscite, was sustained by their own individuality; and third, they could or could not freely choose the path of revolution and sacrifice and show how they provided content to a progressivism that up to that point had only been declared.

From that point on, Cuba was the touchstone for the alignments of the Latin American intellectual field. As American interest in Latin American artists intensified and the culture industry (which the United States was particularly adept at producing) was exported to the Latin American continent, a number of intellectuals demanded a more energetic and precise backing of political pacts: that is, pacts with the revolution.

If anything confirms the hypothesis that this period was marked by an interest in bringing culture and politics together as a common denominator, it was precisely the concern of the United States in the face of this "politicization" of the artistic field, to which it responded with various policies. In this sense, an observation is in order on the specificity of the visual arts and their limited ability to resist US policies of co-optation and seduction with the promise of turning the great Latin American capitals into hubs of international art. Certainly, writer-intellectuals were able to develop more consistent discourses of resistance against the seduction of the various US sponsorships that were to some degree successful in the visual arts. This dependence of Latin American visual arts on the United States was more evident in institutional circuits (galleries, museums, traveling exhibitions) than in the images shown by the artists themselves in their works (Giunta 1995 and 1997). On the other hand, without US assistance, Latin American literature was able to establish itself as a hub of production, recognized throughout the Western world.

3. The Latin American Community of Writers and Cuba

Following the agreements forged at Genoa to create a Latin American Cultural Community, the "first congress of the cultural community of the continent" was held in Arica, Chile, from January 29 to February 6, 1966. An attempt was made to create a more ambitious project than the mere Latin American Writers' Association. The aim now was to create a Latin American Cultural Community.

The congress was convened by Chile's National Commission on Culture and was attended by delegates from almost all of the countries in the region, except for Cuba (which at the time was hosting the Tricontinental Conference), Haiti, Santo Domingo, Argentina, and Mexico. Those present included Braulio Arenas, Enrique Lihn, Jorge Millás, Nicanor Parra, Mario Monteforte Toledo, José María Arguedas, Arturo Ardao, and Ángel Rama. Of those invited, Borges, Carpentier, Rulfo, and Neruda did not attend.

Rama was not very optimistic about the results of the encounter; he wrote with irony: "I am, for the third time, attending the birth of the Latin American Community of Writers" (1966). As the Chilean magazine *Mensaje* acknowledged, "it was—to put it mildly—an assembly with a slim chance of success" (G. B. 119). Nevertheless, its overall assessment of the encounter was positive: "It was what it was meant to be: a starting point, an initial step" (G. B. 119).

In fact, there were predictable disagreements, which *Mundo Nuevo* attributed to an "excess of verbalism" between two opposing groups. On one side were Brother Manuel Sánchez Astudillo (Ecuador) and Hugo Lindo, and on the other, Ángel Rama and Mario Monteforte Toledo, among others. In the "Sextante" [Sextant] section of its first issue, *Mundo Nuevo* avoided commenting on the political aspect of the discussion, but it did report one of the conclusions of the encounter: the decision to declare 1967 as the year of Rubén Darío ("Comunidad cultural" 82). Apparently, however, the Arica encounter neutralized the threat of a politicization that would later become inevitable. It did so by practicing "mutual vigilance between Marxists and non-Marxists" (G. B. 119).

With the purpose of continuing the processes of the institutional creation of the Latin American Community of Writers, the Second Latin American Congress of Writers was held in Mexico in 1967 under the auspices of the government of President Díaz Ordaz. The aim was to promote cultural integration in Latin America, discuss the creation of unions, the defense of professional rights, increase the circulation of works, stimulate bibliographic information, endorse and expand the agreements adopted in Arica, and discuss the Statutes of the Latin American Community and the Charter of the Latin American Cultural Community, among other issues. The organizing committee consisted of José Revueltas, Carlos Pellicer, José López Bermúdez, Marco Antonio Millán, Víctor Gallo, Juan Rulfo, and Francisco Arellano Bellock. Ten Latin American works selected by the congress were to be published and the government of Guadalajara was to grant scholarships for one year to young Latin American writers (Haro viii).

This encounter had not begun on the best note and would end on a worse one. On March 12, 1967, Emmanuel Carballo warned that the host organization was not trustworthy and added that the congress,

> viewed in light of recent revelations made in the United States regarding CIA sponsorship of cultural organizations with ambiguous tendencies, such as the declining Congress for Cultural Freedom, could be considered a sufficiently skillful maneuver to cover up objectives that are contrary to the interests of our peoples (1967).

Carballo was not the only one to hold this opinion; the Mexican writers consulted by *Siempre!* in the survey conducted by Blanca Haro agreed with him. As Fernández Retamar pointed out, Carballo excluded several of the congress organizers from his scathing judgment, such as Carlos Pellicer—who had recently visited Cuba, invited to the "Encounter with Rubén Darío," and had delivered the invitations to this encounter in Mexico—; José Revueltas, who would give them "a tremendous and pleasant surprise;" and Juan Rulfo, who was waiting for them at the airport in Mexico City and was extremely kind to them. The surprise Retamar is referring to was Revueltas's reaction when he announced—after hearing Mario Monteforte Toledo say that the community would include the left and the "clean right"—that he would vote against the creation of an "intellectual OAS" (Fernández Retamar 1967a, 97). *Casa de las Américas* devoted much of its July–August 1967 issue to the encounter. In addition to Retamar's article, it published the declaration of the Cuban delegation and sympathizers, along with four papers presented at the congress, those of José Bianco (1967), Manuel Rojas (1967), Marcio Veloz Maggiolo (1967), and Mario Benedetti (1967b).[30] *Casa de*

---

30 The article, "Ideas y actitudes en circulación" [Ideas and attitudes in circulation] was reproduced in his book *Letras del continente mestizo* [Letters from

las Américas also published the article by Ángel Rama—which later appeared in *Marcha* (1967c).

The "young writers of Mexico," who included José Agustín, Carlos Monsiváis, and Vicente Leñero, in turn issued harsh statements questioning the organization and selection of guests, one of whom was Germán Arciniegas, the former director of *Cuadernos*. This hospitality also surprised Rama, for whom Arciniegas's invitation was particularly unusual since the Americans themselves had replaced him as editor in chief of the literary magazine they financed for Latin America (1967c, 115).

Another objection was the potential to use the community for lucrative purposes, which would benefit only a few. As Gustavo Sainz stated: "The PEN Club worked to sell translations of Onetti, Murena, Vargas Llosa, and the Guggenheim grant for Homero Aridjis. The tug of war over the publishing rights of Sabato and Neruda. A congress here will likely serve to socially connect a whole host of intellectuals who will seldom have such an opportunity to chat in hallways and yawn at conventional conferences" (Avilés Fabila 1967a).

Uruguayan editor Benito Milla[31] also made reference to all these reservations in his coverage of the meeting for the Montevideo newspaper *Acción*, which *Mundo Nuevo* judged to be one of the "most complete and balanced" outlets. According to Milla: "The Mexican press did not seem to attribute much importance to the Congress. Almost all the young writers of Mexico had adopted the same attitude, with a few exceptions, such as the novelist Fernando del Paso and the poet Marco Antonio Montes de Oca." From the outset, Milla was looking to turn things to the advantage of those who were integrated and was critical of those who were apocalyptic. He described Carballo's warning—noting that he had just returned from a trip to Cuba—as "a tale of fear," which saw the hand of the CIA and right-wing conspiracies behind everything (cited in "México, Congreso de escritores").

---

the Mestizo Continent], 9–12, where oddly enough it is dated 1963, which is an obvious misprint (see 1967b).

31 Milla, like Monegal, had ties with ILARI and had already had an intense debate with Ángel Rama about that institution. Nevertheless, he agreed with Rama regarding the lack of interest of the Mexican press in the event.

Juan Liscano, for his part, wrote that days before the congress began:

> extremely different versions regarding its significance circulated. Pro-Cuban leftist intellectuals saw it as an extension of the cultural apparatus of US imperialist penetration. Other writers affirmed that it was a communist maneuver aimed at creating an organization for Latin American cultural integration, to be used for Marxist proselytism (1967b, 4).

In total, more than one hundred writers and critics from the continent participated in the event, which was held from March 15 to 24 in Guadalajara and Guanajuato, Mexico, with an inaugural session on March 15 in the auditorium of the National Museum of Anthropology in Mexico City. Those present included Miguel Ángel Asturias, José María Arguedas, João Guimarães Rosa, Nicolás Guillén, Miguel Otero Silva, Arturo Uslar Pietri, Germán Arciniegas, Jorge Icaza, Augusto Céspedes, Manuel Rojas, Ernesto Cardenal, Mario Benedetti, Nicolás Guillén, Ricardo Molinari, Juan Liscano, Eduardo Mallea, Juan Carlos Onetti, Roberto Fernández Retamar, Ángel Rama, Sara de Ibáñez, Carlos Martínez Moreno, José Bianco, Juan Rulfo, Carlos Pellicer, Rodolfo Usigli, Efraín Huerta, Julio César Chávez, Salvador Garmendia, and Benito Milla. Rómulo Gallegos (a personal guest of the Mexican president) sent a message of support, since age-related ailments prevented him from traveling. Other invitees who did not attend were Julio Cortázar, Pablo Neruda, Jorge Luis Borges, and Mario Vargas Llosa.

According to Liscano, on the day of the inauguration itself, a potential division of the delegates was unofficially discussed. There were apparently behind-the-scenes meetings to avoid demonstrations that would interfere with the proceedings of the congress. The threat came, according to Liscano, "from the large group of writers of various nationalities, arriving directly from Cuba" (1967b, 4).

Ultimately, the rift was made explicit: the entire Cuban delegation, with the support of other participants, read a document in which they announced their decision not to participate in the creation of a Latin American Community of Writers. The document read by Mario Benedetti on behalf of the Cuban delegation stated: "We cannot expect a leftist writer to form part of the same community as a pro-imperialist writer, or a writer committed to national oligarchies, or one who is indifferent to the abuses of the enemy" ("Declaración de los veinte").

The fundamental objection was that the notion of community required the existence of affinities, beyond cultural interest, which were considered insufficient. The critics questioned the idea of conceiving a community on the basis of the professional category: they argued that a community conceived of in this way negated the very project of the writer-intellectual. Retamar stated in his article:

> How is it conceivable that a community like this would not be the product of a community of interests, attitudes, points of view? How is it conceivable that in a community like this Germán Arciniegas and Jorge Zalamea might find themselves face-to-face tomorrow or Juan Liscano and Nicolás Guillén today? . . . This is why, of the participants in the congress, twenty of us, with Uruguayan Mario Benedetti as our spokesperson, have expressed our decision to abstain from participating in the community that was being planned and that was ultimately founded (1967a, 98).

In Benedetti's speech, he thanked Mexico, a country that had not broken off relations with Cuba and, despite certain disagreements, accepted "the good intentions and open-mindedness of those who had conceived of this Latin American cultural enterprise." The "Declaración de los veinte" [Declaration of Twenty] was signed by Roberto Armijo (El Salvador); Mario Benedetti (Uruguay); Alejo Carpentier (Cuba); René Depestre (Haiti); Roberto Fernández Retamar (Cuba); Juan José Folguera (Argentina); Salvador Garmendia (Venezuela); Hernando Guerrero (Colombia); Nicolás Guillén (Cuba); Raúl Leiva (Guatemala); Enrique Lihn (Chile); Carlos Martínez Moreno (Uruguay); Thiago de Melo (Brazil); Álvaro Menéndez Leal (El Salvador); Augusto Monterroso (Guatemala); Marco Antonio Montes de Oca (Mexico); Lisandro Otero (Cuba); Manuel Rojas (Chile); Eleodoro Vargas Vicuña (Peru); and Gloria Zegarra Diez Canseco (Peru).

In commenting on the "Declaración de los veinte" (read "in a slow and monotonous voice" by Benedetti) and the speech by Retamar that preceded it ("he emphasized his country's usual watchwords"), Liscano once again notes: "Almost all the signatories came from Cuba" (1967b, 4–5).

What surprised Liscano, Monegal, and Milla was the special deference given to the Cuban delegation, which was allowed to take the stage along with the board of directors and Guanajuato's municipal authorities. Miguel Ángel Asturias delivered the closing speech of the inaugural ceremony following the reading of the "Declaración de los veinte." According to accounts of those present, Asturias, who was shaken, improvised a speech in which he advocated for the creation of the community, defending the possibility of dialogue, a word that was ideologically prohibited at the time since it formed part of the preferred lexicon of the Alliance for Progress. Rama recalls this, arguing that "it was not credible, given his background, that Asturias could possibly have taken that word to mean a task shared with the Latin American *cipayos*" (1967c).

After extensive deliberations, the situation of the congress was defined. According to Liscano, the "moderate left" prevailed, the congress continued, and the group in favor of "abstention" ended up being a significant minority (1967b, 6). Liscano considered the moderate left to be the sector of writers who, while agreeing with the need for the community to involve a shared and coherent ideological attitude with clear progressive social and political connotations, felt that the task of forming the community was worth attempting. A preliminary draft prepared by this group (consisting of Rama, Rulfo, Ibáñez, Onetti, and Arguedas) proposed that, as a condition for joining the community, writers had to support the Latin American revolution, the struggle against local oligarchies, and the fight against US imperialism. The draft of the preamble for the statutes of the community began with the phrase "Latin America is experiencing a revolution," which was rejected by the majority of the assembly as "propagandistic."[32]

32 The agenda for discussion included the following points: the social role of the writer, authors' rights, the writer and education, the writer and culture, the writer and the means of cultural dissemination, the writer and the Latin American community, the writer's contribution to Latin American cultural solidarity and to the development of a spirit of peace and friendship among peoples, and the integration of Latin American culture into universal culture.

However, the continuation of the congress was, for Liscano, Milla, and Monegal, a kind of Pyrrhic victory. Although the "Declaración de los veinte" remained limited in number to the initial signatories, the secessionist delegation would achieve a major victory when the congress's final declaration incorporated the Cuban requirements and watchwords; the plenary approved a condemnation of the Vietnam War, declared itself against the Cuban embargo, condemned the breach of university autonomy in Argentina, Brazil, Colombia, and Venezuela, and proposed a denunciation of the Camelot project and Project Simpatico aimed at US cultural penetration. Guimarães Rosa withdrew from the vice presidency, regretting the "propagandization" of the congress, and signed a document endorsed by twenty participants (a counter-statement to the declaration of the twenty), protesting the excessive politicization of the congress and calling for priority to be given to issues related to culture and literature. The counter-declaration was signed by Julio César Chávez (Paraguay), Carlos Solórzano, Demetrio Aguilera Malta, Jorge Icaza, Antonio de Undurraga, Fermín Estrella Gutiérrez, Cayetano Córdoba Iturburu (Argentina), Fernando Charry Lara, Ernesto Mejía Sánchez, Benito Milla (Uruguay), Rodolfo Usigli (Mexico), Carmen Naranjo, Francisco Tobar-García, and Juan Liscano.

What Retamar saw as "the positive aspects of the Congress," Liscano and Milla considered a defection of the board of directors, which had enabled the politicization of the event. Thus, Milla states:

> Contrary to what some of the young Mexican writers predicted, to what Carballo had clearly anticipated, and to what the Cubans and their friends undoubtedly feared, the tone of the Congress was predominantly political, its orientation decidedly radical—as reflected in its main political resolutions—and perhaps given such an evident predominance, some of its shortcomings could be established ("México, Congreso de escritores").

Along the same lines, Liscano explains:

> The motions and amendments of the Congress, for the most part, were characterized by a polemic desire shaped much more by belligerent enmity toward US policy than by a genuine concern

> for democracy and culture. Cubans, pro-Cubans, and radicals, although they were in the minority when it came to abstaining on the regulation and implementation of the communities, did succeed during the last Plenary Session, held in Guadalajara, in dominating an assembly that was partly tired or apathetic and partly willing from the outset to play their game (1967b, 6).

Rama also felt that the congress "fiercely debated political rather than literary questions" (1967c). The difference in Rama's assessment was based on the fact that he attempted to contextualize and account for the symbolic power relations in conflict. The politicization that affected the congress was, as Rama indicated, a symptom of the *general situation of the continent*. The same can be said of the Cuban delegation's ability to have its aspirations endorsed. Rama's conclusion was one of uncertainty:

> Whether this culmination has been for the better is another matter. Perhaps the most prudent approach is to wait: the famous waiting period that appears to be mandatory for any new institution in order to see it in action, an approach that, in some cases—like that of the present author—covers up pessimism (1967c, 114–15).

Finally, in Mexico, authorities for the community were chosen: voting took place in the same way as when the communities had been created. Carlos Pellicer, López Bermúdez, Carlos Solórzano, and Demetrio Aguilero Malta were elected as representatives. The Chilean government committed to sponsoring the next meeting of the Latin American Cultural Community.

The fragility of *Mundo Nuevo*, which Monegal was forced to abandon in 1968 and which disappeared, without fanfare, in 1971, after several years of financial and cultural agony, as well as the final triumph of the "abstentionists" in Mexico, are the most notorious signs of the Latin American intellectual corporation's capacity for action and its strategic choices. As Juan Liscano wrote, the struggle, in the end, was between extreme leftists and moderate leftists, a statement that truly reflects the discursive pragmatics of the epoch. From that point on, many institutions attempted to counter others: the best example is the duplication of the tributes to Rubén Darío, one of which, as mentioned above, was held in

Havana. Another took place during the thirteenth Inter-American Literary Congress, which was held in two parts: the first in Los Angeles, from January 18 to 21, the second in Caracas, in honor of its four hundredth anniversary, and was the setting for the first presentation of the Rómulo Gallegos Prize, which would subsequently be awarded every four years. The events in Caracas took place during the first half of August 1967 and were unfortunately marred by the terrible earthquake that struck the city on July 29. On August 7, a roundtable of novelists and critics was held at the Ateneo de Caracas, with the participation of Vargas Llosa, García Márquez (who spoke about *One Hundred Years of Solitude*), Fernando Alegría, José María Castellet, Emir Rodríguez Monegal, Ángel Rama, Uslar Pietri, Adriano González León, and Seymour Menton, and was presided over by Miguel Otero Silva. The roundtable was devoted exclusively to the novel and the future of criticism. The only participant who went off script and gave a political speech was the Venezuelan Adriano González León. On Thursday, August 10, 1967, as part of the same festivities, the Rómulo Gallegos Prize was awarded to Mario Vargas Llosa for his novel *The Green House* at the Museum of Fine Arts (see "Los novelistas y sus críticos," Rodríguez Monegal 1967a, and Liscano 1967c, 2–3).

Juan Liscano had warned in 1967: "What happened in Mexico could be repeated in Chile" (1967b, 9). And, indeed, it was: the Latin American writers' community was created, but its creation was de facto and not de jure, as demonstrated by the failure of subsequent meetings aimed at its institutional consolidation. In reality, the "community" initiative had shifted to Cuba.

The Latin American Writers' Conference, which had been announced in Mexico, was held in Santiago, Valparaíso, and Concepción, Chile, from August 18 to 30, 1969. The theme was "The role of writers in underdeveloped countries." Participants included Juan Rulfo, Augusto Céspedes, Jorge Adoum, Carlos Martínez Moreno, Bernardo Kordon, Claude Simon, Roger Caillois, Emilio Adolfo Westphalen, Carlos Germán Belli, Rosario Castellanos, Camilo José Cela, Leopoldo Marechal, David Viñas, Marta Traba, Juan Carlos Onetti, Ángel Rama, Mario Vargas Llosa, Antonio Cisneros, and the Chileans Nicanor Parra, Jorge Edwards, Humberto Díaz-Casanueva, Enrique Lihn, Pedro Lastra, Luis Domínguez, Francisco Coloane, Martín Cerda, and Waldo Rojas. Carpentier, Cortázar, García Márquez, Borges, and Asturias were absent, and at the last minute, Fuentes, Sabato, Arguedas, and Roa Bastos decided not to attend.

What importance could this conference hold compared to the impressive 1968 Cultural Congress of Havana, where Cuba had been the meeting point of the five hundred most important intellectuals in the world? Among other issues, the encounter in Chile was once again marked by the uneasiness caused by the "snub of the Cuban delegation, which did not reply to the invitation" (Ruffinelli 1969, 29).

The ritual was the "trip *to* Cuba": traveling in the opposite direction made no historical or geographical sense. Although the participants represented "a good literary selection with a broad spectrum of the positions writers are currently defending," the absence of the Cuban delegation was considered serious and, above all, a discredit. The situation in Chile also had an impact on the relative failure of that encounter; the conference was criticized, almost unanimously, for its lack of political independence, having been used for the electoral benefit of the Christian Democratic government in power (Bianchi n275, 223–24).

What happened was that David Viñas quietly left after three days. Then, Emmanuel Carballo did the same, after sending a letter to the president of the Society of Chilean Writers in which he explained that after waiting for several days for the conference to address the points of the agenda previously agreed upon—beyond the social gatherings, which tended more toward *spectacle* than the authentic intellectual exchange of the various ideological positions, and of petty politics in favor of the government in power—*he had decided to leave the conference*. The letter was read at the plenary session on Sunday morning (Ehrmann 109). Marta Traba also complained for the same reasons:

> When we went to the opening ceremony in that turn-of-the-century theater, I expected a writer to welcome us but it turned out to be a minister; then we went to lunch and again I expected a writer to speak, but it was the vice minister. We arrived in Viña, and the sessions were not opened by a writer but by the Minister of Foreign Affairs (Ehrmann 109).

Taking advantage of the presence of the visitors, the Chilean magazine *Punto Final* brought Viñas, Traba, Adoum, Rama, and Carballo together and asked them about various issues related to continental literary output, the role of the intellectual and, of course, the conference they were attending. To underscore the crisis of legitimacy the Chilean conference was facing, *Casa de las Américas* published an article on the roundtable organized by *Punto Final* under the title "¿El único encuentro del encuentro?" [The Only Encounter of the Encounter?].

Jorge Ruffinelli reported that Vargas Llosa introduced the Cuban question, urging those present to sign a "record of the shame and sorrow that the quarantine—the blockade—, this cordon sanitaire that surrounds Cuba, causes Latin American writers." He then presented a manifesto for the liberation of Puerto Rico, which was read by two Puerto Rican women from the independence movement. He even asked the Chilean foreign minister, Gabriel Valdés, who was present, to sign it, but he declined. Finally, Vargas Llosa and others rejected the defense of the representative of Bolivia who justified the imprisonment of Régis Debray, arrested on April 21, 1967, when he was accompanying Guevara in an attempt to create a guerrilla *foco* (Ruffinelli 1969).

Given the context of the increasing entropy of the initiative in the hands of writers and the growing legitimacy of the Cuban Revolution among the Latin American intelligentsia, as discussed above, the Third Latin American Writers' Congress, held in 1970 in Puerto Azul, Venezuela, had less of an impact than the previous ones. The Venezuelan magazine *Semana* was pleased to report its resounding failure on July 16, 1970. Neither the members of the boom nor the most renowned Venezuelan writers of the time, such as Adriano González León, Salvador Garmendia, Caupolicán Ovalles, and Edmundo Aray, attended the congress. *Casa de las Américas* also rejoiced at the failure of this new event ("Sin penas ni glorias" 204).

The most important names of the Latin American lettered city aligned themselves with Cuba and tried, from that point on, to maintain a unified discourse, keeping the differences and discrepancies reserved for the inner circle of family discussions as long as possible. Following the Padilla affair, which brought these discrepancies to light, there was a major split that took place in a different historical-institutional context from the one that had produced the first disruptions in 1966, insignificant compared to the debate that took place in 1971.

4

The Intellectual as a Problem

> The revolutionary intellectual is not distinguished from the intellectual of the bourgeoisie by what he does, by his activity as an intellectual.
>
> ISMAEL VIÑAS, "Aclaraciones sobre repeticiones: '¿Qué es el intelectual?'" (1968, 67)

1. The Dilemmas of Commitment

By the mid-sixties, the conversion of the writer into an intellectual *tout court*, that is, situated fundamentally with respect to the public dimension, had already fully taken place.

Up to that moment, the figures of the critic, the ideologue, the good writer, and the political activist could represent the committed writer-intellectual. Despite the fact that each of these profiles depicts different types of intellectuals, these differences were considered to be nuances or emphases, without affecting or questioning the identity of the intellectual as *progressive*. The notion of commitment functioned as an *umbrella concept* under which the other attributes were grouped. This complementarity of diverse figures marked a particular moment in Latin American intellectual history that can be seen as ending around 1966–1968 when, based on a new constellation of circumstances, the legitimacy of the figure of the intellectual was disputed, either in favor of the intellectual as the critical conscience of society (a kind of residual ideal) or in favor of the intellectual-revolutionary. This second figure of the emerging intellectual began to question the legitimacy of the cultural agenda that had been productive and even successful in the first half of the sixties.

Toward the middle of the epoch, the politicization of intellectuals was expressed with a particular emphasis on commitment. This notion did not involve a concrete program of action, nor was it easily definable. The most significant problem with the notion was the slippage between two extremes: the commitment of the work and the commitment of the author. The commitment of the work involved specific actions in the field of culture and in aesthetic programs, even though the arguments on how a supposed aesthetics of commitment was transferred to the work were not unanimous. For some, committed work could be formulated in terms of realist aesthetics, "avant-garde" aesthetics, or rupture.[33] The advocates of the realist approach to works emphasized the communicative power and the influence of the work of art on the awareness of readers. Those who advocated for the tradition of rupture affirmed the hierarchical parity of the aesthetic series and the political series; they saw it as their task to help "advance" art in the same way that the political avant-garde helped "advance" the conditions of the revolution, and they also viewed artistic-political commitment as involving the appropriation of all of the tools and conquests of contemporary art. To some extent, this is Cortázar's position in his text "Revolución en la literatura y literatura en la revolución" [Revolution in Literature and Literature in the Revolution] published in *Marcha* (1970b, 30–31) and the position taken by *El Escarabajo de Oro* and *El Grillo de Papel*. It is, undoubtedly, also the position of Carlos Fuentes, Roberto Fernández Retamar (toward the beginning of that period), and Juan Gelman, among others.

In all cases, the insufficient development of Latin American literature with respect to "great universal literature" helped to replace other committed traditions of the continent (characterized, for instance, by

---

33 The use of the term "avant-garde" to refer to the artistic production of that period is in itself problematic and merits an analysis that traces the path of the terms, artifacts, and categories that the epoch used to characterize literary production.

the novels of Jorge Icaza or Ciro Alegría) and to invent new ones. As for the commitment of the author, their interventions in the public domain, their conduct, their political ideas, their strategies when facing the enemies of the revolution, it was a necessary guarantee of the general notion of commitment because it always implied some sort of intellectual intervention that *exceeded* the literary or artistic production in question.

Silvia Sigal affirms that the first phase of expansion of the cultural space of the sixties in Argentina—one of the countries that became an initial beachhead in that process of modernization—was not dominated by the idea of committed work. In her book *Intelectuales y política en la década del sesenta* [Intellectuals and Politics in the Sixties], she posits the existence of a split between behavior in the cultural field and options in the political field that gave rise to a type of intellectual who was "politically committed and simultaneously embedded in a system of specific cultural criteria . . . that did not directly refer to ideological-political terrain." What the author seeks to explain is, in her words, the "complex problem of the relationship between an aesthetic avant-garde and a political vanguard" (1991, 192–200). The examples she relies on, such as the Di Tella Institute (the building was inaugurated in 1963), come mainly from the visual arts. But this split between aesthetics and politics is based more on criticisms of the Di Tella than on the way in which many of the artists who exhibited there conceived of their own practices.

My hypothesis perhaps adds some nuance to her statements on this alleged split: in large part because "my" intellectuals are writers and literary critics and also because this view of commitment, as it developed in Latin America (including Argentina) during the sixties, saw the modernization of culture as a truly committed task. Commitment was not simply one of the many components of literature, but rather its *very purpose.* And even within the field of visual artists and among the critics in that field, there is evidence of similar positions. Thus, for example, in *Antiestética* [Anti-aesthetics], Luis Felipe Noé, quoting Sartre—no doubt to argue with those who believed in a "social art" that he felt had lost its artistic quality—wrote that the apparent dualities in the relationship between the artist and their work, on the one hand, and between the artist and society, on the other, "were clarified if one took into account Sartre's definition of the work of art as a social event and individual production." One of Noé's guiding principles was the defense of new modes of criticism that could be perceived and drawn from movements in contemporary art replacing old ones. With these assertions, it is clear that Noé was close to a group of artists who sought to bridge the gap with the "revolutionary" ideals of modernist or avant-garde art. Noé valued the contribution of Pop art in resolving the question of nationalism. According to his hypothesis, Pop art showed that nationalism (an important component of the Latin American left) could not mean any kind of isolationism and even less the act of putting a human face to a localist anecdote (Noé 1965, 66–169).

Oscar Masotta, for his part, in a series of lectures delivered in September 1965 at the Di Tella Institute and later compiled under the title *El "pop-art"* [Pop art], argued that Pop represented a critique of an aesthetic culture like that of Argentina, which considered subjectivity or the "I" as the center of the world's meanings. The insistence on the word "critical" reveals the extent to which the assessment of change and rupture go hand in hand with the intention of producing an ideological reading that would underline the critical and oppositional aspects of modern art. That Pop innovations and, more clearly, their provenance had detractors was natural for the more traditional factions of the left, reticent toward any modernist tendency in the arts considered "decadent." Masotta refers to them, criticizing them, while at the same time affirming the contradiction of considering Pop art reactionary. Masotta's defense of artistic autonomy was primarily a refusal to automatically affirm an "inherent, immediate relationship between politics and art," which, in his words, would only lead to "dangerous cultural terrorism" (1967, 67–68). For this very reason, the convergence of what Sigal calls aesthetic and political vanguards is *symptomatic* rather than *problematic*: it expresses, not the split in intellectual behavior, but a novelty with respect to the terms in which the notion of commitment is understood. For most writers, the task of cultural modernization was part of the agenda of commitment, and many of the writers' own reflections on literature established this relationship as necessary. In any case, the axis of politicization runs through the aesthetic foundations and constitutes the center of all the debates, as seen in the requisite references to political-ideological value that are present in the reflections of Noé and Masotta.

As Julio Cortázar wrote, when asked for his opinion on the duties of the intellectual:

> I insist that I am not demanding that writers become tribunes of the struggle that on so many fronts is being waged against imperialism in all its forms, but they should bear witness to their times—as Martínez Estrada and Camus wished—and their work or their life (*how can we separate them?*) should give testimony to this in whatever form suits them (1967, 11).

Despite being one of the strongest defenders of the role of culture as a mediator, he noted, as if in passing, the real dilemma: the separation between work and life. The issue of the committed work/committed author involves a constant tension, it implies a constant redirection between the two extremes, the stability of which appears to be impossible. Symbolic transactions are only achieved when one of the extremes can be momentarily set aside in order to insist on the other. The inseparability of life/work certainly has an avant-garde tradition. In this sense, the invention of a writer's own "art of living," an invention tied to the process of the modernization of society and the growing separation between spheres of social practices and values, was not absent from the epoch. Commitment was, indeed, one of the key aspects of this *art of living* of the epoch.

It is precisely the moments that can be isolated from these precarious balances that indicate the state of the field. The division made between work and life is completely artificial: one of the main dilemmas of the notion of commitment is that it made it impossible, in all of its versions, beyond specific declarations, to discern between these two extremes: work and life.

The conversion of the writer into an intellectual was, as we have seen, simultaneous to the entry of many of these writers into the market (with a peak moment in 1967), leading them to be known for their books and also for their interventions. This simultaneity of the phenomena affected the understanding of the site of artistic production, both for the reading public, who had access to the ideas and positions of the writers, as well as for the writers themselves, who found themselves at the center of a new scene.[34] The expectations that intellectuals generated around themselves, and which were seemingly validated by the public's growing interest in their works, gave these writers a new *visibility*, that generated what we might call the "expansion of the literary work over the author." The writer's life was inseparable from their work, from literature itself, insofar as it was also open to being read by the same readers that leafed through their books and consumed their opinions and images in the journalistic reports that became a highly cultivated genre in cultural publications.

Initially, these publications were limited to disseminating the works of the writers. In the following stage, interviews replaced the dissemination of texts and constructed another type of text that placed the figure of the author in the foreground. Recalling that moment, Ángel Rama points out in "El boom en perspectiva" [The Boom in Perspective]:

> The public visibility of the writer was favored in the case of intellectual writers; . . . a literary genre that suddenly became fashionable, the literary interview . . . writers of all kinds drew a certain curiosity from the public that emphasized the personal and did not hesitate to delve into their private lives. The attention of the new press voraciously developed the literary interview, photographed writers in their homes, and demanded their opinions on current events (1984, 105).

The flip side of this extreme public exposure was that the writer could be judged from the most diverse domains:

> The Latin American writer now knows that if his essays or fiction or poems serve to make people open their eyes, those open eyes will first look at him. . . . The longed-for repercussion has taken place; the much sought-after echo has finally come to fruition. But what was not entirely expected was that the repercussions and echoes

34 Below we will analyze how the relations and practices of the market reinforce, without intending to, the public exposure of the writer as a person and as an intellectual.

> would be accompanied by a demand, a vigilance, a pressure. In the face of every important event that takes place in this country or abroad, at least a sector of the public wants to know what the writer's views are. It interrogates, exhorts, and pressures him; the plethora of journalistic reports is only a symptom of this attention (1967b, 10).[35]

The vigilance Benedetti refers to in "Ideas y actitudes en circulación" [Ideas and Attitudes in Circulation], a paper he presented at the Writers' Congress in Mexico, where the incidents which so displeased Liscano and Monegal took place, is also projective.

The possibility of a shift from work to life was inseparable from the notion of commitment and, therefore, the inclusion of behavior and *self-vigilance* as part of the intellectual's pact with society was one potential outcome; the *attitude* of the writer-intellectual was the parameter used to gauge the political-ideological legitimacy of their poetic practice. Writers had to place their social relevance in another zone in order to be able to continue writing and legitimizing their literature. This is what Julio Cortázar, for example, did when he was compelled to justify—on an ideological level—the hermeticism of *62: A Model Kit*, and, in exchange, offered to put into writing, in a neo-avant-garde register, his support for the revolution.[36]

Chile's Carlos Droguett was emphatic in this regard:

---

35 It does not limit itself to accounting for the demands of the public, since, in fact, those same demands emerge within the intellectual field itself and express reciprocal vigilance as a dominant note that is established due to the suspicion that intellectuals, i.e., their peers, can be co-opted by imperialism.

36 He did this even though it forced him to break with the writers grouped around *Libre*. In a letter he sent to Haydeé Santamaría—following the Padilla affair—Cortázar says that if being a revolutionary means not taking the easiest path, he is a revolutionary, "because here during the whole Padilla affair, the easiest path was simple and convenient . . . . Instead, you can see that I opted for the least easy; signing that first letter to Fidel, which I still believe to be legitimate from an international perspective, and disassociating myself from the second letter, with all that this implied for me on many levels. And believe me, it has not been easy for me to face the consequences of those acts" (1984, 148–49).

> The writer must offer their life to the revolution, just as those who are not writers offer theirs, because it is the most valuable thing one has, and the same when one is a writer, which in many cases is unfortunately closer to cowardice than to inspiration (*Casa de las Américas*, no. 69, 1971b).

Life or artwork: on those dangerous paths, any crossroads brought the writer face-to-face with this tough choice, as Cortázar had already sensed.

2. The Myth of the Transition

> A new world is in the making, a new type of man is already taking shape. Signs are appearing everywhere. The process unfolds at the center of the fire, but we know there are flowers that open silently after the storm.
>
> Note from the editors, *El Corno Emplumado*, no. 7, July 1963

> To the guerrillas. / To their nameless heroes. / To their martyrs. / To their dead. / To the New Man that is born from them. / Although this is, in the end, the clumsiest tribute that can be paid to them.
>
> Cristina Peri Rossi, dedication of *Los museos abandonados*

The problematic nature of the notion of commitment and the task of the revolutionary intellectual was so intense it gave way to a myth: that of the transition. The myth of the transition can be considered a fiction through which the gap between reality and the expectations placed on it was dealt with symbolically. The programmatic vagueness, the lack of definition of the true role of the intellectual in the revolution and in relation to society, the aesthetics themselves and their integration into the practices of daily life of those who did not have access to the world of literature: everything was explained through the assessment of the transition from the revolutionary seizure of power to the construction of socialism.

The best and most emblematic expression of this is Roberto Fernández Retamar's poem "Ud. tenía razón Tallet... somos hombres de transición" [You Were Right, Tallet: We Are Men of Transition].[37] The poem was one of the most widely circulated texts of the time; it was published by virtually every magazine on the continent from 1965 onward. The word *transition* appears in the title and at the end of the last verse. Between those two points, the poem unfolds the meanings of this concept in the form of a response to a previous conversation; a possible reflection in reaction to a commentary on the present shared by the two speakers, the two poets. Transition is synonymous with a radical heterogeneity that configures the antagonistic spheres in which the opposition between cowardice and heroism is played out:

> Between the whites whose blood you can see circulating, when they are almost polar, past their eyes, beneath their straw-colored hair,
> And the nocturnal blacks, sometimes blue, chosen and purified by horrible tests, so only the best survived and they are the lone truly superior race on the planet; . . .
>
> Between the spattered weaknesses, Saint Peter's denials, almost every day on almost every street,

---

37 Published in practically all Latin American magazines (*Marcha*, no. 1265, July 30, 1965; *Siempre!*, no. 734, July 19, 1967; *Revista de la Universidad de México* XXI, no. 8, April 1967, the *Ruedo Ibérico* anthology dedicated to "Cuba, a revolution in progress," Paris, Ruedo Ibérico; *Margen*—a magazine dedicated to literature and the Spanish language, a publication of the Franco-Ibero-American Cultural and Artistic Association—no. 2 (Fall 1967); *Nuevos Aires*, no. 2, September–November 1970), Fernández Retamar's poem is undoubtedly a key text of the epoch.

> And the heroism of those who've scattered their names throughout schools, farms, defense committees, factories, etc. (Fernández Retamar 2016, 63)

Through repetition, the poet explores the fundamental questions of possibility, duty, and the future in relation to an intellectual identity threatened by its shortcomings, both contextually determined and subjectively defined, and aspirations, the desire to be different in relation to the revolution:

> And the hope that things can be different, ought to be different, will be different;
> Between what we don't want to be anymore, and would've preferred not to be,
> And what we'd like to be still. . .
> (2016, 64)

The juxtaposition of the terms constructs an "apparently" chaotic totality. Each pair defines a group or individual space, public or private attitudes, civic-minded or intimate feelings. In each of these zones, the contrasting elements give the impression of randomly following one another: questions of race, generations of wars and revolution, humiliating or dignified jobs, public virtues and vices, deep feelings, religious beliefs, personal projects, local and national heroes. In this sequence of dualities, only one category introduces the third: class. The excluded third, the one that does not fit into either of the two terms, is precisely the poet or the intellectual:

> Between a class we didn't belong to, because we couldn't go to their schools and didn't believe in their gods,
> And weren't in charge of their offices or didn't live in their homes or dance in their halls or swim at their beaches or make love together or say hello to each other;
> And another class where we asked for a place, but we don't have all their same Memories and we don't have all their same humiliations,
> And it points with its hardened, swollen hands, forever deformed,
> To our hand polished by paper or moved around by numbers (2016, 63)

Whatever their terms, the dichotomies define a before and after of the revolution. In this hybrid, temporal interregnum that is distinguished from both the past and the future, we find not only the poetic subject and his interlocutor Tallet, but also a "we," a pronoun that contains popular representation. The *between* indicates a spatial circumstance that signifies passage, displacement, and movement. As a result, the men of the *between* have a kind of double thinking, at once rooted in what was and also prophetic of what is to come; uncomfortable with the familiar and desirous of the unknown; disencumbered of the old and celebratory of the new. The *between* is a centrifugal movement, an orientation toward an other that becomes part of the "we," or, better yet, the transformation into an other.

In the last lines, at the exact point where the terms of the temporal dichotomy are named for the first time, confronting the past with the future, the poetic logic changes. At this moment the *we* is seen as the protagonist and doer of what was and what is to come, of failures but also of hopes ("Even though we were the past and the future, since if not for us they wouldn't exist"). This is where judgment comes in, the possible acquittal of history, as well as the responsibility to construct it. As if there were a need to offer a coherent explanation to the long descriptions of that ambiguous place that is the *in-between*—a place that has designed the very space of the participants in the revolution—as if the field had to be ceded to history, the poem unravels a series of causes that redeem the men of the transition as action merges with truth and with life. Thus, endowed with legitimacy, the present traces a *continuum* toward the future; the men of the present are the point of union of all times: with revolutionary pride, the poetic subject maintains that transition is the name of history:

> And since we too have been history, and we too have built happiness, beauty, and truth, and we've been present in the light, as today we form part of the present.
> And since, after all, comrades, who knows
> If only the dead aren't men of transition. (2016, 65)

What happens is that the past of the intellectual's training, which has given them access to the world of culture, limited to the few, gravitates around the present of their deliberate revolutionary position. The fact is that it is impossible to erase what one has been:

> My poetics is still dominated by the attitude of the bourgeois I was rather than that of the communist I am . . . it is a good thing that we revolutionary writers embark on the path of future art . . . out of the very entrails of bourgeois culture, accelerating its own collapse and decomposition. (Dalton 1963, 13)

The myth of transition was supported through Ernesto Guevara's authority. In Retamar's poem, in which he concedes that Tallet, a poet of the previous generation, was right, the author conceals the real authority behind the formula of the transition to define not only progress toward socialism, but also the transitional nature of the intellectual's existence, coexisting between the bourgeois world and the new world. In his famous text "Socialism and Man in Cuba," to which Retamar implicitly pays tribute in his poem, Guevara had stated that betting on the future that society was embarking on implied a metamorphosis leading to a specific objective; but he had also recognized the opacity of the processes and intermediate results of these successive transformations. As mentioned above, the article had been sent to Carlos Quijano, who published it in *Marcha* on March 12, 1965. In his work, Guevara refers to the Cuban process of transition as a phase that Marx did not anticipate in the first transitional period of communism or in the construction of socialism. The revolution would lead to an ideal society and that was the promise of the future. For almost everyone, save the most exemplary, the problem lay in the difficult interim period.

Intellectuals and artists have been scrutinizing this message and quoting it extensively since it was first published in 1965. Guevara's text was used to settle two very different issues. First, it offered support in the struggle against socialist realism and submission to the criteria of government officials. Guevara rejected the simplification proposed by government officials that encouraged backing "what everyone understands," responding that what everyone understands is only what government officials understand, annulling "true artistic experimentation" and reducing "the problem of general culture" "to the assimilation of the socialist present and the dead . . . past" (1969 [1965], 165). In that sense, Guevara was in tune with the almost massive rejection by intellectuals of the only existing model of socialist culture, provided by the USSR and the other countries in its orbit, as can be seen in the polemics that pitted the weak positions of the defenders of socialist realism in Latin America against the drive for renewal that characterized, in aesthetic terms as well, the intellectual field of the Latin American left. As previously stated, most Cuban artists disavowed the official Soviet aesthetics, whose conservatism they openly denounced. Guevara had written:

> But at all costs let us not attempt to condemn all post-mid-nineteenth-century art forms from the pontifical throne of realism. That would mean committing the Proudhonian error of the return to the past, and straight-jacketing the artistic expression of the man who is being born and constructed today (165).

Needless to say, these words were music to the ears of the writers, even if the essay contained an accusation that would later be used against them. Second (and more belatedly), he was remembered for his reproach against "the original sin" of intellectuals: not being authentically revolutionary. It is interesting that both emphases within the same text served two different constellations of problems.

As for the myth of transition, it heralded the possibility of leaving behind bourgeois ideas and habits acquired in the process that would lead to the emergence of the new man:

> In this period of the construction of socialism, we can see the new man being born. His image is as yet unfinished; in fact, it will never be finished, for the process advances parallel to the development of new economic forms . . . the reward is the new society where men will have different characteristics (160–61).

As Guevara wrote, the image of that new man had not yet been achieved: the expectation generated by this incompleteness made it possible to address the self-image of intellectuals with all their contradictions, while awaiting their future disappearance. The new revolutionary art and intellectual revealed their unimaginable and utopian nature, what was to come without being able to predict its definitive outline. The possibility of developing a program that would account for the demands of cultural and artistic politicization was then threatened from the outset by a future that was politically well-defined but experientially uncertain. It must be noted that the idea of transition was more concerned with questions of intellectual identity than with aesthetic programs, as it established a certain causality in which experience and biography were situated in the foreground, and aesthetic output as the result of both.

For intellectuals more than for any other category of actors, the formula of transition opened up a comfortable space to deal with themselves as long as reality helped them to *change their skin.* It was thus that the formula "men of transition" in reference to the writers of the here and now circulated widely in intellectual circles.

For Frank Kermode, the myth of transition involves the belief that the epoch itself is one of transition between two main periods and grows into the belief that the transition itself becomes an epoch, a *saeculum.* Kermode proposes that the fiction of transition is our way of recording the conviction that the end, rather than being imminent, is immanent. He goes on to say that our own epoch offers nothing positive and is merely "transitional" (1983, 101–102).

And yet, in retrospect, the period was indeed an epoch, and *furthermore* it was an epoch of transition. The most radical change with respect to expectations was the final result of the processes unleashed at the time. However, this result does not affirm any falsehood with respect to expectations, but instead crudely expresses the state of the relations of force that skewed events in a different direction from the one expected.

The works of art and the aesthetic-intellectual interventions produced throughout the period can be studied as various moments in this territory considered transitional. The keen awareness of the flaws and imperfections caused by the situation of writing and writers on a continent where the separation between cultural producers and consumers and the masses without access to cultural goods accompanied artistic production at every step of the way. The conviction that a new model of society would produce different and better people and new sensibilities reinforced the precarious nature (clearly oriented, nevertheless, toward collective aspirations) of both aesthetic formulas and intellectual behavior.

The *myth of transition*, which also emphasized the defects and class perspectives that intellectuals were expected to shed in a kind of change of skin, resulted in the awareness of a need for permanent vigilance: of oneself, but also of others. The transition as a formula for negotiating between temporary practices and aesthetics (that emerged from the good faith and aesthetic and ideological progressivism of the writers) served for a short period of time to legitimize the process of the conversion from *writer* to *intellectual*. It will cease to be effective when certain forms of progressivism become associated with reformist and even bourgeois ways of being an intellectual, especially the idea of the intellectual as a critic of the society that tacitly founded the notion of commitment. It was at that moment that a debate opened up about the role of the intellectual who could or deserved to be considered revolutionary.

3. In Search of a New Definition

> He went quite a bit further than Henri: he doomed literature itself. Henri continued reading. Dubreuilh went even further: he doomed his own existence.
>
> Simone de Beauvoir (1984, 599)

> Quite simply, when faced with the choice between revolution and literature, we have opted for the former.
>
> Mario Benedetti (1971a, 45)

As the Cuban author Lisandro Otero made clear when giving his opinion on the role of the intellectual in the struggles for liberation in the survey carried out by the Uruguayan journalist Carlos Núñez, the first task was "to abandon *excessive* critical examination." How should this excess be measured? Who would measure it? Otero appears to suggest that excessive critical scrutiny is practically the same as critical scrutiny in the strict sense of the word. And it is no coincidence that from 1966 onward a mass of articles, proclamations, and interventions appeared in which the intellectual family began to discuss its own role, place, and identity, under the heading "the problem of intellectuals." From then on, a sort of discipline began to emerge that approached the intellectual as a political animal, a kind of fervor for *intellectuology*, a discipline which focused on the reflection of the intellectuals themselves.[38] The most notable indication of this problem is the survey on the role of intellectuals in the liberation struggles carried out by Núñez in Cuba, among the writers who participated in the Tricontinental Conference in 1966. If, as had been announced, the advent of a revolution was inevitable: What were intellectuals doing to contribute to this process?

A poem by the Vietnamese leader Ho Chi Minh, which began to circulate as a way of expressing the problem, used a metaphor to formulate the tension between words and actions that lies at the heart of the "revolutionary" view of the intellectual:

> Of nature the ancients loved to sing the beauty: Moon and flowers, snow and wind, mist, hills and streams. But in our days poems should contain verses steely. And poets should form assault teams. (1972, 129)

---

38 This Latin American question regarding intellectual identity converges with the reflection in Europe at the time alluded to in the first chapter: see, for example, *Unión*, Havana, no. 3, 1967, devoted to the theme "Intellectuals in Society." That issue includes an excerpt from the book of the same title by Fréderic Bon and Michel-Antoine Burnier, 45–56, trans. Félix Pita Rodríguez. A dossier of the French magazine *Arguments* is translated in part into Spanish in the book edited in Buenos Aires by Rodolfo Alonso, which includes texts by Edgar Morin, Roland Barthes, and others, under the title *La cuestión de los intelectuales* [The Question of the Intellectuals]. See also the collective text signed by Ricardo Piglia, Ismael Viñas, and Andrés Rivera (1968, 45–52); Ismael Viñas (1968, 61–69).

For literature, then, it was a matter of exploring one's own forms of combat, if indeed they existed: it was not art but man who must be committed, and writers were revolutionaries of ink. All the variants and nuances of this idea can be found, quite easily, in the readers' correspondence to various cultural publications, in the declarations of conspicuous members of the Latin American intellectual family,[39] in the younger generations' questioning of their elders, and in the speeches of revolutionary political leaders. Vituperation or self-criticism was often associated with the various tributes paid by journalists, readers, and writers to the guerrilla fighters who were killed in the struggle. They revealed a broad spectrum of experiences: from clear disenchantment to impotence regarding the role of the intellectuals who had proclaimed their revolutionary faith in those same publications and other platforms. From criticism to self-criticism there was only one step that anti-intellectualism took. Perhaps the cause was, as Roque Dalton states in "Literatura e intelectualidad: Dos concepciones" [Literature and Intellectuality: Two Conceptions], that for too long they had given "a vacation upstairs" to the "basic propositions of revolutionary concepts."

In the process of the politicization of the intellectual, a paradoxical phenomenon ended up confronting the intellectual with the effectiveness of the man of action, whose position is more pragmatic than based on an ethics of saying it all. That is, words and actions can enter into systems of conflict when the certainty that words themselves constitute a form of action that can be associated with the demands of politics deteriorates.

The imminence of the Latin American revolution gradually limited the content of what was understood as "politics." From the idea that *everything was political*, there was a shift to the idea that only the revolution, "the ultimate cultural occurrence," as established by the general resolution of the Cultural Congress of Havana, was political. The only horizon of politics was, from that point on, the revolution. This implied the acceptance of the position of OLAS in the sense that the only path

39 See Brocato (1965, 2–4); Castillo (1966, 28–29 and 16); Collazos (1969a, 1969b, 1970a, 1970b); Cortázar (1970b, 1970c, 1970d).

to revolution was armed struggle, which, incidentally, was spreading throughout the continent.

The step from committed intellectual to revolutionary intellectual can be translated in political terms as the difference between reformism and revolution. The growing demands of revolutionary participation devalued the notion of commitment under which many intellectuals had found protection for some time. The attempt to redefine the role and social function of the intellectual was manifest and, in emphasizing the "revolutionary" requirements of intellectual practice (and not simply the critical, aesthetic, or scientific ones), affected the criteria of legitimacy and validity. The growing opposition between words and actions then exposed the limits of the idea of commitment.

> It is not enough to verbally support the revolution to be a revolutionary intellectual; it is not even enough to carry out the actions of a revolutionary, from agricultural work to defending the country, although these are conditions sine qua non. Intellectuals are also obligated to assume a revolutionary intellectual position (Fernández Retamar 1967b, 11).

What began as a novelty between 1966 and 1968, and intensified as a problem over time, was the attempt to define the revolutionary intellectual; a period that in Cuba, according to Lisandro Otero, coincided with the ideological debate on the social role of the revolutionary intellectual and the crystallization of the consciousness of the revolutionary intellectual as a contributor to shared work rather than as a critical conscience in the face of it (1971). The balance that regulated the extremes of art and life in the relationship writers had with politics was leaning toward the second of these terms as a parameter of the legitimacy of intellectual action. For that very reason, many intellectuals wondered if it was not time to abandon the typewriter and take up arms or, at least, to abandon aesthetic enjoyment for a future in which the triumphant revolution would socialize the privilege of culture.

On a case-by-case basis, the intellectuals basically ended up admitting that none of their acquaintances, insofar as they came from the field of literature, could be considered worthy of the new term. Thus, the question of the relationship between the "revolutionary" intellectual and politics is a subject that, as Cortázar so vividly stated in "Viaje alrededor de una mesa" [Trip Around a Table], "has the power to make us all sit on a doormat of thumbtacks." The discomfort writers experienced in trying on this new suit that did not seem to fit was based on the fact that the requirements for becoming revolutionary intellectuals were associated with a loss of confidence in the mediations inherent to the symbolic practices and, therefore, in all forms of commitment based on specific professional skills.

One of the aspects of the new self-interpretation was terminological in origin: in the rapid and continuous production of theories and interpretations on the revolutionary process in Latin America, the word *vanguard* was co-opted in an exclusive way to refer to the political-military leadership of armed groups. Numerous disagreements (notably expressed at the First OLAS Conference) about who, from a strictly political perspective, should be called the vanguard of the revolution, were resolved, at least in the triumphant verdicts of the corresponding commission, in an apodictic way when it was affirmed that at the conference it had been made clear that the vanguard of the people were those who fight using the ultimate form of struggle, armed struggle. The exclusionary legitimacy of the political significance of the term *vanguard* took an identifying element away from the notion of intellectual. On the other hand, the recognition and title given to Cuba as the "vanguard of the Latin American anti-imperialist movement" left in the hands of its leadership the power to authorize or reject other proposals, both political and cultural, expressed in the name of a revolutionary position.

Starting from this new moment in which the notion of the intellectual as a problem gave way to the devaluation of the committed intellectual—whose profile had been established during the early sixties—, a generalized state of suspicion began to circulate among writers themselves. A novelist present at the writers' encounter in Chile in 1969, overwhelmed by the long debates on commitment and the political efficacy of literature, ended up admitting, overwhelmed: "We are nobody." Leopoldo Marechal added a slight nuance to his colleague's uneasiness with a modest "we are *almost* nobody." This painful dialogue was reported by the magazine *Ercilla* ("Los escritores frente al compromiso" [Writers in the Face of Commitment]) in its coverage of the conference. The cause of this sudden confession of low self-esteem expressed in the plural was a student who attended the deliberations and who, before an audience of literary celebrities, launched a provocation that would neither be the first nor the last: "It seems to me that literature currently plays no role in Latin America." According to the chronicler, the student's accusation against the writers present interrupted the general climate of calm in which the writers and the public had been debating in an auditorium in Santiago de Chile. Carlos Martínez Moreno, one of the attendees, declared: "The most serious thing about all this is that the writer in this is in a position of being suspected of corruption, of softness, of venality."

This state of suspicion invaded the Latin American intellectual family: challenged by the guerrilla vanguards, by the youth, and by a fraction of the field that had taken shape at the beginning of the period, the intellectual community began to realize that things had become strained. The indeterminacies contained in the notion of commitment became contradictions that were difficult to assimilate into the desired identity of revolutionary intellectual. One of the responses developed by the intelligentsia was the constant circulation of discourses that questioned the pretensions of those same intellectuals to be included in the category of revolutionaries. The association of the notion of the intellectual with that of the revolutionary (the "revolutionary intellectual") in search of an immaculate ideological and political legitimacy resulted in a paradox: in determining the revolutionary quality of the intellectual, the history of the problem in the Latin America of the seventies will encounter—rather than a set of positive strategies for action—a growing tendency to erase the identity or specificity of the intellectual character in the terrain of political action.

In other words, the figure of the revolutionary intellectual was reclaimed by those literati who went directly into political activism (which not all of them did) and those who were part of the anti-intellectualist camp and attacked the sharply revealed bourgeois shortcomings of intellectuals. The question "What are intellectuals good for?" has innumerable interpretations and a variety of connotations. Moreover, it is a question that is readily available within the intellectual agenda itself, especially at certain junctures. The availability of this question is mirrored by the availability of one of its answers: intellectuals are good for nothing, or rather, they are not good for what they think they are good for. Or even: the services required by society are not the type of services intellectuals are willing to provide. This set of negative perceptions of intellectual identity can be called *anti-intellectualism.* Anti-intellectualism is one of the predispositions of intellectuals during particularly tumultuous moments in history, when the commitment to action takes on more value than trust in words and any other kind of symbolic practice.

The limits of commitment were perceived both in terms of their inability to reconcile subjectivity with objectivity, i.e., concrete engagement with the world and the fact that they overlooked the intrinsically political quality of symbolic practice. The awareness of these limits expressed in this way can be seen in the objections of Alberto Vanasco to the notion of commitment, particularly the idea that it suggested little or nothing about how to identify in it a prescription for a concrete relationship with the world. Vanasco put his objections in writing when presenting a text/letter sent by Noé Jitrik (1969, 108–111) from France to explain what he understood by "Sartrianism." In his clarification, Jitrik said:

> The idea of commitment, the usefulness of which was undeniable at the time, now appears as an intellectual imposition, an ethical structure superimposed on the literary structure, without trusting it, without dwelling in it . . . this ends up distorting the instrument out of whose intimacy the transformative energy that *changes the reader's existence* must come (emphasis added).

Jitrik proposed defending the creative power of the writer and argued (as did Cortázar, Vargas Llosa, and Fuentes) that the act of writing was already a threat, capable of putting in jeopardy what had already been established.

From the perspective of Latin American intellectual history, a significant aspect of the epoch's internal periodization is the emergence and expansion of anti-intellectualist discourse among the ranks of intellectuals themselves. This emergence and expansion were correlated to the increase in the political radicalization of a fraction of the intellectual field. The development of anti-intellectualist sentiments and ideas characterizes one of the dominant positions of the intellectual field in the second half of the epoch, a period usually referred to as "the seventies."

The discrediting and devaluation that corroded the notion of intellectual were, however, the result of tensions in the process of politicization that had begun earlier. As a series of clichés (nothing new, in fact, since they simply update concepts that were already in the repertoire of the tradition associating intellectuals with politics), anti-intellectualism tends to emphasize the nature of *possession* implied by all cultural competence and to diminish the political importance of symbolic practice.

Why does this statement of the devaluing of intellectuals come across with such force? Undoubtedly, for many intellectuals, the disappearance of the dream of "non-party alignment," of independent thinking, meant disciplined adherence to new party positions, which required a certain homogeneity of spirit and the domestication of the desire for dissidence. Additionally, the urgent need to participate in a broad struggle with immediate effects dispelled the hope of mediation in the mid- to long term, which were also uncertain. The world of denunciation was already effectively saturated by general consensus. The propaganda had been achieved, but what was lacking, no doubt, was action.

I want to stress that the object of this work is not the writers who actually abandoned symbolic practice or reduced it to the time they had left beyond their political struggle. Rather, I am interested in analyzing the discourses of those who continued to produce literature without abandoning their self-proclaimed status of intellectual. Both anti-intellectualism and the "passage to action" are inseparable from the structure of sentiments available at those junctures in which intellectuals are faced with the demands of immediate practical efficacy.[40] An early example of this can be found in Salazar Bondy's statements at the Chilean Congress in 1960. However, from 1966 onward, anti-intellectualism has become increasingly widespread, enjoying a nearly unprecedented acceptance in Latin American culture.

---

40 Lenin's famous *What Is To Be Done?* demonstrates to what extent the notion of the revolutionary intellectual is a practical notion. The exteriority that characterizes intellectuals with respect to society as a whole appears not only as a positive trait but, more importantly, a necessary one, given that it is the intellectual who must become a professional revolutionary.

Anti-intellectualism is a condemnation that expresses the superiority of the political series over intellectual, cultural, and literary activity; it is a discourse—and not necessarily a "sincere" one—that emerges within the intellectual field to abjure itself by confronting its members with other paradigms of value, embodied by the man of action and the man of the people. It involves the problematization of the relationship between intellectual work (in a specifically cultural field) and action, understood in terms of an effective intervention in the political arena. It is interesting that the parameter of effectiveness or usefulness used to measure intellectual action was even more severe than the one used to measure the revolutionary usefulness of the guerrilla fighter, whose value increased with failure and death. As if, in the process of politicizing the discussion about intellectuals, political practice was aestheticized, and the more valuable it was the more gratuitous it became.

Although his reflection focuses on the dilemma of social scientists, Halperin Donghi's description can easily be extended to literati: he formulates the thankless intellectual dilemma as the contradiction between the anticipated practical effectiveness and the dissolution of this practice in the political and even military struggle. It must be noted that Halperin Donghi establishes a distinction between literati and social scientists precisely in relation to the problematic nature of the tension between disciplinary practice and political practice. While for the social scientist the splitting of consciousness would occur internally, for the writer-intellectual, the literary work would function as a way of resolving this dilemma (1984).

However, even writers did not manage to solve the unpleasant dilemma of the practical effectiveness of their specific task. The literary work did not manage to solve this problem, nor did the notion of commitment. As Oscar Terán, who admits to having experienced this tension himself, argued:

> If the logic of history were identified with that of the economy, culture would acquire the residue-free image of the superstructural, and words would be denied all effectiveness. Between the conceptual model and obscure reality there was a gap that intellectuals would never be able to bridge, unless they threw themselves into the purifying waters of practice.

The struggle against US attempts to establish cultural institutions and promote study programs involving Latin American intellectuals generated a new object of criticism: the intellectuals themselves and their vulnerabilities for being co-opted through seductions aimed at both their vanity and their pocketbooks. A system of reciprocal vigilance, which was also self-vigilance, explains the state of suspicion to which Carlos Martínez Moreno refers. As a result of the intellectual's openness to criticism, it was possible to imagine that the figure itself could become the object of criticism. And also possible to understand that one result of that criticism was self-criticism: self-vigilance and the possibility of becoming the object of control of one's own peers. Personal discrediting gained ground over conceptual discussions. Until finally, through a codified system of exclusions constructed in the name of an idealized and theoretically revolutionary intellectual, whose earthly concreteness was beyond the existing literati (at least the living ones), it was the intellectuals as a whole who found themselves called into question.

The visibility and importance of intellectual behavior within the framework of attempts by US institutions to secure their collaboration opened up the possibility of judging the attitudes of writers and their relationship with the United States, as evidenced in the harsh questioning of Pablo Neruda by Cuban intellectuals and the revocation of Nicanor Parra's invitation to serve on a jury for Casa de las Américas as a result of his trip to the United States and visit to the White House. The struggle against imperialist penetration left its mark on the Latin American family and paved the way for ad hominem trials. One of the tensions of the new situation was directly related to the intellectual pretension of adhering to the critical ideal and its desire for autonomy from the powers that be. The demand was now of an assertive, constructive, revolutionary order.

As for the importance it was attributed, in the period immediately prior to this diffusion of anti-intellectualist discourses and the scientific possibilities of reflection on the path of the armed struggle (initially theorized by Debray), it was diminished, inasmuch as these definitions had already been established by the armed vanguard and the struggle itself, which was already underway. It is interesting to note how Debray himself dismissed his previous positions on the importance of theory, with clear anti-intellectualist overtones, in "The Role of the Intellectual," of 1966.

> By what privilege of divine right can the intellectual worker assert his superiority over the manual worker and stand apart from the struggle of all workers against exploitation? For the "intellectual," celestial eternity? And for the communist militant, sterile sweat and terrestrial fragility? . . . Lofty contempt, from who knows what heights, for political commitment is called "bourgeois intellectualism" in political language, "philistinism" in moral language, and in the last analysis, treason. (1970)

Barely a year later, in *Revolution in the Revolution?*, he stressed the natural inclination of intellectuals to make mistakes due to their way of thinking while recalling that Fidel Castro attributed some of the guerrilla's failures to a purely intellectual relationship with the war. He concluded that intellectuals have a natural tendency to perceive the present through a preformed ideology and to experience it through books. He ended by stating, conclusively, that the most decisive of political definitions, the definitive and sole choice, was to join the guerrilla.

Among other defects attributed to the intellectual, anti-intellectualist discourse saw in the problem of intellectual "splitting" a sign of the characteristic self-centeredness of intellectuals, who only through a powerful effort of conscience can come to understand their social responsibility. The difficulty of such an understanding generated in some intellectuals "a political atony that can range from skepticism to desertion," as denounced by the authors of the Second Declaration of the *Casa de las Américas* Collaboration Committee (1969, 3–6). It would thus be students, subjected not only to imprisonment but also to veritable massacres—which the governments usually reserved for peasants and the working masses—, who would serve as the example of a combative and revolutionary attitude.

It is surprising to what extent the history of the complex and ambiguous relationship between intellectuals and politics once again brings to the fore the value of the notion—in this case not explicit—of the "intellectual proletariat" (1993). It was a segment of the intellectual field that was perceived as novel and included students, artists who were still relatively unknown, and the broad group of young people who were increasingly radicalizing toward a revolutionary left that involved active political activism and, preferably, armed militancy.

The "beacon," Sartre, was at the time reformulating his notion of commitment, publicly declaring that he had long been mistaken. In an interview with John Gerassi following the events of May 1968 in France, he argued that the much-debated commitment meant *acts* and not *words*. What illusions could one have about the cultural agenda? Acts and words, literature and action: these new oppositions reflected an antagonism that was both a logical contradiction and actual opposition. The intense politicization that extended throughout the intellectual field was the pattern or the lens through which they reviewed their practices as intellectuals. The political-revolutionary lens necessarily affected the self-image of those who saw themselves in it, eroded the complementarity of socially legitimate intellectual figures, and—most importantly—separated with the precision of a scalpel, the intellectual from the man of action.

The aesthetic approach to the armed struggle had not initially prescribed the concrete participation of intellectuals in the struggle, although the cases of Javier Heraud and Jorge Masetti demonstrated that the possibility was always latent. In general terms, literature and journalism had largely contributed to aestheticizing the guerrilla phenomenon without the obligation for their authors to join the struggle. Consider, for example, "Reunión" [Meeting] by Cortázar; *Los fundadores del alba* [*The Breach*] by Prada Oropeza; the dozens of reports on guerrilla leaders; *País portátil* [Portable Country] by Adriano González León; and *La guerrilla tupamara* [*The Tupamaro Guerrillas*] by María Ester Gilio.

This aestheticizing vertigo of the revolutionary struggle at the same time contributed to abandoning the pretensions of the political effectiveness of the aesthetic practices themselves. What for literature and journalism was a particularly relevant theme shed light on the most comfortable aspect of the work of writing: while the writer's imagination led his characters into combat, exalting their spirit of sacrifice and bravery, men of flesh and blood exposed themselves to fatigue, hunger, and death for the sake of the revolution desired by all. The phenomenon of the path of the armed struggle became the main event against which intellectuals were to measure themselves, their trial by ordeal.

Che Guevara's death was accompanied by intense weeping and a barrage of poetry. The first anniversary of his fall in combat triggered a poetic eruption on the part of professionals and amateurs. What is most remarkable, however, is the appearance, in conjunction with the tribute to the fallen guerrilla, of a new model of *poiesis*. A poem by Híber Conteris, dedicated to Guevara, who was shot in October 1967, ended as follows:

> But he goes on and this is his war / and we must go on with no excuses. / To open the jungle that closed on his footsteps / to set up camps once again / to sow where napalm burned / to retake the land where they say / you gave your life up and go on living / definitively / Che, my brother. (1968)

Seeking to accompany a radicalized public opinion, often reflected in the letters from readers to newspapers and magazines, the anti-intellectualist discourse had an almost definitive opportunity to unite and solidify after the fall of Guevara, a figure whose light cast a shadow of disrepute on other models and whose death placed the continent's intellectuals in check. In all publications, from October 1967 onward, it was common to find a proliferation of essayistic and poetic texts and articles that bordered on the self-justification of their authors, expressing shame for not taking up arms. Writers felt this blow very strongly, and many considered themselves the primary beneficiaries of this sacrifice, read as a call and a challenge, since it would only achieve its full value by producing successors. The readers' letters in several political-cultural magazines were filled with phrases conveying the message that shame could only be redeemed by taking up the arms that Guevara had left behind.

Those who could express themselves in words, whether as readers or contributors to the publications, expressed their desire to fall or to have fallen like Guevara, whose tomb, they said, inspired in them both courage and fear. It is true that many readers found the words of poets insufficient. One of them wrote the following to *Marcha*: "Miss Vilariño, Mr. Conteris, Mr. Onetti, Mr. Gutiérrez: Che's death is not a topic for stylistic flourishes or erudite praises." In response to the criticism of the collaborators, the editor's note used the same arguments: "The reader enters into a false opposition . . . he also writes comfortably seated at his desk" ("Correo de lectores" 1968). This event, perceived as a landmark, served to rethink the past and rewrite recent history: "Che Guevara's death marks a turning point in the revolution," declared the

Casa de las Américas Collaboration Committee in an attempt to give a chronological account of the state of the Latin American revolution and the position of intellectuals a year and a half after the events in Bolivia, which led to a notable decline in guerrilla conflicts on the continent. The effect that the failure of guerrilla warfare in Bolivia had on the various movements of the armed struggle exceeds the scope of this work, but it should be noted that the disappearance of Che coincided with a general decline of guerrilla warfare in Latin America (which would later experience a revival in the form of urban guerrilla warfare, especially in Argentina and Uruguay). Before Guevara, Luis de la Puente y Lobatón had fallen in Peru, Fabricio Ojeda in Venezuela, Turcios Lima in Guatemala, and Camilo Torres in Colombia. The strengthening of the various national armies, trained in US academies to enact new and forceful forms of repression with US aid, made them virtually forces of occupation in their own countries. The governments developed highly equipped anti-subversive units, and the armed forces set out to ensure internal order, generalizing the use of torture as never before.

Oddly enough, the actual retreat of the guerrilla movements (which were forced to deal with the deaths of their most important leaders) was not reflected in the political-journalistic discourse. On the contrary, increasing emphasis was placed on the need to continue with the successful predictions and to confirm the path of the armed struggle—blocked by the repressive machinery of the armies, fine-tuned by governments, in their joint defense of the political and economic interests that opposed the change of the status quo—as the only possible way forward. The figure of the martyrs placed the guilt on those who had not yet taken up arms and forced them to create a new revolutionary dictionary, from which the term "defeat" was definitively eliminated and replaced with the more neutral "contest," recalling in passing that the Cuban Revolution had been born from the Moncada disaster, a true symbol of revolutionary sacrifice:

> Twenty years after the attack on the Moncada Barracks, when the echoes of that struggle still resound in every corner of Latin America, when the oppressed peoples of our continent are still engaged in the tough struggle for liberation, we feel the need to recall that event, still in force, as a starting point for what will become

> a liberated America, a socialist America. The Moncada continues to be an example that should be kept in mind in order to properly assess revolutionary actions in the Americas. Without leaving aside the marvelous experience it offered us, we must keep it present in order to correctly interpret the revolutionary ebbs and flows, which have caused many ideologues to fall behind the times due to their haste in judging the struggles of our peoples, that sometimes began by losing a battle. ("XX aniversario del asalto al Moncada" 1973, 50–51)

The controversy in which Francisco Julião, a Brazilian leader from the Northeast and creator of the peasant leagues, found himself questioned was highly indicative of the dominant positions within the Latin American left. Julião described that historical moment as the triumph of the counterrevolution, in contrast to the most optimistic visions, which predicted exactly the opposite. Based on his diagnosis, the Brazilian leader argued in favor of the democratic consolidation of the system and, therefore, proposed that the left should rely on elections as a way of moving closer to the state, in a sort of tactical anticipation of new suitable conditions of struggle (1970, 16–17). As a sign that politics as a positive value was restricted to the lofty ideal of the revolution, the proposal was attacked by several intellectuals as an unforgivable defection or betrayal. Political leader Paulo Schilling replied that Julião's positions disqualified him from being considered an agitator and that he could scarcely claim the title of "firefighter" (1970, 22).

Something similar happened to Carlos Quijano, who published sidebars in *Marcha*, in which he expressed his opposition to many actions of the Tupamaros, especially kidnappings. Issue 1466 reprinted a letter, under the title "Rehenes y atentados" [Hostages and Attacks], that Peter Kropotkin had sent to Lenin in 1920 in which he declared his opposition to the use of hostages. These famous sidebars earned Quijano a passionate reader's letter written by one of the weekly's contributors. Híber Conteris criticized Quijano, "in the name of what *Marcha* was and continues to be for the men of my generation," for not standing in solidarity with those who "decided to embark on a form of struggle that, sooner or later, will have to be waged not only here but in the rest of Latin America."

As an explanatory and affective matrix, the revolution actually transcended the limits of politics and aesthetics. Revolution, both for the people and for the writer faithful to it, was the end of all exiles, the magmatic return to the native country, to home, to one's own, to full health; the return—for both an entire people and an individual—to continuity with oneself, to the sun of history (Depestre 1967, 38–41).

The revolutionary space envisioned in this way allowed for only one privileged protagonist at that juncture: the revolutionary leader, the guerrilla fighter. The intellectual, however, was left with the role of exegete and often censor, which anti-intellectualist sectors practiced in order to disqualify other intellectuals. This is precisely what the declaration of the Cultural Congress of Havana (1968) expressed when it postulated that the revolution treated intellectuals more severely simply because of the presence and proximity of the guerrilla example. If the existence of rural guerrillas placed the blame on intellectuals, the phenomenon of the emergence of urban guerrillas, which increased that proximity, accelerated the problematization of intellectual relevance understood in terms of political efficacy.

The expression *revolutionary intellectual* also concealed aspirations of emulation—literati could not be equated to heroes—and became an oxymoron: its two components were vehicles for two contradicting values so that one had to be eliminated or, at the very least, subordinated to the other. In short, just as it is social consensus that sanctions intellectual identity, revolutionary identity is also based on external recognition, that of revolutionaries already recognized as such, pure revolutionaries, such as Fidel or Che. The supporters of Latin American anti-intellectualism quickly went down a path that consumed all positive assessments of culture. From the rejection of certain "elitist" forms of culture, they moved on to questioning culture itself. Of course, this meant rejecting the space given in certain intellectual circles (modernized and attuned to worldwide theoretical trends) to "linguistic speculation" which considered the most important characteristic of the century to be "structuralist ideology," instead of highlighting the emergence of socialism. It was in these terms that Fernández Retamar polemicized in *Casa de las Américas*, establishing a causal relationship between structuralism and the bourgeois position of class in the intellectual universe. In this way, in "Calibán" (1971, 121–51), Retamar attacked theory and ideology, on the one hand, fusing them into one, and, on the other, his antagonists Carlos Fuentes, Severo Sarduy, and Emir Rodríguez Monegal. Along the same lines, José Antonio Portuondo affirmed that structuralism was the most recent fetishization of bourgeois idealist symbolism, and Oscar Collazos devoted his article "Escritores, revolución y cultura en América Latina" [Writers, Revolution, and Culture in Latin America] to justifying his distrust of culture, accusing the new theoretical paradigms disseminated by certain intellectuals of promoting "the delirious celebration of a formalism that once again tempts us in the name of science" (1971, 110–19). The heights of culture become the equivalent of the cliché of *clean hands*, and culture itself, a symptom of fear of action. Any comparison, in any epoch, between the misery of the world and a work of art forces the same recognition. The solution is, perhaps, to ask if the comparison is valid. For Collazos it is:

> What does the Marquis de Sade mean for the tortured Brazilian worker, student, or sergeant . . . . What does structuralism mean for the young man massacred in Caracas? What is the interior monologue to the man sentenced to twenty years in prison, accused of subversion and plotting against institutions? What did Bataille, Lévi-Strauss, *Tel Quel*, or *The New York Review of Books* mean to the fifteen students recently assassinated in the city of Cali? (1969)

This anti-intellectualist devaluing assembled an entire repertoire of new rejections: cosmopolitanism, erudition, foreign culture, and writers fond of "exquisite luxuries": "Why do we care about Joyce, who is so often followed and imitated? He is a product of British, Irish, Dubliner, and of course European culture." Guillén's outburst (1971, 8) is inevitably related to what Carpentier said about Joyce in 1967. In a lecture delivered in Geneva and reprinted in *Casa de las Américas* as "Papel social del novelista" [The Social Role of the Novelist] (Carpentier 1969, 8–18), he analyzed Joyce's mastery of language and praised *Ulysses* as a book "that has not ceased to fascinate us for over thirty years." Personal differences are, logically, possible, but we can also see here the rereading of a cultural tradition and, along with it, of the figure of the writer in relation to society.

Only politics in the strict sense would actually allow for a change in class, that is, to no longer be a petty bourgeois, a condition that "irremediably" characterizes the intellectual, as they incessantly and guiltily stated. The domain of art and literature, restricted to a minority of the social body as a practice and object of consumption, was thus perceived as an intrinsically autonomous sphere, that is to say, not socialized and incapable of it. If society as a *public* had been a fervent aspiration at the beginning of the epoch, what occurred after that was the radicalization of the demand according to which *culture* is a social space if and only if society as a whole were capable of *producing it.*

Even if a structural distinction can be identified between variants of art for art's sake and those of a social art (the calls to abandon the pursuit of art, with its rhetorical and ideological component, only served to devalue art without hindering its existence), the way in which the social status of art was addressed simply separated its autonomous zone from the rest of social practices. In other words, anti-intellectualism affirmed the powerlessness of culture to carry out those actions or, as Ismael Viñas argued, there were no formulas to teach "how to be a political activist through one's own work." From prison, the Peruvian peasant leader Hugo Blanco wrote a letter addressed to "the revolutionary poets and poet revolutionaries" in which he appealed to his "comrades, poet comrades," calling on them to resurrect César Vallejo and Javier Heraud "because we need them urgently." And he added: "We need poets who write on demand" (Blanco 1969). Certainly, writing "on demand" was far from the aesthetic ideal of the great majority of writer-intellectuals, as far as producing poems that could be "sung by the militiamen in combat," as the Turkish poet Nazim Hikmet had proposed in an interview with *Lunes de Revolución* (Hikmet 1961).

Asturias, Carpentier, and Vargas Llosa acknowledged this cultural deficiency at a roundtable held in Paris in May 1967 to discuss the question of the Latin American writer. On the one hand, they confessed the powerlessness of art to bring about social transformations, underlined by the fact that the great majorities of people that interest the writer are neglected by the cultural market. Although they confirmed the separation between the writer-intellectual and his milieu, they continued to expound old convictions associated with the critical ideal: that the work of the writer constituted a vocation of renunciation and combat, that the function of the Latin American novelist was to produce protest literature against an unpleasant reality (a protest, of course, that could not be likened to propagandistic denunciation), and that literature contributed to raising the awareness of the masses. However, the gap between writer and society made it indispensable to refer to the *problem* of the writer, which can only be solved through their insertion in the revolutionary process, as the Cuban experience had shown. In fact, there was nothing literary about the solution that Vargas Llosa—in a meeting held in Paris in 1967—proposed for Peru, "the rifle and the mountain" (Híber Conteris "El escritor latinoamericano").

"Hasn't the time come to decide that thinking-writing is not enough?" Carlos Núñez's question in his *Crónicas de este mundo* [Chronicles of This World] was predetermined. Here a clear split can be proposed between cultural conduct and political conduct. Vargas Llosa's rifle and mountain were the solution for Peru, but they were not, as the writer himself acknowledged at the time, "the solution for Latin American literature." Revolution and literature are traveling down separate paths: it no longer appears necessary to draw up an aesthetic program in tune with politics. The new situation assumes writers will write "as they feel and what occurs to them" as long as when the "moment of the concrete and effective struggle arrives, provoked and generated by politicians and men of action, they throw their papers to the wind and fight," as the playwright Ricardo Talesnik said (Morandi 1970).

The call to produce strong and beautiful works that would respond "with epic force to man's ever more demanding need for art," as Hugo Blanco had claimed, should not prevent us from noting that the call was then, as always, accompanied by an adversative clause. Even if writers were writing on demand, their works would serve to help *revolutionaries* march in song:

> All the factors that best define and sustain our responsibility and our legitimacy as writers would come to nothing, for us and our books, if we did not make the necessary efforts to be authentically revolutionary. A new vision of the intellectual, thinker, and man of action, a man of truth and profound tenderness, is already offered to us in the figures of Fidel Castro and Ernesto Guevara, of Fabricio Ojeda and Douglas Bravo, of Régis Debray and Amilcar Cabral, of Frantz Fanon and Camilo Torres. These examples show that serving the revolution is presently the greatest of duties and the very source of Latin American honor (Depestre 1967, 38–41).

Strictly speaking, it is the very absence of the role of literature itself that anti-intellectualism posits, given that it views the role of revolutionary as exclusive. The absence of that role not only fails to neutralize art; it is tantamount to fulfilling an opposite role. The result is a conception of art as an integrating sphere, a vehicle for the ruling classes through its ideological components. Anti-intellectualism attributed this state of affairs a provisional character: it formed part, so to speak, of an assessment of the situation. It did not propose, in the abstract, the definitive abolition of all hope with respect to artistic creation. History (the long, almost eternal duration of the so-called transitional period that extended between the bourgeois and the new man), and not theory, eliminated the possibility of an art that was also revolutionary. And yet this salvaging of art in the long term provided new arguments for anti-intellectualism. Once again, it was not art but artists who were to blame for the present.

Anti-intellectualism only partially affected the word "intellectual," protecting it when applied to "true intellectuals," such as Fidel or Che Guevara. To a large extent, anti-intellectualism was a functional response of the intellectual field to the partisan leadership, and of the partisan leadership to the intellectual field at a time of imbalance in favor of political leaders. The term was made positive based on the exclusion of those who traditionally used it as a self-designation involving a social legacy, whereby intellectuals were the object of a de facto, global, and tacit delegation (Bourdieu 1984, 61–64). As a structure of clichés and sentiments that was widespread in leftist culture toward the end of the period, anti-intellectualism was also the historical response to a specific set of expectations and concrete situations.

Within it, however, a distinction must be made between a strong and a weak variant. It is not that anti-intellectualism was in opposition to an outright defense of the intellectual, but instead a less virulent criticism, steeped in negative connotations and blame. In fact, anti-intellectualism forced all progressive intellectuals into a kind of judicial *reversal of proof*. Since history showed that every intellectual risked becoming a counterrevolutionary in order to defend themselves, each intellectual had to demonstrate not *what they were*, but *what they were not*, and to be perpetually prepared to show their loyalty to revolutionary positions.

Anti-intellectualism implied both an acceptance and a diagnosis of the transformations taking place in the public sphere: the fact that intellectuals were addressing a minority of peers within their circle and that the majority could no longer be won over through cultural criticism or art. Thus, the suspicion that their claims to representation had been tainted from the outset completely affected the social identity of intellectuals and pushed them toward anti-intellectual positions. Positioned as they were in a public space from which they intended to address not only their peers, these intellectuals found themselves compelled to gauge the validity of their message in terms of their ability to influence society. From the realization that their effectiveness could not be compared with that of true revolutionaries, and excluding from the ranks of their peers those who, through recognition in the publishing industry, had become *professionalized*, anti-intellectualism argued the illegitimacy of claiming the right to speak for others or on behalf of others: instead of challenging their interlocutors and winning them over to their cause, it was the intellectuals who challenged themselves to fulfill the ethical imperative of justice and equality that they had proclaimed as the specific morality of their task, but not through words. A state of guilty self-observation led them to take on their condition as a product of privilege and to "deconstruct" it, showing that any defense of specificity for their work hid sectorial interests.

The climate of anti-intellectualism stigmatized all those who postulated the specificity of their task and demanded freedom of creation and criticism within socialism, without being subject to the control of political power, as bourgeois, counterrevolutionaries, or mercantilists. For anti-intellectualism, literature was a luxury that had to be relinquished because, in the end, only revolutionaries were needed to carry out the revolution. Anti-intellectualism was also a product of the difficulty of finding a formula to balance the antagonism between literature and action, called into question by the collapse of the model of commitment. In this sense, an anecdote published in *Marcha* by journalist Carlos Núñez from Havana is revealing: an intellectual complained to Ernesto Guevara because he could not find a way to promote the revolution through his specific line of work. Guevara asked him: "What do you do?" The intellectual answered: "I am a writer." "Ah," replied Guevara, "I *was* a doctor."

"There is a moment when artists' gestures of rupture, which are not able to become acts (effective interventions in social processes), become rituals" (García Canclini 23). This observation, which aims to describe the trajectory of the avant-garde, is perfectly applicable to "revolutionary" discourses. Anti-intellectualism understands it this way, starting from the basis of a ritual truth in the statements of intellectuals but engaging in other gestures of rupture that fail to become actions. Faced with the devalued ritual of discourse, the only option that appears to remain is to shift into action. However, this also implies a change of terrain. Anti-intellectualism had an aspect of self-flagellation, with a rhetorical character that may even overshadow the sincerity of its discourses. An attribute of subordinates? The voice of a guilty conscience? Masochism? A necessary prolegomenon to initiate non-figurative combat against the bourgeoisie and its armies? Although the question of abandoning literature in order to politicize the role of the intellectual was raised, it should be noted that most of the discourses collected here belong to writers who, in very few cases, actually stopped writing, although they fervently devoted themselves to the anti-intellectualist ritual.

The revolution brought intellectuals face-to-face with the mirror image of reality, and there was no need to panic if they did not look their best (Dalton 1969). What was to be done? The answer was:

> For a Latin American writer, to become unalienated does not mean finding their reflection in the mirror as a Marxist Baudelaire, but rather to see themselves as the progeny of an illiterate and barefoot, tubercular and humiliated people, who, beginning to see themselves as ugly on all sides, know that they have embarked, through a revolutionary historical transformation, on the path that will allow them to achieve, through liberated work (and shoulder to shoulder with all members of society), the fulfillment of their human comprehensiveness at the highest level of their times (Dalton 99).

Thus, there were two sets of idealized practices and knowledge between which the anti-intellectualist intellectual placed themselves: the pure revolutionaries and the masses. Between the actions of one and the suffering and oppression of the other, the condition of the intellectual was revealed as ineffective with respect to the one and privileged with respect to the other which therefore rendered their words *illegitimate*.

4. The Global Reach of Anti-intellectualism

> A theorizing intellectual, for us, is no longer a subject, a representing or representative consciousness.
>
> GILLES DELEUZE (Foucault 1977, 206)

Although anti-intellectualism presents its own characteristics in Latin America, the trend has a worldwide scope. In the European theoretical field, the decline of humanist Marxism and the rise of structuralism tended to challenge the positioning of the intellectual that derived from the theory of commitment. In this case, an "integrated" society—with little room for change—also blamed the intellectual, reminding them of their lack of effectiveness in bringing the proclaimed leftism to fruition. The issue that the French magazine *L'Arc* devoted to the decline of Sartrism is a clear illustration of the new direction:

> The language of reflection has changed. The philosophy that triumphed fifteen years ago is fading today in the face of the human sciences, and this fading is accompanied by the appearance of a new vocabulary. We no longer speak of "consciousness" or "subject," but of "rules," "codes," "systems;" we no longer say that individuals "construct meaning," but that meaning "comes" to individuals; we are no longer existentialists but structuralists (Pignaud 1966).

According to this view that states that an enormous transformation has taken place—the theoretical consequences of which are not yet clear—Sartre becomes, in 1966, an isolated, displaced, and ultimately uncomfortable character. What is clear is that the discomfort is a sign of the times, which also affects Sartre's position as a philosopher. The weight that the "crisis of history" and "crisis of the subject" acquired as a result of new theoretical paradigms determined, in part, a change of direction in Sartre's positions. In response to the various articles published in *L'Arc*, his belief in the potential of literary commitment became more nuanced. He assigned literature a secondary role, affirming, above all, the importance of concrete changes in the political and economic system. Sartre intervenes in a specific context, his own and that of his intellectual field, denouncing a new *betrayal of intellectuals*. By making the role of literature secondary, he responds to his detractors whom he denounces for abdicating their responsibility to history in the theoretical movement of negating it in the name of structure. In the conception of contestation or combat at the level of language or, in Sartre's terms, "literary positivism," he sees the symptom of a demise at the level of politics. From the statement "the real is what prevails," art and literature lose weight and reality at the same time. The new perspective and founding value of intellectual practice is the revolution and, as Sartre says in the interview granted to *Libre*, from the revolutionary's point of view, the success of the revolution ranks above all else ("Entrevistra con Jean-Paul Sartre" 1972, 8).

It is impossible not to mention in this outline of the situation the climate of the Chinese Cultural Revolution, also charged with a strong dose of anti-intellectualism. The traditional struggles for legitimacy in the cultural field were translated in those years into political-ideological terms, perhaps with greater intensity than ever before. Undoubtedly, in each case, these were confrontations between political power and a concrete intelligentsia that should not necessarily be elevated to universal maxims. In short, the political culture of those years unquestionably contributed to thinking of the social world as a system of irreconcilable contradictions. Therefore, if the Chinese Cultural Revolution surprisingly won the support of intellectuals who also defended explicitly literary policies, as was the case of the *Tel Quel* group, it was also encouraged by a series of clearly anti-intellectual certainties that pitted the idea of intellectual privileges against authentic revolutionary positioning.

As part of the requirements of the Cultural Revolution, intellectual workers (as well as political leaders) were forced to periodically descend from their high positions and go to work, one month a year, in factories and farms. These privileged groups were encouraged to perform manual labor so as not to lose contact with workers and farmers. One of the highly rhetorical formulas used by Mao Zedong to justify the proletarianization of culture ("sew flowers in your brocade or send coal to fight the cold?") posed, for many, a real and serious problem. Based on a sharp opposition between politics and culture, it was logical for Maoism (and a substantial part of the Latin American intelligentsia) to postulate that all the theses in the arts that privileged aesthetic over political criticism were bourgeois.

As a result of this kind of intransigently binary logic—the relationship between Latin American anti-intellectualism (in its less anti-culturalist version) and the Maoism of the 1966 Cultural Revolution—intellectuals found themselves trapped in one of the characteristic tensions of modernization: innovation on the one hand, democratization or popularization on the other, favoring the latter:

> The social and economic base has changed, but the arts as part of the superstructure, which serve this base, still remain a serious problem. Hence we should proceed with investigation and study and attend to this matter in earnest. Isn't it absurd that many communists are enthusiastic about promoting feudal and capitalist art, but not socialist art? (Zedong 10–11)

Chinese rhetoric, accusing the Soviet world of being revisionist, bureaucratic, and bourgeois, helped remove the classist content from the political debate. An inevitable terminological shift took place: the new binary opposition to the term bourgeois would no longer be proletarian but "revolutionary." The Uruguayan Mario Sarandy Cabrera, on his return from China several months before the beginning of the Cultural Revolution, disseminated in Latin America some of the elements of what would soon call into question the effectiveness of intellectuals. In his article "Yo que vuelvo" [I Who Return], he proposed debating the importance of literature and its *actual* value, warning that it was "dangerous to overestimate the role of the writer in transformations" since "intellectuals are nothing in the eyes of the people" (1965). Sarandy Cabrera, faithful to Maoist precepts, insisted, a few years later in "Revolución y literatura, por su orden" [Revolution and Literature, in That Order], on a scenario where these premises constituted more widespread convictions: "Art transforms or it is useless." For this reason, it is important to reject the idea that "literature and revolution can speak to each other as equals" (1968; 1970, 29).

The progressivism of the sixties raised the status of manual labor, characteristic of the masses of workers and peasants, while also safeguarding the critical and modernizing dimension of intellectual work. The impact of the growing development of mass culture led many progressive intellectuals to defend the threatened values of "high" culture and to consider disseminating and democratizing it—rather than questioning it—a part of their political activism.

The minority nature of reading and writing skills, on the other hand, was considered only in its elitist aspects by the "revolutionary" intelligentsia. While the work of the people continued to be extolled, intellectual work lagged behind. This led to an *asymmetry in value* according to which, if the effectiveness of non-intellectual work in building the new society was valued, the merits of intellectual practice were devalued.

In other words, for the left, it was initially not about questioning the value of intellectual practice, but of raising the value of manual labor. This move to glorify popular work and knowledge represented a moment of equilibrium between the two poles. Anti-intellectualism took charge of influencing one of the extremes to the point of devaluing intellectual work. Guerrilla fighters and the people were the two points of reference against which the problematic figure of the intellectual was outlined in the negative.

5

Cuba, Homeland of the Latin American Anti-intellectual

A revolution is not a stroll through a garden:
it is a cataclysm, wrenching to the core.
But more than anything else, it is the
dazzling possibility of changing life.

Roberto Fernández Retamar
(Benedetti 1967d)

For a writer it is harder to accept than to reject.

Lisandro Otero (1966)

1. The Trauma of the Debates

The Cuban Revolution of 1959 was a completely new and unique process; in fact, it was the first socialist revolution carried out without the participation of the Communist Party. The Cuban revolutionary process was never static, nor did it move linearly in a single direction. Instead, it was rather erratic and subject to numerous political and ideological shifts, motivated, among other things, by the economic, political, and ideological struggle between the United States and the USSR.

The (communist) Popular Socialist Party of Cuba was founded in 1925, when Stalin was beginning to dominate both the party and the Comintern, and it was associated with the Communist International until its dissolution in 1943, at which point it channeled its loyalties toward the USSR. It was undoubtedly one of the most important communist parties in Latin America. Although it did not view Fidel Castro's struggle in the Sierra Maestra with particular sympathy, once the revolution had triumphed, it began to gain increasing influence within the revolutionary government, and with the visit of the Soviet Deputy Premier Anastas Mikoyan to Cuba on January 31, 1960, the era of the Cuban-Soviet agreements began. On August 15, at the session of the Organization of American States (OAS) held in San José, Costa Rica, the United States succeeded in pushing through a resolution condemning Cuban policy, declaring that "totalitarian" states were incompatible with the continental system. Known as the "Declaration of San José," the OAS declaration nevertheless disappointed the United States, as the US State Department had hoped for a more explicit condemnation of Castro and Cuba (Thomas 1656). In response, on September 2, 1960, Castro called a national General Assembly of the Cuban people and read, before an audience of one million people, the document that would become known as the First Declaration of Havana, in which Cuba, "free territory of the Americas," rejected the document dictated by US imperialism, defended national self-determination, sovereignty, and the dignity of the peoples of the continent, and repudiated US interventions and invasions, while declaring that the aid offered by the Soviet Union in the event that Cuba was attacked by pro-imperialist military forces constituted an act of obvious solidarity. Soviet solidarity had the opportunity to deliver in April 1961, on the occasion of the Bay of Pigs invasion, which had been prepared with backing from the CIA and the US government and carried out by Cuban dissidents trained by the United States in Guatemala. On April 16, on the occasion of the burial of the victims of the bombing of the Havana airport that had preceded the Bay of Pigs invasion, Fidel maintained that the Americans were attacking Cuba because they refused to accept the socialist revolution.

Given this context and despite reciprocal misgivings between Castro's followers and the communists, a rapprochement with the party was inevitable. In a country without political organization and without institutions, Castro must have felt a very strong temptation to turn to the Communist Party, beyond his general agreement with the communists on issues of nationalism and the United States (Thomas 1565). This rapprochement was necessary and even crucial. The socialist honeymoon could not last forever. The country's economy was facing difficulties that stemmed in part from an administrative vacuum and a lack of organization. It had to be remedied quickly. Discussions were held regarding the creation of a party of the revolution that would mobilize energies at all levels and introduce discipline into all aspects of productive life (Karol 65).

Establishing a *party of the revolution* was complicated, marked by old grudges and diverse positions: there was a moment in which Castro's historic followers were replaced with communist bosses and one wave of leaders gave way to another. The revolutionary government put longtime communists in cultural positions: for example, Edith García Buchaca was appointed director of the National Board of Culture and Juan Marinello, rector of the University. García Buchaca, then director of the National Council of Culture (until the trial against sectarianism), provided the following instructions for literary criticism: criticism of intellectual work, when it is directed at the enemy, at the writer, or artist in the service of the imperialist, counterrevolutionary forces, must be devastating criticism, not only in terms of arguments and content, but also in terms of the language used, in relation to its form. In contrast, when critiquing the work of a friendly writer or artist, it must be done in a friendly tone and not in an aggressive or contemptuous one (Rama 1971a).

For many Cuban artists, the problems began there since the Cuban communist cadres followed Moscow's directives and aesthetic programs to the letter. At the time, this generated a certain level of concern among artists: Cuba was becoming a socialist country, did that mean losing the freedom of the two previous years?

What sparked the first discussion, the first schism, between Cuban artists and leaders was the banning of the short film *PM (Pasado Meridiano)* by Orlando Jiménez Leal and Alberto "Sabá" Cabrera Infante. It was an exercise in free cinema—inspired by the style of Albert and David Maysles and the film *Primary*—shot with a handheld camera, blending documentary and experimental techniques, and made with rather primitive means: an old wire recorder to which a long cable for newsreels had been added, clippings of virgin film, and a budget of five hundred dollars. The film, lasting almost fourteen minutes, documents the nightlife ambience in the city's popular bars in the heart of Havana's Black quarter. The direct sound features music, singing, speech, and the street in a montage of scenes saturated with rhythm and frenetic activity. The short begins and ends with the arrival and departure of the Regla boat, one of the many endless night tours evoked by Guillermo Cabrera Infante, the film's intellectual mentor, in his novel *Three Trapped Tigers*. It is a pilgrimage to the bars and cabarets that captures Havana's inhabitants having a good time on a night in the late sixties. The Cuban Institute of Cinema Art and Industry (ICAIC, for its acronym in Spanish) banned its screening on the grounds that the film expressed tendencies removed from and even contrary to the revolution. Apparently, the film was not well received because it gave an impression of life in Havana as free and easy at a time when the city was supposed to be on high alert, expecting an invasion (Thomas 1713). As a result of the debates sparked by the ban and the generalized uncertainty about the revolutionary directives for art and culture, there was a series of meetings between members of the government (including Fidel Castro himself) and a group of intellectuals; the meetings took place in the National Library Assembly Hall on June 16, 23, and 30, 1961, and, on this last date, Castro delivered his famous speech "Palabras a los intelectuales" [Words to the Intellectuals]. In addition to Castro, the meeting was attended by the president, Osvaldo Dorticós; the minister of culture, Armando Hart; and his wife, Haydeé Santamaría, president of Casa de las Américas; Carlos Rafael Rodríguez; Edith García Buchaca, head of the party's cultural apparatus; and Alfredo Guevara, the director of ICAIC.

The *PM* incident had the strongest resonance, but in reality there were several discussions on aesthetic matters. The extremes of these debates, to greatly oversimplify the question, were the proposal of an art more or less related to socialist realism on the one hand and, on the other hand, "that of the great majority of artists, the defense of an art that did not renounce the conquests of the avant-garde" (Fernández Retamar 1967b, 13). However, a review of the works of fiction that were awarded Casa de las Américas prizes between 1960 and 1962 explained the fears of artistic dirigisme expressed by the great majority of Cuban writers and artists. In 1960, José Soler Puig—"a chronicler of the heroic city where he was born" (Santiago de Cuba), as Rodríguez Feo described him in his prologue to the reprint of *El caserón* [The Ramshackle House] (1977, 9)—won with *Bertillón 166*, a novel with epic, historical, and testimonial dimensions focusing on the clandestine struggle against Batista. In 1961, the prize was awarded to the novel *Tierra inerme* [Defenseless Land] by Dora Alonso, which evoked the pre-revolutionary Cuban past, especially peasant misery. The author had been a war correspondent during the Bay of Pigs invasion. In 1962, the Casa de las Américas Prize was awarded to Daura Olema's novel *Maestra voluntaria* [Volunteer Teacher], which recounted the conversion of a bourgeois girl into a revolutionary, a conversion that was sparked by the awareness she gained in her role as a literacy teacher. These texts, with their positive heroes, satisfied the demands of ideological purity but were certainly not the artistic program most artists had hoped to see encouraged.

This is reflected in the very long conversation that a group of writers from the supplement *Lunes de Revolución* had with Nazim Hikmet in June 1961, just days before the meeting with Fidel. Calvert Casey, José Baragaño, Edmundo Desnoes, José Hernández, César Leante, Heberto Padilla, Walterio Carbonell, Virgilio Piñera, Ambrosio Fornet, and Jaime Sarusky raised concerns and expressed their doubts to Hikmet, who offered solutions to their dilemmas. To begin with, the question arises as to what it means to serve the revolution as writers and intellectuals. Educating, propagandizing, narrating reality, and writing good literature figure as equally valuable aspects of the task. The predominant verb tense is future: Edmundo Desnoes wagered that:

> the intensity with which one understands the revolution and what is happening *will be reflected* in literature, more or less intensely, in line with the life and experience one has, it *will be reflected* in the work. ("Conversatorio con el poeta turco Nazim Hikmet")

Hikmet, for his part, claimed that a song could be written for the militiamen to sing while marching, and that this song would be a very high work of art within its genre.

In this way, there are already signs of the emergence of elements that would later serve to construct the transition myth, for example when José Hernández states in that collective discussion that the revolution has an impact on men shaped "by the old society," with a series of ideas and habits that are difficult to erase, causing "a tremendous struggle between their past, their present, and what he thinks their future should be." Virgilio Piñera speaks openly of "the writer's fear in the face of revolution" and suggests dominating it as one would do when breaking in a horse. In general terms, uncertainty about the present is repeatedly reflected in the hope for the future that characterized the discussions. Heberto Padilla expresses it with a declaration of optimism along the same lines as that of Desnoes and his colleagues: "The readers will come later. Of that I am sure. And we will write for them with clarity, with objectivity, with love." It sounds strange coming from Padilla, but those were his words.

Following the meeting at the National Library, writers and artists who feared that socialist realism would be imposed on them by decree were apparently reassured by the promise that the revolution would leave artistic output to their discretion. "Words to the Intellectuals,"—which tends to be remembered for the statement "*Within* the Revolution, everything, *against* the Revolution, nothing"—was in reality a completely ambiguous discourse that could be read as either proposing total aesthetic dirigisme or granting absolute freedom to create the art of one's choice. The program summarized in that apothegm was broad and indefinite, except that it placed the criterion of revolution before any other, and, naturally, everything depended on knowing what or who would advocate for that revolution, which was considered to have the ultimate rights. Undoubtedly, the place of the writer and the artist became uncomfortable and infinitely open to interpretation, and so did the possibilities of art.

According to Rama, "Words to the Intellectuals" was a transactional text that allowed Cuban cultural life to function for a decade (1971a, 49). Fernández Retamar interpreted it as an affirmation that the revolution would not impose any regulations in questions of art "there being no more limitations for it than for counterrevolutionary propaganda" (1967b, 12). In Carpentier's view, Castro's message meant: "Create as you please, you are completely free. I ask only one thing of you, that you not be counterrevolutionaries" (1970, 55).

However, the artists' concerns did not instantly vanish, and all indications suggest that the discussions continued, as evidenced, among other things, by the discourses of those who advocated for a form of art directed by the cultural apparatus closely tied to power and favoring the formula of socialist realism. See, for example, the following opinions:

"Socialist realism, which does not underestimate beauty in art, understands it as a vehicle of truthfulness, as a path to knowledge, and as a force for the transformation of the world. Ideological content is important in all arts, but in literature more than in any of the others. Sinful slips in literature are incomparably more serious" (Aguirre 1963). Or the controversy over Fellini's *La dolce vita*, criticized by the communist leader Blas Roca, director of the newspaper *Hoy*, who published an attack against the film (that he had not personally seen) in which he argued that a film of that nature should not be shown in a socialist country like Cuba. Alfredo Guevara, director of the ICAIC and the main person responsible for banning *PM*, responded harshly, forcing Roca to retract his statement. The interest generated by these discussions was reflected in several articles published outside of Cuba (Rama 1964d).

An attempt was made by several institutions (including Casa de las Américas) to take advantage of all available opportunities, due more to the sidelining of hardcore communist leaders than to "Words to the Intellectuals," to explore all aesthetic horizons without limit.

Although it is true that in the cultural summary of 1961, no reference was made to *PM* or to the incidents provoked by the film in the article that *Casa de las Américas* dedicated to cinema (Manet), Desnoes nevertheless laid out a solidly argued defense (evidence that such an argument was necessary) of non-figurative painting. He acknowledged that, for the "average viewer," it could be exasperating to be unable to find a recognizable figure in a painting or sculpture, yet, he argued, non-figurative art was not only a delight in itself and freed the public from naming things, but also helped them enjoy figurative works and countless aspects of everyday life more thoroughly so that anyone who did not understand non-figurative art would not fully enjoy traditional painting either (1961a, 132).

And just as Desnoes justified abstract art, López Valdizón destroyed the novel *Maestra voluntaria* (which had received the Casa de las Américas Prize in 1962), describing it as a "report of poor literary quality" in which the reader would find "neither fiction nor beauty" (55–56). In the articles mentioned above, there is a clear intention to accompany the revolution without giving up the absolute availability of techniques, procedures, and aesthetic orientations. The review of Italo Calvino's *Il visconte dimezzato* [*The Cloven Viscount*] may be useful to highlight "the utter effectiveness that can be achieved by a Marxist narrator using expressive means that bear no resemblance to those advocated by socialist realism" (Llopis 75). The process of opening up to new aesthetic horizons was neither obvious nor peaceful; the fact that Calvino's first novel, *Il sentiero dei nidi di ragno* [*The Path to the Spiders' Nests*], was about resistance and guerrilla warfare against the Nazi-fascists undoubtedly operated as a principle of authority to show that an author could combine the realism of one text with the fanatical aesthetics of another, without the need to follow "the canons of realism or other canons" (Llopis 76).

In that same issue of *Casa de las Américas* (no. 17–18), Antón Arrufat repudiated the attacks on writers who did not write for the majority. Arrufat's argument was that the intention of making "art for the people" almost always concealed a sense of contempt for the people. The author carefully leaned on Engels, quoting his letter to Minna Kautsky in which he advised her that the more the author's political opinions were hidden, the better the work of art would be (78–80).

The arrival in Cuba of illustrious visitors who were committed to modernizing Latin American literature served to neutralize political dirigisme in artistic matters. In addition to the growing Latin Americanization of its troupe of authors and problematics, *Casa de las Américas* (and also *Unión*) set out to update the discussion on Marxist aesthetics based on new readings, such as those of Adolfo Sánchez Vázquez, who—based on the *Economic and Philosophic Manuscripts of 1844*—stipulated the need for the artist's free creation, arguing that only by creating freely in response to an inner need, could the artist achieve the true objective of art, defined as the affirmation of the human essence in a sensible concrete-object. Sánchez Vázquez not only criticized the dogmatism of Soviet aesthetics but also postulated that the *value* of art should be measured by its *potential for rupture* (1962, 3–24 and 1964, 8–23).

The lecture Julio Cortázar gave in Havana focused on those same paths: writing for a revolution, writing within a revolution, writing in a revolutionary way—Cortázar affirmed—did not mean, as "many believe, to obligatorily write about the revolution itself. If the writer, responsible and lucid, decides to write fantastic or psychological literature, or a return to the past, his act is an act of freedom within the revolution, and for that reason it is also a revolutionary act." Cortázar ended with a warning directed at the hard-line communists: "Beware of the easy demagogy of demanding a literature that is accessible to everyone" (1962–63, 12–13).

The Latin American intellectual family, in which Cortázar occupied a privileged position, contributed greatly to the establishment and dissemination of new perspectives based on hitherto unknown, underestimated, or recent contributions to Marxist aesthetics. A clear example of these contributions is Cortázar's insistence to Retamar (in private correspondence that was only made public in the magazine's tribute to the writer following his death) that *Casa de las Américas* publish a particular article. In a letter dated July 3, 1965, in Paris, Cortázar wrote to Retamar:

> I am sending you something that I think is quite good: the essay by Fernández Santos. You will see that it is long, perhaps too long for a single issue (that is, if you decide to publish it); perhaps it could be presented in two issues, although it would be a pity because the essay is organized in such a way that all the background set out in the first part luminously clarifies the second. . . . What I find interesting in this essay is that the criticism of "cheap" or tendentious Marxism is wonderfully supported by the bibliographical references. You will see that the thesis is not new; but as Gide used to say, although everything has already been said, nobody listens, and we have to start all over again. I believe that for many Cuban writers and artists, who may be slightly confused about the theoretical aspects of their craft, this essay will clarify a great many things (1984, 20).

On December 24, in another letter to Retamar, Cortázar praised the magazine and commented: "It is good news for Fernández Santos that his essay will appear very soon; he was a little anxious and told me so several times" (1984, 25). On May 7, 1966, Cortázar insisted:

> When leaving Paris, Fernández Santos phoned me. He wants to know what is going on with that essay I sent you some time ago. He is a little apprehensive and wonders if one of those fanatics you know might have branded it as "revisionist" or something similar;

> you already know that I don't understand anything about politics, but as far as I can recall, F. S.'s work was unobjectionable as constructive criticism and as a defense of those values that you and I both share (1984, 39).

The article in question finally appeared in the September–October 1966 issue and is perhaps the most significant and representative reflection of the aspirations of Latin American writer-intellectuals. To begin with, because the erudite article (sprinkled with quotations from prestigious and new authors) opens by directly proposing the invalidity of the question "What is literature for?", an anti-Marxist question by definition, the symptom of an instrumentalist and utilitarian prejudice or the derivation of a vulgar and positivist Marxism or of the degenerated Marxism of the Stalinist era. Fernández Santos's main theoretical guide was Adorno's *Notes to Literature*, and therefore, not surprisingly, he insisted on defining literature as a meaningful and autonomous structure, within the historical and social totality, whose artistic truth had no relation to its ideological, conceptual, or political content. His conclusion was that the rationality of art was the rationality of negation and that its most intimate and authentic voice was that of the "Great Refusal."

After his visit to Havana, Emmanuel Carballo sent *Casa de las Américas* an article in which he pointed out the shortcomings of the old left in considering, from a current perspective, the opening up of artistic possibilities (1963). Roque Dalton, a member of the Salvadoran Communist Party, went much further by proposing that one of the tasks of artistic creators should be the cultural education of party members and even suggesting they instill a love for St. John of the Cross, Henri Michaux, and Saint-John Perse in the Secretary of Organization of the central committee (1963, 17). The line of thinking that tended toward modernization and a defense of the principle of autonomy—basically understood as the artists' principle of self-determination or, in other words, the principle of the non-intervention of political leaders in the aesthetic field—managed to establish the validity of its *canon*, with the help of Guevara in "Socialism and Man in Cuba." So, for a time, Cuba appeared to be the promised land of the writer-intellectuals, not only for its revolutionary achievements in terms of social justice but also because it provided a space full of institutions that were open to art. (Take, for example, the exhibition of the Parisian Salón de Mayo in Havana in 1967). In this regard, the best proof of the excellent conditions enjoyed by artists can be seen in the explicit acknowledgment by an anti-Cuban publication such as *Mundo Nuevo* when it admitted that intellectuals and artists were the most favored by the new regime and recognized the new possibilities that the revolution had opened up for art. It had no choice but to acknowledge: "The important thing is that in aesthetics you can do what you want" (Fejtö 57).

But it is also true that the debates created temporary uncertainties and left some traumatic aftereffects. In the words of Cortázar in another letter to Retamar, "the bad habits of the past are weighing too heavily on the present" (1984, 72). Guatemalan Mario Monteforte Toledo, on returning from Cuba, demonstrated a certain degree of concern for the traumatic burden of the debates on art and the role of intellectuals. Although he made it clear that the Cuban Revolution had developed in an era in which "Stalinist brutality and ideological schematism are but an unpleasant memory," he also warned:

> I would be overly optimistic if I were to say that Cuban intellectuals have already completely won the battle for freedom. In the country's bookstores there is a significant lack of important books that have been produced and are published in the Western world. There is not a single foreign newspaper for sale . . .

Monteforte regretted that none of the texts submitted for that year's Casa de las Américas Prize referred to the current situation and expressed his wish for works to be produced that would "critically address some of the defects of the regime and evaluate the impact on the milieu," while at the same time commenting that several political leaders "expressed their displeasure because the painters do not paint enough works with proletarian themes and the poets do not write more about workers and peasants." In conclusion, Monteforte's article conveyed the concern of certain intellectual sectors in Cuba that feared that dirigisme would become institutionalized in the future. In fact, Monteforte himself had come up against several of the measures that were perhaps the critical issues he was calling for in the literature of Cuba's present. In his article he referred to the "incident" that occurred "not long ago regarding homosexuality. Homosexuals were persecuted, imprisoned, harassed, and subjected to the harshest manual labor. A false revolutionary machismo reacted against them as if they were Cuba's worst curse. Julio Cortázar and the great Uruguayan critic Ángel Rama were there at the time and, along with other Cuban writers, *complained to Fidel* about the atrocity that was being committed against individuals who are not to blame for their condition. Twenty-four hours later the repressive measures ceased" (emphasis added). Here we can see how, on several occasions like this one, conspicuous members of the Latin American family protested to Fidel. This indicates the influence they had or believed they had over some aspects of the Castro revolution.

With respect to the fears of the "modernizers" regarding the specter of Stalinism and its potential to sow fear in Cuba, Carballo put it this way: there was no censorship on the island, but there was self-censorship. In his opinion, writers became inhibited and perplexed:

> They do not want to lower the quality of art or over-structure the current possibilities of the Cuban reading public . . . *Costumbrismo*, idealistic realism, and critical realism are formulas that are used all too often . . . they [the writers] are asked to put into practice optimism for a not-so-distant future. And optimism and literature are like a mismatched couple: sooner or later they end up divorcing (1966a, XIII).

Cuban writer and critic Lisandro Otero responded rather angrily to the panorama described by Carballo, accepting that there were fears among artists, while at the same time anxiety to see the emergence of true revolutionary literature. He also recognized the traumatic impact of the debates, the weight of the past in the present, which had had negative consequences since "hesitant writers allowed themselves to be won over by fear and retreated from the revolutionary positions they were leaning toward," while revolutionary writers adopted a defensive attitude of justification (1966, 205). But Otero's response included some *new* issues that should be taken into account: he found, as a *positive* counterpart of the debates on freedom of creation, that the identity and role of the writer in the revolution had been reconsidered, that the ideological struggle had forced them to "revise old texts and submerge themselves in new sources." That, in short, it would contribute to "the formation of a revolutionary aesthetic" (205). Otero criticized, without mentioning their names, the well-known positions of many Latin American writers of the "family." Describing those who believe that "literature is a constant form of insurrection, insubordination, rebellion" as writers of the bourgeoisie, he summoned the ghosts of Carlos Fuentes, Vargas Llosa, and Cortázar.

Like Otero, Fernández Retamar maintained that, although dogmatism was an evil that threatened the revolution and was based on convenience and ignorance, he nevertheless spoke out against an anti-dogmatism that under the pretense of combating dogmatism with a "friendly mask" in reality concealed its position against the revolution (1967b, 13).

Otero's objections against the famous heavyweights of Latin American literature are explained and based on the framework of the struggle against the cultural facades and rifts caused by the appearance of *Mundo Nuevo*, symbolic of the wave of projects financed by US foundations for sociological studies and the dissemination of cultural output. The demand for an incorruptible intellectual conduct coherent with the anti-imperialist postulates became more intense and involved the rereading of previous behaviors. All indications point to the need for a kind of memento. The great public exposure of many writers, which led them to view themselves or be viewed as characters or celebrities, likely forced them to recall the backseat role they had played in the Cuban Revolution. That memento warned those who believed they had the right to set themselves up as critical consciences or "men who say no" that their judgments and interventions were far from infallible and that it was always easier to talk than to engage in combat.

2. 1968: A Year Divided in Two

An increasingly overt dispute between revolutionary leaders and intellectuals, and also among intellectuals themselves, over the control of culture radically changed the idea of collaboration between the Cuban state and its intellectuals. It also established a principle of distrust with respect to the very notion of artist and intellectual. The issue of *Casa de las Américas* published immediately after Ernesto Guevara's death was entirely devoted to the "situation of the Latin American intellectual," as if operating on the assumption that honoring Guevara also implied revising the intellectuals' own laurels. It also included a series of documents associated with the "General Declaration of the First Conference of the Latin American Solidarity Organization." Point fourteen states: "The Cuban Revolution as a symbol of the triumph of the armed revolutionary movement represents the vanguard of the Latin American anti-imperialist movement." And it ends by affirming or, more accurately, ratifying Castro's statement from the Second Declaration of Havana, in which he maintains that the duty of every revolutionary is to make the revolution, obviously without drawing professional distinctions. The pretensions of the revolutionary intellectual were thus "officially" subsumed under those of the revolutionary in general.

The issue of *Casa de las Américas* dedicated to intellectuals reveals the coexistence of two types of discourse and a failure to hide the growing antagonism between contrasting positions. On the one hand, Vargas Llosa and Cortázar insist on distinguishing the inherent heroism of the writer and intellectual (for the mere fact of being one) and politicize their own experiences of exile in a progressive sense. Cortázar states:

> Today, every intellectual is potentially or effectively a part of the Third World since their very vocation is a danger, a threat, a scandal to those who slowly but surely place their fingers on the detonator of the bomb. (1967, 11–12)

And Vargas Llosa, in his contribution to that issue, "Sebastián Salazar Bondy y la vocación del escritor en Perú" [Sebastián Salazar Bondy and the Writer's Vocation in Peru], writes that "the Peruvian writer who does not desert, who dares to be one, is exiled. All our creators were or are, in some way, at some time, exiles" (1967b, 19).

On the other hand, the magazine's editorial (representing the power of collective and official pronouncements) affirms the inevitable and radical political, social, and economic transformation of the Latin American continent at the forefront of which "we will see new intellectuals who, like Fidel Castro, Che Guevara, Camilo Torres, Luis de la Puente, and Fabricio Ojeda, will become leaders of the people." Carlos

Núñez follows this same line of the redefinition of the positive axis of the notion of the revolutionary intellectual when he wonders whether Fidel Castro and Che Guevara do not represent, without "them or us knowing it, the true figure of the intellectual, elevated to its highest incandescence" (1967).

René Depestre affirms the dangers of the Christian West, which takes possession of Third World intellectuals, turning them into "pseudo-intellectuals," "pseudo-men," "mini-revolutionaries," "zombies of culture and revolution," and Mario Benedetti, one of the most prestigious political—though not literary—intellectuals of the time, moderately but insistently presents several of the lines of the anti-intellectualist thesis (particularly the inseparability of work and life in judging the militant commitment of artists and intellectuals). He does so by questioning the parameters of aesthetic legitimacy which others use to shield themselves and reminding us that although the slogan of the total freedom of creation allows us to overcome the "opaque and interminable history of socialist realism," we must not trust "that hypothetical demarcation, that improbable dividing line that many intellectuals, *playing it safe*, attempt to draw between the literary work and the human responsibility of the writer" (1967e, 19).

1968, "The Year of the Heroic Guerrilla," was a year split in two for the Latin American intellectual family and also for Cuba. The first half marked the climax of the euphoric alliance between intellectuals and the revolution. The second marked the beginning of the dissolution of those ties. Toward the end of the previous year, the Cuban-Soviet disputes had intensified. In fact, on behalf of Cuba, only the minister of public health attended the celebrations of the fiftieth anniversary of the Soviet revolution. Neither Castro nor Dorticós were present, and their absence was related to Cuba's refusal to accept the guidelines of the CPSU with respect to the armed struggle.

On January 2, fuel rationing was introduced, and Fidel Castro declared that the dignity of the revolution prevented him from requesting an increase in the Soviet oil supply. Two days later, the Cultural Congress of Havana, which had been established in September 1967, began to meet ("Hacia el Congreso Cultural de La Habana" 167). The congress is witness to the convergence of two antagonistic conceptions of intellectual work that will eventually clash: there are overlapping disputes that are more or less explicit, but also two ideals, one that is becoming residual, while the other is emerging and will become hegemonic. It is not a coincidence that Carlos María Gutiérrez, who covered the congress for *Marcha*, entitled his article "Mala conciencia para intelectuales" [A Bad Conscience for Intellectuals]. The general resolution of the Cultural Congress of Havana stated: "To defend the revolution is to defend culture," and added that change could only come about through armed struggle. The unavoidable duties of the Third World intellectual include participating in the struggle "that begins by joining the fight for national independence." If the defeat of imperialism is the inevitable prerequisite for the achievement of an authentic culture, "the cultural event par excellence for an underdeveloped country is the revolution." Most importantly it included the affirmation that only those who, guided by the great advanced ideas of the time, were willing to face all risks, and for whom death was none other than the ultimate possibility to serve their homeland and their people, could be called *revolutionary intellectuals.* Participating in literature, art, and science was a weapon of struggle in itself, but the "revolutionary gauge of the writer" was determined by their willingness to share in the combative tasks of students, workers, and peasants. (It is revealing that, after referring to a variety of intellectual practices, the revolutionary gauge is a parameter applied specifically to the writer.)

The Cultural Congress of Havana ended up affirming: "The old conceptions of the cultural avant-garde take on an even more specific meaning. To become part of the cultural avant-garde within the framework of the revolution implies *militant* participation in revolutionary life."

Despite attempts to the contrary, this bad conscience spread like an oil spill. The "revolutionary offensive" that Fidel Castro proclaimed on March 13, 1968, involved the nationalization of all private businesses and services and the general mobilization of the labor force for agriculture, particularly sugar production. It was announced as a cultural restructuring, according to which greater discipline, dedication to the task, and humility—in other words, a more rigid framing of cultural forces—were to be placed at the service of a markedly voluntarist effort for the intensification of the revolutionary process that was, at the same time, required given the country's complicated economic situation and the goal of confronting underdevelopment (Rama 1971a, 57).

Many circumstances led the country to make dramatic decisions: the militarization and prioritization of the economic battle. An unexpected event determined a direction that was perhaps already being anticipated in the revolutionary process: the rapprochement with the USSR, scandalously expressed—for the many who would defend the independent character of this revolution—through Cuba's support for the invasion of Czechoslovakia by the troops of the Warsaw Pact on the night of August 20–21, thus violently interrupting the process of building a socialism that was independent of the USSR. This came to the surprise of almost everyone, including the Cubans themselves, who "spoke as if their leader had already condemned the actions of the USSR" (Karol 575). However, on August 23, Castro declared that he was in favor of the invasion: the generalized attitude of the intellectual family was to conclude that Stalinism was being revived and that the plurality of socialist formulas had no validity when it came to countries linked to the Soviet Union's defense system (Rama 1971a, 56). It was easy to imagine the feeling caused by this shift if one recalls that the controversial escalation of the Cultural Congress against the sclerosed pseudo-Marxist church had begun earlier that same year. Moreover, this abrupt change took place immediately after and on the occasion of the Soviet invasion of Czechoslovakia, at a time at which the revolutionary credibility of the USSR had reached the lowest point in its history (Karol 551 and 534).

The internal political situation was complicated: Cuba suffered fifteen major attacks in 1968, the sabotage of twenty-five businesses and warehouses, and thirty-six school fires. On September 28, Fidel Castro announced that no counterrevolutionary would be allowed to live. On October 7, for the first time in seven months, two Cubans, accused of being CIA spies, were sentenced to death. Ten days later, five hundred young people, "the young men dressed in flowered shirts and tight pants, the young women in miniskirts and high boots, were arrested by the police in Havana's downtown" ("Pas de feuilles de vigne pour Fidel Castro" 90). According to the prime minister, these young people believed they were living under a liberal *bourgeois regime* and not in the midst of an ongoing revolution. According to *L'Express*, following the invasion of Czechoslovakia, Castro became convinced of the harmful role that intellectuals could play since they were all too inclined to support any attempt at liberalization.

A scandal that started small but grew to be massive emerged in late 1967 and early 1968. *El Caimán Barbudo* became the scene of a heated controversy between Heberto Padilla, who had returned from Europe in 1966, and Lisandro Otero, vice president of the National Council of Culture, and the team of young intellectuals who ran the publication. It all began with a survey on *Pasión de Urbino* [Urbino's Passion], Otero's recently published novel, which Padilla attacked[41] while defending Cabrera Infante's *Three Trapped Tigers*: "a figure who at the time had not yet issued the ridiculous and indecent opinions that he would later send to *Primera Plana*, but who already appeared to be a worm[42] in his actions and affinities, and not exactly a silkworm" (Benedetti 1968b). Padilla argued that he had wanted to compare the two novels "to illustrate, by means of an indisputable example, the differences that exist between literary talent and vulgarity." The comparison was not only a provocative one on the part of the poet, it also had a precedent: *Three Trapped Tigers* had won the 1965 Biblioteca Breve Prize and *Pasión de Urbino* had come in second place. Both were published the same year, one in Spain, the other in Cuba.

Padilla's problem, apart from attacking a government official and colleague, was to broach the subject of Cabrera Infante, who since 1965 had been a cultural attaché in Brussels. Padilla did admit that several friends warned him he might be defending a "guilty party," but he demanded that such guilt be proven before he issued his own opinion. Did he force the issue? Had he imagined what could happen?

His position was more than rebuffed when, on July 30, Guillermo Cabrera Infante decided not to wait for anyone to prove his guilt. With fanfare and stridency, he made several explosive declarations against the Cuban Revolution:

---

41 The novel in question is a story of family and economic passions, centered on the character of a Catholic priest and set in total timelessness and independence from recognizable historical events. The collection's backlist included texts by Alain Robbe-Grillet (*Jealousy*), Aleksandr Solzhenitsyn (*One Day in the Life of Ivan Denisovich*), Carson McCullers (*Reflections in a Golden Eye*), and James Joyce (*Interior Monologue of Ulysses*).

42 Benedetti uses the word *gusano* here, which means "worm" but is also a derogatory term for anti-Castroists and anti-revolutionaries.—Trans.

> in an incredible Hegelian cabriole, Cuba had taken a leap forward but had fallen backward. . . . Now, in the poor clothes of the people, in the bastard cars (except, of course, the official limousines or the fast late model Chevrolets of the premier's caravan), in the hungry faces, it was clear that we were experiencing, that we were, underdevelopment. Theoretically, socialism nationalizes wealth. In Cuba, through a strange perversion of practice, it was misery that was socialized. . . . Cuba no longer exists for me except in memory or in dreams and nightmares. The other Cuba (even that of the future, whatever it may be) is truly a dream that turned out badly. . . . Even if this pandemic were to reveal itself one day as only an epidemic . . . not an endemic but a controllable outbreak, after this prolonged bout of Castro-enteritis the country would be so morally exhausted, so depleted of its spiritual resources that to return to it would be like spending the rest of one's life at the bedside of a patient who may never wake up from his coma (1968, 49).

Cabrera Infante's defection was highly publicized and rapidly disseminated by all the international news agencies. His political differences with the revolution, as evident in the above quote, had been expressed in a highly aggressive way. The fact that in his article he referred to the situation of Severo Sarduy (who had left Cuba early, not as an exile but as a scholarship holder, bound for France, and who, according to Cabrera, had spent two years with no papers "until he had no choice but to become a French national") exacerbated the fear that this gesture would be repeated. To counter this and as a warning, there was a generalized repudiation of a significant—though far from homogeneous—portion of the output of many Cuban writers of the previous few years. 1968 was also, to put it in a typically Cuban way, the "Year of the Conflictive Awards." In October, the National Union of Writers and Artists of Cuba (UNEAC, for its acronym in Spanish) summoned Cuban writers to its annual literary contest, in which both foreigners and Cubans served as jurors. In theater, the prize was awarded to Antón Arrufat (a gay writer who had directed *Casa de las Américas* in its early days) for the play *Los siete contra Tebas* [The Seven Against Thebes], which received three votes. In poetry, the winner was Heberto Padilla, for *Fuera del juego* [Out of the Game]. In both cases, these were books that "even before appearing had already been the object of violent criticism," as *Casa de las Américas* revealed some time later when it published the volumes ("Unión de libros").

In *Los siete contra Tebas*, Arrufat described, with few precautions other than the translucent veil of the characters of Greek tragedy, "the bloody conflicts between revolutionary power and the counterrevolutionary forces in exile, justifying the actions of the latter aimed at restoring legality" (Tuttino 1968b, 7).

Heberto Padilla won unanimously according to the jury consisting of J. M. Cohen, César Calvo, José Lezama Lima, José Tallet, and Manuel Díaz Martínez. The jury even stated that no other book submitted had sufficient merit to rival the winner, so it agreed not to give honorable mentions to any other candidate. Among its merits, mention was made of its intense exploration of the key issues of the period and its critical attitude with respect to history. Acknowledging UNEAC's objections, the jury emphasized that some of the poems objected to had been previously published in various magazines (*Casa de las Américas* and *Unión*, among others) without generating negative reactions ("Dictamen del jurado"). But according to the UNEAC committee, Padilla's poems attacked the Cuban Revolution, making strategical use of referential ambiguity to avoid suspicions about his true target. Many of Padilla's poems were judged as openly provocative and irritating or, at best, inopportune. UNEAC's intervention and many of the terms it used can be questioned, especially the attack on Padilla based on the reading of the poem "El abedul de hierro" ["The Birch Tree of Iron"]—which had originally been published in *Unión*, in September 1966—, in which Padilla criticizes the Soviet revolutionary process. UNEAC responds:

> It is frankly shocking that the Bolshevik revolutionaries, men of unblemished purity, true poets of social transformation, are portrayed with a lack of historical objectivity, disrespect for their actions, and disregard for their sacrifices. ("Declaración de la UNEAC")

The conflictive aspect of the awards did not end with the cases of Padilla and Arrufat. The 1968 Casa de las Américas Prize in the short story category was awarded to *Condenados de Condado* [The Condemned of Condado], by Norberto Fuentes, and earned a glowing commentary in the magazine:

> Rather than relying on two writers, Norberto Fuentes appears to escape the pitfall of the political pamphlet by relying on two books: *Red Cavalry*, by Isaac Babel, and *The Burning Plain and Other Stories*, by Juan Rulfo. The greatest discovery of the book is not in the theme itself, in its specific character of national epic, but precisely in the transcendence of those frontiers, in the leap to the universal that pulsates in the immediate and the everyday (Benítez Rojo 159).

Revolutionary literature once again appeared to be within reach, as had happened with the short stories of Jesús Díaz two years earlier, without it being mentioned again as an example later on. Not surprisingly, Norberto Fuentes's work would eventually make its way into the *Index*. This time the objections also reached Casa de las Américas, which had awarded the book a prize. Norberto Fuentes would not publish his next book in Cuba: *Cazabandido* [Bandito Hunter] was printed in Montevideo. On October 6, 1968, before Cuban television cameras, Haydeé Santamaría defended the institution's award policy by defining quality as the exclusive criterion for award-winning works and the international prestige achieved by the Casa de las Américas awards. In her statements, Santamaría commented on the jurors' surprise when they learned that the main interest of Cuba and of the institution she presided over was to recognize the best works, without prioritizing themes or genres.

As evidence of a new series of changes in cultural policy, Lisandro Otero, vice president of the National Council of Culture, at the annual meeting of writers in Cienfuegos in early November, announced that there would be no place in Cuba for those who tried to promote "Czechoslovakian-style solutions," in a comment that also represented a direct allusion to Padilla. This is how *Primera Plana* understood it: "The jab was biased, but no one had any doubts about its intended target" (Heberto Padilla's presentation, "Respuesta a Cabrera Infante" 1968). A few days later, articles began to appear in the magazine *Verde Olivo* that, in addition to questioning several cultural institutions, aesthetics, and authors, reinterpreted Fidel Castro's "Words to the Intellectuals" and stressed the sin of intellectuals (not being authentically revolutionary), as diagnosed by Che Guevara in "Socialism and Man in Cuba." Signed with the pseudonym Leopoldo Ávila, the articles in *Verde Olivo* (organ of the Revolutionary Armed Forces of Cuba) were dedicated to attacking

Padilla, Arrufat, and, in the last of the series, "Algunas corrientes de la crítica y la literatura en Cuba" [Several Trends in Criticism and Literature in Cuba], the low political standard of Cuban artistic circles, which had substituted the possibilities of a critical approach "with elegant verbiage that barely covers total emptiness and undignified schemes."[43] *Verde Olivo* accused Arrufat of having put the hero and the traitor on the same level, of "celebrating insolence" and "applauding infamy." In a way, these criticisms are similar to those that will be used to object to the book by Norberto Fuentes. Ávila mentioned that when he was the director of *Casa de las Américas*, Arrufat had published a poem by José Triana in which sexual inversion was described with "the most vulgar details." Triana was a member of the jury that awarded the prize for the theatrical work in question. According to Rama, Leopoldo Ávila was the nom de guerre of an "identity that was never revealed and therefore remained associated with Luis Pavón, the director of the weekly" and vice minister of culture in 1971 (1971a, 60). In his autobiography Heberto Padilla also made the same association (1989, 54). According to Lourdes Casal, the pseudonym corresponds to José Antonio Portuondo (7). However, Rama's hypothesis is more convincing since Pavón used the same language as Ávila and attacked the same targets, as seen in his opinion pieces ("Literatura y revolución: Encuesta," 142–45).

Casa de las Américas, which had tried to resist the process of condemnation in which it found itself involved, sought to defend itself from the movement driven in particular by the Revolutionary Armed Forces and which called into question a decade of cultural policy, in addition to the institution's awards. In 1967, for example, UNEAC had awarded the poetry prize to José Yánez (one of the writers who would be forced to deliver a self-criticism in 1971 at Padilla's "invitation") and the novel prize to Reinaldo Arenas (*El mundo alucinante* [*Hallucinations*]), who was also in a complicated position with the revolution and, to make matters worse, homosexual.

---

43 The importance of Ávila's opinions was highlighted by the fact that his article was reprinted in several other Cuban publications: *La Gaceta de Cuba*, no. 68 (November–December 1968); *Unión* IV, no. 3 (September 1968).

Certainly, by the time the Cultural Congress was held, the debates had reached their climax. Even Mario Benedetti, in his lecture at the Cultural Congress of Havana, had expressed the need to "reconcile" intellectuals and men of action, speaking, naturally, on behalf of the former and implying that they were not exactly on good terms. In a rather audacious intervention, he maintained that "not all revolutionary intellectuals end up as soldiers" and that one of the duties of the revolutionary intellectual was "not to invent a bad conscience" (phrasing in a rather odd way the slogan that the duty of every revolutionary intellectual was to make the revolution). And, he added, part of that duty was not "to allow others to invent it." Benedetti positioned himself against what he called any "sectarian threat" and reaffirmed the critical ideal by postulating that "the indocility of the intellectual enriches the revolution" (1968c, 116–20).

It is true that his arguments did not change much after that point, and his compatriot Carlos María Gutiérrez praised him for this:

> How difficult it is for us to renounce what has been incorporated into the blood and mentality of intellectuals of transition from their bourgeois origins; to consider themselves the conscience of society . . . to be transformed, as Mario Benedetti believed at the Cultural Congress of Havana, into "a vigilant conscience, an imaginative interpreter, a critical provider." It is no coincidence that Benedetti, with his acute sensitivity for the social and his aptitude for grasping the parameters of human behavior, after a year of having lived deeply inserted in this new process, believes that this concept is relative and requires nuances or revision (Dalton et al. 107).

Adolfo Sánchez Vázquez's statement, like that of Benedetti, also pointed directly to the relations between intellectuals and leaders, although in terms of "aesthetic avant-gardes" and "political avant-gardes." In his talk, he tried to demonstrate the need for the harmonious coexistence of both avant-gardes and to show that the bourgeoisie (rather than socialist leaders) has the most interest in hindering it (1968, 112–15).

According to Rama, not only did the Cultural Congress not formulate any aesthetic doctrine, but the debates dealt "mainly with the revolutionary attitudes of intellectuals" (1971, 53). Rama *artificially* subdivides the problem into two since the *aesthetic doctrines and revolutionary attitudes of intellectuals* were the very terms of the positions in the discussion: in one case they were insisting on the validity of the cultural agenda, while in the other, they were aspiring to eliminate it. Moreover, the Cuban organizers expressly stated that they did not want an academic debate but were hoping for a concrete response to the main question, which was latent in all aspects of the agenda: How can an intellectual serve the revolution? (Karol 434).

In fact, Carlos María Gutiérrez (whose article "Mala conciencia para intelectuales" was not published in the literary section of *Marcha* but rather in the main body of the weekly tabloid) stressed that the congress invited the intellectuals to discuss their responsibility to the Third World and the role they must play in the liberation process of underdeveloped countries, and maintained that the concrete issue with which the congress confronted intellectuals had one name only and that name was *revolution*. Gutiérrez also maintained that the intellectuals of the underdeveloped world no longer had any doubts about their course of action: "Choose revolution and reject the cultural colonization of the capitalist West."

The "Llamamiento de La Habana" [Havana Appeal] was written and presented by Ralph Miliband and Marcel Liebman. It was the subject of a lengthy discussion in the first commission and was put to a vote the day before the congress ended. The following day, before the general assembly, which was to approve the adopted resolutions, a version of the "Appeal" was read out that was so different its authors had a hard time identifying it. A paragraph had been added evoking Guevara as an example and calling on intellectuals to take part in the guerrilla war. Miliband objected to the changes made without his consent. After several hours of consultations, an extraordinary plenary assembly was called, in which José Llanusa, president of the congress and minister of education, apologized for the incident. Later Carpentier read the original "Appeal." According to the quotations cited in Carlos María Gutiérrez's column, it appears that it was the corrected version that was disseminated among Latin American readers.

In the balance of forces, we can see the margin of action of *Casa de las Américas*, which did not publish the most anti-intellectual presentations delivered at the Cultural Congress of Havana that were disseminated some time later. These include Ambrosio Fornet's contribution, published in an official anthology of texts on culture and politics, a sort of canon of revolutionary criticism, which started off with Castro's 1961 speech, "Words to the Intellectuals." In it, Fornet rejected as insufficient the intellectual pretension of equating their political responsibility with their artistic responsibility:

> When intellectuals of a country in revolution demand concrete responsibilities from others, it is because we have accepted our own and are willing to account for our actions. I am not only speaking of our civic responsibilities. As intellectuals of an underdeveloped country in revolution, teaching literacy, learning how to handle weapons, and harvesting sugarcane are already part of our basic duties. . . . Although our aesthetic tastes are almost the same, our perspective has been completely transformed. . . . On discovering our reality and, along with it, the ineffectiveness of the theoretical instruments we had hastily incorporated in the course of our readings and travels, we understand what we are not . . . intellectuals are compelled to be, above all else, *critical of themselves* (1980, 316–19, emphasis added).

In fact, it is in this same book where positions at the time considered typical of sectarianism are "officialized," such as "Apuntes sobre la literatura y el arte" [Notes on Literature and Art] by Mirta Aguirre, a text that proclaims the virtues of socialist realism, "which does not underestimate beauty in art," and warns that ideological content is important in all the arts, but more so in literature, where "sinful ideological slips are more serious." It also includes a talk delivered in 1974 by José Antonio Portuondo entitled "Itinerario estético de la Revolución" [Aesthetic Itinerary of the Revolution], in which he unequivocally disqualifies the Cultural Congress of Havana, that, according to the author, "served to convince many to become revolutionaries and 'show' us what we should do. The negative consequences were that some young people, seduced by these prominent figures, sought to engage in a hypercritical activity and confront the revolution" (1980, 180–81).

In its November 1968–February 1969 issue, *Casa de las Américas* responded to the attacks elusively. The editorial column reviewed several years of activity to emphasize that its task had been to disseminate the revolution among the continent's intellectuals and the rest of the world, inviting innovative artists of the highest level to Cuba, without limiting itself to a particular theme. However, it did coincide in one respect with the ideological condemnation of certain artists proposed by the Revolutionary Armed Forces: "Those who approach the revolutionary process from a confused perspective that is simply nihilism or skepticism do not have the right to express the revolution" ("Editorial" 1968–69, 7–9).

Dedicated to commemorating the tenth anniversary of the revolution, the issue included an extensive survey ("Literatura y revolución" [Literature and Revolution]) of writers, artists, and critics—neither Heberto Padilla nor Norberto Fuentes responded—, in which the various positions and also the authority of each one, measured in terms of their capacity to polemicize, can be gauged. A significant portion of Luis Pavón's response is aimed at discrediting certain Cuban writers: he comments that Virgilio Piñera "repeats himself to the point of monomania" and Arrufat "repeats Piñera with more obscurities, greater reticence and amphibologies." Pavón is very pessimistic about the state of Cuban literature:

> some novelists have been won over by the tendency to adopt new techniques that are so poorly assimilated that the result is quite ridiculous, and in others, the search for success through pornography and sensationalism has hampered their best intentions. There are cases that are even more regrettable: prize hunters like Norberto Fuentes and others dispute the pages of our cultural magazines and publications of the revolution, with superficial, clumsy, and, of course, nonrevolutionary works and judgments. . . . [Poets like Retamar] fortunately help us forget certain displays of indolence in revolutionary poetry and the most pathetic demonstrations of hostile indolence to the revolution of the last or penultimate Padilla ("Literatura y revolución: Encuesta" 143).

But Pavón highlights his aesthetic ideals, clearly ideological in nature: "Our narrative knows no work of greater beauty, sincerity, and grace than Comandante Guevara's *Pasajes de la guerra revolucionaria* [*Episodes of the Cuban Revolutionary War*]" ("Literatura y revolución: Encuesta" 143).

3. Explicit Formulation of Anti-intellectualism as Subordination to the "Revolutionary" Directive

> The Latin American intelligentsia has not fully complied with the ideological-cultural tasks that the emergence of socialism in the Americas entails.
>
> ROQUE DALTON (*El intelectual y la sociedad* 96)

> And what am I? The angry leader retorted: What were you doing while everyone around me welcomed the distribution of work and tools? And the man replied: I was contemplating your work and marveling at your judgment and fairness. The leader, moved, answered him: You, sit on my right, for you are the poet.
>
> PABLO ARMANDO FERNÁNDEZ (1968, 182)

As 1968 drew to a close, Cuba found itself in a defensive position and a state of unrest, more threatened than ever before due to counterrevolutionary sabotage, the US blockade, and economic restrictions. In the words of Benedetti: "The revolution consciously adopts a state of mind in which humanistic culture becomes secondary." And he ends up accurately predicting the future: "Given this state of mind, it would not be illogical to expect an increase in the social pressure on intellectuals in Cuba" (1968b, 30). The Cuban leadership called 1969 "The Year of Decisive Effort." The slogan alluded to the significant efforts called upon to achieve the goal of the ten-million-ton harvest of sugarcane. It is also important to remember that, starting in 1965, Cuba had made investments to reach, in 1970, this tremendous objective that would ensure its international purchasing power. But as the poet Cintio Vitier commented to Ernesto Cardenal, not only was an economic goal at stake in the ten-million-ton harvest, but "the entire national honor was at stake" (Cardenal 10). In 1968 and 1969, Cubans experienced a real sugar obsession. The entire country's workforce had been mobilized and recruited and was quickly militarized in an attempt to make the challenge of the sugarcane harvest a success. This militarization can be seen in the July–August 1969 issue of *Casa de las Américas* devoted to praising the armed forces. Each writer and columnist is presented according to their military rank, and the issue includes an anthology of texts produced at the Military School, illustrated with photographs of military training exercises. The appeal to the population for volunteers did not distinguish between intellectuals and non-intellectuals, so for the former, revolutionary heroism was measured in terms of an action planned by a centralized organism rather than the autonomous or specific play of cultural practice governed by its own actors.

Armando Hart, the minister of culture, invited by Fernández Retamar to write an article in commemoration of Lenin's centenary, sent the magazine a letter in response (dated January 3, 1970, "Año de los Diez Millones," in Santa Cruz del Sur) explaining that, although he was mortified at not being able to respond to Retamar's expectations, he could not write about that or any other subject. In particular, writing about Lenin would require an effort and care that he was unable to muster because "I am here, *in the middle of the battle for the harvest and processing of sugarcane*, trying to reach every harvester, operator, and technician" (Hart 1970, 164).

In the March–April 1969 issue, the *Casa de las Américas* Collaboration Committee issued its second statement based on the need to reread and reinterpret the past. It proposed "a change of perspectives" grounded in the belief that it was witnessing a new juncture, a major milestone: the disappearance of Che. It is both strange and symptomatic that Guevara's death nearly two years after it took place still held such significance and generated new interpretations. Problematizing its 1967 declaration, the committee now affirmed the need for revolutionary intellectuals to participate in direct action ("Por una nueva vanguardia latinoamericana").

Of all of this, what is most interesting is the shift in direction of *Casa de las Américas*: from that point on, its task was to insist on the nature of the change in situation and the attempt to revitalize the mission of revolutionary intellectuals; to participate, develop, and disseminate thinking capable of incorporating the broad popular masses into the tasks of the revolution; to create works that, as Régis Debray had said, would wrest the privilege of beauty from the ruling class. Of particular significance was the misunderstanding that the declaration of the Collaboration Committee generated in European progressivism, which the Cuban magazine took pains to clarify. This emphasis can only be understood in the light of subsequent discussions. On April 11, 1969, the Italian weekly *Rinascità* had published a commentary on the aforementioned declaration of the *Casa de las Américas* committee, understanding it as an attempt to form new intellectual avant-gardes. In response (issue no. 56), the Cuban magazine felt compelled to express its disagreement, pointing out that at no time did the committee's declaration refer to intellectual avant-gardes, but rather to the establishment of a new *political avant-garde*. From a careful reading of the document in question, the opinion formulated by *Rinascità* does not appear to be misguided. Indeed, they were talking about intellectuals, not politicians. The shift in the issue, with retrospective validity, explains the progression of the debate between intellectuals and the revolution. The sympathetic reference to the Italian publication does not obscure the fact that a whole host of negative signs were emerging around "the foreign" ("La Casa por fuera").

Casa de las Américas appeared to be at a crossroads, and in its efforts to maintain some sense of equilibrium, expressions revealing the existence of a new context began to emerge somewhat chaotically. In the same issue that published the second declaration of its Collaboration Committee, *Casa de las Américas* announced the publication of the two books that had won awards from UNEAC that had sparked the first Padilla affair and the reaction of Leopoldo Ávila, citing a few excerpts from his article. In a clear dispute over cultural and aesthetic criteria between opposing groups, *Casa de las Américas* lamented UNEAC's publication of the "unfortunate poem 'Reseña deportiva' [Sports Review]" included in the book *Poesía inmediata* [Immediate Poetry] by Roberto Branly ("Unión de libros" 165). The poem's resemblance to the tone of Fidel Castro's closing speech at the 1971 Congress of Education and Culture and to Heberto Padilla's poem "Viajeros" [Travelers] is curious, to say the least.

The poem attacked the juries of the Casa de las Américas Prize and took a stance in the debate on the privilege of intellectuals, clearly expressing a perspective that affirmed the almost innate parasitism of intellectuals. It also declared the tepidity of the literary profession, coupled with the complicity of "the jurors," who would later appear capitalized, *Jurors*, in order to offer an even clearer opposition to the only legitimately capitalized word, *Revolution*.

> The jurors come from everywhere: from the winter and the snow / from the tropics full of fruit and imported machinery; / they come with their books, their magazines and their data, / always preceded by the corresponding "curriculum vitae;" / the jurors, smiling, land, descend the stairs / with their ears perked up and their respective travel bags at the airport; / the jurors arrive, they are put up in first-class hotels, / they eat à la carte, hold beautiful and profound dialogues, / with bureaucrats dedicated to the half-hearted task of making literature; / the jurors, with astonishment, witness a *bembé*, they are taken to and brought from / the "Chori" in Varadero when the rain clears up and the jellyfish have gone; / they are taken on tours of studios and art schools. / And then, the members of the jury give interviews to the press, / they are photographed, microphone in hand, / they stock up—if they are not fully leftist—on Marxist phrases, / and in the round tables, most especially, they make allusions to the "Camelot" plans, / to "Mundo Nuevo," alienation, the CIA, / the jurors drink several "daiquiris" / at the "La Torre" restaurant, / they travel from cocktail to cocktail, all rose-colored, / they admire the absence of "Stalinism" and the prevalence of "Pop art," / they have friendly conversations, one-on-one, with promising youth, / and with the promising elders who no longer have any promise; / from time to time, when they have time, / they remember, perhaps, that they are jurors, they act the part / and read an original, they underline it or one of the four copies, / with their slogan, as is well known, in a sealed envelope with the contact details / of the unpublished senders, anxious, in the shadows; / and, finally / the gentlemen of the Jury, in a solemn act, / play the lottery, and out of anonymity / a new clamorous name, if not a worn-out one, / emerges into the world of letters. / Then,

> after another new itinerary, after banquets and feasts, / after performances of ballet and concrete music / —death, by golly, to dogmatism—; / after shows of pure creole folklore, / the gentlemen members of the Jury, / calmly close their suitcases, / and return, showered with love, / —without having genuinely experienced, / what a people in Revolution truly is— / to the aluminum and cement of the airports.

Casa de las Américas cautions him to remember "that the attitudes of those men (with the usual exceptions) put an end to the hardly imaginary adventure of *Mundo Nuevo*; that the CIA has indeed infiltrated intellectual circles; and, above all, that many of those jurors, for the mere fact of coming to Cuba, lost their jobs, were fired, etc."

Given the weakness generated by the cultural advance of other sectors, represented by the opinions of Luis Pavón, among others, *Casa de las Américas* made explicit changes to avoid confrontations with the political leadership. In the presence of the jurors assembled to decide the winners of the 1969 literary contest, Haydeé Santamaría confirmed that that year, "as every year, *Casa de las Américas* has limited itself to choosing the jury from among the best" (they included Ángel Rama, Alejo Carpentier, Oscar Collazos, Jean Franco, Paco Urondo, David Viñas, Roberto Fernández Retamar, and Noé Jitrik). However, she announced a novelty in the selection criteria of the jurors from that point on: "Next year we will try to have each juror come from the country where they were born, that is, from Latin America" ("Últimas actividades de la Casa de las Américas" 167).

It is worth noting that in 1969 UNEAC established a new literary award. It was called the David Prize, after the nom de guerre of the revolutionary martyr Frank País, to be awarded to *unpublished* Cuban poets and artists, in other words: new, young, with little cultural capital, and with a literary output that emerged after the triumph of the revolution. The declaration of anti-intellectualist principles was institutionally formulated at the roundtable in Cuba on May 2, 1969, as a reflection on the first ten years of the revolution, in which the overall theme was precisely intellectuals, evidence that this was one of the main issues to be resolved within the revolution. Participants included Cuba's Roberto Fernández Retamar, Ambrosio Fornet, and Edmundo

Desnoes, Uruguay's Carlos María Gutiérrez, El Salvador's Roque Dalton, and Haiti's René Depestre. It can be said that anti-intellectualism acquired its philosophy and reached its climax at that meeting; one of the main postulates outlined consists in the acceptance of the superiority of the political leadership, and the affirmation that the revolutionary intellectual is precisely the one who accepts that superiority.

Thus, in order to neutralize the force of anti-intellectualism, these intellectuals had to subordinate themselves to government institutions and the political leadership, which, according to Carlos María Gutiérrez, "without knowing much about literature, painting, or music, appears at this historical moment to propose cultural solutions that really correspond to the needs of a socialist revolution" (Dalton 112–13). "Revolutionary," in this sense, refers only to the intellectual who accepts as necessary his subordinate position with respect to the state and its institutions. Since an avant-garde (the revolutionary government) already existed and was defined in exclusionary terms of political leadership (including the dissemination and creation of aesthetic standards for artistic production), the promotion of new avant-garde groups was not only unnecessary but uncomfortable since their very existence tended to question the state policies in practice.

The anti-intellectual faction of intellectuals developed the hypothesis that the only thing they retained as intellectuals was the *name*, while the *role* of revolutionary intellectual had been fulfilled, in practice, by leaders and political cadres. The Uruguayans Carlos Núñez and Carlos María Gutiérrez were part of the non-Cuban group that most strongly exacerbated the anti-intellectualism of the island in a dynamic that also included other "external" intellectuals, who from their most comfortable positions incited their Cuban peers to prove themselves, at least publicly, willing to affirm time and again that they were "nobodies." The reason of war, the raison d'état, gave rise to a sort of declaration of a "state of siege" on the activity of intellectuals. Oddly enough, the most virulent anti-intellectualism was spread by non-Cuban intellectuals, who were, so to speak, more Catholic than the pope, presumably as a way of emphasizing their support for a revolution they had not helped triumph.

In May 1970, in a dramatic speech, Castro announced to the country that the planned objective had not been achieved due to errors and technical defects related to crucial political deficiencies. In his speech he criticized the excessive verticalization of the leadership and publicly acknowledged his responsibility for the failure. Castro, who had cut sugarcane himself, delivered a self-critical speech entited "Discurso sobre la zafra" [Speech on the Sugarcane Harvest], before a crowd that wept with him. After the failure of the *zafra* (sugarcane harvest), the Cuban intellectual community was united by an even stronger anti-intellectualism and, of course, would demonstrate a greater tendency to engage in self-criticism.

It was logical that the definition of the intellectual as the critical conscience of society would be abolished, as it was. An identity of this kind was possible in societies that required criticism by nature, not in a reality immersed in revolution, where any production, thought, policy, or intervention became, *merely by virtue of its site of enunciation*, "revolutionary." Or, in its opposite variant, "counterrevolutionary." In a kind of positivism that linked the context to the practices, thoughts, and interventions that took place in it, if the revolution had come to Cuba, everything that came out of it was immediately revolutionary: customs, clothing, art, discourses, fashion, aesthetics, etc. Cuban revolutionary society was by definition *uncriticizable*; so, it was also logical that the critical yearnings of its intelligentsia should be turned against it.

There is no lack of evidence to suppose that the political also served as a disguise, as a rhetorical system, and as a paradigmatic mode of argumentation in this struggle for cultural legitimacy. Undoubtedly, the emergence of new generations of writers and new aesthetic trends had, at times, a similar character to that of competition within the intellectual field anywhere in the world and at any time. The difference was that, in this case, success would require, more than in any other circumstance, support from the state since the intellectuals had no means of mediation that were entirely their own or that they entirely controlled.

Evidence that this discussion could also take place in the aesthetic domain can be found in the commentaries on the book *Tute de reyes* [Kings' Game], by Antonio Benítez Rojo, that received the Casa de las Américas Short Story Award in 1967. From a very different perspective to that of Leopoldo Ávila, the reviewer celebrates the fact that, for once, a quality work won the award (Arenas 145–52). The manifesto of a group of "new" poets, who were adolescents when the revolution triumphed, expresses a desire for the recognition of new literary voices; the voices of those who, because they had not actively participated in the revolutionary struggle, were at risk of not being considered eligible to claim their rights to aesthetic existence ("Nos pronunciamos" 1966). The usual competition between established authors and newcomers in the intellectual field was coated, to some extent, in political disquisitions. Undoubtedly it was for this reason that the *newcomers* argued that legitimacy was strongly anchored in the revolution, even more so than for the *men of transition*: "Thirteen years of our life—undoubtedly the most important ones—have been years of the combative and victorious revolution . . . without it we would not be able to explain ourselves" ("Nos pronunciamos" 1966). One of the signatories reframed the justification in terms that are hard to refute: "The circumstance itself provides a weapon: to be situated *in* the revolution and write *from* it" (Víctor Casaus). Lacking a childhood in which the superstructural effluvium instilled in them the good news of the revolution, the intellectuals who until then had dominated the cultural institutions could hardly undo the perfect logic whose elements they themselves had helped construct after having prophesied the ideological health of their heirs; an interesting—fictionalized—story that addresses the difficulties the younger generation had in terms of accessing the intellectual field during that period, is represented by Jesús Díaz's novel *Las palabras perdidas* [The Lost Words].

The choice between revolutionary and bourgeois, logical from the perspective of the Cuban context, spread rapidly outside the island. This particular situation gave rise to an anti-intellectualism with universalizing pretensions (or at least Third World validity). That the definition of the revolutionary intellectual in the context of the Cuban Revolution would inevitably lead to anti-intellectualism is to a certain degree implicit in the Marxist notion of avant-garde, since it demands, on the one hand, the indispensability of theory for the emancipation of the present and, on the other, condemns the theoretician for being situated in the comfortable bourgeoisie or the university academies. It also enters into conflict with the typical ideology of intellectuals, assigning a fundamental value to the culture of critical discourse and the exaltation of these same intellectuals before the obedience and discipline required by the military demands and dangers of the avant-garde (Gouldner 106–7).

Processes of repositioning that had been taking place simultaneously and not antagonistically (despite the existence of disputes, however bitter they might be) converged in an antagonism that in many ways encapsulated the positions that were subsequently adopted: "with Cuba or against Cuba." This meant for a whole group of intellectuals, whether explicitly or implicitly, that they embraced the consequences of the new cultural policy and the redefinition of the intellectual, establishing a clear and dichotomous separation between two types of intellectuals: those who supported the revolution and those who were against it. In short, the fact is that the whole series of discussions on the role of the intellectual in Cuba ended up favoring the positions of the Revolutionary Armed Forces and their cultural institutions as a corollary of the process of the militarization of culture and its control by the state. It is true that belonging to the left had conferred almost exclusive legitimacy on intellectual practice, but this was vague and amounted to simple adherence. To be enacted by general consensus required new topics that were not unanimous. It was then dismissed as a matter of conscience and became a legal issue that had to be defined by everyone. For a broad sector of intellectuals, one of the fundamental topics from 1968 onward and particularly after 1971 was the unequivocal support for the positions that were formulated in Cuba with respect to intellectuals. The development of anti-intellectualist tendencies on the island turned out to be an infernal machine for generating exclusions. The authors and works that were (this time) hailed as "revolutionary" almost inevitably became betrayals because, in the end, the anti-intellectualist logic was a weapon that the intellectuals turned on themselves. It is surprising to what extent exclusion was disguised as repetition. Yesterday's accuser became tomorrow's accused, and the changes of fortune and position were, in many cases, unpredictable. Nothing could be further from the imagination of the historian of this period than to read the bitterness of Lisandro Otero speaking of his position in today's Cuba; the Cato of the seventies now an outcast:

> In Cuba, the treatment of artists who have their own opinion is very subtle. There is no direct repression: exile or censorship. My book *Árbol de vida* [Tree of Life] was not published, but it was not rejected either. . . . As for me, I am a "ministerial adviser," with a high salary. But in actual fact, I am isolated (Fogel and Rosenthal 417).

It seems that the memory of those *anni horribiles* also weighs heavily in Cuba. François Maspero stated not so long ago that all the Cuban writers with whom he had been in Cuba were of the opinion that literary creation in 1989 was experiencing its best moment in ten years and that the debate on the role of the intellectual in the revolution had been relegated to the history of the "terrible seventies," "an expression that reappears in discussions quite naturally" (Maspero 213). In a similar assessment, though made by someone "on the inside," it was stated that, after a longer than desirable and advisable period,

> the broad outlook, the serene reconsideration, the recognition of a brotherhood that appeared to have been erased allow us to resume the path that intellectuals had not even attempted to abandon. And quite a few years went by under those conditions, years during which, though neither the salary nor the basic conditions to ensure daily life were lacking, the editorial silence and the absolute lack of participation in the country's pusillanimous cultural life did tremendous damage to all the intellectuals involved in a situation that could have been avoided. But furthermore, prejudice permeated everyone, including those who apparently could have benefited from a more comfortable and convenient situation. There was a deterioration in the creation and dissemination of works and cultural events that filled the celebration of history, the jubilee of the revolution, with sadness (César López 83–84).

In retrospect, the analysis of the factors that led to the deterioration in intellectual activity and caused the fracture of the Latin American intellectual family, focused on Cuba, led to its designation as the "gray quinquennium, by one of its protagonists" (Fornet 1987, 148–53).

The Cuban positions continued to reveal their strength before, during, and after that period. The ideological legitimacy of the directives emanating from the island was particularly notable and, on the other hand, increasingly definitive. One symptom of the unquestionable legitimacy of the revolution, in this case embodied in its cultural institutions, was that Vargas Llosa—as he had done when awarded the Rómulo Gallegos Prize in consulting with Haydeé Santamaría on whether or not he should accept it—and Cortázar took advantage of the meeting of the *Casa de las Américas* Collaboration Committee in January 1971 to gauge how much support Cuban cultural institutions would give to the fledgling project of the magazine *Libre*. According to Goytisolo, at the annual meeting of the Collaboration Committee, Vargas Llosa and Cortázar presented the *Libre* project in an attempt to secure the participation and undoubtedly the approval of Cuban writers. However, the writers "limited themselves to listening to their arguments without making any commitment in terms of their involvement" (Goytisolo 1983, 17). Cuba continued to be as much the focus of ideological-cultural authority in 1971 as it had been in 1966. Vargas Llosa and Cortázar were merely repeating the gesture that had been made at an earlier time by Emir Rodríguez Monegal, who had also attempted to ingratiate himself with Cuba's intellectuals, knowing that the success or failure of the *Mundo Nuevo* enterprise depended on their approval or disapproval, as later proved to be the case.

In his novel *El vientre del pez* [The Belly of the Fish], which is virtually a rewriting of *Los niños se despiden* [The Children Bid Farewell], Pablo Armando Fernández tells the story of an intellectual who, finally "converted," ends up actively and voluntarily participating in the ten-thousand-ton harvest. The image the narrator paints of the protagonist is not particularly benign. Like many Cuban intellectuals, the intellectual in *El vientre del pez* had returned to Cuba once the revolution had triumphed. The narrator of the book evokes the intellectual world with considerable contempt, juxtaposing it with the hard work of the *zafra*:

> The literary gathering at Germán and Idia's house, although excessively controversial, was intelligent, and the nights in which dawn often came as a surprise, spent incessantly discussing the same topic, each time more corrosive, were enjoyable . . . . There was no lack of excessive, insubstantial erudition, snobbish attitudes, irony, and caustic commentaries that generated complicated situations. . . . The uprooting was posed in terms of creation: the preference for foreign authors—from Europe or the United States—and for a cosmopolitan theme. Paris, New York, or London, Stockholm, Berlin, or Madrid were frequent subjects in poems, stories, and novels. The years of absence necessarily opened a gulf between these writers and those of the previous generation. The debate that began in the

> early days of the triumph of the revolution seemed inexhaustible, even if it currently took place at home and among very close friends. The diatribe, the challenge, and the polemics had disappeared from the newspapers and magazines, but the controversy became increasingly virulent as a new generation wielded its weapons, rejecting those who immediately preceded them, to glorify writers whose works had achieved recognition in the thirties and forties, especially those who had come together around the magazine *Génesis*[44] and its director (1989, 143–44).

The traumas experienced at that time, as can be seen, did not immediately dissipate over the years.

44 The reference to the magazine *Orígenes* is obvious.

6

Alternatives to the "Padilla Affair"

> As if the time that has passed and the revelations accumulated since the 20th Congress of the Communist Party of the Soviet Union had been in vain, and a fatal machine once again embodied the old specters.
>
> Ángel Rama (1983, 231)

Following the Padilla affair in 1971, the personal relationships that united the Latin American intellectual family soured. This idea can be found repeated in two similar versions. Juan Goytisolo (1983, 12) wrote that from that point on "the Hispanic cultural community would become a world of good guys and bad guys." For his part, Jorge Edwards (1989, 35) declared that "Latin American intelligentsia was irremediably divided between Castroists and anti-Castroists" (*Vuelta*, no. 154). There is a clear consensus that what had been a kind of unitary bloc, despite certain disagreements, had fractured. However, the Padilla affair was simply the most visible and public moment of a rift that Latin American intellectuals had already been attempting to repair on their own without drawing too much attention to its existence.

We had left Heberto Padilla playing the role of *enfant terrible* and *provocateur* of Cuban literature; and unemployed, since in 1968 when *Granma* had dispensed with his services due to his controversial declarations. However, Padilla relented and, once Guillermo Cabrera Infante's statements against the Cuban government became known, he even confronted his former colleague. The Padilla versus Cabrera Infante controversy took place between December 1968 and January 1969. Padilla (1968, 88–89) accused him of playing the role of "every counter-revolutionary who attempts to create a difficult situation for those who have not chosen the same path." He maintained that Cabrera Infante, "who was said to be so confident and energetic, now offers me the three options of betrayal. But I am here, participating with my life and my work in the construction of a more dignified and just society."

In his reply, Cabrera Infante (1969, 64–65) declared: "I believed I was repaying Padilla a literary and human favor and instead I have committed a nameless crime . . . I have chosen free will, while Padilla chooses history and slavery."

Cabrera Infante suggested, referring to Padilla's poem "En tiempos difíciles" [In Hard Times], that the latter had not only given up poetic language but also a poet's dignity and modesty, denying having had anything to do with his past misfortunes:

> Padilla's "difficulties" did not begin with (*were not because of*) my interview (*Primera Plana*, August 16, 1968), far from it. . . . Nor did these difficulties begin with the controversy over the inclusion of my novel *TTT* in the Castro *Index*, which Padilla settled a year ago with Lisandro Otero. . . . Nor did Padilla's persecution begin when he published a poem, "In Hard Times," in the same *Ruedo Ibérico* anthology in which Retamar declares himself a "man of transition". . . . This recklessness was committed by Padilla in an issue of *Casa* magazine in homage to Darío. . . . As with the reviews commissioned by *Caimán* on the novel by commissioner Otero, Padilla "did not conform to what was asked of him" with his poem, and although Retamar attempted to persu(ad)e him, he insisted on publishing it. . . . However, Padilla's dangers did not begin then. Like chronic illnesses, they merely worsened (65).

After a year without employment, Padilla wrote a personal letter to Fidel Castro, a step that would seem unusual in many other places. More unusual is that he received a reply the following day and was allowed to choose the job of his choice at the University of Havana. It was as simple as that; "the job he chose, that's the one they gave him," says Ernesto Cardenal (1972). Everything suggested that he had been rehabilitated and welcomed back into the bosom of the revolution. In 1969 he was on the poetry jury of the David Prize; he had published at least one poem ("En la muerte de Ho-Chi-Minh" [On the Death of Ho Chi Minh]) in the magazine *Unión,* no. 4–69; and, as Maurice Nadeau (1970, 38) affirmed—with few details about what had happened—those episodes he had been involved in had not prevented Heberto Padilla from "preserving his crown, living in Cuba, and continuing to write." Moreover, at the UNEAC, Padilla had given a reading of his book *Provocaciones* [Provocations], a title that directly alluded to the *Verde Olivo* article in which he had been attacked ("Las provocaciones de Heberto Padilla" [The Provocations of Heberto Padilla]), and the reading had apparently been a public success. In fact, Enrique Lihn (1971, 6), in an "open letter," told him: "I realized that this reading, which was even attended by the cultural *attaché* of the People's Republic of China, was a very important milestone in your trajectory as a revolutionary poet."

But Cabrera Infante was right when he said that Padilla's problems were a chronic ailment, which, like any chronic ailment, could always get worse. And Padilla's ills would certainly get much worse. The facts, which are very well-known, can be summarized succinctly: on March 20, 1971, Heberto Padilla was arrested and accused of engaging in counterrevolutionary activities. After thirty-eight days in jail, he presented himself at UNEAC to publicly admit his mistakes and, in the process, those of his friends and colleagues. The poet was introduced by José Antonio Portuondo, then vice president of UNEAC, since the president, Nicolás Guillén (as Portuondo explained), was ill. In a long speech of almost two hours, Padilla said he had made a lot of mistakes that were "really unforgivable, really reprehensible, really unspeakable" and, after acknowledging his failings, felt "truly light, truly happy after this whole experience." In his speech Padilla accused himself of counterrevolutionary bitterness, of an excess of vanity and opportunism that had led him to establish ties with virtually anyone in order to be successful abroad, of having slandered the Cuban Revolution before anyone willing to listen to him (especially foreign visitors), and ended by affirming that his experience in prison had helped him to become a staunch defender of the revolution. Throughout his speech he gradually mentioned his circle of friends and invited them to acknowledge their mistakes (César López and Pablo Armando Fernández, among others, presented their own self-criticism in that session). In the case of Norberto Fuentes, whom Padilla called upon to retract his positions, Fuentes declined the invitation, stating that he was and had always been a revolutionary writer. Padilla's self-criticism was transcribed in *Casa de las Américas,* no. 65–66, March–June 1971, which provided only the part in which Padilla spoke without the comments of the other invited writers. *Libre* printed the complete version sent to Prensa Latina. In it, we can read the invitation to Norberto Fuentes to offer a self-critique and his response, in which he states he had no reason to do so. According to Rama, just as there was a Padilla case, there should also have been a Fuentes case. If that did not happen at the time, it was, according to Rama, because "he was not useful for the Cold War since he had declared himself a revolutionary, did not contact foreign correspondents, etc." (1983, 231–61).

Instead of exhaustively summarizing the accusations and the self-disqualifying hyperboles of his self-criticism, I am interested in highlighting the central themes of his speech, which form the basis of the broad anti-intellectualism. The topics can be summarized as follows: the cultural sector has lagged behind in the revolution; writers are vain by nature; Cuban intellectuals have not been generous with the revolution. The flaws that Padilla monotonously threshed out in his confession exceeded, as can be seen, the merely personal:

> I have to confess that, thinking about our cultural sector, I came to the conclusion that—save some exceptions—if there is a sector that politically lags behind in the revolution, it is culture and the arts. We have not risen to the level of this revolution. . . . How many harvests have been attended by a significant number of writers? . . . However, when it comes to demanding, gossiping, protesting, criticizing, most writers are the first in line (Padilla 1971b, 108–9).

However, by the way the matter was discussed publicly, there is no doubt that Padilla's situation (which contained a series of overtones that extended beyond the poet's fate) was circulating quietly below the surface within the Latin American intellectual family. As stated in *Casa de las Américas* (no. 65–66, March–June 1971), there were discussions that had reached "even the very heart of the former Collaboration Committee of our magazine."

According to Ángel Rama (1971, 59), this clash of positions, however, generated exponents on only one side, the one claiming that the work of art should have militant political content. Rama stated that he had not seen "any theoretical text supporting the opposite position." This opposite position would be held, from then on, by a fraction of that united front that was now splintering.

What the consequences of the Padilla case reveal is the density and complexity of the circulation of discourses within the Latin American intellectual field and the extent to which the era problematized the gap between discourses that circulated privately and those that circulated publicly.

It is worth citing a paragraph from Padilla's self-criticism that is quite telling:

> this is the man who objectively worked against the revolution rather than for its benefit; this is the man who, when he issued criticism, did not criticize the organization he was supposed to criticize, but criticized the corridor, criticized his comrade, with bad intentions. People will say to me that they were private criticisms, that they were personal criticisms, that they were opinions, but in my view that's not important. I think that if I wanted to be a revolutionary writer and a critical writer, my private opinions and the opinions I express to my friends should have the moral weight of the opinions I express in public (97).

Similarly, the Sierra Maestra guerrillas interviewed by German writer Hans Magnus Enzensberger in Havana in 1969 criticized the policies of the former Communist Party, but only did so in private because, as Enzensberger wrote, "the subject is taboo in the public sphere."

It was also taboo, or rather anti-strategic, to hold open and public discussions on the new cultural direction of the revolution. As José Mario (1973) wrote in the prologue to *Provocaciones* [Provocations]: "The writers of the self-proclaimed left were afraid to speak out about Cuba, afraid to appear as traitors." The diffusion of the Padilla affair forced many to speak out: for or against the Cuban Revolution. It is likely, in any case, that the path of Cuban cultural policy would have offered other occasions that generated the same reactions.

One of the phrases that Benedetti (1971c) used to describe the public dissemination of the Cuban Revolution's cultural policies (and not Padilla's problems) is illustrative: "The bomb finally exploded." It is very similar to Rama's wording (1971a, 50) when he declared that the debate had left "the cenacle or the committee where we had it safely *contained*" (emphasis added). In fact, Cortázar's recently published collection of letters reveals in a letter to Vargas Llosa that the Argentine writer formed part of a group that, in 1968, was circulating a kind of petition among colleagues to try to defend Padilla in the situation caused by the problematic and controversial award given to *Fuera del juego*. Cortázar asked Vargas Llosa to join the crusade in Padilla's defense while commenting on the letter that

> Fuentes, Goytisolo, and I have prepared, based on certain reliable information that we have recently received. I am not commenting on it because I understand that its reading is sufficiently clear; we have thought that in no way should it be an open letter, but rather a request for information. And that it should only be signed by a few writers who are friends of Cuba and well-known everywhere. I think things are serious enough that we cannot remain silent. In January I will join you in Havana, for the meeting of the magazine, and there we will likely have the answer to this letter; in any case that is my hope.

Everything indicates, therefore, that it was an old discussion carried out surreptitiously that was now becoming public knowledge and had to be addressed.

Padilla's self-criticism—viewed in light of his subsequent exile and the decision to publish the novel *En mi jardín pastan los héroes* [*Heroes Are Grazing in My Garden*] and later his autobiography *La mala memoria* [*Self-Portrait of the Other*]—appears as yet another strategy that reveals the gap between the content of the various discourses depending on the degree of publicity of their circulation. Moreover, the Padilla affair exposed the fantasies of part of the intellectual family, while at the same time denying them. When news of his arrest became known, several members of the "family," supported by a significant group of celebrated foreign intellectuals, convinced that they could turn to Fidel

Castro once again and change the course of events, wrote a letter to the leader expressing concern over the poet's arrest. Conceived and drafted by Goytisolo and Cortázar and endorsed by a total of fifty-four signatories who feared that the writer's arrest would mean the reappearance of a process of sectarianism, the letter concluded by ratifying the solidarity of the undersigned:

> with the principles that guided the struggle in the Sierra Maestra, and which the Revolutionary Government of Cuba has expressed so many times through the words and actions of its prime minister, of comandante Che Guevara, and of so many other Cuban leaders (Padilla 1971b, 96).

In response, the shorthand version of Padilla's self-criticism (1971a) circulated through Prensa Latina Cuba. It did not help anyone, not the Cubans, not the Latin American family, not even Padilla himself. This "grotesque mea culpa" (in Juan Goytisolo's words (1983), "a parodic remake of the Stalinian processes" and "an authentic Ubuesque montage that would have filled [Alfred] Jarry himself with rapture") served as a sign of alarm that convinced part of the family that they should intervene more emphatically. It was this conviction that helped inspire the text of the second letter sent to Fidel Castro. Lobbying activities and meetings brought together the most eminent members of the family in Europe. On May 4, 1971, the attacked drafted a new letter to which several signatures were added (Resnais, Pasolini, Rulfo), bringing the total to sixty-two—but also including some notorious defections (particularly those of Julio Cortázar and Carlos Barral)—and sent it to the newspaper *Le Monde*.

Padilla's self-criticism may be regarded as cynical, considered a parody or reiteration of an easily recognizable style of writers' self-criticism during the periods of the Soviet purges. If the use of dissonant and even ridiculous adjectives in Padilla's mea culpa suggest an association with parody, it nevertheless touched, with unusual and notable restraint, on an issue that should be mentioned. That is the point where Padilla (1971b, 103) argued that his expectations were that "I would be respected, that I was a first-rate intellectual, and that I was a politically astute mind with great insight." That was what he believed, what the

Latin American family believed he had been entrusted with, and what was *his duty*. However, that was not in the Cuban government's plans at the time.

This time, it was a letter of dissent. Communicating their "shame" and "anger," the signatories stated, in the "Second Letter to Comandante Fidel Castro," that the "pitiful" text signed by Padilla could only have been obtained "through methods that are a negation of legality and revolutionary justice." What they called "a pitiful masquerade of self-criticism" reminded them of "the most sordid moments of the Stalinist era." Only an exceptionally close relationship to the recipient could explain the final paragraph: "We would like the Cuban Revolution to return to what once made us regard it as a model within socialism."

Why would the signatories express such solidarity with Padilla? Or, rather, were they in solidarity with Padilla? The letter was dated May 4. If José Revueltas, in pre-trial detention in Mexico, in his letter dated May 3 had made a reference to the speech delivered by Fidel Castro at the closing of the First National Congress of Culture, the signatories of the letter of the 62 must have known about it as well.

Between April 23 and 30, 1971 (a period that partially covers the days of Padilla's imprisonment and his public self-criticism), the above-mentioned Congress took place in Havana, where the ideological-cultural criteria that characterized the new Cuban context of the relationship between intellectuals were officially and programmatically proposed. The type of anti-intellectualism advocated by the Congress implied the absolute dismissal of any possibility that the "man of the future"—referred to in the declaration—could come from the ranks of "existing intellectuals." The Congress proclaimed the need to maintain "the monolithic ideological unity of our people;" to combat "any form of deviation among the young"—"extravagant aberrations," "homosexual deviations"—and; most especially, criticized the actions of the cultural institutions that took aim at a perfectly recognizable target: the "negative cultural influences that strive to penetrate our milieu" ("Declaración del Primer Congreso Nacional de Educación y Cultura" 1971).

In his closing speech at the Congress on May 1, 1971, Fidel Castro was even more explicit. He alluded to a rumor that was circulating at the time, that he would refer to "that" in his speech. "That" was "those scumbags," to whom he did indeed refer. The "scumbags" in question were Latin American intellectuals, scoundrels who instead of serving in the trenches of combat "lived in the bourgeois salons enjoying the fame they had gained when in an earlier stage they were capable of voicing some of the problems plaguing Latin America." These intellectuals were nothing more than "sub agents of cultural colonialism," waging a war on Cuba. In a shift in meaning that was valid for both sides in the conflict, the relationship was portrayed as one between judge and jury. Accustomed to judging literature as jurors for the prizes awarded by Cuba, many of the family's intellectuals felt like judges qualified to deliver their opinions on broader and more general issues. Castro made it very clear when he challenged them, saying that there would be no more "little contests" in which they would assume the role of judges. "To play the role of judges here you have to be real revolutionaries, real intellectuals, real combatants! . . . And the magazines and contests are not suitable for phonies."

Castro denounced that a small group of conceited impostors had monopolized the title of intellectual to exclude those whom they claimed did not fit the definition. Castro's words went to the heart of the problematic definition of intellectuals: that it is a self-definition par excellence.

Thus, the Padilla case was merely a trigger, in the sense that there were already many existing "fissures" that had been kept secret in association with a deeper discussion on the redefinition of new intellectual models. Once war had been declared on the group that dared to send letters criticizing this or that aspect of the Cuban government's decisions, the intellectual family had to define its positions, and it did so by using the Cuban Revolution as its center of reference. As Skármeta affirmed (1971), there was no Latin American intellectual "who had not experienced the most bizarre things in the past month." All intellectuals, both well-known and less known, had to make public statements in a sort of *Latin Americanization* of the new Cuban context.

The strange thing is that in many cases the positions were limited to the Padilla affair, leaving out any reflection on the more fundamental issues where Padilla's fate was not the focus. This is the case of the opinions of Rodolfo Walsh (1971) who questioned the 62 foreign signatories, wondering how in three weeks, half an ocean away, without proof, and in stark contradiction of the evidence of the French correspondent who physically examined Padilla, the 62 intellectuals concluded that his self-criticism could only have been obtained through torture. Naturally, Walsh was right; they had no way of knowing this, but they had suspected it for some time, which explained the speed of the reaction, which was related to the underlying issue.

The months that followed Padilla's arrest and self-criticism were full of public statements and positions, widely disseminated by Latin American magazines and newspapers. On May 5, Vargas Llosa (1971) wrote to Haydeé Santamaría to resign from the *Casa de las Américas* Collaboration Committee. In her reply, Santamaría (1971) reminded him that in January of that year, in a declaration that Vargas Llosa himself had signed, a decision had already been made to replace the committee with a long list of collaborators of the magazine and the institution, due to the differences in criteria that divided the committee. It should be noted that this third statement was not published by *Casa de las Américas*. It may be that those in charge were waiting to see how far the balance of power would tip, in a back and forth in which they also participated. Additionally, it is interesting that the issue of the magazine following the Padilla affair was delayed a few months; issue 64 corresponded to January–February 1971, while issue 65 was not published on the corresponding date (April) but in a double issue that covered the months of March to June (no. 65–66), as if perhaps in that short period there was a chance that there might be a change in what was to come.

Maybe there was hope that this would happen. The issue of *Casa de las Américas* prior to the eruption of the Padilla affair is reminiscent of the art of a tightrope walker: dedicated to Peruvian literature, it brings together texts by Luis Loaiza, Rodolfo Hinostroza, Antonio Cisneros, Alfredo Bryce, César Calvo, and Vargas Llosa, among others; it is the last issue in which the Collaboration Committee appears; and the section "Al pie de letra" praises Enrique Lihn, Jorge Edwards, and Rodolfo Hinostroza and reproduces fragments of a report on Vargas Llosa ("Con Vargas Llosa" 1971, 193–94) that appeared in the Colombian magazine *Cromos*. However, when commenting on the 1970 Casa de las Américas awards, Ambrosio Fornet refers to the winning novel, *Sacchario*, by Miguel Cossío Woodward, criticizing the path taken by Cuban novelists up to that point. According to his main arguments, the "traitorous fidelity to the cause of literature" did not serve Cuban literature and there were other writers, the "comrades of the boom," who had even begun to claim that they were the ones producing revolutionary literature. *Casa de las Américas* (in "El maquillaje del lenguaje" [The Makeup of Language]) also begins its polemic against the emergence of a new perspective of literary criticism that valued the linguistic aspects of the work, which for the magazine was nothing more than a new critical catchphrase: "The current linguistic trend generates a great deal of confusion that could be avoided with better information."

Once the positions on the Padilla affair were known, the editorial in issue 67 of *Casa de las Américas* argued: "The capitalist press unleashed a slanderous campaign against Cuba, with the collaboration of dozens of colonizing intellectuals with their colonized followers full of rambling ideology."

It was then that the tally of their own and others on the battlefield began: *Casa de las Américas* ("Suplemento: El caso Padilla" [Supplement: The Padilla Affair]) opted to reproduce only the statements that were favorable to Cuba: "As for the hostile texts, we dispensed with them; the empire had already taken charge of disseminating them copiously."

Indeed, the statements made regarding the case were copious as well as obligatory. Many intellectuals aligned themselves with the Cuban leadership, among them Mario Benedetti, Oscar Collazos, Rodolfo Walsh, and Gonzalo Rojas, who in statements to Prensa Latina had said: "The original sin of the intellectual and the suspicious nature of the letters sent to Fidel are a new low," an opinion published by *Casa de las Américas* and not by *Libre*.

Also in favor and once again in statements made to Prensa Latina (which was overwhelmed with cables and interviews), Carlos Droguett affirmed: "One cannot be a truly free writer to judge a revolution from afar, from the comforts of Paris, London, or Barcelona." In a later contribution, Droguett reaffirmed his position: "For us writers, Cuba is our real poetic art."

For his part, in a telegram sent to Juan Goytisolo, Salvador Garmendia (1971, 134–35) stated bluntly and briefly: "I express my full support for the Cuban revolutionary process and reaffirm that unproven accusations of torture and procedures contrary to human dignity feed a defamatory campaign against the revolution unleashed by US imperialism."

As on previous occasions when an author and his texts were reiterated in the network of Latin American magazines, the opinions quoted and requoted were reproduced almost infinitely. It was the hot topic on which everyone had an opinion. No reader of any publication on the continent read these opinions less than twice, since they were transcribed and retranscribed during the months immediately following the scandal's outbreak. Not surprisingly, the weekly *Siempre!* covered it as well. In the various issues dedicated to the topic of the hour, it devoted itself to seeking the opinion of a large part of the Mexican intelligentsia, which was divided. In May 1971, it published the opinions of José Revueltas (which *Marcha* and *Libre* later republished), Octavio Paz, Carlos Fuentes, and Eduardo Lizalde. *Siempre!* even organized a survey, conducted by Federico Campbell, to which Homero Aridjis, Juan Bañuelos, José Carreño Carlión, Edmundo Domínguez Aragonés, Miguel Donoso Pareja, Salvador Elizondo, Isabel Fraire, Juan García Ponce, Argelio Gasca, Jaime Labastida, María Luisa Mendoza, Marco Antonio Montes de Oca, José Emilio Pacheco, and Umberto Valverde responded. Two issues later, the subject was still being discussed.

Juan Manuel Torres (1971, XXI), who sided with Cuba, proclaimed that "the Cuban Revolution has ceased to be a carnival where anyone could wear the mask of a revolutionary. . . . Perhaps the protests would have been fewer, or none at all, if the person involved had not been an intellectual. No one would have worried about an office worker or a peasant; but in the case of an intellectual, the alarm bells could not remain silent. Does anyone truly believe that an intellectual cannot be an enemy of the revolution? Everything that has happened is healthy. It is healthy that the Cuban Revolution openly distrusts Cuban intellectuals and intellectuals from abroad. It is healthy that the Cuban Revolution clearly identifies its enemies. . . . Consciously or unconsciously our intellectuals are doing great harm to the revolution." Gerardo de la Torre wrote: "Now, the harshest and most malicious criticisms are directed against the leader, the caudillo of the Cuban Revolution . . . I do not know what our intellectuals expected from Fidel Castro after having launched themselves against him and against the Cuban Revolution. That he would thank them for their courageous, excessive, and hasty criticism? That he would invite them to spend a vacation on the island so that they could patch up and strengthen the projects of the revolutionary regime? For his part, Germán List Azurbide (1971), affected by the same feeling of injustice inflicted on the revolution by an intelligentsia that considered its *caste* privileges as natural, argued: "All those who, like that Heberto Padilla, are sure that their intellectual worth is so great it makes them untouchable, have raised their voices, claiming, with haughtiness and petulance, the right to make of their particular asset, their talent, whatever they please. This is the same or even worse—since they do it with full awareness of the cause—as the owners of latifundia all over the world do when anyone dares to touch their sacred property."

There were collective statements by nationality: Chileans, Peruvians, Uruguayans, Cubans. In essence, these statements coincided with the opinions expressed by Fidel Castro in his May 1 speech, with the declaration of *Casa de las Américas*, and with the letter written by forty-one Cuban writers ("Declaración de escritores cubanos") against the "slanderous letters sent to the prime minister" by the "mouthpieces of imperialism" whose "petulant counterclaims and 'little bits of advice'" they found unacceptable, and concluded by affirming that, when it came to ideological clarifications, those who did not align themselves with the Cuban Revolution had opted for the enemy camp.

For his part, as he had done at one point with Cabrera Infante, Padilla again left his defenders without arguments, in a response to the signatories of the *Le Monde* letter (dated May 24, 1971), with the accusation that "*for some time now*, every opportunity they get, they throw their poisoned darts at Cuba" and that they are "always playing the role of judges of our revolutionary process."

On the other hand, there were those who stressed the critical ideal of the intellectual and who therefore, to varying degrees, broke with the Cuban Revolution's new cultural policy. This group included Vargas Llosa, Carlos Fuentes, Marta Traba, José Revueltas, Ángel Rama, Adriano González León, Octavio Paz, Eduardo Lizalde, Enrique Lihn, and Juan García Ponce. Establishing a strategy that did not fall into the regime of categorical opposition was a complex task. Attempts were made, without much success, by Haroldo Conti (1971), who stated in declarations to Prensa Latina that he found the Padilla affair "inflated to the point of excess;" and Isabel Fraire, who commented that "the letter signed by Heberto Padilla is a dishonor to those who wrote it, a dishonor to those who signed it, a dishonor to the recipient, a dishonor to those who published it, a dishonor even to those who read it. The only thing that Padilla's confession, authentic or not, confirms is that ten years of revolution are not enough to change human nature. The leader, overwhelmed by the disproportionate responsibility and the pressures placed on a country that is beginning to transform itself, loses all sense of proportion."

In an open letter to Retamar, David Viñas wrote: "I disagree with both of the fundamental, polarized, and antagonistic interpretations of the Padilla affair that have been discussed so far. I disagree with the assessments of Stalinism by those who wrote to Fidel from Europe, but also with those who, from the opposite side, label the first as pro-European in order to disqualify their judgments. To insult in this way (rats versus torture) is to change the conversation." These "intermediate" positions turned out to be problematic, and there were long silences and a certain disconnect between those who formulated them and the Cuban intelligentsia, which expected stronger support for its positions.

All the same, it was not so easy for the "outsiders" to consistently hold a position. Federico Campbell (1971) commented that several Mexican intellectuals refused to respond to his survey, alleging various reasons: that the questions about their positions on the Padilla affair were counterrevolutionary, that nothing could be signed against Castro, that there was a lack of information to express an opinion, and that "intellectuals have no right to defend the right to criticize as long as we are not willing to kill ourselves or let ourselves be killed for that right in the same way that revolutionaries have given their lives."

At first glance, it is easy to see a gap between the collective and individual declarations. With the exception of the letters from European and Latin American intellectuals to Fidel Castro, the other collective declarations gain strength from their numbers rather than the prestige of their signatories. On the other hand, of those who make individual statements, the vast majority possess greater cultural capital, prestige, or authority. It is interesting to analyze particular strategies: from the retraction and self-criticism of Luigi Nono (who regrets having signed the first letter and explains his error as an example of the intellectual contradictions that will only be overcome "with the militant practice of the organic Marxist intellectual within the working class") to the more complex and sophisticated approaches of the most prestigious Latin American writers, many of whom perhaps agreed with the opinion of José Mario (1973, 10), who believed that writers feared losing the public they had created for themselves through their support for the island. The most interesting tactics from the point of view of the pragmatics of discourse were those of Julio Cortázar and Gabriel García Márquez.

Nevertheless, it is worth analyzing the strategies of the magazines, which do not necessarily coincide with their particular representative figures: *Marcha*, for example, includes a wide range of opinions, both for and against, but the leadership of the magazine itself, despite regretting the Padilla affair (because of the importance it was given in Cuba and the effect that had beyond the island) and not exactly praising Castro's speech, describes the episode as a mishap in the path of the Cuban Revolution, which "does not detract from its significance, nor does it diminish its virtues or tarnish its heroism. It continues to be the vanguard of our revolution. Even in its errors, because at its own expense, it warns and teaches us" ("Introducción" 1971, 4).

The case of *Siempre!* is more explicit (or more graphic). Taking advantage of the usual expressiveness of the weekly's cover illustrations, the cover of issue 936, June 2, 1971, shows a promontory representing the island of Cuba, with a sign indicating: "Socialism is being built here," and a giant statue, whose sculptor, standing on one of the arms, is Fidel Castro himself. Standing on a small boat christened *Calliope* and floating in the sea, Heberto Padilla breaks a toe of the gigantic metal colossus that represents Cuban socialism.

Casa de las Américas, for its part, reveals a complete alignment between the collective or individual statements published and the magazine's criteria. The Argentine magazine *Panorama*, in "Intelectuales vs. Fidel: Cartas de un joven poeta" [Intellectuals vs. Fidel: Letters from a Young Poet], argued that, following Padilla's self-criticism, the anti-Castro supporters ran out of arguments, recalling that the Cuban intellectual circles, although they detested Batista, had generally participated very little in both the struggle against the dictatorship and in the triumph of the revolution. And he concluded, ironically: "The fate of the young poet Heberto Padilla in Cuba does not seem nearly as severe as that of the young poet Javier Heraud, who died with the guerrillas in Peru, or that of the young poet Otto René Castillo, who died with the guerrillas in Guatemala."

For *Nuevos Aires* it was a relatively common event, in a country going through a revolution, that a citizen suspected of counterrevolutionary activities would be detained. In its view, those who were worried about Padilla are victims of the belief that "Stalinist deformation is a natural development in all socialist countries," concluding that indications to the contrary have not prevented this belief. In recalling the roundtable on intellectuals and revolution, held in Havana in 1969 and commented on extensively in this work, it stated:

> The seriousness of this freely assumed attitude, which leads to the acceptance of a *desired and admissible subordinate* attitude, where the accent is placed on the social responsibility of the writer, suggests that this self-critical, conscious, and modest path will be highly profitable for the future of the relations between the revolutionary powers and their intellectuals.

The truth is that with the Padilla affair the honeymoon between most writer-intellectuals and the Cuban Revolution reached a critical point. From that point on, the Latin American family would be divided between those who supported the revolution (and accepted as a definition of revolutionary intellectual those who took the side of the working class, took part in the revolutionary struggle, and accepted the directives of the revolutionary political leaders) and those who returned, with determination and deliberation, to the intellectual tradition sustained by the critical ideal. When the label of revolutionary intellectual was reclaimed (based on the organic imperative) by the "men of action" or, failing that, by those who accepted the directives of the men of action, the division of the intellectual field was considered, according to the positions of the groups within it, as an antagonism between "revolutionary intellectuals" and "bourgeois intellectuals," for the group identified with Cuba, and between "intellectuals subjugated by the state" and "critical intellectuals," for the group that attempted to revive the wounded identity of the intellectual as a critical conscience of society.

Minerva and the Flying Horse: Pragmatics of Discourse

The realm of the sayable is hard to publicly violate but it can be *circumvented* by a certain type of speech. That realm establishes a pragmatics of discourse that individuals must respect, unless they invent their own ways of transgressing or eluding it. In 1971, Lezama Lima resorted to some bizarre language to avoid attending Heberto Padilla's self-criticism session, creating through verbal distance a real physical distance that finally allowed him to overcome the persistence of those who "invited" him. It is safe to say that he was aware that this strategy worked well since he had tried it before.

Ten years earlier, following the meetings with Fidel Castro at the National Library, when a decision was made to hold the First Congress of Writers and Artists of Cuba (in June 1961), *Lunes de Revolución* transcribed the statements of the writers prior to the congress in the article "Un congreso de escribas y artistas" [A Congress of Scribes and Artists]. In general, unanimously edited for the same content and style, the opinions on the future congress outlined by various writers in the first-person singular coincided with the "Manifesto of Intellectuals and Artists," which declared that to defend the revolution was to defend culture and highly praised the possibilities that both the congress and the creation of the National Union of Writers would generate for Cuban culture.

Lezama Lima's response was unique in that collection of opinions:

> It seems as if Dante, after joining the guild of pharmacists, since there wasn't one for poets, had to take an ectoplasmic, worldly stroll to find in the Alchemy of the verb a place for his guild stupefaction. The alchemists, in search for a golden essence, an extratemporal drop, equated themselves with the poets in their eagerness to create a body amid the fragments of the metaphor and the totality of the image. The artists' new abode spreads through the organized voice of a congressional virtue, where the severity of the canon of forms takes on the andantino of a march that leads it to the joyful melody of its eternity. The congressional essence is a rich diversity that culminates in the chorus of total unity. In this rendezvous with the fascination of a fate, we will see that when a revolution acquires its

> state figuration, that is to say, a convergence of state and people, the artist must develop the fullness of their image. House for the image and congress for the revolutionary creative forms. Hurrah, midday light, temple for the definitions of the Minerva who sculpts the flying horse.

In a way, it was a strong affirmation of uniqueness, which he was permitted because he was Lezama Lima and affirmed "I am Lezama Lima." There were not that many individual strategies capable of standing outside that community of voices to say something different from what everyone else was saying.

An epoch or a problem can be studied, as proposed in chapter 1, taking into account the pragmatics of discourse and the complex and heterogeneous strategies in which the word is inscribed, following the process of capturing speech, as Michel de Certeau put it. The Padilla affair, for example, revealed the value that intellectuals (producers of discourse par excellence) conferred to silence or to the confinement of their opinions in conciliabules of peers.

An excellent example of the thematization of the discursive pragmatics that can help establish a writer's political vocation can be found in Simone de Beauvoir's novel *The Mandarins*. This text is situated in a relationship that bears a surprising analogy with the problems discussed here on intellectuals and revolution or intellectuals and politics. A reading of it reveals a surprising fact: the similarity between the dilemmas of some of the postwar French intellectuals, as fictionalized by Simone de Beauvoir, and the obsessions of Latin American intellectuals toward the end of the period, at a time when the demands of politicization became more radical and the revolutionary character of intellectuals was associated with demands for greater instrumentality and effectiveness of symbolic practices. *The Mandarins* provides an exhaustive typology of the dominant discursive pragmatics following the Second World War among the French intelligentsia in the context of the Cold War and the expectation of leading the country to socialism. It covers all stages of speech and silence; illocutionary strategies, such as denunciation, dissimulation in speaking, silence, denunciation, concealment; and also the great dilemma of politicized writer-intellectuals (to write or not to write?).

These pragmatic considerations are exemplified in the characters of Robert Dubreuilh (a kind of shadow of Sartre) and Henri (a figure behind which Albert Camus can be glimpsed). Dubreuilh, for example, is faced with the choice, as the editor of a newspaper, of whether or not to denounce the forced labor camps in the USSR, which as an *object of discourse* belonged to the "reactionary" press. Experiencing the tensions of an ethical debate that divides him internally and in which he involves his wife and narrator, Dubreuilh is presented with the dilemma of reconciling the problem of speaking or remaining silent or, in the terms of his general dilemma, reconciling his identity as a critical intellectual and a revolutionary or progressive intellectual, based on the existence of the USSR and Dubreuilh's position as a fellow-traveler of the Soviets.

Once the problem has been set out, Anne, narrator and wife, reminds her husband that *as an intellectual* he had made the commitment to "tell the truth." This leads to a significant ellipsis. "*And as a revolutionary*?" What is omitted suggests the extent to which politics, *for intellectuals*, can be associated with dissimulation, propaganda, or secrecy. Truth as a supreme value defended by intellectuals can run up against the limitations established by political reason or reason of state.

Simone de Beauvoir's work addresses the way in which the intellectual desire to intervene in politics affects the identity of the intellectual as a critical conscience, thus problematizing the very notion of the intellectual, illustrating the dilemmas of the relationship between the intellectual and politics. The book involuntarily examines the future as it refers to the concerns and debates the Latin American intelligentsia was engaged in for fifteen years: the value of art and aesthetics, the class determinations of intellectuals, the relationship between tradition and the need to invent new, urgent forms of collective expression, the problematic relationship between intellectuals not aligned with a party or movement and political leaders, the need to resort to new knowledge, the merit or demerit of an intellectual identity ("I'm an intellectual, period. And it annoys the hell out of me when they make that word an insult").

In Latin America there are plenty of examples of this type of debate over speaking out or remaining silent. One example is Carlos Quijano, who, when questioned about the fact that his weekly did not criticize US and Soviet policies equally (which he opposed on many fronts and, it must be said, was also criticized in *Marcha*), replied that criticism of the socialist camp was dealt with extensively in the "pro-imperialist" press. This is also the case of the criticisms (which circulated privately and later became public) of many of the policies of the Cuban Revolution: in many cases, the silencing of much of the reticence of Latin American intellectuals toward various positions taken by the Cuban leadership was a self-imposed strategy so as not to show weakness in the face of anti-Cuban positions.

The article that Juan Goytisolo dedicated to recalling the *Libre* experience reveals that many of the traumas it generated remained (and still remain), as can be seen in the bitter criticism he dedicated to García Márquez and Cortázar for having, in his view, petulantly abandoned the ship in which the *Libre* "devotees" were sailing.

Rather than commenting on the ethics of these diversion strategies, it is interesting to analyze them. García Márquez, for example, developed his own strategy by eluding the idea of being an intellectual. In fact, of the most visible writers of those years, García Márquez was the only one who did not clearly put himself in the position of an intellectual. The interview he granted to Ernesto Schoó in Mexico in 1967 is an example of how, from very early on, García Márquez established for himself the position of the writer-star described by Jean Franco (1984, 122–29). The clothes he would wear to go for a walk or to look more photogenic, the autographs he would sign or not sign on his imminent visit to Buenos Aires were part of the public image that García Márquez constructed and that, in this case, fit perfectly with *Primera Plana*'s journalistic style (Schoó 1967, 52–54). In one way or another, the Argentine weekly helped García Márquez find appropriate ways to construct his image, which he then continued to use.

The main focus of Goytisolo's criticism of García Márquez is with respect to the position he adopted on the Padilla affair. García Márquez was not in Paris when the first letter to Fidel Castro was sent, but his friend, compatriot, and editorial secretary of *Libre*, Plinio Apuleyo Mendoza, included García Márquez's name among the signatories, assuming that he would support the letter. However, the author later refuted his support and had his signature withdrawn from the "Letter of the 54." Goytisolo's rancor toward García Márquez came from the fact that the latter, using a strategy of "headlong flight," managed to avoid the painful sensation described by Foucault in *The Archaeology of Knowledge*, which consists of coming up against what one does not want to say. In his evaluation of the errors he had committed, Goytisolo regretted having insisted on the *Libre* project, since the magazine had been born out of "lobbying" and "commitment," and recognized that his support for the Cuban Revolution had, for years, been lacking in conviction and enthusiasm, opinions and feelings. Goytisolo felt that the terms of that letter sent to Fidel Castro were insufficient, and in his view:

> he had not been able to fully respond to the challenge: instead of analyzing point by point the accumulation of regressive options that in recent years had transformed the Cuban Revolution into a repressive and totalitarian system, he focused the discussion on the spectacle of the UNEAC, although at the last minute we partially corrected the error and added, following Enzensberger's advice, a paragraph that should in fact have been the main focus of our reflections.

The paragraph in question is the following:

> The contempt for human dignity implied in forcing a man to ridiculously accuse himself of the worst treachery and vileness does not alarm us because he is a writer, but because any fellow Cuban—peasant, worker, technician, or intellectual—could also be the victim of similar violence and humiliation.

This addition was key because it anticipated the potential and inevitable objections that the revolution would present in response to a group of writers and intellectuals who simply embarked on a defense of their interests, which is what it did anyway, in spite of the paragraph included at the last minute.

García Márquez did not issue a direct opinion on the Padilla affair. His public opinion was limited to an interview granted to *Diario del Caribe* when he was on his way to New York where he would receive an honorary doctorate in literature from Columbia University. His position revealed a subtle handling of the tactics of enunciation, inclusion, and exclusion that, thanks to the use of pronouns, shifts the responsibility for his own discourse. When asked how he would be viewed by Latin

American writers who had broken ties with Castro, García Márquez (1971) replied: "The conflict of *a group* of Latin American writers with Fidel Castro is an ephemeral triumph of the news agencies." The reporter's cross-examination sought to determine whether García Márquez included or excluded himself from that group ("What, then, is *your* position on the letters of protest by intellectuals to the Cuban prime minister?"), to which García Márquez replied: "I did not sign the letter of protest because I was not in favor of sending it. However, at no time will I question the intellectual honesty and revolutionary vocation of those who did sign the letter" (emphasis added).

The journalist's interest in knowing where his interviewee stood on the issue became increasingly insistent. He asked: "Are you with or against Castro regarding the case of the poet Heberto Padilla?" and received the following response: that García Márquez did not believe in the sincerity of the poet's self-criticism; that if there really was a "seed of Stalinism" in Cuba, it would soon be revealed by Fidel Castro himself, and that neither he nor the "writers who protested the Padilla affair" had broken ties with the Cuban Revolution.

Later, García Márquez defended the Cuban Revolution as a personal friend of Fidel Castro, but he also served as an intermediary to get several dissident writers out of Cuba. Much later he had to once again demonstrate his qualities as a strategist in the case of Ochoa and the De la Guarda brothers, friends who were tried and convicted for drug trafficking in 1989.[45] His relationship with the Cuban Revolution was of an almost personal nature, based on a friendship with its top leader and detached from group commitments, a position that could also be sustained thanks to the fact that, as a writer, García Márquez stood out among his Latin American colleagues in terms of prestige and celebrity, sealed by the fact he had won the Nobel Prize for Literature.

Julio Cortázar was, of all people, the one who ended up struggling the most with what he wanted and did not want to say. In fact, it was he who engaged in the most controversies: from defending Padilla when *Fuera del juego* generated objections to the discussion he had with Arguedas, the

45 See Fogel, Françoise and Bertrand Rosenthal 1992, 90, 93, 124–25, 142, 156, 306–7, 399.

debate he was forced into when he and other writers were questioned by Oscar Collazos (1969a, 1969b), and, later on, the objections of David Viñas (1969, 734–39). In his arguments against Collazos's objections, Cortázar, in "Literatura en la revolución y revolución en la literatura" [Literature in the Revolution and Revolution in Literature] practically omitted his explicit audience and based most of his perspectives on the assumption that Che Guevara and, therefore, Fidel Castro, would support them:

> Few will doubt my conviction that Fidel Castro or Che Guevara have established the models for our authentic Latin American destiny; but in no way am I willing to admit that *Human Poems* or *One Hundred Years of Solitude* are inferior responses, on a cultural level, to those political answers. (By the way: What would Fidel Castro think of this? I don't think I'm deceiving myself if I assume that he would agree, as Che would have agreed.)

Cortázar was one of the writers who promoted *Libre* magazine and demanded that Cabrera Infante be barred from participating. He not only signed but also wrote the first letter addressed to Fidel Castro when the news of Padilla's arrest became known. However, he did not sign the second letter, which was a response to Padilla's self-criticism and had practically implied a declaration of war, from the "Rive Gauche," on the Cuban Revolution's cultural policy. According to Goytisolo (1983, 22), if Julio Roca's interview with García Márquez had been a prodigious exercise in acrobatics, the prize for the "despicable and grotesque" went to Cortázar for his text "Policrítica en la hora de los chacales" [Polycriticism When the Jackals Come Calling].

Cortázar offers an invaluable opportunity to describe the realm of the sayable and the pragmatics of discourse associated with it. On the one hand, he abandoned group strategies and developed personal forms of communication regarding the complex issues that affected the intellectual family. On the other, his strategy included the "literaturization" of his discourse. It was no coincidence that his manifesto-text on the Padilla affair was a poem. At the same time, he accompanied it with a (private) letter to Haydeé Santamaría.

In "Policrítica en la hora de los chacales" Cortázar laid out a formula for compromise that combined what was to be said, what was intended to be said, what could be said, what could not be said, and the genre through which it could all be said. Cortázar understood the importance of rhetoric and discovered that negotiation was ultimately possible, provided that the appropriate means were found. If literary discourse was in crisis, the thematization of that crisis was the way in which the discourse could be momentarily defended. Cortázar understood that the field of friends and adversaries had to be dereferentialized and rebaptized, that many of the questioned words (self-criticism, for example) could be restored through some type of hyperbole or excess that could only be found in the "aesthetic" aspirations of the discourses. Thus, "self-criticism" is both multiplied by and, at the same time, hidden in "polycriticism": one of the nerve centers of the intellectual component (criticism) is maintained, while affecting the whole universe of the polemicists. Several fragments of the lengthy poem-declaration-manifesto demonstrate this:

> What is the use of writing good prose / what is the use of presenting reasons and / arguments / if the jackals keep watch, if the pack hurls itself / on the word, / mutilating it, taking what they want and leaving / the rest . . .
>
> Jackals are wise in telexes, they are the scissors of infamy and / misunderstandings /
>
> So no, it is better to be what you are, / to say what burns your tongue and your stomach, / there will always be someone who understands this language from the depths, / as from the depths emerge semen, milk, / ears of grain.
>
> And for whomever expects something else, defense / or a subtle explanation / recidivism or escape, there's nothing easier / than to buy the newspaper made in USA / and read the comments to this text / the versions of Reuters or UPI / where know-it-all jackals will give you / the satisfactory version . . .
>
> I'm not making excuses for myself / or for this language / . . . and I share my experiences and my feelings / my suffering and my hopes.
>
> . . .
>
> It is hard for me to use this first-person / singular and even harder for me to say: this is the way it is, or that is a lie. . . .

> I understand Cuba as one understands / a loved one, / the gestures, the distances, and so many differences / the fury, the shouting: above all the sun / the freedom. . . .
> And it all begins with the opposite, with a poet / imprisoned, / with the need to understand why / to ask and to wait; / what do we know of what is happening, / so many of us who are Cuba. . . . You are right, Fidel: only in the struggle; / is there a right to discontent. . . . It is now that I exercise my right to choose / to be once again and more than ever before / with your Revolution, my Cuba, in my own way.

As seen above, the political context provided the basis for cultural practice, even for those for whom this turn of events was not valid. Even Juan Liscano (1967b, 6), when he wrote about the 1967 congress held in Mexico, ended his article by apologizing for having focused more on the political than the cultural issues. This gesture shows that the dominant modes of legitimization and interest extended beyond individual desires.

The question that remains is how to know what is being silenced. Throughout a long survey of periodicals, I found two ways to determine how certain public interventions had to be verified in other spaces. Both possibilities involved Cortázar in a leading role. The first verification of the existence of two modes of circulation of antagonistic discourses for the same enunciator became possible as the period ended (bringing about changes with respect to the sayable): it is related to the protocol of the exhumation of documents that were restricted for a time, a frequent practice in the case of states that even have laws concerning how long documents can remain secret. In 1984, *Casa de las Américas* published part of Cortázar's correspondence with Cuba. Many of these letters shed light on the problems of intellectual autonomy during the period and the importance of the Cuban *nihil obstat* to legitimize interventions. The best example in this case is Cortázar's correspondence regarding *Mundo Nuevo.* In his letter dated December 24, 1965 (*Casa de las Américas,* no. 145–46), Cortázar wrote:

> I take very good note of your letter to Rodríguez Monegal. . . . I presume he will tell me about the magazine in question. . . . Although I was aware of the origins of that publication, your letter clarifies

> a few things for me. It will be interesting to see what Emir does in response to our attitude, because, although I hardly know him, I understand that he is an honest and lucid man (25).

January 23, 1966, he added:

> I have remained attentive to Emir Rodríguez Monegal's problem. I had lunch with him, and he gave me a copy of his response to your letter. So you know his point of view; yesterday, by chance, I ran into him in a restaurant (he was there with Mario Vargas, to whom he must have been explaining the problem, since Emir wants all his friends to be well aware of the matter, just as you do). He repeated to me that he wants to go to Cuba to speak with you and the folks from Casa; I hope he does because it would be the only way for everyone to get a clearer view of this matter, which seems to have been tainted since its inception. Emir has had the intelligence to avoid asking for my collaboration and has limited himself to giving me his perspective. My hope now is that he will go to Cuba, and the future will determine what comes of this matter (31).

Cortázar, who had refused to participate in *Mundo Nuevo*, asked Retamar in a letter dated July 21, 1966: "What finally happened with *Mundo Nuevo*?" He added that his friends in Paris told him that the first three issues were unobjectionable "from the point of view you imagine" (41) and that he had only seen the first issue. That first issue of *Mundo Nuevo* that Cortázar claimed to have seen included Fejtö's piece, which in no way disguised his antipathy toward the Cuban Revolution—and which had been harshly criticized at the time by Fornet—, no doubt the "*from the point of view you imagine*" that Cortázar was referring to. Why the question? What Cortázar was proposing, since Monegal insisted on asking him for contributions, was that if the magazine remained "in a worthy position" he would submit his article on *Paradiso*, the novel by Lezama Lima that had first been removed from Cuban bookstores and then put back on the shelves thanks to the involvement of Cortázar and his friends. The letter concluded by stating that he would not give Monegal a definitive answer until he had Retamar's opinion. On February 17, 1967, Cortázar commented to Retamar that all of Paris was talking about the latest revelations concerning the CIA and *Mundo Nuevo* funds, "which merely confirm what we all basically knew when we last met up," and affirmed that he would see Monegal "to clarify my point of view on *Mundo Nuevo*" and that he would talk to Carlos Fuentes to "clarify the meaning of the criticisms" (44) that had been leveled at him in *Casa de las Américas*. He promised to send an "official" letter soon.

The limits of the Cortazarian ideal of promoting the Che Guevaras of literature, as he had proposed in his discussion with Collazos, were abruptly revealed when it was necessary to comply with the discipline of political authority.

The second opportunity to verify the limits of the sayable was far more unexpected. What could be more unexpected than the chance encounter, in a Parisian library, of issue number 1 of *Mundo Nuevo*, profusely, freely, and privately annotated in the margins by Cortázar himself, who was evidently telling the truth when he claimed to have read it? His handwritten notes on the interview with Carlos Fuentes take on a tone that is far from militant rejection. Instead, he expresses a complicity that reveals—from one friend to another—that he is grateful for the praise lavished on him; he includes Marechal among the writers who inaugurated a humoristic vein in Latin American literature, he adds San Martín's name alongside that of Bolívar, and does not hesitate to use the interjection "che,"—closely associated with Buenos Aires—in this case more closely associated with argentinian humorist Pepito Marrone than with the protagonist of "Reunión." So, it was only within the intimacy of a private reading that Cortázar had space for the laughter that the gravity of his times forced him to stifle in public.

7

Breaking Family Ties

1. The Market and the Vanity of the Writer

> Since even I find myself embarked on this ship we call the boom, I have only one desire: that someday we forget that word!
>
> Julio Cortázar (1975, 86)

The historical determining factors of the so-called boom included the heightened self-awareness of the role of the writer-intellectual as a public figure; the expansion of associations of intellectuals on the continent and the friendships that generated phenomena of horizontal recognition; the emphasis on Latin America as an entity that transcends national borders; and the dissemination of Latin American output by critics at the continental level. However, not all Latin American writers had the same luck in the market or with critics. The distinction between established and unestablished writers marked clear differences between them. History may have been different if market conditions had not changed, but the fissures in the Latin American intellectual bloc drained away some of the energy that this bloc could have used to promote new authors, while at the same time, new economic circumstances threw the Latin American publishing world into crisis. The extraordinary market phenomenon that took place between 1960 and 1967 was intense but very short-lived; the fact is that it was unable to incorporate new names into the ranks of the established. Between the late sixties and early seventies, national publishing houses were replaced with large multinational book publishers. In 1971, Henri Charrière's *Papillon* was the best-selling book in Latin America, and many Latin American publishers were practically bankrupt. The truth is that the market reorganized the authors' space according to its own dynamics, and one of the consequences was confrontation.

A survey of the adjectives used by the group of those who, following the Padilla affair, aligned themselves with the Cuban Revolution to attack those who dared question it, provides a common denominator of epithets, particularly related to the writing profession: "snobbery," "vanity," "egocentricity," "hypertrophy of the ego," "individualism," etc. The new constellation justified the rereading, from an accusatory perspective, within the intellectual field itself, of the Latin American "boom": this is an essential framework for situating the debates that pitted Latin American intellectuals against each other in 1971.

More study is needed on the impact that the literary market had on the ideologies of the writer and on the configuration of aesthetic-ideological debates in the Latin American intellectual field. As long as the cultural agenda proved viable, the first interpretation of the avalanche of success of Latin American literary works was celebratory; authors had finally found an audience, and critics could at last regard Latin American literature—thought of years before as only an unrealized prospect, project, or historical desire—as finally existing. Latin America went from being a geographical or political reality to also becoming a cultural reality, which, through its literature, captivated reading audiences all over the world. During the times when the cultural agenda was in force, the great majority of writers spoke out against any kind of dirigisme in the arts, especially Cuban artists, mainly because they argued that socialism stood to lose the most as a result of that policy. Needless to say, the panorama changed after Cuba's alignment with the Soviet Union and the proposal to create revolutionary art that would reach the masses, within the framework of the above-mentioned discussions.

Moreover, once a set of novels and authors was established, it became clear that an author's chances in the market did not improve according to their revolutionary quality. The way in which works reached readers was far from transparent, a mere vehicle for communication between authors and readers, and even farther from being governed by the mere voluntarism of their producers. Society, the people, and the public were not the same thing. The literary work was (is) also a commodity and as such was (and is) linked to consumer society and its forms of media manipulation. A cover of *Primera Plana* in 1968 bore the title "Editors: The Dance of Millions," and the article on the topic highlighted a figure who had been more or less hidden up to that point but who was extremely influential: the editor. The weekly underlined a fact that had become luminously evident: "The Word has rare properties: one of the most consistent is to make us forget that books are bought and sold, that they are also merchandise." As a commodity, it was hard to see how a literary work could have any revolutionary function.

Market recognition traced a division between famous authors and others. We could say that beginning with the "boom" (a word in heavy circulation since 1967; Monegal mentions it in his paper "Los nuevos novelistas" at the 13th Conference on Literature in Caracas and in his article "Diario de Caracas"), a transition had taken place "in less than ten years, from its most radical exaltation to an equally resounding negative" (Lafforgue). What was this process through which the Latin American family drew a particularly odd line between established and unestablished authors? In the pages of *Mundo Nuevo* (one of the magazines most associated with the boom) Monegal expressed his gratitude for the dissemination of Latin American literature by *Visión*, a magazine on Latin American affairs published in the United States and part of the ideological apparatus of the Alliance for Progress, but he took the precaution of rejecting any suggestion that the success of Latin American literature implied a source of economic income for its authors. According to the Uruguayan critic, the only lucky one had been Pablo Neruda, "who has seen the editions of his books increase by millions." Monegal's most significant observation was contained in his warning ("Las buenas intenciones" 1972) that it was not wise to "foster the illusion that there is a club of Latin American writers who live off their royalties."

Nevertheless, the idea of a club and even a mafia began to circulate to describe the writers who had had better luck in the market and space in the press. The word mafia came into widespread use in Mexico following the publication of Luis Guillermo Piazza's 1967 novel *La mafia* [The Mafia]. In it Piazza referred to

> a supposed vague, diffuse, and mysterious group of supervisors of culture that everyone attacks and to which everyone would like to

> belong . . . [and that] repeats itself from place to place: Buenos Aires, with the *Sur* group, Bogotá with the followers of Marta Traba and the Nadaistas, Caracas with the Techo de la ballena, Montevideo and *Marcha*, Paris and *Les Mandarins*, London and the Bloomsbury Group or the irate young people who are now mature and very meek.

The new mafia to which Piazza then alluded was the recently formed mafia of the boom: to the question "Why do you believe that this group or most of it (Cortázar, Vargas Llosa, Fuentes, Donoso, Viñas, Cabrera Infante, Carpentier, and now García Márquez, who has left for Barcelona) prefers to live in Europe while continuing to write about Latin America?" Piazza replies: "That does not include everyone who is there nor is everyone there everyone there is . . . the inclusion of Donoso is a joke on Fuentes's part, the inclusion of Viñas is a cruel joke, a mockery" (R. Castro 1967, VII).

As *Primera Plana* had observed, 1967 was a decisive year in terms of the potential for the recognition of Latin American texts and the establishment of professional writers. From then on, García Márquez (and some other writers) would speak a language in the lexicon of which words such as "print run," "translations," "copyrights," and "representatives" would stand out and be reiterated, and they would even provide advice from established authors to the up-and-coming. Meanwhile, in 1968 the Argentine publishing industry was exporting 11.5 million dollars; the Mexican industry, 11.2 million; *The Death of Artemio Cruz* was being exported to Denmark; in four months 20,000 copies of the Italian edition of *A Change of Skin* were sold out; the Feltrinelli publishing house was about to publish *The Time of the Hero* and was preparing the Italian translation of *One Hundred Years of Solitude*, a novel that in two years was to sell over 200,000 copies.

The existence of such a sizable market turned an eminently quantitative phenomenon into a qualitatively relevant fact with unexpected effects on intellectual life in Latin America. To the extent that in the three years between the first and second editions of *Los nuestros*, Harss was able to maintain that time had made itself felt in that very short interval. The point was that what had come to be called the boom in Latin American literature turned out to be a phenomenon that had "more to do with a publishing and advertising revolution than with a true flourishing of creativity . . . [and that] in multiplying loaves of bread, there is no shortage of swindlers, parasites disguised as rivals, and broken promises."

Within the context of the revolutionization of the intellectual, how must the system of war metaphors that Tomás Eloy Martínez (1968, 40–49) used in *Primera Plana* to present the "exiled novelists"—in whose view "the words of their novels are long-range rifles, intercontinental rockets that do not miss their target"—have sounded? The piece on Fuentes, Cortázar, Vargas Llosa, García Márquez, Cabrera Infante, and Sarduy was presented as a description of "their firing ranges, their types of artillery, and the secret clocks that are fitted into their projectiles."

As early as 1969 this process of the corrosion of the foundations of literature and acclaimed literati can be documented; Juan Carlos Martini (1969, 29) states in an article in the magazine *Macedonio*: "Because most of the writers of the current Latin American narrative claim to be on the 'left' and to repudiate the sad social reality of our people; and yet we have seen that this does not ensure anything in terms of art, and therefore, anything in terms of change." The problem for writers, especially when they were doing well, was that they needed the treatment prescribed by Benedetti; that is, "a dose of modesty." This remedy was intended to remove *vanity*, which, according to Benedetti in an interview (Lavín Cerda 1969), was and would be "for a long time yet, our weakest flank, the most propitious area of our territory for the enemy to turn into a base of operations, for its penetration." It was that context and this demand that prevented Cortázar and Vargas Llosa from having a pleasant experience in Paris when they agreed to participate in a roundtable on the topic "Intellectuals and Society." According to Cortázar (1970a), they were harassed and attacked with arguments similar to Benedetti's, except that this time the objectors were present and their attacks were direct; the attendees launched themselves against him and Vargas Llosa, showing signs of a "depressing sectarianism." Almost as "a guarantee of their past and future work," they demanded that the writers commit themselves to a militant intervention in the social struggle or to the creation of a work with a revolutionary theme connected to the sociopolitical context, in which the literary language used did not exceed "the comprehension level of the average reader." Cortázar's argument that the more revolutionary a work was, the more it was ahead of its time, a fact that, he complained, "many colleagues in Latin America" seemed to ignore, was to no avail. Their protests went unheeded, and, it seems, both writers were accused of being escapists, traitors, and irrelevant.

In 1969, Benedetti warned that the narrators of the boom, those who had given an accurate "diagnostic of the continent," would end up dazzled by "the publishing boom and the publicity." The weapons that Tomás Eloy Martínez referred to were only toy artillery and not even necessary since in Europe they were not at any risk. On the contrary, he argued, many were gladly circulating around Paris with the hope of being "boomized," and he pointed out that those included in the boom were living in Europe, while those who had plenty of merit but were left out of the phenomenon were living in Latin America, such as Onetti, Rulfo, Arguedas, Roa Bastos, Marechal, Viñas, and Sabato ("El boom entre dos libertades"). In line with *Primera Plana*'s reports, an issue of *Visión* magazine offered a "special report" on the new Latin American narrative under the title "Triunfos y penurias" [Triumphs and Hardships]. The analysis attributed the success of Latin American narrative *to publicity*, calling into question an assertion that had become a watchword of the intellectual family and that dated the origins of interest in Latin American literature to the Cuban Revolution. So it was not the revolution? Roque Dalton took care to refute *Visión*'s opinions: on the one hand, he attacked the myth of the hardships that, according to *Visión*, acclaimed writers would have suffered while living in European garrets. On the other, he rejected the capitalist view of literature presented by *Visión*, whose purpose, he denounced, was "to try to get the attractive accumulation of figures in dollars and 'production and marketing glory' into the heads of Latin American writers in order to create in them an awareness of their identity of interests within the capitalist system" (1969). Dalton did not display great confidence in the ability of his colleagues to resist the temptations of the market, an institution which he judged to be very powerful in perniciously working on writers, alienating them and leading them to believe in the "autonomy of their social role," inciting them to believe, erroneously, that they had a *direct* relationship with their public. He went so far as to posit that this false belief could more easily attack those who, "with the aim of 'preparing themselves' for the promised land they entered following the publication of their first book of sonnets, have become effeminates, prostitutes, alcoholics, or changed their voice" (1969).

The controversy that pitted Arguedas and Cortázar against each other in 1969 was a symptom of the distrust of the professionalization of the writer: that discussion viewed as problematic a series of situations that had become unacceptable as a matter of principle, such as, for example, the fact that many acclaimed authors lived in Europe. In the opening chapter of *El zorro de arriba y el zorro de abajo* [*The Fox From Up Above and the Fox From Down Below*], Arguedas criticized Cortázar and many other "professional," "erudite," and "cosmopolitan" writers. Cortázar accused him of resentment in "Un escritor y su soledad" [A Writer and His Solitude]: "In recent years the prestige of these writers has exacerbated a kind of resentment on the part of the sedentary, which translates into a search—nearly always in vain—for the reasons behind these exiles and an emphatic reaffirmation of staying in situ." This accusation prompted a response from Arguedas (1969) opposing the idea that "the essence of the national is best understood from the high spheres of the supranational." Arguedas distinguishes between those who plan a novel with the honorarium in mind and those who, like him, live to write.

From Cuba, it became clear that Latin America itself was haunted by the specters of divas. The new literature, as was evident in the course of a few years, had distributed prestige and resentment (Donoso, in his novel *The Garden Next Door*, depicts in a very illustrative way the experiences of writers in the market). It was also noted that those who had contributed most to the prestige of the Latin American novel, now well established "worldwide," created their works in contact with the cultures of core countries and quickly developed writers' ideologies shaped by the weight of their acclaim, and even dared to affirm that they were the ones who made "revolutionary literature," as Ambrosio Fornet (1971) put it. The critical perspective regarding the market was more easily observable from Cuba, a country where, following the revolution, the literary market had been eliminated, the publishing industry was in the hands of the state, and not only the payment of royalties but also the idea that supported the very existence of those "rights" was abolished. But for other reasons as well, Ambrosio Fornet's commentary mentioned above began with the phrase: "Convinced that we had nothing new to offer them," which is very illustrative of why Cuba developed a particular aversion to literary output from the continent that did not come from the island. (It should be noted that it also developed quite a dislike for those who did come from Cuba: perhaps therein lies a crucial explanation of the problem of Cuban literature after 1959).

Jean Franco argues that "it was natural in the early sixties to expect Cuba to provide a revolutionary aesthetic" (1977). Indeed, the wait was long: "Waiting for Godot" was *Primera Plana*'s explicit title for an anthology of Cuban short stories (published by Arca in Montevideo in 1967). Where was the revolutionary literature? The best storytellers lived outside Cuba and had broken relations with the government (Guillermo Cabrera Infante and Severo Sarduy), and Lezama Lima was on the fringe of the revolution. The wait for a revolutionary literature in Cuba was almost a nightmare; "a hell of a problem," as Mario Benedetti confessed (in Lavín Cerda). Emmanuel Carballo recounted that President Dorticós had told him that the Cuban authorities also "believed that simply because the revolutionary struggle had triumphed, art and literature would reflect the content and objectives of the revolution. They soon realized that this was nothing more than wishful thinking."

Lisandro Otero also referred to the "natural impatience" to see the revolutionary epic reflected in literature, acknowledging that, upon seeing that this literature had failed to appear, the writers had been pressured:

> I am not going to describe in detail all the subtle or direct ways in which this pressure was exerted. The Revolutionary Government remained completely on the sidelines and continued proclaiming and defending its policy of respect for the creative freedom of artists (1966).

However, years later, he considered this stage and the waiting itself to be over:

> During the first decade of the revolution, we proclaimed that Cuba was fertile ground for the emergence of a new and experimental art in which formal audacity would serve as a vehicle for revolutionary content. That new art was nowhere to be seen. The intellectual became the guardian of aesthetic forms, forgetting the political content (1971).

At the time, *Casa de las Américas*, in its "Editorial," also referred to a sort of mandate that was hanging over Cuban writers: "As the Cuban Revolution is about to celebrate eight years in power, many still wonder: Can we speak of a Cuban literature of the revolution?" The fact is that, as texts appeared that could be considered the "seed" of this new revolutionary literature (such as *Así en la paz como en la guerra*, *Los años duros*, *Condenados de Condado*, to name a few examples of texts that were said to represent the new literature, product of the new society), the internal disputes in the intellectual field eliminated, one by one, the supposed future values of this revolutionary literature. Except for when it was submitted for evaluation by juries in the case of awards, it had virtually no space "outside" the consideration of its own Cuban peers, which made it easier for many intellectual debates to turn into practices of cultural commissariat. If we think of the notion of collective capital, that is, the symbolic capital accumulated over the course of history through the actions of successive generations for certain professions, which according to Bourdieu (1992) makes it possible to measure the degree of autonomy of the field, we will see to what extent the battles within the Cuban field and the successive erasure of achievements ended up annihilating this collective capital. In "Situación actual de la cultura cubana" [Current Situation of Cuban Culture], Benedetti acknowledged, without satisfaction, that it was true that Cuban culture in those first ten years had not produced "the great revolutionary work to which such an exceptional experience and process are entitled," and added: "Distance is undoubtedly needed for ironic writers to emerge, and exile perhaps to make that distance possible." Benedetti realized that these expectations had been detrimental to Cuban literature, while at the same time criticizing the functioning of the publishing industry, which turned the book into a commodity (Lihn and Marín 1970). Some time later, he once again referred to the "great impatience" of all revolutions to see "the artistic products that reflect them blow up," but at that time he shifted the problem to a later occasion, stating: "I believe that what Fidel Castro said in a recent speech is also applicable: 'We're taking it slow because we're in a hurry'" (González Bermejo 1971, 149–55).

Much later, Cuban cultural institutions embarked on a curious revision of the Cuban literary canon to affirm that Cuban revolutionary literature had emerged where "the critics least expected it." The editor of the volume *Literatura cubana (1959–1978)* [Cuban Literature (1959–1978)] mentioned both that it was a collective volume by specialists who had worked "closely with the various directorates of the Ministry of Culture," which sought to "reveal the achievements obtained throughout the revolutionary process in the area of culture," and that *Paradiso* was "an example of pre-revolutionary literature." The best exponents were therefore the documents and speeches of Fidel Castro and Che Guevara. "La historia me absolverá" [History Will Absolve Me], the speech delivered by Fidel and the text of his defense during the trial for the attack on the Moncada Barracks, would have been "the best example of what we will later be able to recognize as literature of the Cuban Revolution." According to the official version, the main texts of the revolution included a range spanning from "the most representative speeches of the leaders to the testimonial texts, with one of the most moving examples being the *Diario del Che en Bolivia* [*The Bolivian Diary of Ernesto Che Guevara*]." The Second Declaration of Havana, on the other hand, was an example of "the highest aesthetic hierarchy, beyond its political efficacy and ideological diaphaneity" (Arias).

The situation of debate in Cuba, along with the fact that other writers from *abroad* claimed the literary laurels for themselves, helped foster a climate of hostility and even resentment toward those who had brought Latin American literature to that maturity so highly praised just a short time earlier. Criticism of the market and the market writer was crucial to the ideological devaluation of the novel as a genre; in an interview Benedetti conducted with Retamar, the latter argued that there had been a narrative boom rather than a poetic one because poetry was less marketable. It is clear that only a discrediting of the genre could make a defense, such as the one Juan Carlos Martini Real attempted, plausible. He argued that, although the novel should still be considered a "modality of mature and reflexive expression in relation to the productive forces of the development of societies," it was affected by a problem of the times because it had leaned toward a "*préciosité*-style formalism," examples of which were *Hopscotch* and *Three Trapped Tigers*. As the use of language, narrative techniques, and "verbalism" became more sophisticated, the distance from the essence of the struggle for emancipation became more pronounced:

> The boom, *One Hundred Years of Solitude*—like modernism in poetry—brought Latin American literature up to date in the Western world. However, in its intricate and lavish content, it already contains or proposes questions and weaknesses that are now decidedly emphasized. . . . The paths of García Márquez—like those of Cortázar, following *One Hundred Years of Solitude* and *Hopscotch*—have now been closed off; without the potential for more exhaustion, they reached their culmination as an aesthetic solution. . . . They made the Latin American narrative phenomenon possible, including the potential to depart from mere indigenism, academicism, or primitive and falsely political naturalism that surrounded the process. Ideologically, they responded to the intellectual who, from the Hilton Hotel, applauded or celebrated the bearded revolutionaries who descended, triumphant, from the Sierra Maestra (1972, 142).

Thus, criticism of the market blended perfectly with the anti-intellectualist climate, which in its clearest and most severe versions was generally supported by writers occupying a secondary or marginal position, revealing that the public opinions of writers not only arise from social demands but also from the symbolic benefits associated with their own logic and the conditions under which they practice their profession. The irruption of a market that bestowed acclaim began leading literature and the intellectual-writer in the opposite direction of the demand for politicization. In addition to aesthetic and ideological arguments, certain writers in particular were the main target of Cuban attacks. The intellectuals aligned with Cuba developed a specific vision in which the novel, the market, and the avant-garde were united, and which served to attack the writers who focused all their attention on personal promotion, narrators who had ceased to fulfill their role. Juan Marinello would speak of narrators of "alienated and alienating ideology" (1971) (and he was particularly critical of Vargas Llosa, whose idea of the writer as a lifelong rebel he found to be of "rampant immorality"), who in "an astute, albeit superficial manner," Fernández Retamar would say (referring to Carlos Fuentes), proposed "the tasks of the right with the language of the left" (1971).

2. Free or Revolutionary?

> This revolution, like Christ, has come to divide "father against son and son against father, mother against daughter and daughter against mother, mother-in-law against daughter-in-law and daughter-in-law against mother-in-law."
>
> Luke 12:53 (cited by Ernesto Cardenal 1972)

> The impostors will be against Cuba. The truly honest and revolutionary intellectuals will understand the justness of our position.
>
> Declaration of the First National Congress of Cuban Education and Culture

The processes of rupture and conflict among intellectuals toward the end of the period were virulent and quite public. The dispute was presented as a confrontation, within the left, between the "usurpers" and the "genuine" inhabitants of that common space from where this revolutionary creed was more or less stridently proclaimed. Drawing this border was, therefore, a highly important operation, the precise surgery that contributed to dividing the hitherto consensual bloc of the Latin American intellectual left. Although the Padilla affair brought to light profound differences, the origin of this divide lay in the disagreement over the definition of the revolutionary intellectual. The rupture of the left-wing intellectual camp did not mean a break with progressivism *per se*, but rather disagreement over the repertoire of themes, attitudes, concepts, and topics that defined it. For the anti-intellectual group, the value attributed to the idea of revolution—which took the Cuban Revolution as an example—resignified and devalued the self-described "progressive" positions that did not recognize the intellectual's obligation to submit to the decisions of the leaders. For the group of intellectuals who opposed it, who were seeking to revive the notion of the intellectual as the critical conscience of society, the submission or subordination of intellectuals to political leaders represented another way of betraying an identity.

The fracture entailed a strong rereading of the immediate past that encompassed all possible objects: works, authors, genres, writers, attitudes, and aesthetics. The public death of the consensus that brought the Latin American family together marked the end of a period within the epoch, the main characteristic of which was the associative ideal of intellectuals. Pierre Bourdieu aptly names and defines the main characteristics of the intellectual debates centered on politics. The anti-intellectualist group can be compared to what Bourdieu terms "responsible intellectuals," those who in the name of their responsibility tend to reduce their thinking to militant, and often anathematizing, views. The group of critical intellectuals is equivalent to what Bourdieu calls "free intellectuals," those who in the name of freedom exhibit a propensity for terrorism and who would gladly transfer into the political arena the wars to the death that are the wars of truth taking place in the intellectual field. And, more interesting still, he refers to the strategies of certain second-tier intellectuals (from the point of view of the criteria in force within the intellectual field), especially the opportunity to take revenge, in the name of popular demands, on intellectuals who had sufficient symbolic capital to claim their autonomy in relation to the powers that be (1984). The description of these two types of intellectuals fits very well with the two camps that were seen as confronting each other in Latin America.

It is important to consider, within the history of Latin American intellectuals of the period, not only the arguments that pitted them against each other, but also the concrete configurations of the intellectual field and the field of alternatives available to writer-intellectuals. In other words, this will enable an analysis of who and why they had the right to speak, where the notion of truth that conferred legitimacy to their discourse came from, and from what institutional spheres it came. The most clearly defined group that engaged in the discussion against Cuba's allies consisted of those who had formed part of its loyal ambassadors and were later grouped around the magazine *Libre*. Concerned about the direction the discussion on the role of the intellectual in the context of the revolution was taking, a group of writers (the most famous, those whose literary works were by then the most widely recognized by the public and their own peers) conceived the project of the magazine in 1970. Even then, the position of these authors was already *anachronic* in terms of the trend of radical politicization; as their first editorial stated, they were motivated by the desire to formulate "revolutionary demands in a critical tone" ("Editorial" 1971).

In *El boom doméstico* [The Domestic Boom], Pilar Donoso recounts two of the most important events she witnessed in early 1971: "The magazine *Libre* was founded and Mario Vargas Llosa changed hairstyles." This statement is interesting insofar as it captures the truth of *Libre*: its firm, solemn, and serious intentions combined with the intimate interweaving of personal relationships among its Latin American members, all writers, all established, almost all of them eminent figures associated with the boom. Hence the importance of the union in defense of the "free" intellectual and their willingness to participate in any debate in which the intellectual's situation was threatened. The reason for grouping around a new magazine, according to one of its founders, was to break with the mentality of the besieged fortress that was attributed to Cuban writers and which, according to the members of the magazine, was "detrimental to their interests" (Goytisolo 1983, 13–14). Such a statement of purpose is typical of the century-long tradition of intellectual ideology. Who decides here what is beneficial and what is harmful to others? There is no doubt that Goytisolo was sincere in declaring that *Libre* intended to reinforce "the position of intellectuals." The problem was that his opponents sought to reinforce the position of something considered more important: the revolution. It is not a question of taking one side or the other; nor even of considering that the defense of the revolution was really based on the arguments of those who claimed to defend it. It is impossible to know what would have become of *Libre*, whose editorial board consisted of many of the intellectuals who had complained to Fidel Castro about Padilla's arrest and self-criticism (Claribel Alegría, Ariel Dorfman, José Donoso, Hans Magnus Enzensberger, Enrique Lihn, Juan Gelman, Teodoro Petkoff, Ángel Rama, Francisco Urondo, Mario Vargas Llosa, Jorge Edwards, Octavio Paz, and Severo Sarduy, among others), if the project had not come up against that case or, even worse, if its most conspicuous members had not been responsible for turning the Padilla episode into "the

Padilla affair" (in fact, the first issue of *Libre*, in 1971, was largely dedicated to the publication of documents on the Padilla affair, and the second proposed a debate on the topic of "freedom and socialism").

We know that it initially sought the approval of Cuban cultural institutions. We know that Vargas Llosa and Cortázar asked for that support at the last meeting of the *Casa de las Américas* Collaboration Committee in early 1971. Thanks to the Padilla affair, certain details that had not been made public until then became known, such as, for example, some of the disagreements that marked that meeting in Havana in which Viñas (1971, 23) objected to "the characteristics of the proposal for the magazine *Libre* that Cortázar and Vargas Llosa were bringing from Europe." In the analysis of *Libre*, what interests us is not so much the set of aesthetic-ideological strategies as the constellation on which the failure of those strategies is based; not so much the way in which the intellectuals of *Libre* define the relationship between politics and culture (in response to the relationship that many Cuban intellectuals had proposed, at least since 1969) as the positioning that determines its rhetoric and the objects it submits for discussion. In short, what is of interest are its weaknesses, if we take into account that the magazine emerged as part of the attempt to theoretically and ideologically support the validity of a notion of the intellectual (the intellectual as critic) that was heavily discredited. Its procedures are those of *justification*, which signals from the outset the rhetoric of its weakness. In the first place, the magazine was published in Paris at a time of strong opposition between Europe and Latin America and when the fact that many Latin American writers had chosen to reside on the old continent was being questioned. In other words, this came at a point when a de facto and ongoing situation—that the most famous writers of the continent were living and writing in Europe—was becoming unacceptable de jure, as can be seen in Viñas's emphasis in rejecting the proposal that Cortázar and Vargas Llosa brought *from Europe*, even before Fidel Castro publicly spoke of living in Europe as a problem. The Latin American essence of *Libre*, published on a "continent in decline," in response to Spanish author Juan Goytisolo's decisive convocation, and with a markedly international list of collaborators, was thus challenged. *Libre* was also the magazine of the Spanish writers of the diaspora or semi-diaspora imposed by Franco's regime: the Goytisolo brothers,

Manuel Vázquez Montalbán, and Jorge Semprún, among others. The participation of Spanish intellectuals served to some degree to legitimize their discourse through the presence of those who were subjected to persecution or censorship in their own country. In any case, it was through this dispute that the Parisian publication's Latin American reference fundamentally operated; it was also Latin American because its conditions of possibility and its failures were determined by the general situation on the continent.

While in any collective publication, the enunciation is problematic in terms of attribution—we cannot forget the disclaimer that clarifies, with variations, that the opinions expressed in the signed texts only reflect those of the author, a warning that is not free of irony within the context of a process of redefinition of intellectual commitment—, in *Libre* that enunciation was even more problematic. Its collaborators were, for the most part, Latin American writers and critics who up to that point had maintained close and friendly ties with Cuba: Cortázar, Vargas Llosa, and Rama had been members of the Collaboration Committee of *Casa de las Américas* until its dissolution in 1971. Other *Libre* collaborators had participated in the ritual "trip to Cuba" to sit on a jury or receive an award from Casa de las Américas. Most of them were anthologized, congratulated, invited, honored by Cuban publications: Italo Calvino, José María Castellet, Adriano González León, Noé Jitrik, Roberto Juarroz, Enrique Lihn, Carlos Monsiváis, Octavio Paz, Rubén Bareiro Saguier, Daniel Moyano, Gabriel García Márquez, José Donoso, Ernesto Cardenal, Claribel Alegría, José Emilio Pacheco, Rodolfo Hinostroza (who also lived in Cuba), Luis Loayza, and the Goytisolo brothers. A few were former friends but already proven adversaries or uncomfortable figures when the publication began: Carlos Fuentes, Jorge Edwards, Teodoro Petkoff, Hans Magnus Enzensberger (mentioned by Padilla in his review as a sort of foreign contact with whom he had had numerous conversations that may have resulted in an essay by the German author against the Cuban Communist Party). And a few members who were no doubt openly irritating for the island's institutions: the Cubans Carlos Franqui (revolutionary journalist, founder of the 26th of July Movement, former director of the newspaper *Revolución*) and Severo Sarduy.

A problematic and complex enunciation, since the reactions to the Padilla case placed certain members of *Libre* on opposite sides. This was the case of Ariel Dorfman and Antonio Skármeta, who left *Libre* after three issues, and of Cortázar, Juan Gelman, and Francisco Urondo, who left before the fourth and last issues. The disappearance of Wilfredo Lam's name in the second issue seems to be due to the fact that Lam never consented to be included, as *Casa de las Américas* reported. The continued presence of Salvador Garmendia and Carlos Droguett, who explicitly held positions opposite to that of the most conspicuous group at *Libre* and who continued to be part of its staff until the end (perhaps because that end was abrupt), is surprising. In response to the schism, *Libre*'s strategy consisted in not reducing its number of collaborators, expanding its staff with each defection, so that the visual mass of the nomenclature produced an impression of fullness identical to the beginning or greater (the magazine began by displaying some fifty signatures and ended up adding ten to the initial ones). Susan Sontag, Jean Genet, Jean-Paul Sartre fulfilled the decorative role of being reported on in several installments, but even so they had a more relevant presence than some of the other names listed there. It is hardly the list of names that allows us to determine the *we* that held *Libre* together. (Moreover, as the magazine is a relatively aborted project, any analysis of their eventual participation would be purely counterfactual.) The safest approach would be to analyze, in each issue, the responsibility of the rotating editorial board and to define this *we*—never refuted by *Libre*—as the one attributed to the Cuban side, in which Carlos Fuentes, Juan Goytisolo, and Vargas Llosa played a fundamental role.

On what was the authority of the members of *Libre* based? To begin with, they formed an active part of the constitution of the Latin American family. Second, they were famous and had gained prestige with their works. They were *acclaimed* by critics, the market, and the public. It was therefore logical that they would seek to defend their professional autonomy politically (since at the time politics was the focal point around which all discourse orbited). *Libre* thus emerged at the intersection of a fortuitous historical situation (the Padilla affair); a strong institutional factor; the market (and its subsequent exhaustion for the new Latin American literary generations); and the strangeness and loss of legitimacy that its imprint gave to its texts. Defending the validity of their criteria as proven and recognized by the public, the intellectuals of *Libre* postulated their identity as critical intellectuals and reclaimed the agency that had been attributed to them for their works. They thus opposed the severe anti-intellectualism that emanated from the intellectuals of the revolution themselves and that only accepted the figure of the intellectual if it accepted a subordinate role with respect to government institutions and the leadership of the revolution. It was precisely in rejecting this state of affairs that *Libre* made its *petitio principii* in the editorial of the first issue, declaring itself against those "sectors whose idea of the writer's commitment always contains something of a military, if not bureaucratic, nature." The emphasis on the defense of the "freedom of criticism and creation" by the acclaimed writers, came to be considered by their opponents as a perfect example of the ideology of the uncompromising, individualistic, and fatally bourgeois writer, disengaged from the requirements of the revolution. At the same time, most of the established writers tended to think of their place in the market in terms of sociopolitical legitimacy. Defending market approval as society's plebiscitary approval of their works was also a way of challenging the hegemony of the Cuban Revolution's cultural policy guidelines, in which the state replaced the market, including the literary market.

Logically, *Libre* did not defend the market for the market's sake, because although it was partly due to that institution that it had come into being, that was not enough to antagonize the Cuban state: to the revolution/market opposition that neutralized them, *Libre* offered the comparison between the "ideal socialist state" and the "real socialist state," embodied by Fidel Castro and the countries of the Soviet orbit in general. Because if there was something pragmatic or not entirely suicidal in *Libre*'s venture, it was its alliance—albeit symbolic—with Chile under the Popular Unity party, without whose existence the hegemony of the "Cuban approach" could not have been discussed in even strictly cultural terms. The Allende government inaugurated a new political model for the transition to socialism that eliminated the need for the armed vanguard. In Peru as well, the experience of Velasco Alvarado, defended in *Libre* by Carlos Delgado and Héctor Béjar, former guerrilla commander of the Movement of the Revolutionary Left (MIR, for its acronym in Spanish), seemed to challenge the undisputed Cuban hegemony in political matters, although, of course, neither of these experiences was on par with the Cuban Revolution. With respect to the men of action, a figure that was essential during this period when conceiving of a cultural publication in Latin America, *Libre* relied mainly on the experiences and guidelines of Pompeyo Márquez and Teodoro Petkoff, founders of the Movement Toward Socialism (MAS, for its acronym in Spanish) in Venezuela. This incorporation allowed them to establish an analogical view of historical processes in socialist states whose central notion was that of Stalinism, conceived as the specter that threatened any revolution.

The confrontation between the two sectors of intellectuals can also be analyzed as the result of a complex distribution of cultural capital, which in turn was tied to the question of geographical capitals. The issue, which had already been outlined in the discussion between Arguedas and Cortázar, became even more polemical. Support for Cuba, with some exceptions, was mainly expressed by writers who lived on the Latin American continent, while the intellectuals who criticized the Cuban Revolution had settled abroad: almost all of them lived in Europe, and from there they responded to the commitments of a market that was not entirely unfavorable to them. To see and criticize this capital in the possession of intellectuals was easier for those who possessed less of it and who were more violently anti-intellectualist, denouncing the "Midases who live off literature because they turn everything they write into dollars" (Romualdo 1967, 75). These Midases were the least inclined to consider the situation in this light and therefore tended to defend not so much the market as the possibilities of circulation it offered to their works, which they saw as conveying a worthy message. Anti-intellectualism was not only the result of free *choice* but also of *placement*. As Pierre Bourdieu (1992) explains, the foot soldiers of the intellectual world always produce a disenchanted image of it; for the lesser intellectuals, no one is great. They are the best situated to discover contradictions and weaknesses: the dominated regions of the field of cultural production are very often inhabited by a sort of rampant anti-intellectualism.

The result of the breakdown of the international leftist intellectual bloc was a new, emphatically negative vision of Europe, centered on the notion of the decline of an old world, withdrawn into its old and faded glories, incapable of understanding the effervescence of the new continent and its revolutionary transformation. It also implied the end of the illusion that the left could maintain the avant-garde canon intact. Rubén Darío, whose figure had been venerated and celebrated on his centenary at the initiative of many intellectuals who had gathered in Cuba in 1967, was soon after subjected to the ups and downs of this rereading and became an involuntary victim of the repudiations that followed. An example of this can be found in the words of Nicolás Guillén:

> Unamuno, who could not stand modernism and vigorously rejected whatever cosmopolitanism, emptiness, and external brightness there was in it, always had certain reservations about its top "hierarch" . . . . Unamuno wrote this eighty-two years ago, but it is still valid today and seems to continue vibrating like an arrow in certain "cerebral" brains of our time, as convoluted now as they were then.

The weakness of the new magazine was ostensible and self-evident. To begin with, it assumed a war between two types of alliances in the intellectual field, already asymmetrical in terms of their power: a strong alliance with a state cultural policy, against a weak alliance of intellectual positions with no other support than their own prestige and individually weakened by the personal choices of each member of the group. Another weakness of *Libre* was its financing, a weakness acknowledged in the justificatory tone of a footnote in the editorial of the first issue, where it was made clear that the economic support provided by Albina de Boisrouvray (granddaughter of Patiño, the Bolivian king of tin) "does not imply any kind of commitment on the part of the publication and was accepted in view of the fact that A. de B., also a contributor to magazines and weeklies such as *Il Manifesto, Le Nouvel Observateur, Politique-Hebdo*, and *J'Accuse*, shares *Libre*'s aims."

This defined a rare conjunction of modernity and anachronism since the modernizing pretension of *Libre* (a magazine of writers apprised of the most recent theoretical and literary novelties, with a rotating editorship and therefore a non-hierarchical structure of enunciation) was set against the archaism of the private patronage that made it possible. The clarification of those in charge of *Libre*, backed by Pilar Donoso's description of the proven progressivism of the financier, who lent "help to this group that espoused ideas opposed to those of her family," did not convince the Cuban polemicists, for whom Boisrouvray would never cease to be a member of a "family enriched with the sweat and blood of Bolivian workers and peasants" (Marinello 1971, 214–51). It is revealing how precisely in the midst of the controversy over the financing of *Libre*, *Casa de las Américas*, in issue no. 65–66, March–June 1971, gives an account of the end of the Argentine magazine *Sur*, acknowledging Victoria Ocampo, its director and patron, who, in spite of having waged a clear and well-defined campaign against the Cuban Revolution, "instead of devoting her ample wealth to perfumes, she devoted it (in part) to ensuring that Argentina had a magazine and, later, an up-to-date publishing house." All reasons for which "it would be unfair to deny what Latin America owes her."

On the other hand, Juan Goytisolo's statement that the magazine's purpose was to lend "critical support" to the Cuban Revolution is hard to sustain (the idea of including Cabrera Infante in the magazine was no longer a sign of confrontation, but rather an outright declaration of war), especially if one takes into account another of *Libre*'s weaknesses, perhaps the most notable: filiation. Given its precursor, *Libre* remained associated with its image as the offspring or appendix of *Mundo Nuevo* (although there were other less problematic and controversial ones, such as the magazine *Margen*, launched in 1967 and warmly welcomed by *Casa de las Américas*). This precedent was both "endorsed" by its opponents and "recognized" by some of its members. From Cuba, the efforts to delegitimize *Libre*'s voice were based primarily on the lineage that linked the new publication with the one directed until 1968 by Rodríguez Monegal. "Mundonovism" was, therefore, one of the persistent justifications to attack *Libre*'s ideological authority. Fernández Retamar in "Calibán" recalls: "Those writers already had a suitable organ; the magazine *Mundo Nuevo*, financed by the CIA. That publication, that brought together those men and others very similar to them—such as Guillermo Cabrera Infante and Juan Goytisolo—, is soon to be replaced by another that appears to have the same team, plus a few additions: the magazine *Libre*" (264). Or, in "Ellos escogieron la libertad" [They Chose Freedom]: "Even the most pessimistic expected something better from this melancholic birth, which is more like *Mundo Nuevo* than *Mundo Nuevo* itself... It is sad to see that caution and hypocrisy have prevailed over gratitude and that the name of its putative father, E. R. Monegal, does not appear in the list of *Libre*'s collaborators. It is true, however, that the firm pillars of *Mundo Nuevo*, Juan Goytisolo, Carlos Fuentes, and Severo Sarduy, are present, ensuring continuity."

Nonetheless, the immediate filiation between *Mundo Nuevo* and *Libre* was problematic. Although the chronological continuity between the two publications was symptomatic (the final issue of *Mundo Nuevo* was dated March–April 1971; the first issue of *Libre*, September–October–November of the same year), the former was far from being the expression of "the best Spanish-speaking writers," as its alleged offspring claimed to be, and its lack of prestige was already indisputable. It could be said, following Emir Rodríguez Monegal's resignation as its director, that the next issue of *Mundo Nuevo*, in its affirmation of a new stage in which ideas will be more important than people, delivers a declaration of principles that does not succeed in hiding the refusal of the "big names" to collaborate with the publication. Other reasons that could justify a certain hiatus between the two magazines were the presence in *Libre* of Julio Cortázar (in the first three issues, with his defection in the last), who had flatly refused to collaborate with *Mundo Nuevo*, and that of Ángel Rama, who was the main organizer of the campaign against that magazine, from the pages of *Marcha*, and whose articles denouncing the CIA financing of *Mundo Nuevo* were regularly reproduced and lauded by *Casa de las Américas*. Parisian, however, like *Mundo Nuevo*, with the participation of some the same "mainstays,"[46]

---

46 The spectral advice of Monegal himself, the most emblematic absent presence of the magazine in all of its strategic exclusion, once again reveals not only the limits of the sayable but also the question of who is or is not authorized to speak. Monegal reveals how close he is to *Libre*: "I tell him (Goytisolo) that the magazine still seems shapeless to me, as if it were an accumulation of texts, with no greater plan or meaning. The signatures, even the most illustrious ones, and there are some, are mired in an overall vagueness. Perhaps the fact that each issue is directed by a different team contributes to this haziness . . . . Later, at a cocktail party at the Chilean embassy, I speak with Plinio Apuleyo Mendoza, a Colombian writer, a close friend of García Márquez, and the secretary of *Libre*, about the magazine's problems. Apart from the Cuban boycott, exacerbated by the capitalist origins of the funds, *Libre* also has the

Libre shared deep affinities with the former, especially with respect to its conception of literature and would have endorsed, had the opportunity presented itself, these statements by Monegal (1966b, 20): "We must abandon the very old-fashioned, apocalyptic idea of a disjunction between words and actions. A writer's actions are in his words. Those are his only true actions. In some parts of Latin America, these things have not yet become clear."

The *Mundo Nuevo* experience helped those involved in *Libre* to understand that its chances of survival were tied to the sympathy that the project could elicit in Cuba. But the efforts of Vargas Llosa and Cortázar in that sense were in vain. Defensive strategies were already at play in the discussion over what to name the publication; the title had to be vague but open to connotations and, nevertheless, polemical. *Blanco* was apparently the initial suggestion, but it was rejected out of fear that it might be seen as having racist overtones. Limiting the semiosis of the word itself on a terrain that was particularly conducive to the ideological interdiction of language was typical of the period, which saw the endless codification of rhetorical strategies considered safe in speeches designed to achieve public resonance. As far as the intellectual historian is concerned, the best documents have been lost: far more information and substance would be gained through knowledge of the elusive private discourse, safeguarded by peers who have unanimously become the guardians of *correct* revolutionary discourse in a climate governed by mutual suspicion and the fear of the infiltration of "the bourgeois" into the language, which would only finally disappear from words when the long-awaited "new man" became flesh and blood. The conviction that one belonged only to the uncomfortable group of "transitional intellectuals" made vigilance more acute. Any false step would reveal

---

issue of its very high price. For a magazine that seeks to be read by the young revolutionaries of Latin America, its cost (two dollars for a single issue) is prohibitive. We discussed the possibilities of lowering it. The most practical solution would be to reduce the number of pages in each issue, which would not be difficult because they publish a lot of filler material. Another solution would be to print it somewhere cheaper than France. Local booksellers have told me that the second issue (the third one has not arrived yet) has hardly sold." "Nuevo Diario de Caracas," *Zona Franca*.

the counterrevolutionary vestiges of their bourgeois origins. If, on the one hand, words—exposed to the realization of their ineffectiveness in the face of other forms of action—lost value, paradoxically they did not lose their importance, evidenced in the excessive control with which they were dispensed. For if they could not compete in effectiveness with "pure action," they would instead be one of the battle horses for the counterrevolution. The magazine's definitive name, however, was no more palatable. *Casa de las Américas* asked itself, judiciously: *Libre* (free "of what? of whom?"). And in the only major commentary dedicated to the magazine once it was published (*Casa de las Américas*'s strategy was to avoid referring to it directly), the question of the name was key:

> Such a beautiful term, it does not cease to be widely manipulated, and is, above all, the battle horse of capitalist ideologues. . . . It would be hard to find a more revealing name than this, the defenders of intellectual free enterprise who, comfortably situated in the free world, would gather to give lessons on revolution to the poor underdeveloped peoples ("Ellos escogieron la libertad" 1971).

Did the founders of *Libre* have Sartre's phrase in mind—"the freedom of writing implies the freedom of the citizen. One does not write for slaves. The art of prose is bound up with the only regime in which prose has meaning, democracy" (1949)—and were they planning to take advantage of it in relation to their positions on Cuba? If they were counting on the ideological support of a figure like Sartre (who joined the staff in the last issue), their gamble was futile. The lengthy report on Sartre (published in the fourth issue) proved it. If *Libre* succeeded in obtaining a denunciation of the Soviet system, it was strongly qualified by the statement that the opposing intellectuals of the East were liberals rather than true democrats and that, moreover, they were more interested in obtaining the freedom to write what they wanted than in promoting the development of a revolutionary process. To which Sartre added: "To write only what one wants, without taking into account what is going on, is bourgeois." And, although Sartre did not agree to offer a "libertarian" judgment on Cuba (he argued that he was too distant from the events), he gave the impression that the Padilla affair simply expressed greater control over culture than before. The image that Sartre gave to those associated with *Libre* was categorical when he affirmed that intellectuals could do "something more useful than writing novels or poems" and that "the success of the revolution counted above all else." Regarding Chile, *Libre*'s proposed counter-state, Sartre expressed skepticism regarding the possibility of achieving socialism through legal means: "There can be no revolution without revolution, that is, without violence."

The confrontation was a complex question of capitals: Paris versus Havana. Or a play of mirrors to find the object "Latin America." It was a matter of rehashing cultural heritage and traditions: if Latin American adversaries lived in Europe, Europe became an "other" to Cuba. The *Latino-Parisians* reflected in the Cuban mirror. And a new refraction of the object: the mirror of the geographical location that from that point on determines the gaze; two synecdoches for "Latin America." It will be revolutionary to live where one was born and counterrevolutionary to prefer the European Olympus. In the case of *Libre*, the force of this apothegm determined a tactical decision: its editor in chief, given his geographical location, had to counteract the uprootedness of the other figures. The task fell to the Colombian Plinio Apuleyo Mendoza, on the recommendation of García Márquez. It was also a question of the confrontation of cultural capital with political or revolutionary capital. It was the possession of good cultural capital that allowed writers the "freedom" they claimed and facilitated the formation of specific ideologies of exclusive circulation within the group of well-known writers (both through the mechanism of prizes and the market). One of the main components of this literary ideology consisted in attributing a specific critical power to *good* literature. On the other side was the possession of political or revolutionary (or even *military*) capital that could only be acquired by fighting in the war, since, as Nicolás Guillén (1971) said, "is someone who has not heard the whistle of lead or smelled the smoke of rifles really in a position to punish or forgive, that is, to judge?" In its first editorial *Libre* proclaimed the intrinsic ideological legitimacy of its cultural capital:

> A simple reading of this first issue of *Libre* can be more informative than any reasoned statement of intent: when a magazine brings together writers *such as the authors of these articles* and those who

> will collaborate in future issues, its objective cannot lend itself to misunderstandings or hasty interpretations.

For this reason, it eliminated the ties between politics and literature (so as not to redouble the political aspect already implicit in the latter) in each published article and juxtaposed the two topics by contiguity. In short: a *Libre* writer would preferably discuss literature, as seen in the interviews with Borges, García Márquez, and Donoso. This type of discourse produced a style of reporting that was very different from that of other more radical publications, not only Cuban, in which the definition of the revolutionary intellectual was determined according to other criteria. On the other hand, to talk about politics *stricto sensu* there were the politicians: Héctor Béjar, Pompeyo Márquez, and Carlos Delgado addressed questions of Marxist and revolutionary theory and the political struggle in their respective countries. The strength of *Libre*'s writers was, even for their adversaries, literature itself. The dispute between the two intellectual groups was defined politically along the lines of the analysis of the Cuban situation, but in literary terms it was presented as a dispute over the legitimacy of the literary production associated with one or the other. This conflict was a strength rather than a weakness for *Libre* and thus represented a difficulty for Cuba of assuming, without initially denying, the hegemony in terms of the literary quality of the authors or of denying it with a certain argumentative deficiency. Ultimately, it was always possible to claim, on the one hand, that one group possessed *literature* and, the other, *revolution*.

In stating its purposes, *Libre* had declared that it hoped to be a springboard for the *best* Spanish-speaking writers and the implementation of a "revolutionary" endeavor on all the levels that are *fundamentally accessible to the word*. It was precisely this pretension of bringing together the best writers that brought Benedetti into the discussion, and in an interview with González Bermejo he stated:

> I have also lived in Europe, and I have seen that the authors of the boom are practically presented as second-tier authors: their books appear in the middle of summer, when neither the public's attention nor the critics are at their best, and furthermore the promotion given to these works is frankly inferior to that of European authors.

> So, where does the boom take place? In Latin America, where this second- or third-rate European promotion, based on little more than provincial criteria, becomes a major success.

The very notion of the validity of cultural capital was called into question: anti-intellectualism placed the focus on the means required for the acquisition of the cultural expertise that characterized intellectuals and concluded that they were accessible to very few. Culture as such was conceived of (and, as a good, *possessed*) as an unacceptable privilege within the context of a society in which the effort of many sectors contrasted with the wasteful and superfluous quality attributed to art. The self-reflexivity regarding its own condition that characterized anti-intellectualism, in addition to the perceived cutting of the ties of representativity with respect to the underprivileged classes, made the intellectual's possession of symbolic capital (and in some cases, also pecuniary capital, whether or not derived from the former) visible to the intellectual.

Once the belief that intellectuals were inherently productive critics had been partially destroyed, it was assumed that they possessed a form of capital that, unlike other types of capital, could not be expropriated. The differential quality of this capital, or rather, its novel view of culture as capital (along with the practices and skills associated with it) problematized the class attribution of the intellectual. Anti-intellectualism posited that, like all accumulation in the capitalist world, this too should be seen as generated exclusively and fatally through inequality. Knowledge, stemming from an education that its bourgeois condition assured the intellectual, became a pure negative difference. This symbolic *surplus value* made the intellectual suspicious of themselves, thinking that they were suspect in the eyes of others. In each intellectual resided part of the sacrifice of their people. In the first conference of the Latin American Solidarity Organization, it was put in the following way: "Intellectuals cannot set out to resolve this situation—of misery and exploitation—on a personal or sectoral basis, but rather in relation to the people as a whole, through whose sacrifice, whether they know it or not, they have been educated."

On the other hand, efforts to weaken the notion of quality that those of *Libre* claimed for their literature were made in theoretical, political, ethical, and even scientific terms. In his closing speech at the

First Congress on Education and Culture, Fidel marked the boundaries: on one side, the revolutionary writers, on the other, those who "from Paris look down on them because they see them as apprentices, as poor and unhappy people who do not enjoy international fame" (Castro 1983d [1962]). Two members of *Libre* were spared Castro's insults. Carlos Droguett (1971a; 1971–72), who had declared that Cuba was the true poetic art for writers, establishing distances with *Libre*'s clearest line, and Salvador Garmendia, who agreed with the anti-intellectualist positions expressed by the Cuban line: "If artists are not capable of breathing anything but the air of bourgeois liberalism, then artists and writers will be useless pawns in a revolutionary process."

Several issues of *Casa de las Américas* directly and indirectly polemicized with *Libre*. Logically, the most interesting attempts to discredit the adversary were not those that resorted to invective or insult, but those that sought to strip the *Libre* writers of the laurels that allowed them to confront the state and Cuban cultural institutions. The right to criticism was then doubly disputed, multiplied by the rejection of the legitimacy of the literary criticism of *Libre* writers, an area frequented by Vargas Llosa, Carlos Fuentes, Goytisolo, and Cortázar, and which had not been disputed previously.[47] Analyzing several of the texts by Vargas Llosa (his reading of *Tirant lo Blanc*, in particular), critic Carlos Rincón, in *Casa de las Américas*, raised a legal question, the *quid juris*, in response to the criticism of writers:

> With what right, from what theoretical point of view does Vargas Llosa speak, what credentials does he have to back his word on what is nothing more than an operation to define, using his own bourgeois ideological criteria, the whole of Latin American literary production (Rincón 1971, 39–59) . . .

47 "It seems that *Amaru* is going to make it a healthy tradition to include in each of its issues a valuable critique by the Peruvian novelist of one of the most notable novels currently being published." "Artes y ciencias" 1968, 154.

to end up denying any right to writers (within the context, of course, of the existence of a clear political discussion) to postulate a truth about their works and those of others.

The literature that had been so highly praised in the early sixties was then devalued through ideological-political disagreements, an argument that was used to bury—like funeral rites of the past—all the production from Carpentier to García Márquez, who at one point was presented as the best writer in the Spanish language, a sort of Colombian Cervantes. The interesting thing about these deliberate mirages is what they acknowledge regarding the position of the other gaze, even more than what they express through their own gaze. In this case, the dispute to see who is more modern that was taken on by "revolutionary" intellectuals played with the recognition of the conception that the "critics" had of themselves. Both the aesthetic and political discussions were carried out, in their most interesting version, in theoretical terms. In *A Contribution to the Critique of Political Economy*, the Marxist category of use was revealed as a theoretical weapon capable of confronting the concept of "quality" literature held by those of *Libre* and the possibilities of proposing an instrumental-functional vision in order to legitimize revolutionary culture. On the other hand, implicitly resorting to the analogy (a resource that will be rejected as anachronistic when proposed by *Libre*) between two historical moments (1920s Russia and the Cuba of the time) and two political leaders (Fidel Castro-Lenin), Adolfo Sánchez Vázquez (1972, 14–19) recalls that, while

> for the most audacious artists of the time the fundamental task was to revolutionize art, for Lenin the first thing was to revolutionize the social and cultural conditions that, one day, would make a true revolution in art possible. . . . As a revolutionary political leader in the concrete historical circumstances of a backward country that in the midst of unprecedented difficulties is building a new society, Lenin declares he is in favor of art that, at that moment, is more useful to the revolution: art with direct ideological content, even if it is linked to more traditional forms and means of expression.

It is true that Sánchez Vázquez warned that Lenin's aesthetic tastes could not be elevated to the condition of normative principles, though *Casa de las Américas* did not invalidate his article, which could bring Castro and Lenin closer, even with their flaws.

For his part, from the pages of *Libre*, Goytisolo attempted to elaborate a theory that assimilated "intertextuality" to "commitment," close, in some respects to Cortázar's concept of "revolution in literature." Meanwhile, Vargas Llosa, in his literary statements and essays (particularly *García Márquez: Historia de un deicidio* [García Márquez: Story of a Deicide], fragments of which were published in *Libre*) sought to phylogenetically discover the irrational components (i.e., neither deliberate nor controlled) of artistic creation, likening the writer to a rebellious god. From this he derived a poetics of intertextuality (Sarduy, Donoso, Goytisolo); a defense of thematic indetermination; the defense of the specific revolutionary character of art and the idea that the transformations in the literary system were homologous to the transformations in the social system (Cortázar), basically as the repudiation of all programmatization of social realism, of content-driven literature, and of the revolutionary intention defined by the cultural institutions of the state and against any poetics that could be associated with Zdhanovism.

Libre's anthology of Peruvian poetry was preceded by the criterion that had guided the selection: they were texts whose "formal rigor, cosmopolitanism" distanced them from "the unbridled, painful, Stalinist aesthetics" (Hinostroza 1971–72). *Libre*'s choices in theoretical and critical matters (the *Tel Quel* group and Barthes, in particular) were criticized as false revolutionary pretensions of an idealistic and fetishized theoretical corpus. In fact, it was precisely because those loyal to *Libre* relied on them that the "revolutionaries" rejected them as a distortion of reality. For *Libre*, however, it was a matter of defending a single essential, non-negotiable condition of literature, which meant that the social and aesthetic function of art could only be achieved in absolute autonomy from the power of the state. It was there that the aesthetic-ideological and political criteria of *Libre* were defined. Literature would be autonomous—that is, it would establish its own laws—and anti-mimetic. It would thus be intrinsically subversive in its own right, and the writer, as a perpetual *hors-la-loi*, would be the critical conscience of society.

From Cuba, "*libre*" literature was seen as a new tactic of subjugation invented by imperialism for the purposes of colonization: literature was a monster that had to be controlled. For *Libre*, it was literature and not the state that represented the public spirit. The neutralization of its critical power leads to the death of that spirit, *Libre* replied, citing Marx. They no longer have politics there, only repression, the ground zero of all politics: that was the gist of Fernando Claudín's reply (1971–72, 6). Claudín argues, citing Marx, that censorship kills the public spirit. In reality, the "free" and the "state" camps both defined themselves in relation to the same theoretical body (Marxism) but choosing certain blocks of quotations strategically, claiming for themselves the true interpretation and practice that separated the texts. It was common to find the voices of Antonio Gramsci, Rosa Luxemburg, Lenin, and Marx arguing with each other from different battlefronts.

With the two mirrors facing each other, competing to reflect Latin American reality instead of forming a single image, they sought to shatter that of the enemy. Critics and authors knew and cited the canonical texts and could hardly take seriously the fierce opposition between the Mukarovskians and the Lotmanians of the "revolutionaries," or the Barthesianism and Telquelism of the *Libre* group. It should also be noted that the theorizing bias was a general feature of the second stage of this epoch, and therefore not restricted to this episode of intellectual debate.

In this theoretical battle, *Libre* had to relinquish what had been one of its most risky gambles: the legitimate legacy of Ernesto Guevara, several of whose unpublished texts *Libre* published in its first issue, compiled and presented by Carlos Franqui with the explicit intention of highlighting Che's "significant warnings" about "the dangers of sectarianism and the abuses of authority." The mere pretension of disputing that legacy with Cuba revealed the high regard that the writers of *Libre* had of themselves and their power to dispute a succession with a state.

Given its weak position vis-à-vis its adversaries, the four issues of *Libre* were in fact a process of retreat or "deflection" of discourse, attempts to grasp key questions regarding the definition of the intellectual, politics, and the relationship between literature and the state. The first issue (under Juan Goytisolo's direction) opened with a dossier on "the Padilla affair." The last one (directed by Vargas Llosa) closed with a sincere expression of support for reconciliation with Cuba. The difference is not the reference but the tone, the physical space given to the topic (many pages in the first issue; a few in the second; none in the third; in the fourth, only Yurkiévich's final column) and, more importantly, to defeat. *Libre* came along too late to understand an essential aspect of the moment in which it was intended to intervene, something that Haroldo Conti (1971) knew well: that, at times, silence was a great advantage. The second issue (edited by Jorge Semprún) engaged collective enunciation in the design of a survey on the topic of "Freedom and Socialism," attempting to open a debate that would leave behind the "anecdotal" aspects of the Padilla affair and focus on the relationship between culture and society, the role of the intellectual, and the scope of the concept of creative and critical freedom, where the position taken is provided in the statement preceding each question, such as the one that preceded question "b": "Marxism-Leninism recognizes the advisability of criticism and debate as a means of overcoming the contradictions that arise in a socialist society. How far can the freedom of criticism extend? Do existing institutions offer valid means for this to take place?" The introduction to the next question of the survey stated: "The bureaucracy's own repressive tendencies tend to come into conflict with the intellectual sectors, whose education and level of culture make them more sensitive to the problems of socialist democratization."

All of the answers relied heavily on Marxist theory and the effort to define the relationship between writers and the public in political terms was notorious. A new and highly original argument defined the freedom of creation as a response to a general social demand, which exceeded the circle of authors. Thus, the castration of the writer, it was argued, was equivalent to the castration of the reader. The only one to reject the survey's terms and assertions was Salvador Garmendia.

Another deliberate way of talking about Cuba was the reading of Norberto Fuentes's texts *Cazabandido* (which, owing to the objections received, had to be published in Uruguay) and *Condenados de Condado* (Casa de las Américas Prize 1968) reviewed by Julio Ortega (1971–72, 147). The main purpose of reviewing them was to dispute the (post-1968) Cuban interpretation, which accused the texts and their author of being anti-revolutionary. In contrast, for the *Libre* reviewer, those texts attested to "the socialist affiliation of the author and, more than that, his personal and active intervention in the process of the revolution itself." It is worth mentioning that *Marcha* also sought to defend Fuentes and consequently embarked on a polemic (without casualties) with the Cuban interpretations. Jorge Ruffinelli, in charge of the weekly's literary section, welcomed the appearance of *Cazabandido* (the name of the Cuban military operation that defeated the counterrevolutionaries in the Escambray and the title of the book by Norberto Fuentes, who had covered that military campaign as a journalist and in which he revisited the original material from *Condenados de Condado*). If in 1968 the objections against *Condenados de Condado* had already been significant, it goes without saying that this time the new book (and the same defects) once again became the center of debate. Fuentes was reproached for not clearly taking the side of the revolutionaries in his texts on the fight against the Escambray mercenaries. Later this reproach would become even more serious when voiced by Armando Quesada, editor of *El Caimán Barbudo*, who regarding Padilla's self-criticism described it as "a book that harms the interests of the armed forces in power since the attack on the Moncada that brought this revolution to triumph." Ruffinelli had praised the presence of a new sparse and subtle narrative language that reflected the complexity of human motivations in an "objective" and anti-idealistic way (1970, 29). González Bermejo (1970, 30–31) found in this praise the key to failure and argued that in the Escambray there had been good guys and bad guys, so it was ideologically unacceptable to treat both in the same way. In attempting to escape pamphleteering, Fuentes fell into ideological indifference. Ruffinelli, for his part, argued that it was impossible to solve the problem of writers and literature in discussions of that type, much less through canonizations such as the one sought by socialist realism.

There was not much more support for *Libre*. The last two issues did not seek politics out to the same degree and sought them out elsewhere. An interesting response or initiative was the inclusion of a dossier dedicated to the topic of "women's liberation," an oblique mirror image of *Casa de las Américas*' homage to women.[48] *Libre* prepared a questionnaire tying the theme of women to the critique of socialist states. The Cuban perspective of exalting revolutionary women as exceptional

48 Dedicated in part to "Women," with articles by René Depestre, Isabel Larguía, John Dumoulin, Ana Ramos, Margaret Randall, and Julio Huasi, no. 66–67 (March–June 1971): 35–112.

beings was theoretically undermined by the more radical positions of the feminist movement (Rosana Rossanda and Susan Sontag, among others). Rossanda stated that in socialist countries, "except in material terms—and even then—the situation of women and the family has changed very little. . . . To conclude from this that socialism does not offer a solution to the problem seems to me to be absolutely abusive since it is tantamount to admitting that socialism would be what it is in those countries." Susan Sontag, for her part, referred to the fact that "women will be emancipated only through a general revolution that will profoundly change consciences and upset the basic structures of society." That revolution must reject "the ideology of unlimited economic development" that is "shared with equal enthusiasm by the countries belonging to the capitalist bloc and those belonging to the socialist camp," and that "it must challenge and remake the traditional, fundamentally authoritarian moral habits common to both capitalist and communist countries. It is a fact that none of the countries that tend to act in accordance with the Marxist legacy have radically reconsidered the problem of the status of women."

In a certain sense, *Libre* sought to approach politics from the point of view of the exhaustion of institutions, making a politics conceived in class terms no longer possible. That is why it paid particular attention to the emergence of what have been called "new social subjects" (certainly also because it was edited in Paris) with their own logics of antagonism and combat: women, Black writers, and gay writers were present in *Libre*, perhaps not with the strength they later achieved to question the hegemony of globalizing theories, but certainly enough to mark their presence. It is in this sense that its need to broadly redefine the idea of emancipation, "not only political and economic but also artistic, moral, religious, sexual," should be read.

Perhaps *Libre* was not aware of the support that the Cuban positions generated outside the island. The massive support of many writers and artists for the Castro revolution no doubt unsettled the publication and determined its short life. The declarations of support for Cuba and repudiation toward *Libre* are innumerable and in the majority, at least in the public discourse.

The story ended with Cuba's victory over *Libre*; a triumph that broke the ties within the very group that organized and maintained the publication. The unexpected last issue (unexpected because nothing in that issue indicated that it was the last) contained the chronicle of a press conference held in Paris by Cuban cultural and intellectual authorities. The tone was intended to be neutral, objective, stripped down: the language of the reporter disappeared behind the direct style used, devoid of quotation marks or any indication of quotes or otherness. For example: "At the front of the auditorium stand Juan Marinello, José Antonio Portuondo, Cintio Vitier, Guillermo Castañeda . . . According to the answers, formulated in a frank and direct way, the revolution does not privilege any artistic form, it does not pretend to impose formulas. . . . There is no official aesthetics regarded as imperative dogma. . . . The revolution does not demand an exclusively militant art but, above all, expressions of a high artistic level. . . . The intention is not only to raise the level of cultural production, but also to extend it to all people" (Yurkiévich 1972, 140).

The reporter added a minimum of commentary to conclude: "I believe we should consider what has been expressed at this conference as steadfastness and commitment by the Cuban Revolution to its intellectuals and artists. The relationship with Latin Americans in exile remains to be clarified. I vote for the total reestablishment of a mutually respectful dialogue, for a move from invective to analysis, from enervation to constructive criticism, coinciding in principles and tolerant with respect to possible divergences in practices" (142). Apparently, the question of the Latin American exiles would remain without clarification, and dialogue would not be possible, at least not in *Libre*. That was the last page of its last issue.

It was evidently easier for intellectuals to closely align themselves with a state than to trust in their own less solid ties to obstruct individual paths. It is paradoxical that Goytisolo (1983) would later judge the colleagues who abandoned the endeavor and reconciled with Cuba in terms that were curiously similar to those of the accusations received: "Comfortably installed in the bourgeois democracies, the standard-bearers of the supposed revolutionary cause . . . celebrated or covered up with their complicity each of its oppressive measures, even the most aberrant." And he also disqualified his former adversaries with the same arguments that were used against *Libre*:

> As we would later discover to our surprise, the followers of the official Cuban line, who stigmatized the inconsistency and frivolity of the violet liberals, would be very careful not to analyze, in accordance with Marxist doctrine and as a matter of basic honesty, their own social relations and practices, their real and concrete way of life: the fact, for instance, that they preferred a US scholarship or a professorial course in California to a prolonged stay without prerogatives of any kind in that political laboratory, where their dreams of a harvest without empires or slaves, nourished at the expense of the labor of others, ran the risk of dissipating. The experience of those months with *Libre* thus revealed to me that the high degree of artistic knowledge of some of my colleagues did not necessarily correspond to their intellectual and moral rigor.

The final, involuntary game of mirrors culminated in a paradoxical assimilation: *Libre*, like Cuba, became an island, and its members, "classes of one," authentic islets, without a shared language.

A review of the history of Latin American writer-intellectuals reveals that the debate between those forms of the missionary imperative, those posed in terms that privileged the critical nature as well as those that privileged the revolutionary nature of the intellectual, were interrupted by processes that exceeded the dynamics of the field itself. None of these ideals succeeded in fulfilling their purposes because the conditions of intellectual practice changed very quickly.

The fact that the discussion of two different models resulted in diatribes rather than principles, that the will to persuade was to some degree abandoned, did not help clarify the problem of the social function of intellectuals, nor did it make it possible to explore the transformations that at that very moment would radically modify the possibilities of intellectual practice. One by one, Latin American magazines ceased to exist, except for *Casa de las Américas*. If continental unity appeared to be affirmed from the point of view of a political tragedy embodied by the succession of coups d'état, the intellectuals who forged the Latin Americanism of the time were forced into a sort of Latin American conditioning imposed by external circumstances. The associative ideal was abandoned, and there is no telling whether or not the future holds a new rallying call.

8

The Poetics and Politics of Genres

1. Novel: Realism? Avant-garde?

> The terms realism, fiction, and language should be revised and updated in relation to the new objectives proposed by the novel.
>
> Noé Jitrik (1960)

> The words realism, realist, lend themselves to confusion or, at least, they are frequently used with a sense of confusion. . . . A question of vocabulary, a tragic question of vocabulary.
>
> Louis Aragon

> The new, the creative, and, therefore, the truly revolutionary is rupture, negation. . . . You can choose not to write surrealist poetry these days, but you cannot write poetry as if Surrealism had never existed; you can create true realistic art today—and I stress the word true to set it apart from what in the name of realism is the negation of realism and of art itself—but today to be realistic you have to assimilate the contributions of the most diverse aesthetic tendencies—from impressionism to abstract art.
>
> Adolfo Sánchez Vázquez (1964)

The aim of this chapter is to analyze how the intellectual history developed in the previous chapters can be linked to a history of the practice and interpretation of literary genres at the time and how the growing politicization of the intellectual field affected the appreciation of the aesthetic and ideological values of the various genres.

Roberto González Echevarría states that, after the disappearance of figures such as Alfonso Reyes, Pedro Henríquez Ureña, Mariano Picón Salas, and José Carlos Mariátegui, Latin America lacked meaningful literary criticism. However, according to González Echevarría, this deficiency was not so grave since literature itself constituted true Latin American critical thought (1985b, 33–35). It is not my intention here to discuss in detail whether Latin American criticism of the period was or was not on par with literary production. It is not impossible to think that the conception of *criticism* implicit in González Echevarría's reflections implies knowledge, objects, and perspectives that are very different from those that at the time formed the basis of the work of Ángel Rama, Carlos Real de Azúa, Antonio Candido, and Adolfo Prieto.

The period was not spared from the cliché whereby many writers complained that critics were not up to the level of their work, especially at a time when certain texts were beginning to be formulated in dialogue with the emerging structuralism. "I am not surprised that no one understands a Leñero structure, for example, if very few know what a structure is," said José Agustín (in Caso). And Carlos Fuentes declared from Paris: "You cannot call a man a critic if he does not know languages, if he has not read the works of his specialty, if he does not know who I. A. Richards, Epsom, Foucault, Barthes, and Wilson are" (in Alberto Diazlastra). Mexican authors were perhaps the most explicit in their critiques of the backwardness of criticism, although the cliché of the writer versus critics can also be seen as sometimes masking issues of the competition for approval. Fernando del Paso, whose novel *José Trigo* was accused by critics of being hermetic, stated: "It would be bad if they spoke well of my book because among the defects of criticism in Mexico is that of establishing myths." And as a prominent example of the critical myth, he pointed to Carlos Fuentes as "a better writer than his critics think" but "not as good as his critics have led him to believe." He also mentions that the public, who purchased 4,500 copies of his novel in only five or six months after its publication, was much more lucid than the critics. Juan García Ponce said then what González Echevarría would later propose: that criticism was literature itself. For his part, José Agustín challenged the bad faith of the critics, who silenced Cabrera Infante so as not to embarrass Cubans Lisandro Otero or Roberto Fernández Retamar, whom he considered members of a "deplorable official culture that is going through a stage of self-sufficiency and servility" (in Caso). (Incidentally providing an interesting example of the objects that constitute discursive taboos at a given moment).

Undoubtedly, the literary criticism of the time had not developed an aspiration of scientificity such as the one generated by the impact of structuralism, around 1968. A good example of this is the trajectory of Ángel Rama, who only began recommending the reading of the Russian formalists in 1970. Forgotten for forty years, the formalists had emerged on the heels of structuralism and had gained universal fame as the seed of a methodological revolution as important as the one carried out by Lévi-Strauss and Roland Barthes (Rama 1970).

Critics such as those mentioned above held significant importance in the debate on the politics of writing, not only through the influential political-cultural journals in which they participated, but also by discussing—in the same forums as the authors of fiction whose work they were concerned with—the undertaking of what would be called "the new Latin American novel." Furthermore, there are few moments in the history of Latin American literature in which literary criticism has had more weight and importance, not so much in terms of *how* to read (with what methods, knowledge, or tools) but in terms of how it *proposed reading*, what literature it put into circulation among a continental mass of readers. Undoubtedly, this criticism participated in the construction of a criteria of aesthetic and ideological validity that, in practice, contributed to the hierarchization of certain genres and the demotion of others. In this sense, the critics, in general—at least until 1967—*were strongly betting on the novel* and, judging by the results, they were successful: the novel was *the* genre through which Latin American literature showed that it was on par with the great literatures of the world. The Latin American novelistic explosion was a phenomenon that surpassed all expectations, as Augusto Roa Bastos (1969–70, 45) pointed out. In the process of establishing the novelistic genre, critics and authors were great allies, and often the authors did not differ from the critics since they cultivated criticism with frequency and fluency.

The novel as a genre seemed to enter the cultural agenda of writer-intellectuals (and critic-intellectuals), almost as a matter of course, to the extent that it was a privileged combination of the two highest values of the critical intelligentsia of the time: social aspirations and the impulse toward the new. The superiority and efficacy of the novel were at play on several levels, ranging from the renewal of literary languages to its potential as a means of understanding the world. While it is relatively simple to understand how the novel could be conceptualized in relation to progressive aspirations and the radical transformation of society, describing how the impulse toward the new was conceptualized is more complex. As for the first point, the novel's effectiveness was linked to the fact that the genre was conceived as a generator of consciousness based on a work and a quest for objectivity. In Adolfo Prieto's terms:

> Virtually everything is possible for the novelist, which means that the novelist has perhaps the most notable responsibility in this undertaking of configuring the broad outlines of our reading public. The novelist can take on tones of voice, interpret irrational residues, penetrate, objectify, become the living conscience of each of the readers addressed: and the novelist can address everyone (1956, 153–54).

For Noé Jitrik, the novel was one of the privileged instruments of human life: the here and now entered into it not only as places, cultural objects, contemporary problems, but also as formal ones (1959). According to these ideas, one of the most ambitious goals of a novelist should be "to take a fragment of reality, experience it dramatically, and give it meaning in order to project it onto the reader as fiercely as it has been received by the author" (Rama 1964e). In the novel, one conscience (that of the writer) was put in relation with another (that of the reader), and the genre, with its burden of objectivity, could be conceived as a means of transforming the consciousness of the audience. For this reason, it was important for each author to take sides and take a position. The genre of the novel was perfectly "positioned," capable of representing a totality that the experience of the world could only give in a fragmentary way. This conviction, which unites such dissimilar views as those of Lukács and Bakhtin, attributed to the novel an enormous power to account for the "real," the "contemporary," and the deep web of causalities and determinations that united the seemingly discontinuous. Carlos Fuentes's *La región más transparente* [*Where the Air Is Clear*] is a good example of the novel's ambition to structure and make sense of history through the *petite histoire*. The subjectivity of the author, immersed in social life, was an essential factor for the genre to mediate between the creator and the intended recipient of the message. According to Roa Bastos:

> In the depths of subjectivity, where the pressure of reality discovers and manifests new modes of its *objective* essence and unprecedented possibilities of *interhuman communication*, the writer is not isolated from the social context (1969–70, 51–52, emphasis added).

Undoubtedly, the strong impulse toward the new that is visible in most of the novelistic production of the period has led recent critics to use the term "avant-garde" with a certain frequency to designate the innovations of the novelistic production of the period. El Techo de la Ballena in Venezuela, along with Colombian Nadaism and the movement of concrete poetry in Brazil, were perhaps the only experiences animated by a true "avant-garde" spirit, in terms of experimentation and rupture with the distinctive features of the art institution. It is interesting, therefore, to analyze the repertoire of concepts that accompanied the publication of novels as dissimilar as *Where the Air Is Clear*, *Hopscotch*, *The Time of the Hero*, and *One Hundred Years of Solitude*, to give some significant examples, as they emerge from the critical development of the period.

During the first years of the epoch, literary critics and novelists established the importance of the genre of the novel in terms of both a vocation for realism as well as a "tradition of rupture," as an editorial in *Casa de las Américas* put it, quoting Octavio Paz's oxymoron ("Editorial" 1967a). How could both critical justifications coincide in their assessment of the importance of a genre? Any approach that seeks to account for how writers and critics conceptualized the aesthetic impulse strongly oriented toward the new, which was characteristic of the epoch, must acknowledge the horizon of problems, traditions, and even traumas that helped to shape verbal artifacts in order to describe what that novelty consisted of.

I would like to briefly outline the horizon of thought in which the literary criticism of the period was inscribed. The constellation is complex. To begin with, we cannot underestimate the weight that the experience of the Russian avant-garde and the revolutionary leadership had in the historical and aesthetic memory of Latin American artists and critics of the epoch. The promise of the union of the artistic avant-garde and the political avant-garde defined a euphoric moment of the Bolshevik revolution, which ended badly for avant-garde artists. At present, it is hard to imagine to what degree the outcome of these relations could have influenced the dual aspirations of Latin American literature at the time: revolutionary and experimental aspirations.

A good part of the communist intelligentsia and the Western "fellow travelers," witnesses of the shipwreck of the avant-garde aspirations to accompany the process of the October Revolution, refused to accept the dictates of socialist realism, but they did not dare to establish almost immediate ties with the avant-garde movements as the Tel Quel group would do, without giving up on defining themselves within the theoretical framework of Marxism ("Tel Quel nous répond" 50–54).

For a long time, there was a sort of vacuum to verbally conceptualize an aesthetics of rupture, an ideal of novelty, and new forms of artistic criticality associated with the desire to contribute, through artistic practice, to the revolutionary transformation of society. On opening any Latin American political-cultural publication at random, the scholar will find the reiteration of a series of names that lent authority to artists and critics: Lucien Goldmann, Roger Garaudy, Enrst Fischer, Jean-Paul Sartre, and several Italian critics—whose importance cannot be underestimated—, such as Galvano Della Volpe (who had published his *Critique of Taste* in 1960) and Cesare Luporini. These were some of the men whose formulas served to describe a new aesthetics that, countering official Soviet perspectives, sought to rescue the modernist works and authors that were fundamental milestones of the art of this century.

Soviet culture had punished Kafka, Proust, Joyce, and Beckett by labeling them decadent artists. "Decadence" was the word that divided the socialist family on issues of art. The epoch saw a lively discussion within the socialist camp about the appreciation of modern art. Western intellectuals asked themselves: Can we leave Kafka in the hands of the right? Will we have to give up the achievements of modern art? Héctor Schmucler wrote that the idea of decadence had been "one of the most difficult stumbling blocks to overcome" and that, among other things, it prevented "explaining the impressive presence of Joyce, Kafka, and Proust in world culture using the cold Lukacsian framework" (1963, 48). Within this context, several encounters took place as part of East/West dialogue and promoted by the European socialist intelligentsia. One of these encounters was focused precisely on the notion of decadence, and it led to the widespread proposal to eliminate that term from artistic evaluation. A select group of the most prominent intellectuals expressed their complete disagreement with anything that would force them to renounce modern art. At a meeting held at the editorial office of the Czech literary magazine *Plamen*, Ernst Fischer argued that only if they were left in the hands of the bourgeoisie could Beckett and Proust become enemies of the left ("Entretien à Prague sur la notion de 'décadence'" 71–85). The French communists of *La Nouvelle Critique* took care to ensure that their position against the Soviet *Index* and in favor of the modernist *refusés* was clear: "When Sartre demands a permanent visa for Proust, Joyce, or Kafka in socialist countries, naturally, we are on his side since we grew up with them intellectually" (Gisselbrecht). They also noted that the fall from grace of these authors was yet another product of the deformations of Stalinism: "The ostracism of these artists (Proust, Kafka, Joyce), which ultimately implies a certain involuntary lack of culture, is not inherent to communism" (Gisselbrecht).

Along with other positions that theorized on art from a Marxist perspective, Roger Garaudy's famous book *D'un réalisme sans rivages* [On Realism Without Borders], published in 1963 (and translated into Spanish by Raúl Sciarreta, a member of the Argentine Communist Party), extended the notion of realism in such a way that it encompassed practically all artistic manifestations: it is hardly by chance that Garaudy himself acknowledged that for his book he had chosen to comment on works and authors that "for a long time we had been forbidden to love in the name of overly narrow standards of realism." As Sartre declared in an interview, "Marxist culture must undergo expansion, that is, it must take things from the bourgeois and *restore* them as

Marxist things" ("Rinascità entrevista a Sartre" 153). The broadening of the aesthetic spectrum, carried out in the name of that realism whose non-truth resided in its amplitude, held that, as Garaudy put it, "there is no art that is not realistic, that is, that does not refer to a reality that is external to it and independent of it; the definition of this realism is extremely complex" (1964, 167).

On the other hand, the meaning of the concept "avant-garde," like that of "realism," was not very clear. After all, in 1956 Roland Barthes had written:

> Our dictionaries do not tell us precisely when the term *avant-garde* was first used in a cultural sense. Apparently the notion is quite recent. . . . Because, from a historical perspective, this protest [of the avant-garde] has never been anything but a proxy. The bourgeoisie delegated some of its creators to tasks of formal subversion, though without actually disinheriting them. . . . The *avant-garde* is in fact another cathartic phenomenon, a kind of vaccine intended to inject a little subjectivity, a little freedom under the crust of bourgeois values. . . . No, to tell the truth, the *avant-garde* is threatened by only one force, which is not the bourgeoisie: political consciousness. It seems that no sooner is the *avant-garde* won over to the necessity of revolutionary tasks than it renounces itself, agrees to die. . . . It can propose new techniques, subvert our complacencies, enrich the dramatic vocabulary, awaken the realistic author to the need for a certain freedom of tone, rouse him from his usual apathy with regard to forms. (89–91)

Barthes was thus highlighting the complexity of the relationship between the aesthetic avant-garde and the bourgeois world, although he was also concerned with establishing the need for artists not to despise the formal qualities of art that the avant-garde had helped bring to the fore. And Hans Magnus Enzensberger required the immediate elucidation of the term "avant-garde," *which had never been done up to that point* (1974, 22). Latin America was part of this debate. Juan Carlos Portantiero wondered how to conceive of the struggle for a new art on the "threshold of a new civilization." Although he recognized that avant-garde art had emerged as a negation of the bourgeoisie, he added that the avant-garde negation also implied a detachment from the people, but that did not mean that its formal achievements could be denied since they were achievements in knowledge. Furthermore, he denounced "the conservative masters who have taken possession of the term (realism) and have intoxicated it with false content," and he criticized the over-estimation of nineteenth-century realism, "which has caused enough damage to Marxist literary criticism" (Portantiero 20, 41, 45, 61).

The question was not so much denying the label of *realism* (in fact, there would be talk of a "new" realism that would be extended to include all artistic manifestations), but the novelty was eliminating the "prescriptive" nature of its definition. What happened then was a process of radical resemantization that preserved the word ("realism") but separated it from realist aesthetics and its normative significance. In some ways, the result was the verbal phenomenon that every "novelty" faces: the absence of a word that records it as such. At the beginning of the epoch, the first conceptualization of the novelistic genre that began to arouse the interest of the continent's readers was expressed in terms of a "new realism," correlative to the moment of the cultural agenda that assigned itself the task of constructing a literature, perhaps because, as César Fernández Moreno ("Reportaje literario en Buenos Aires: Situación actual de la novela" [Literary Report in Buenos Aires: Current Situation of the Novel]) opined, realism was "the only possible vein in the Americas."

This way of thinking about the aesthetics of the novel as a genre was expressed through the slogan "deeper zones of reality," which became a workhorse of critical assessment, along with the Sartrean notion of "authenticity." The emphasis placed on definitions of "realism" to describe the works that burst onto the literary scene after *Where the Air is Clear* (1958) and *Hopscotch* (1963)—and without minimizing the impact of novels such as *Pedro Páramo* (1955) and *Explosion in a Cathedral* (1962)—is surprising. The *terminological* challenge in favor of realism was remarkable, whether one spoke of "new realism," "the realism of today," "deeper zones of reality," "an exploration of the layers of the real," etc. As Yevgeny Yevtushenko said, for example, realism could have hundreds, if not thousands, of different forms, and it could also be figurative and non-figurative. This unbridled realism, without borders, critical, experimental, formally careful, thematically unrestricted, and not based on a specific *message*, served as the foundation for the novelistic program. Drawing on Auerbach, Della Volpe, and Garaudy, Jaime Rest described this aesthetic as a realism of critical intent, highly aware of the artifice of form, whose model could very well be Bertolt Brecht. To clear up any misunderstandings, Rest distinguished two types of realism: One, which he sought to overcome, was illusory and useless for the purposes of reflection since it "distracted" and "hypnotized." The other, in contrast, embodied the new artistic rationality and was critical and novel. According to this formula, that emphasized the formal values of the work (since formal perfection "is not at odds with the precise description and criticism of the social environment"), "a realist is a creator whose work makes it possible to evaluate the objective conditions of the society in which they live, even if it formally distorts the external appearance of the world."

The *new realism* also involved the search for a tradition of rupture; Paz's oxymoron is highly significant, since it manages to express this double valence of the new as "realist avant-garde" and "avant-garde realism." The most frequently used formulas presented the renewal as a new realist-modernist aesthetic: as an emblem of the resulting figure, similar to the ideal postulated by Carlos Fuentes, for whom the new Latin American novelist must be at the same time a Balzac and a Butor. The new realism, or the blend of Balzac and Butor, sought to overcome folklorism and nationalism, that is, an anachronistic state of the genre, which prevented the transformation of Latin American literature into a universal literature. That transformation was postulated in terms of the opposition between an old realism and a current realism: "The crude and stuttering realism once employed has also disappeared: today's realism ranges from the psychological to the magical, passing through the critical and the behaviorist" (Carballo 1966b, V). The double valence connoted by the term "realism" (between the new and the old) was present in the corrections prescribed by the critics. Just as he affirmed that realism was the only possible vein in the Americas, Fernández Moreno warned that this realism should not be "photographic but dynamic" ("Reportaje literario...").

In part, for the critics, to speak of a "new realism" was to include a newer category than that implied by the notion of "avant-garde." The term "avant-garde" referred to the historical avant-gardes and was a throwback to forms and styles that were forty years old, thus implying an *archaism*: "To speak of the avant-garde in 1964 is old-fashioned and outdated. While it is true that there are valuable and still exploitable procedures of the avant-garde, they must be subordinated to a message worthy of interest" (Rama 1964e). On the other hand, the connotation of the term "avant-garde," whether positive or negative, was an obstacle to the need to communicate with a relatively illiterate society. On a continent that barely ensured minimal literacy for the majority of its population, the aspiration of avant-gardism further restricted the circuit of the reception of works of art. In that sense, the way in which the question of readership was posed was completely at odds with the fragmentation of the public that was characteristic of the avant-garde movements. For critics and writers, it was also a matter of reconciling the tensions between their own education and their aesthetic choices with the necessary approval of an art that could communicate. The communicative qualities of the narrative works had to be set against the background of a new phenomenon: mass culture, a development already identified as crucial by Adolfo Prieto (1956, 86–93).

For Latin American critics, what basically mattered, then, was the search for a new and unique artistic expression, which meant it was crucial to recover and explore, without limitations, other aesthetic horizons tied to the avant-gardes and modernisms and to more recent developments in the novel of the United States. In short, to the art of the twentieth century. As Calvert Casey confirmed, within the group of Cuban writers who were active in the early sixties, many of them expressed their reality and the reality of their country through a technique that essentially belonged to recent US literature. "Some through many years of immersion in the United States (Humberto Arenal, Edmundo Desnoes) and conscious reading of what the followers of Gertrude Stein have written, others through constant reading of a powerful literature and the occasional inevitable trip (Cabrera Infante, Luis Agüero)," concluding then that it was so remarkable that it made all others pale in comparison. One of the models valued by critics and writers was precisely that of the US school of Southern narrators, dominated by Faulkner on the one hand and Erskine Caldwell on the other (and which influenced Robert Penn Warren, Truman Capote, William Styron, Tennessee Williams, Carson McCullers, Thomas Wolfe, and Katherine

Ann Porter), to whom *One Hundred Years of Solitude* and the literature of Onetti are so indebted.

Finally, were "integration," "conservation," "development," and "overcoming" not Roger Garaudy's key words (1964, 29)? Critics and novelists undoubtedly detected the existence of something "new" in Latin American literature and were of the opinion that constant renewal was one of the principles of artistic creation (Rama 1965b). This dimension of "the new," which was often insisted upon, was conceptualized in terms of the recovery of the horizon of all modern literature. The new was based on the appropriation of previously existing literary traditions (even if they were not Latin American), as well as on the "renewal" of the relatively old terms of aesthetics, which were being taken care of by the Western Marxist intelligentsia. In fact, Juan Carlos Onetti was seen as a forerunner of the new realism, when in 1942, with *Tierra de nadie* [*No Man's Land*], he "established the first crude X-ray of this new human reality" (Rama 1964f), and Rodríguez Monegal, emblematic defender of the tradition of rupture, maintained—in line with Rama—that Onetti's "model" literature had extended the frontiers of realism in Latin America (quoted in Oviedo 1972, 45), which shows that the word realism did indeed circulate as a *mot d'ordre* and critical password. No one can doubt that Rama and Monegal, two of the most important critics of the period, fought explicitly for the modernization of Uruguayan and Latin American literature. Both sought to think about the basis on which a tradition could be invented. Both, although in this case with strong ideological differences between their trajectories and positions—including their assessment of Borges, whom one disseminated and situated in the Olympus of Literature while the other dismissed as an irritating ideologue of an unbearable conservatism—, were (occasionally exaggerated) actors and witnesses of the growing politicization of intellectual and aesthetic practice. For Rama, the literature of Borges is a closed literature, a superficial game, a symptom of creative frigidity. Nevertheless, it is more accurate to venture that the two indispensable Uruguayan critics resemble—more than the characters of *The Magic Mountain*, Settembrini and Naptha "but in Spanish," as Cabrera Infante's *calembour* suggests (1989, 56)—the theologians of the Borgean tale: in paradise, Emir Rodríguez Monegal knew that, for the unfathomable divinity, he and Ángel Rama (the orthodox and the heretic, the hater and the hated, the plaintiff and the victim) formed a single person. The two stipulated that the program of a new literature, with universalist ambitions, necessarily entailed a crossover with other literatures. Onetti's great discovery, according to Rama, was that any renewal of literature must start from a *foreign* influence. Rama made a veritable *program* out of this affirmation. Likewise, for Monegal, a new tradition entailed an indispensable link with world literature, preferably Anglo-Saxon.

This search for a new aesthetics was basically in opposition to the *criollista* novel, which was considered a remnant of the nineteenth century and which typified characters and landscapes: gauchos, *llaneros*, Indians, *guajiros*, jungles, plains, and pampas. In the words of one Venezuelan critic, the new novel

> has left behind the poncho and the *chiripá* depicted with the stasis of a folk museum, the endless plains of the depredations of a woman in her fifties, or the contagious spell of the jungle that was feared as an artificial deity (Loveluck 27).

This statement was part of the generalized rejection, shared by critics and writers, of *costumbrismo*, nativism, ruralism, folklorism, and the role that the international division of artistic labor seemed to assign to Latin American production. The search for internationalization and the incorporation of foreign traditions (a rich and diverse search that differed according to the individual trajectories of each writer or the various national literatures) marked the path of a modernization that could lead Latin American literature to become part of the "greats" of the world. That was the context in which the first narrative experiments were read. Monegal clarified:

> Certainly, the so-called new novel is far from being a homogeneous aesthetic, just as that of the previous masters, such as Rulfo, Carpentier, Borges, or Asturias, was not. *Pedro Páramo* is the paradigm of the new Latin American novel: a work that takes advantage of the great Mexican tradition of the land but metamorphoses it, destroys it, and re-creates it by means of a profound assimilation of Faulkner's techniques (1969, 25).

Although critics noted and celebrated the new narrative techniques employed by the new novels, the novelty of the procedures was framed within this supposed new realism. The Chilean critic Fernando Uriarte emphasized how, in his opinion, the "Hispano-American novel" had incorporated great changes in point of view, "a new perspective, a horizon, a repertoire of unknown panoramas, tensions, and palpitations of life," which constituted "a historical change in the genre" (147). This historical change did not seem to affect the view of the novel as realist:

> The current type of *realist* novel, with its experiences of great vigor and precision, enveloping, dense, structured with a disorienting and complicated technicality, multiple points of view, i.e., in perspectives on life and the nuances of its change [so that] if the Spanish American novel today displays unforeseen, surprising peculiarities; if it displays density and strength; if, moreover, it is written with fluency and authentic language, it is because it is all suitably related to a real situation that is accepted without hesitation (Uriarte 152–53).

The jurors who awarded the Biblioteca Breve Prize to Vicente Leñero in 1963 applauded *Los albañiles* for its "idiomatic, structural, and social-realist virtues" and praised the use of the technique of the shifting point of view, the dismantling of the story, the sensitivity involved in "writing" a polyphony of voices from other times and settings, from different individuals and social strata (all connected to the dimension of the new), without the perception of novelty attenuating the novel's *social-realist* virtues. Vargas Llosa's *The City and the Dogs* was also read in this "new realism" format. Rama presented it as a novel that boldly went beyond *costumbrismo* and conveyed the totality of reality in an authentic way through modern structures (1964f). With new realism, technical renewal and the departure from *criollismo* and regionalism were taken for granted. Using similar arguments (although not for the novel, in this case), Roberto Fernández Retamar, in considering conversational poetry superior to the anti-poetry of Nicanor Parra and his followers, postulated that the former implied a "new realism" while clarifying that it was a label that should not be feared since it was "enriched with the conquests of the last forty or fifty years." And he added that he found the movement toward realism "ostensible" in all contemporary arts, especially in the new novel. He concluded by affirming that the energetic tempos of the action were well suited to this realism (1969, 251–62).

In reality, the word "avant-garde" did not belong to that dictionary and, when employed, its use was as labile as that of the notion of realism, designating, in a similar manner, the impulse toward the new that characterized aesthetic reflection and narrative production without opposition between the two terms. In sum, both words served as artifacts rather than categories. This is evident in Rodolfo Walsh's statements:

> Realism is not necessarily opposed to avant-gardism. When the exhaustion of themes or forms weakens the depiction of reality and its interpretation, the realist author is forced to become avant-garde. The avant-garde is therefore the form that realism adopts in a historical context of exhaustion. This situation cannot be forced, nor is it mandatory that each stage have an avant-garde. When an attempt is made against the grain, the result is simply anomalies or oddities that momentarily pass for avant-garde. . . . In Latin America the realist writer is in the avant-garde when he or she makes the invisible visible: the empire, the class struggle, the meaning of human relations, and the feelings of individuals. Carlos Fuentes and Vargas Llosa, the best Cortázar, are realism and avant-garde, without any contradiction in terms (Bignami 1973a, 58–59).

When used, the word "avant-garde" (like "new realism") could mean the desire to produce an art that drew on the technical repertoire and procedures of modern art. In this sense, we can read a commentary on *The Green House* in which Vargas Llosa's strategy was described as the assimilation of the conquests of the avant-garde in a new context (Larco 58–59). "Assimilate the conquests of contemporary art" was another of the slogans repeated by writers and critics of the time in all variations and nuances. This insistence reflected the existence of the aesthetic "taboos" that the new left struggled to break.

Alejo Carpentier was undoubtedly one of those who most explicitly built bridges between the past of the avant-garde and the program of a new Latin American novel. In fact, he explicitly and critically referred to the postulates of André Breton—who had dismissed the novel from the avant-garde program, considering it an inferior genre—with the condition that it be enriched by the "marvelous" (31). Based on these formulations Carpentier likely developed his notion of the marvelous real of the Americas (from which he derived his expression "marvelous realism"), which played a key role in the search for a specifically Latin American aesthetic. In reality, what critics and writers set out to do *did not have a name.* In the end, with the exception of conceptualizations such as Carpentier's marvelous realism or Sarduy's neo-baroque, the new novelistic projects were not formulated in very precise conceptual terms. The best example of this insufficient conceptual framework is that the new novelism could be described with the phrase "escribir así" [write *like this*] In a letter from Julio Cortázar to Roberto Fernández Retamar, dated August 17, 1964, in Paris, on the topic of the enthusiasm that Retamar felt after reading *Hopscotch*, Cortázar declares himself "shaken" by the "marvelous phrase" the Cuban had used to refer to the novel: "So one of us can write *like this*?" (1984, 17). In fact, Cortázar makes the expression his own and does not attempt to define the procedures, themes, or techniques it holds implicit.

> It doesn't matter that it was I who wrote *like this*, perhaps for the first time. The only thing that matters is that we are coming upon a time in the Americas in which one can begin to write *like this* (or in another way, but like this, that is, with everything that you imply in underlining the word) (1984, 17).

Later Cortázar would replace the vague "like this" with a conceptualization of the "revolution in literature," which could be considered a quasi-avant-garde *ars poetica*, in which he argued that writers should be the Che Guevaras of literature (1970b).

Thus, for some time the description of what was happening to the novel was limited to an idiom, the connotations of which, without needing clarification, seemed nevertheless to be understood by the group of writers who wrote *like this.* Considering the explosion of the Latin American novel as a privileged genre, it can be concluded, then, that what was new, rather than a homogeneous aesthetic, was basically an *institutional novelty*: the creation of a canon to which recent works greatly contributed and to which the major innovators of the immediate past were added. *What was new was the consolidation of the novel as an object of reading and cultivation*: from 1960 to 1970, Mexican, Argentine, Uruguayan, Colombian, Chilean, etc. narrative produced a "Latin American novel." If until then, as it was said, there had been novels but no novelistic studies, as of 1967 that criticism was no longer valid.

However, the situation of the novel was to shift from that point on. Ariel Bignami made a distinction between an avant-gardism of evasion and a true avant-garde (in the same way that Rest had drawn a distinction between illusory realism and critical realism). The true avant-garde, according to Bignami, could be exemplified in "*the most profound realism of our days*, as represented by the new Latin American narrative" (1973b, 33). The peculiar assimilation between the "true avant-garde" and "deep realism" was not an eccentricity on the part of Bignami and revealed that the appeal to the categorical revision proposed early on by Jitrik (1960) did not have immediate echoes. However, what is important to retain from Bignami's phrase (and Rest's divisions) is that the field of objects (unified under whatever name) included a "good" and a "bad" version of things. Good realism/bad realism, good avant-garde/bad avant-garde. If for a long time the term realism was the password that an "epochal threshold" used in order to designate the object "novel," that was in turn being devised on the horizon of modernism and in the interests of experimentation, it could be said that the "epochal awareness"[49] that was simultaneous to several ideological confrontations in the intellectual field reached the point of positing an opposition between realism and avant-garde (which, moreover, was not new in the history of art). The good and bad versions, also expressed in terms of "true" and "false," served as well to divide the waters and to justify certain artistic experiences self-defined as "avant-garde," as was the case with the collective exhibition *Tucumán Arde* [Tucumán Is Burning] staged by visual artists in Argentina.[50]

The awareness of the innovation introduced by the novels considered part of *new realism*, along with the attraction exerted by the

49 The concepts of "threshold" and "epochal awareness" come from Jauss 1996.

50 See Giunta, 1994, and Longoni, 1995.

emergence and diffusion of French literary theory, made two tendencies visible within the mainstream of the Latin American novel: one more attentive to the critical potential of writing; the other more attentive to the critical potential of its subject matter. The two were often combined, as in the paradigmatic case of *Los fundadores del alba* [*The Breach*], which recounted Guevara's campaign in Bolivia using "experimental" techniques. Two superimposed tendencies, one emphasized the representational procedures that were more typical of realism (in the strict sense), the other emphasized the experimental aspect and more precise work with language. Octavio Paz noted these two tendencies when analyzing the literature of Mexico's younger writers (they can also be seen in the rest of Latin America). Paz called one "social criticism" and the other "verbal creation" (Embeita, cited in Glantz), to which Margo Glantz ascribes the concepts of *onda* (wave) and *escritura* (writing), respectively. These two approaches reached a strong point of divergence and each of them gradually deepened its tendency (Glantz).

The best example of the existence of both tendencies is the decision that the jury of the Barral prize for the novel made to refrain from awarding the prize in 1972. The jury consisting of Félix de Azúa, José María Castellet, Salvador Clotas, Gabriel García Márquez, Carlos Fuentes, Julio Cortázar, Mario Vargas Llosa, and Carlos Barral determined that the novels presented were either "highly complicated in stylistic terms, almost hermetic, difficult to understand" or excessively propagandistic, in which the jury felt they could discern the "autobiographical experiences of frustrated guerrillas." Faced with this material, the jury deemed it necessary to strike a balance, declaring that "renewal is fine, as long as it makes sense and is legible" (Benedetti 1972, 31, and García Grau 31). This event and these observations reveal the exhaustion of novelistic expectations and establish new objects of reflection on the state and the future of the genre.

2. Cuba and the Question of the Avant-garde

> The avant-garde is born in Europe out of the crisis of the capitalist world. It so happens, however, that our backward societies do not and cannot present similar crises. Are we therefore going to dispense with what the avant-garde has conquered? Are we going to confine ourselves to wild and deplorably folkloric expressions? . . . In our case, the term *revolution* is added to the terms *avant-garde*—in itself quite conflictive—and *underdevelopment*. It is a question of creating avant-garde art in an underdeveloped country undergoing a revolution.
>
> ROBERTO FERNÁNDEZ RETAMAR (1967B, 15, emphasis in the original)

> Avant-garde is not gratuitous difficulty, but rather subversion in the face of outdated attitudes and models. This use of simplicity is, in the best sense of the word, subversive.
>
> MARIO BENEDETTI (1967D and 1967C, 210)

> We must sacrifice, if necessary, genres, schools, styles, the whole aesthetic, in the face of the mortal urgency of creating this consolidation of a new relation of productive forces.
>
> EDMUNDO DESNOES (Dalton et al., 39)

The epigraphs at the top of this page should generate a sense of perplexity. For Cuban writers (more than for their colleagues on the continent), the revolution brought as a great *promesse de bonheur* the union of the literary and political avant-gardes. The possibility of conceiving of that union or mutual flourishing, as it was once envisaged, was facilitated by the existence of a political avant-garde recognized as such and which had even been theorized as a "vanguard," in the broad, military sense of the term. That same phenomenon may have been repeated in Argentina at the end of the epoch, when the appearance of core groups of political activists that sought to form political avant-gardes gave rise to a desire to create an artistic avant-garde that could be combined with the political avant-garde. Perhaps for that reason, many Cuban artists focused more on renewal with an aesthetic vocabulary in which the word avant-garde could appear more frequently, although, as we have already seen, the aesthetic debate was not always easy in the context of the Cuban Revolution. Nevertheless, many Cuban artists nurtured the hope of being able to repair what Sánchez Vázquez had called the "historical error of the Marxist-Leninist avant-gardes" that, by rejecting modern forms of expression, caused the artistic avant-gardes to turn away from politics (1968). The artistic disputes between defenders of the "aesthetics of rupture" and the "great rejection" and defenders of (socialist) realism further blurred the possibilities of using the term "realism." Cuban visual arts and cinema, because of their audacious commitment to renewal, were disconcerting to European critics. In 1967, the London gallery Ewan Phillips presented the exhibition *Contemporary Cuban Art*, in which works by Amelia Peláez, René Portocarrero, Raúl Millán, Fayad Jamís, Luis Martínez Pedro, Mariano Rodríguez, and Raúl Martínez (who exhibited the famous series with Fidel Castro's face, which was inspired by Andy Warhol's Campbell's soup cans) were shown. Antonio Cisneros described the heterogeneity of styles, techniques, and currents of the exhibition in which the following were mixed:

> flowers and leaves and fruit like a Baroque stained-glass window forged in the Colony, Fidel's face seven times, Martí's face seven times, the Cuban flag seven times; dreams, viscera, shadows, Tachism, Surrealism, Abstractionism, a popular Virgin, Pop, Expressionism, and the rest as well (66).

It does not matter whether the works exhibited were *avant-garde* or not, since it seems evident that the meaning of the term is far from being clear. What is worth noting is the surprise of British critics at the freedom and cosmopolitanism of the works, which led them to point out that Cuban socialism had gotten rid of the old schemes of social realism, which was undoubtedly one of the most important gambles of the Cuban artistic field, displaying the radical originality of its political and aesthetic revolution. A French guest at the Cultural Congress of Havana was surprised by the presence of the new and modern expressions: in poster art, in the ties with Pop, in cinema, which displaced the linear narrative, chronology, and history through an experimental montage. Instead of what was "expected" (a mass of documents, statistics, and photos), the "Third World" exhibition showed the presence of Vietnam in Pop posters, neon heads with the image of Guevara, and the presence of all modern methods of animation (Parmelin 1669).

The defense of an avant-garde art developed underground and sometimes secretly, reaching its climax in 1968, when the conditions for the use of the word "avant-garde" to refer to art found their historical limits in Cuba: the key question was whether it was possible to create a "new" art or literature (conceptualized as avant-garde, experimentalist, or not) on an economically and politically dependent continent, and in countries in which the only possible audience for artistic output was recruited from the ranks of the middle class. Nothing could be further from the people than this or any other type of art. For this reason, Roberto Fernández Retamar stated that he should recant his hypotheses about the mutual flourishing of the artistic avant-garde and the political avant-garde on the grounds that only revolutionaries could be considered "avant-garde." He further stated:

> I have less confidence today in univocality, in the clarity of an expression such as "aesthetic avant-garde," which brings with it so much confusion. In Europe, the meaning of that term, referring to a specific epoch that is no longer this one, has been clarified considerably, as far as I can tell. With respect to the current literature and art of the capitalist countries—since the expression originated in them, it comes from them—what exactly does aesthetic avant-garde mean today? And in socialist countries, especially the underdeveloped ones, such as Vietnam, Korea, or Cuba? . . . That is why I believe that to clarify things it might be helpful to begin by

> dispensing with a nomenclature that has proved ineffective (Benedetti 1971b, 12).

Years later and to clear up any misunderstanding, he defined the term "avant-garde" as "susceptible to so many misunderstandings and so many vain polemics" following "academic criteria" to narrow it down, to reduce the term "avant-garde" to Miklós Szabolcsi's definition in his paper for the Fifth Congress of the International Association of Comparative Literature (held in Belgrade in 1967), that is: "The well-known movements of revolt . . . between 1905 and 1938" (Fernández Retamar 1974, 119).

As an explanation of the phenomenon of the complex relationships between the artistic avant-garde and the political avant-garde (when both coincide at a given historical moment), I find the distinction made by Susan Buck-Morss between *vanguard* and *avant-garde* quite interesting. This distinction serves to resolve the misunderstandings surrounding the problem of the relationship between the political and aesthetic avant-gardes and, therefore, the ties between intellectuals and politicians. Referring to the contrast between Lukács's experience in the Budapest Soviet and Adorno's discussions of Marx with his literary circle in Berlin, Buck-Morss observes how two clearly antagonistic conceptions emerged regarding the role of intellectuals, who according to Lukács were to be the vanguard of the revolution, while for Adorno they constituted the revolutionary *avant-garde*. According to Buck-Morss, "despite the common Renaissance-military origin of these words, their meanings had diverged in history," given that, specifically, the "military connotations of the term *avant-garde* had become purely metaphorical by the nineteenth century" and "it applied to literary and aesthetic praxis rather than sociopolitical praxis." The *avant-garde* rejected the bourgeois cultural tradition, but whether this rejection functioned as social protest was in many cases a secondary consideration. The notion of the party vanguard implied that the role of the intellectual was one of leadership and political instruction, while the *avant-garde* model defined the intellectual as an experimenter, permanently challenging dogma, meaning that their leadership was more exemplary than pedagogical. What mattered, therefore, "was not"—according to Buck-Morss—"the bourgeois origins of the techniques, but the critical attitude which the intellectual brought to them" (32–33).

I have attempted to show how the political-ideological situation dismissed that *promesse de bonheur*. Along with the abdication of the hope of an aesthetics of rupture (that would make it possible, on the other hand, to once again celebrate a writer like Rubén Darío), the renunciation of the use of the *word* "vanguard" was associated with a precise meaning of the *expression* "vanguard." What was being discussed in the name of questioning the *vanguard* was the artists' claim to self-regulate their own production, regardless of the type of works they produced. Not only was the *political* vanguard the only one that could be considered a *legitimate* vanguard, but it was also an ideological impertinence that artists or artist intellectuals—if only because they were united by the same signifier—could or would equate themselves with *their* political leadership, to whom they were not peers but subordinates. Thus, without a program expressed in distinctly avant-garde terms, there was a paradoxical moment when the word "vanguard" reappeared, almost out of nowhere, to be objected to in ideological terms. This appearance, with negative connotations, can be seen in the words of Ambrosio Fornet, who, in 1968, in his lecture at the Cultural Congress of Havana, titled "El intelectual en la revolución" [The Intellectual in the Revolution], had warned: "We must put to the test the formulas that reach us with the label of the vanguard." The same Fornet, a year later and with the approval of a solid core of intellectuals of revolutionary authority, declared that until then intellectuals had only been "vestals of the form, underdeveloped guardians of the vanguard" (1980, 318).

The generalization of anti-intellectualist discourse called into question the cultural agenda (that had already been achieved) and not only experimentalism or the impulse toward the new. The new Latin American narrative was attacked *in toto*. It was natural that the emergence of a theoretical discourse imported from France and disseminated by certain critics and authors—a discourse that, in very brief terms, affirmed that the only important thing in literature was language—should prove, in that context, particularly irritating for the "revolutionary" faction of the intellectual field. The idea of an equivalence in value between aesthetic modernization and ideological commitment also became problematic, as demonstrated by the trajectories of Sarduy, Cabrera Infante, and, much later, Vargas Llosa and Carlos Fuentes, who, unlike the anti-intellectualist group, were able to conjure the ghost of Borges and have him on hand as a precursor. Especially irritating was an intervention by Carlos Fuentes when he introduced a discussion originating in Europe, in which some of the critics questioned (once again in history) whether or not the genre was on the verge of extinction. The European discussion of the novel began in the late fifties and lasted for some time: among other examples are the texts of Nathalie Sarraute, Alain Robbe-Grillet, and Group 63, dedicated to the experimental novel in Italy; its death certificate was drawn up on more than one occasion. In fact, Leo Tolstoy had commented in his diary in 1893: "Not only is the novel not eternal, but it is already passing away."

In his book, Fuentes asserts:

> What has died is not the novel, but precisely the bourgeois form of the novel and its term of reference, realism . . . several great novelists have shown that the death of bourgeois realism only heralds the advent of a much more powerful literary reality (1969, 17).

What was irritating about Fuentes's book? Undoubtedly, the idea that the novel was "myth, language, and structure" and that the great novelists who could aspire to the construction of a "more powerful" literature demanded a "diversity of verbal explorations" that characterized precisely the established Latin American writers (although not only them), including Fuentes himself (1969, 30–31). The mention of Jorge Luis Borges as the founder of literary modernity on the continent, which elicited an angry response from Fernández Retamar ("Borges is a typical colonial writer, representative among us of a class that no longer has any strength. . . . It is odd that the writing/reading of Borges should have met a particularly favorable fate in capitalist Europe"),[51] could not be considered a real novelty in Latin American literature at the time. Although Borges's political positions made him particularly inconvenient (especially in the Río de la Plata region), his status as a "master" was fully recognized by the new novelists, from Cortázar to García Márquez. The inclusion of Guillermo Cabrera Infante and the theoretical scaffolding provided by new French literary theory, the

---

51 1971, 255–56.

contention that approval would be deadly for socialism, and the claim that the authors he discussed were the ones who would kill the bourgeois novel, were, on the other hand, sufficiently provocative. But even if Fuentes disputed the category of realism, *he never replaced it* with that of the avant-garde.

And although there had not strictly been "an avant-garde," some works that had been thought of in terms of innovation and modernization were reclassified as "avant-garde," and this time they were set against an aesthetic program of recovering representation and communicability. A more traditional concept of representation strongly included the denunciational and thematic aspects linked to the revolutionary objectives of literature. From 1968 onward, a kind of polemic between realism and the avant-garde appeared as the central focus of the debates among critics and writers. The existence of this debate is paradoxical since Latin American narrative works were neither realist nor avant-garde in the classic sense of these notions.

The polemic was directly associated with the configuration of the Latin American intellectual field and the new aesthetic currents that were gradually becoming dominant in Cuba and were connected to different modes of anti-avant-garde aesthetics. The problem, perceptively identified by Juan García Ponce, was that the "definition of avant-garde did not accept definitions" (in Caso). And just as there was a historicist and innovative anti-avant-gardism at the beginning of the period, there was another that attacked experimentalism in ideological terms. Basically, it criticized writers such as Carlos Fuentes, Vargas Llosa, and Julio Cortázar, who, in their attempt to politicize the word, had defined it as equivalent to subversion and criticism, or critics such as Ricardo Piglia, who had asserted that Latin American literature was a permanent rebellion against language's original structures and a new attempt to conquer reality with language ("Prólogo" in *Las crónicas de Latinoamérica* 8). These positions suddenly found themselves confronted with new aesthetic-ideological foundations that disqualified what those novels had introduced into the art of Latin American narrative. The radically pre-revolutionary anti-avant-gardism that went hand in hand with anti-intellectualism stressed the tension between the communicative efficacy and the aesthetic efficacy of the work of art.

The anti-avant-gardism of the beginnings highlighted the anachronistic nature of the avant-garde and a certain "poverty of ideas" of those who used that label without any knowledge of the cause. The anti-avant-gardism that shaped the next stage of criticism and intellectual history was closely linked to a dual criticism: against the hermeticism of an art for the few, but also against the Latin American novel, which in its day had been declared foundational, authentically American, which had been "like this" (according to Cortázar and Retamar), and disseminated with the label of *new realism*. Whether well theorized by critics and writers or not, it was the novel that had succeeded in getting a public to turn to its authors, "seeking in them the expression or enlightenment that cannot be found in either political or military leaders" (Vanasco 6). But not only the public, since the genre was also a pedagogy for the new writers: Antonio Skármeta affirmed that the connection of Chileans with Latin American narrative in that initial period "until the success of Cuba, the publication of *The Time of the Hero* preceded by the publicity hype of the ingenious Seix Barral prize, the Hopscotchization of the universe by Sudamericana, was practically null," and that they therefore despised the Latin American literature they had known up to that point (1984, 267).

However, once they were integrated into the circuit of mercantile production and consumption, those same novels were reclassified as "avant-garde," giving rise to a discourse that challenged avant-gardism and also questioned the sterility of the aesthetic debate of previous times and the harm it had caused to the constitution of a truly revolutionary aesthetic program:

> From 1966 onward, a misdirected "avant-garde" established a false dilemma and delayed the process of the consolidation of a critical current that a generation of young authors and directors had initiated three years earlier. The realism versus avant-garde polemic diverted attention and confused aesthetic and ideological values. Realism became synonymous with conservatism, reaction, and avant-gardism with the revolutionary, the new (Morandi 23).

The perception by those in the theater, a genre I have not addressed so far, is symptomatic, since new genres and artistic forms were to take the place of the novel. The theater, which prescribes other, collective modes of reception, could nurture hopes of politicization that would not necessarily be rejected by the political avant-garde. The search for a new language, considered legitimate and even indispensable, was associated with *excessive ingenuity*, the individualism of artists, and ideological vacuity or, worse, with disinterest in social issues. Since the anti-intellectualist discourse presented the European as decadent (returning to a word disqualified after long and onerous polemics), the literary aesthetics that made use of certain concepts recently coined in France sounded unwise to certain sectors of the critical intelligentsia.

The trial of the boom involved a strong re-hierarchization of the map of genres, attacking the novel and novelists in particular, contrasting their "gratuitous" work with the sacrifice of the people and the revolutionaries:

> While García Márquez writes *One Hundred Years of Solitude*, in 1966, a Colombian priest, Camilo Torres, dies as a guerrilla fighter in the mountains, making use of the violence that the writer overlooks or declines to portray in his book. As if the geniality, technique, and vision of a Borges were transplanted to the tropics and shown off in the hands of a great magician, who also claims to be a leftist, in order to embrace all the contradictions of colonized intellectuality, complicit in the unrest and misfortunes of a people adrift. The bewitched mystery of García Márquez has a name: mythologizing the present (Martini Real 1972, 141).

The tension between the attempt to democratize culture and the attempt to revolutionize it was the central focus of the discussion on the avant-garde and politics. Many writers had to strike a precarious balance between their elitism and their sincere political reformism to take a stand against the theoretical challenge that the expansion of public life and the growing participation of the masses in it posed to their aesthetic affinities and political positions. The gap between mass culture and elite culture, which was in the process of irreversibly deepening, is a key factor in contextualizing the debates. The growing segmentation between the circuits of the consumption and production of culture made the separation between artists and the public more complex and profound, especially within the horizon of the revolution, where the aim was to bridge this gap. In any case, criticism was not limited to the question of the presumed avant-garde. The discrediting of the acclaimed novelists also entailed that of the conceptualization of the presumed realism that had served as a foundation for them. Criticizing in its entirety what he called contemporary bourgeois aesthetics (a term that included Garaudy, Fischer, and company), José Antonio Portuondo wrote:

> In the face of the growing abstractionism of contemporary art, Marxist aesthetics first opposed an unbridled defense of realism, especially of socialist realism, which from a perfectly valid aesthetic category in Gorky had become a narrow political carte blanche in the hands of Zhdanov and Khrushchev. It was then translated into the analysis of "modernism" and the "avant-garde," ranging from complete negation (Lukács) to historical justification (Fischer). An extreme position that broadens the frontiers of realism until any expression, however abstract and alienated from the real it may be, is the one adopted by Garaudy (1972, 12).

In closing, Portuondo referred, in no less disparaging terms, to the "growing interest of bourgeois ideologues in Marxism" (1972, 12), by which he meant the new literary critics and theorists who stressed the importance of language and established new categories, such as *écriture* and *structure*, and defended the absolute autonomy of the artistic work. The disparagement encompassed the structuralism and incipient post-structuralism that dominated French criticism and quickly seduced Latin American criticism in the countries that had more contact with the metropolitan centers.

Out of this constellation emerged the manifest and contradictory efforts to resolve the problems arising between taste and ideology, between the consequences and differences, between legitimate success and popularization, cultural fashions and aesthetic rigor, between the adoption of a pro-Western tradition and a Third World ideology, between the cultural industry and mass media, without being trapped in the uncomfortable cage of the mandarinate. The bid for new genres thus constituted the fundamental operation of political or revolutionary art as it was conceived in the second period of the epoch once anti-intellectualism had become hegemonic.

3. Communication, Truth, Revolution: The New Formats of a Revolutionary Art

> Perhaps the best news would be the birth not so much of new works but of new genres.
>
> ROBERTO FERNÁNDEZ RETAMAR

> Our narrative is bogged down and cannot find its way out. A political writer is more important than a literary writer.
>
> RODOLFO WALSH
> ("Boletín con los del premio")

Europe could afford certain luxuries; not so the Latin Americans, who could (and should) leave Proust and his new conquests for later, given that the leaders were asking for poems on demand and the revolution required syllabaries, songbooks, and collective rituals that would strengthen the spirits of the combatants and the morale of the governed. It was time for "emergency lyrics." Enzensberger's proposal, which was along similar lines, had been well received in Cuba (where he had traveled several times until Padilla accused him of being a foreign spy) and in its zone of influence. Enzensberger spoke of the "exhaustion" of literature, its limited influence on social life, and called on intellectuals who claimed to be well-meaning to contribute to the education of the people to raise awareness and bear witness to how some were struggling to change the world (1969, 149–61).

According to Andreas Huyssen, Enzensberger may have been right to criticize the revolutionary "histrionics" of the left, which sought to make up for its own incompetence by issuing invitations to the funerals of literature. But he also recalls his own revolutionary histrionics that led him to ask writers to devote themselves to producing social pedagogy rather than lamenting the state of high culture (Huyssen 151). The anti-intellectualist faction of the Latin American intellectual family also generalized critiques of the shortcomings of culture, as understood by artists who had conceived of their engagement as part of a new cultural agenda. The proposals that emerged from the First Congress on Education and Culture were extremely clear in this regard: education should be given full priority. Also because of the breakdown of the intellectual family and the entry of Latin American narrative into the market, the novel gave up its privileged place in the view of that faction of the literary field. The revolutionary proposals demanded an art shaped by events, ideally made by all and for all. Lisandro Otero wrote a report for Unesco ("Cultural Policy in Cuba") in which he highlighted precisely that tendency:

> In literature, a novel movement has grown from the literary workshops whereby literature is brought to the people, not only through periodicals and books, but by teams of poets and storytellers arranging gatherings in work centers and public places to read their works. . . . Thus, literature is taking on a new dimension in the encounter of the creator and his work with the people (Otero and Martínez Hinojoza 33).

At the same time, the word "pamphlet," which had been emblematic of what revolutionary art should not be, was exorcised of its negative connotations. According to Fornet, it had been the fear of the political pamphlet that had paralyzed Cuban literary production: "The current Cuban novel has taken great pains to avoid slipping into pamphleteering. But today we have the terrible suspicion that it took too many pains" (1971, 183). For his part, Ronald Portocarrero affirmed that the word had already lost its pejorative character and that the fear of being accused of pamphleteering was a fear of cowards and nothing more. Just as the writers grouped around *Libre* did not (and could not) defend the market for the market's sake, the "revolutionary" fraction of the literary field did not seriously defend the political pamphlet either. Because of their background, their readings, their expectations, such a defense was implausible and also disingenuous. When presenting the 1971 Casa de las Américas Prize to Manuel Cofiño López for his novel *La última mujer y el próximo combate* [The Last Woman and the Next Battle], Manuel Rojas said that the award-winning text possessed extraliterary virtues, that it was a constructive, measured, clean work. Portuondo described it as the "happy realization of a revolutionary novel, understanding as such that form of narration in which the creative imagination is at the service of a clear and definite political intention: to expose the dialectic birth of a socialist conscience" (1971). He highlights the living contradiction of the magical, pre-scientific world, responsible for that marvelous real, which Carpentier began to cultivate and which culminates in *One Hundred Years of Solitude*." The magical realism that goes from Carpentier to García Márquez is a magical and pre-scientific conception of reality that opposes the revolutionary and the very new parameters imposed by the Marxist-Leninist interpretation of reality itself" (1971).

How can we conceive of the rare case of a literature with *extraliterary* qualities? The challenge was not a simple one. This is reflected in the system of restrictions or taboos that paralyzes literary discourse, clearly illustrated in the lyrics of "Playa Girón," a *protest song* (according to the term used at the time) by singer-songwriter Silvio Rodríguez. With each verse addressed to his colleagues in the various artistic and intellectual fields (poets, musicians, historians), the text formulates all the forms of *what to do* in order *not to do* something out of place: this "out of place" is so broad that it encompasses almost everything: the sentimental, the "beyond the avant-garde," the political pamphlet. The first verse, addressed to the poets, speaks of the greatest restrictions or taboos. The following verses—given that the text, despite its questions, manages to move forward—establishes its "story" about the sailors of the fishing boat that spent several months on the African coasts. The questions about how to proceed become increasingly rhetorical, without ceasing to be the main compositional principle, both aesthetic and ideological, of "Playa Girón":

> Fellow poets: / considering the latest events in poetry / I wish to ask—urgently— / what kind of adjectives should be used to write / the poem of a ship without getting sentimental, / far from the avant-garde and the obvious pamphlet / should I use words / like Flota Cubana de Pesca and Playa Girón? / Fellow musicians: / considering those polytonal and audacious songs / I wish to ask—urgently— / what kind of harmonies should be used to write / the song of this ship with men of little imagination / with men and only men on deck / black and red and blue men / the men who crowd the "Playa Girón." / Fellow historians: / considering how implacable the truth must be / I wish to ask / what I should say, what borders I must respect / if someone steals food and then gives his life, what do I do? / How far does the truth extend: / How much do we know? / They should write—then—the history, their history / these men of "Playa Girón."[52]

Around 1969 and 1970, a commitment to the cultivation of new literary formats and genres, such as testimony, poetry, and protest songs, became widespread among the anti-intellectualist group. In 1969, Miguel Barnet, quasi-founder of the testimonial genre with *Biografía de un cimarrón* [*Biography of a Runaway Slave*] (1966), devoted a long article to testimony in the magazine of the Union of Cuban Artists and Writers. In it he wrote:

> There is nothing more controversial, more misleading, and oppressive than the definition of the novel. Novel, so to speak, is a double-edged sword. . . . The old term novel has served, like so many other terms, like so many other nomenclatures, to bring the whole of Western art into a closed circle. . . . What we now call the novel, with all its trappings, fails us, it is not effective, it is of no use to us. . . . So-called fiction is gradually losing its substance, it is no longer useful (102).

52 Cited in Cardenal 89–90.

In that work he quoted Enzensberger and coincided in criticizing the aristocratic and elitist character of the "laboratory" novel, a novel that in his opinion was a dying machine that was intended to be revived "with a new crank"—a crank that is later "patented and bears the name of the *new novel*" (105). In Barnet's view, since Martí, Latin American writers had been trying to break away, trying to inaugurate. The results of those attempts were unsuccessful: "Some, attempting to be so 'unique,' have gone to spend the night in the heights of Matías Pérez's balloon, others, attempting to be so purist, have fallen into the well of indigenous waters, never to resurface." What Barnet proposed was a *foundational literature*, to which he could contribute with what he called the "testimony novel," one of whose merits was the "suppression of the self, of the ego of the writer or sociologist" (105–9), which, as seen in the arguments of anti-intellectualism, was the "natural" defect of acclaimed novelists. The novel-testimony, or simply testimony, would replace the exhaustion of the novel as a tool of knowledge. In testimony, knowledge of reality prevailed and the author-witness imbued it with a fundamentally historical meaning (110).

It is no coincidence, then, that in 1970, *Casa de las Américas* inaugurated "testimony" as a new category in its annual literary contests. The testimony of urgency and reality would perhaps fill the void in Cuban revolutionary literature. The rules of the genre, to participate in *Casa*'s contest, stressed the importance of direct documentation and of the author's knowledge of the facts. The first winning work in the new category was *La guerrilla tupamara* [*The Tupamaro Guerrillas*], by María Esther Gilio, emphasizing the fact that, at a time when Uruguay had become "radicalized," the need for communication became more intense:

> Is it possible to write a story, a novel, about the Tupamaros and the struggle in Uruguay? Clearly, it is. However, it is legitimate to think that these anonymous, courageous, and austere Uruguayan combatants are, in their expression of rebellion, an aesthetic manifestation that deserves the dedication of a writer to capture them in living reality and bear witness to that experience. We do not deny, of course, that in fiction (short stories, novels) the writer can also engage in the revolutionary struggle. But it is in testimony where

> the elements found in society are gathered, ready to enter the linotype and be massively disseminated (Andrade 172–73).

A new pedagogical emphasis, which stood out in the resolutions of the National Congress of Education and Culture (1971), was better suited to the tasks that writers could fulfill in transmitting and disseminating revolutionary morality. That is why so much emphasis was placed on the "communicative" aspects of the texts and on the defense of a propagandistic literature that would emphasize the communicative aspects of the message in order to reach the widest possible audience:

> The possibilities for communication must be intensified. We must try, by all means possible, to stop poetry from being a recalcitrantly elitist activity. . . . To this end, young Cuban poetry has taken—has begun to take—two complementary paths: the creation of direct poetry, which draws on and begins with the concerns and issues of the revolution, and the use of any means of mass communication (Casaus and Rivero 108).

Eduardo Galeano (in an interview with Jorge Ruffinelli) renounced his short stories and explained his shift to writing documentary, explanatory, and denunciatory texts, or "militant essays" in his own words, such as *Las venas abiertas de América Latina* [*Open Veins of Latin America*]. In that sense, the revolutionary writer, pressured by the historical moment, had to write not what he wanted but what he considered "necessary." In any case, Galeano displayed the characteristic tension of the moment, affirming that he did not share the inferiority complex of the writer as opposed to the man of action, and repeating the rather overused formula that said that writing could be a potential form of action. But in order for that to be true, Galeano found that he had to abandon fiction (in Ruffinelli 1971a, 30–31). Rodolfo Walsh had said that the concept of the novel was in crisis: it was surpassed by testimony and denunciation as artistic categories suitable for the new juncture (Link 1994, 55 and 59). Even the greatest representative of the novelistic genre, Gabriel García Márquez, declared that he would no longer write novels and that instead of cultivating the genre that had made him famous, he would write short stories or "novelistic reports" in the style of Truman Capote (González Bermejo 1970). The new interest in protest songs, poetry (that had previously resisted the market), testimony, and journalism arose from the possibilities these formats and genres had of extending the conditions of production and reception. According to songwriters, committed songs complemented the process of liberation through denunciation (Viglietti). A song can replace a book, affirmed the Catalan protest singer Raimón during his visit to Mexico. The system that limited book culture to an elite could not prevent people from listening to songs that "were about reality." The range of the audience was greatly expanded by this genre to which many poets contributed (Suárez).

Between 1969 and 1971, the political-revolutionary appeared to be embodied more effectively in poetry than in the novel. The loss of the ideological legitimacy of the narrators of the boom (because of their, at best, ineffectiveness), given the genre's predisposition to incorporate itself into the market and its publicity apparatus, enabled this *transition.* Years earlier, the subjective nature attributed to the poetic genre—"the subtle temptations of the ego" (Peri Rossi 1970)—appeared to distance it from politics and restrict it to accounting for the pure subjectivity of the lyrical subject. From that point on, new poetic bases were formulated for a genre, closely aligned with protest song, that—instead of being measured in terms of the verbal and structural prowess that proved the narrative's ability to revolutionize language—was defined as "more akin to socialism." Mario Benedetti was preparing his anthology *Poetas comunicantes* [Communicating Poets] around that time and stated that communicative poetry renounced the pretensions of posterity. Around 1971 there was talk of a "poetry boom" (both in *Marcha* and in *Casa de las Américas*), which was very different from that of narrative, especially because it had nothing to do with the market: "Two remarkable occurrences characterize this year . . . that poetry—a perpetual outsider for so long—has taken the lead in literary activity and that its current firm and indefatigable promoter is the newest generation of our literature" (*Marcha,* no. 1561). Ernesto Cardenal, one of the most celebrated Latin American poets, commented that poetry had faced a reaction against subjectivism and now dealt with current affairs (a word that could be the key to this new reformulation of political genres that includes cinema, poetry, testimony, and song).

Current events, conversation, testimony, and simplicity as a synonym of maturity seemed to constitute the new norms of the genre; a poetry "made of events, people, and things, real places, dates, figures," in the words of Cardenal (in Benedetti 1970a). There was even the paradox of a poetry not made of words, of the convenience of "saying things, not words" (Fernández Retamar in Benedetti 1971b), a phrase that summarized the antinomy between discourse and action, between intellectual and revolutionary. Despite the significant amount of rhetoric implicit in these formulas (consider the poetic production of these same authors, especially that of Cardenal and Gelman), they themselves seemed to suggest that poetry was not really a trade (or at any rate, not a restrictive one or one that implied a knowledge acquired through years of reading). Poetry could attempt, in some cases, to "rescue" the novel. An experiment in this sense was Mario Benedetti's novel in verse, *El cumpleaños de Juan Ángel* [*Juan Ángel's Birthday*], which also touched on the guerrilla theme at the height of the armed struggle of the Tupamaros in Uruguay. This attempt was very well received on the other side of the Río de la Plata. In fact, the unsigned review that appeared in issue 5 of *Nuevos Aires* recommended it as revolutionary literature:

> In a return to the epic, like Homer with Troy, Benedetti shows us the Ulysses of our times; of course, today's heroes—in the absence of gods on Olympus and shields or swords that are invincible in battle—possess less mythical but more concrete weapons: the total conviction that there is only one way to seize power: the armed struggle, and that there is only one receiver of that power: the people. Juan Ángel could be (or should be) *any one of us*: a human being with all of his or her contradictions, joys, and anxieties who, at last, chooses his revolutionary fate, the most elevated condition for mankind. Juan Ángel has joined the Tupamaros and faces his first battle; on the threshold of this battle, Benedetti ends his story. There is no need to go any further; one knows who, in the long run, will win. We do not want to fall into easy dithyrambs; we simply say that *Juan Angel's Birthday* seems to us to be one of the most politically and aesthetically important texts of these years. We believe that Benedetti's aim was to combine both aspects and to achieve full author-reader communication. And he has succeeded, in its entirety.

One of the dangers of this new poetry was *infantilization*. The embodiment of the genre conceived for its affinity with the political and expressed in the fact that it did not require special skills could have been Magdalena, Ruffinelli's "child poet," or Carlos María Gutiérrez, the novice journalist of *Marcha* who astonished everyone by winning the Casa de la Poesía prize in 1970 without having previously written a single poem. The jury's rationale (in a year in which Uruguayans swept the awards) was the high quality of poetry through which *Diario del cuartel* [Prison Diary], the winning collection of poems, expressed the passion and significance of the Latin American revolutionary struggle through "personal experiences." These personal experiences unfolded in a space recognized as particularly "revolutionary": prison. Benedetti said that Gutiérrez did not consider himself a poet because, for him, the revolution was more important than poetry, although, for his compatriot, it was precisely this conviction that made him more of a writer (1970b). At the other end of the scale, Rama, who by then was already living outside Uruguay, described Gutiérrez's book as "an applied and scholastic task that I believe is beginning to border on the art of the taste of civil servants and that is—for adults—like those poems that enchant wet nurses and that they pass on to children" (1971a).

Ruffinelli's child poet was named Magdalena, and she wrote poems about Camilo Torres (who had been a friend of her father's) and the Latin American revolution. She published a collection of poems—*La palabra del rocío* [The Word of the Dew]—, with a poem-prologue by Pablo Neruda and an introduction by Gonzalo de Freitas. According to Ruffinelli, the precocious poet was born in California, her parents were Chilean, and the family had lived for many years in Montevideo. In 1969, at the age of eight, she wrote "Camilo Torres en su tumba" [Camilo Torres in His Grave] (Ruffinelli 1971b):

> He lies in his grave
> Camilo
> Nettles cover your chest
> Camilo
> A cold corpse is reflected. It was
> Camilo
> You mercifully defended the poor

and died for them
          Camilo
Already your true face
has risen to heaven
          Camilo
Only your corpse seems
to wait for your return
          Camilo
          Camilo Torres

The new poetry (the procedures and themes of which Magdalena captured with great insight) pushed an aesthetics of blood or self-flagellation to its extreme: the repression of the poetic word as a result of unfulfilled revolutionary duty, precisely as a result of writing literature. It was, in the versions that could adopt the *interpretations* of the know-how of the genre expressed by Ernesto Cardenal (but not of his own poetics), an anti-intellectualist poetry that expressed the contradiction between two conflicting forces: that of writing and that of the rifle. This "aesthetics of blood," in the antipodes of Artaudian cruelty, can be illustrated with a fragment of "Tracción a sangre" [Traction in Blood], by poet Silvia Herrera:

You still have to suffer so much
poor sunken corner of the world . . .
you start to ask for
your own blood,
young and dead. Oh
she's not dead I
know
she's not dead, she's not dead she's not
dead, that's why she's running through the streets and I'm screaming with her...

The politicization of society was accompanied by a remarkable increase in sensory *stimuli* carrying the message and good news of the revolution. Among them, there were an enormous number of musician-poets who cultivated the protest song genre: it was a worldwide phenomenon.

From Joan Baez and Pete Seeger to Georges Moustaki, Georges Brassens, the Quilapayún group, Violeta Parra, Daniel Viglietti, Víctor Jara, Los Olimareños, Carlos Puebla, Armando Tejada Gómez, César Isella, Alfredo Zitarrosa, each with their own style and quality, combined the massiveness of the recital and the ideological exploitation of the mass media in a growing recording industry that had a greater impact than the printed word.

Cuba was the host of the first world meeting of "protest songs" in Varadero in 1967. The songs referred to the liberation struggle, the Vietnam War, racial discrimination, and social and political denunciation. At that meeting, in which popular and sophisticatedly modern musical forms coexisted, there was a discussion about giving the genre a new denomination: "revolutionary song," "song of struggle," "new song," "testimonial song." An ideal in which the new, the struggle, testimony, and revolution came together with the idea that the boundaries of the arts were being transgressed and subverted. This was expressed in the final declaration of the Varadero meeting: song, due to its particular characteristics, possesses an enormous capacity to communicate with the masses, as it breaks down the barriers that, like illiteracy, hinder dialogue between artists and the people they form part of. Thus, the *protest song* was defined as a weapon at the service of the people, which is why Casa de las Américas became the headquarters of a center to collect, classify, and disseminate the materials of a particularly "revolutionary" artistic expression.

The controversy in which the novel was embroiled was challenged by other literary genres. However, none sparked such expectations of politicization as those of *new political cinema*.

In fact, Ambrosio Fornet claimed that the timidity of Cuban literature, caught between two fears (social realism and avant-garde hermeticism), should be contrasted with the impetus of documentary cinema (1971). In his manifesto *Eztétyka da fome* [*Aesthetics of Hunger*], written in 1965, the most important Latin American filmmaker and creator of Brazilian *cinema novo*, Glauber Rocha (who lived in Cuba from late 1971 to December 1972 and collaborated with the ICAIC), maintained: "Our originality is our hunger." Although economic conditioning plunged the Third World into philosophical impoverishment and powerlessness, hunger and misery could be taken as the main argument for a new, fundamentally violent aesthetics:

> Hunger in Latin America . . . is the essence of our society. . . . only a culture of hunger can qualitatively surpass its own structures by undermining and destroying them. The most noble cultural manifestation of hunger is violence. The moment of violence is the moment when the colonizer becomes aware of the existence of the colonized. . . . The love that this violence encompasses is as brutal as violence itself, because it is not the kind of love which derives from complacency or contemplation, but rather a love of action and transformation" (13–14, 1983).

Rocha's film *Terra em Transe* [*Entranced Earth*] won the Luis Buñuel prize at Cannes, awarded by the Spanish critics and the international federation of film companies. In Locarno, Switzerland, it received the grand prize and the critics' prize, and in Havana it was considered the best film of 1967. Commenting on Vietnamese film production, especially the short *Cô giáo Hanh* [Teacher Hanh], José Rodríguez Elizondo (1967) portrayed political cinema as an art of the people that had "nothing to do with pure art or with art for the exquisite," which, of course, had no connection with an "art of butterflies or daisies," and which found its artistic material everywhere, especially "in the craters left by bombs." *Cô giáo Hanh*, in addition to being a "weapon of combat," was, according to Rodríguez Elizondo, in keeping with the best modern European cinema, which was unknown in Vietnam.

The opposition between cinema and literature is often traced back to 1968, the year of the consolidation of political documentary cinema, which took its cameras to where relevant events were taking place. As Alfredo Guevara, director of ICAIC, declared, 1968 had been the year of Cuban and revolutionary cinematographic maturity, thanks to the enormous production of documentaries, many of which were shown in the Documentales 69 festival, the program of which stated that "of all the artistic manifestations associated with the work of the revolution, it is the documentary that has been the most consistent and organic." Although that year saw the release of feature films such as Tomás Gutiérrez Alea's *Memorias del subdesarrollo* [*Memories of Underdevelopment*] and Humberto Solás's *Lucía*, *Casa de las Américas* (no. 53) stated that the "quality" and "effectiveness" of ICAIC's work lay mainly in the production of documentary films and in the contributions of Santiago Álvarez, one of the genre's great innovators. What's more, the magazine reconsidered the relationship of the revolution with the arts, drawing on a precedent with considerable authority. It thus declared:

> It was not the first time that a revolution had understood the extraordinary relevance of cinema. Lunacharsky has told us how Lenin commented to him: "You, who happen to be the protector of the arts, should remember that, of all the arts, the most important for us is the cinema" ("El documental cubano" 1969, 162).

In September 1968, the constitution of *Marcha*'s film department clearly established the terms of what could be considered political art: it was not going to film "sunsets or reflections of light on the waves." Not sunsets, reflections of light on the waves, butterflies, or daisies: people resisting. The New Latin American Cinema movement had its inaugural moment at the 1967 Viña del Mar Festival in Chile, where the conviction that political cinema could become a weapon for the revolution began to take shape. Commenting on the 1969 Viña del Mar Festival, the Argentine weekly *Panorama* wrote:

> If Latin American cinema were to be judged by what was shown at the recent Viña del Mar Festival, one could deduce that its revolutionary ferment is tremendous. Almost all the material shown at the festival was motivated by the goal to attack and change structures, with the illusion of turning a cultural product into a rifle.[53]

---

53 Cited by Mariano Mestman in "Notas para una historia de un cine de contrainformación y lucha política," *Causas y Azares*, Buenos Aires, no. 2 (Autumn 1995): 144–61. Ministerio de Cultura de Nicaragua, ed., *Hacia una política cultural de la revolución popular Sandinista* (Managua: Área de Literatura y Publicaciones, 1982).

Cinema could make use of its immediate visual impact as well as its capacity to process the immediacy of events. Its modes of exhibition could also be conceived in terms of *acts*, as emblematically expressed in a number of manifestos of the Cine Liberación group and the film *La hora de los hornos* [*The Hour of the Furnaces*], by Fernando Solanas and Octavio Getino, which circulated clandestinely in Argentina and in which, during the second part, a voice-over invited the audience to pause the projection in order to discuss the images. The invitation declared: "This is not a film, this is an act of liberation."[54] The timeliness of the themes, the strong aestheticization of violence, and the search for high-impact images were the characteristics thanks to which this new cinema could be called "political." Just when the concept of intellectual commitment and the demands of radical politicization were entering into crisis, the concept of the intellectual's autonomy was broken, and the intellectual had to take on the role of political activist. It was posited that cinema (and no longer the word) formed part of this militancy.

Of this cinema, as of one of its precursors, Joris Ivens, it could be said:

> He senses the focal point of world events. He brings to light resisted truths. The Civil War in Spain, the Soviet Union, Cuba, Vietnam. He is a Marxist-Leninist of conviction. . . . He considers the script of his films like the plan of an offensive.

In 1969, this New Latin American Cinema received the attention of Europe and the world at various festivals. Glauber Rocha won the best director award at Cannes for *O Dragão da Maldade contra o Santo Guerreiro* [*The Dragon of Evil Against the Warrior Saint*]. *Cahiers du Cinéma* devoted special issues to *The Hour of the Furnaces* by the Argentines Solanas and Getino (founders of the Cine Liberación group); to Glauber Rocha; and the Bolivian film *Yawar Mallku* [*The Blood of the Condor*]. Other films, such as *La primera carga al machete* [*The First Charge of the*

---

54 See Ana Longoni 1995, "Sobre una antirrevista en el año del Cordobazo," *Causas y Azares*, no. 2 (Autumn 1995): 136–43. The film was presented in Pesaro, Italy, in July 1968, and thus began to circulate in international encounters. See Longoni 1995 and Mestman 1995.

Machete], from Cuba, or *Macunaíma* and *Os inconfidentes* [*The Conspirators*], from Brazil, demonstrated new aspects of Latin American originality. Thus, "the sad era in which 'Latin American cinema' meant rural melodrama, clouds at dusk, *zamba*, conga, tango, and marimbas" (Echegoyen 1969) came to an end. It is interesting that the acclaim for this new cinema was expressed in the same terms in which the new novel had been applauded.

The importance of cinema was proportional to the space dedicated to it in many political-cultural publications. *Marcha* usually dedicated the last issue of each year to assessing the state of each artistic expression. Generally headed off by literature, issue no. 1505, the last of 1970, gave priority to cinema (literature was given a single page, which was also the last).[55]

The new modes of political art appeared to suggest that they democratized not only (collective) reception but also production; as the Cuban filmmaker Santiago Álvarez said, to make films you didn't need to be a genius, anyone could do it. David Viñas made a similar suggestion when he proposed taking cinema as an example of collective work. Political cinema eliminated the problems present in individual writing, such as "Balkanization at the personal level" through a process of the "dissolution of individuality and its replacement by a pseudonym that characterizes those who work collectively, dissolving all the dogmas of literary theology: sacredness" and the "theological vision of literature: the writer as creator" ("¿El único encuentro del encuentro?" 1970, 160–61).

4. The Literatures of Politics in Cuba

Revolutions represent a unique case of the relationship between literature, power, and politics, which deserves to be analyzed. This means thinking about what literature and power do together when politics and aesthetics establish a space for collaboration based at the same time on

55 Aharonian 1979, 25; "Cuba documental" 1970, 27; and Solanas, Getino, Sanjinés, Litin, Handler, Álvarez, Meyer 1970, 14.

values that formulate, for literature and literati, politics as a necessity. This rare phenomenon (in the literal sense, scarce and unusual) forces us to conceptually define an object in a circumstance. First of all, because it highlights, as a cliché of the theoretical language, the expression "the politics of literature." It seems to refer to the intrinsic and specific efficacy of symbolic and artistic production as such, to the political modes of being of literature and art, *independent of their historical forms of institutionalization.* In order to explore an avatar of the historical relationship between literature and revolution, in which different strategies of production, circulation, and reading operate, it is helpful to get rid of the set expression and look for a more generously descriptive one, in which the unusualness of the data shines through. These forms of collaboration between literature and power can be called "the literatures of politics."

For some time, the Cuban Revolution was presented as a revolution without theory, in part because its outbreak and subsequent evolution were of a vertiginous and changing dynamism. The expression of this completely foundational nature was embodied in the phrase "we are greener than palm trees," a clear allusion to the unpredictability of the process of shaping the new society and an appeal to the creativity of that process, to its character of absolute innovation. The revolution also brought together, from the beginning, an immense majority of artists and intellectuals, and not only Cubans. The abrupt turnaround of the political, social, economic, and cultural reality was the undreamt-of realization of the surrealist program: *to change life.* The moral primacy of the political leaders was undisputed. But—and this is the first problem that the revolution posed to writers—creativity and innovation first appeared to be attributes of political power, of its strategies and struggles, rather than of art and artists, who were placed one step behind. The assumption that the merits of art would never equal those of the revolution, widespread among politicians and artists alike, generated a kind of permanent sense of deficit in the face of the magnitude of the collective struggle.

The legitimacy of the new political power, its major representativeness, could not but play a major role at the cultural level: on the one hand, as a *producer* of criteria for the ideological and aesthetic validity of literature, as a privileged and active *reader*—both implicit and explicit of concrete works—, and also as a *critic* comparing the degree of suitability linking the programmatic with its realizations. Until then, for Latin American writers, the ability to reflect on the critical character of literature was guaranteed by the conception of the state as the writer's natural "other." This led to a second problem: the need for an affirmative accompaniment breaks with an age-old tradition. It is not a coincidence that a significant part of the literary production of the early years of the Cuban Revolution makes reference to the outrages of the Batista dictatorship and preserves its critical tone, a symptom of the difficulty of finding a political logic in accordance with the literary logics that emphasized the critical power of literature. The forms of the physical institutionalization of literature underlined this direction: the weight of political power in the regulation of matters concerning art took the form of the abolition of the literary market. This new institutional framework left the final word in the creation of "revolutionary" cultural institutions in the hands of political power and fostered a new profile of the intellectual, often, but not always, included in the state apparatus as a civil servant. The collaboration of artists with the revolution took on different forms: 1) participation in collective tasks—the most symbolic of which was the *zafra* or sugarcane harvest—, in literacy, or in assuming responsibilities in public administration; 2) the strictly cultural civil service; and 3) the strictly literary; paradoxically, the least comfortable. From this comes a third problem. The egalitarian logic of the revolution is underpinned by an ethics that is contrary to the preservation of professional privileges, derived almost exclusively from class origin. Hence the discomfort of writers in fulfilling the double role of "anonymity" in the collective task of the masses and at the same time trying to do what is expected of them, in their specific field: to make a "revolutionary" contribution.

In this context, where the very notion of intellectual field finds its historical limit since it presupposes a relative degree of autonomy with respect to the field of power, the duty was imposed on writers to create a literature that corresponded in excellence to the excellence of the revolution. So how could writers escape the trap of the "sad craft" (the useless craft of literature) within the context of such a political process? This is how Antón Arrufat (1963a) defines literary work in his poem "Playa Girón":

> With my useless hands
> that can do nothing but write,
> I would like to gather your heads, my brothers, my compatriots, the heads blasted off and shattered by shells,
> . . . I, whose sad trade is waiting for others to live for him, for their blood.

The main features that characterize "the literatures of politics" can be summarized as follows:

1. *Acceptance of co-authorship or a strongly embodied form of implicit reader practically superimposed on an empirical first reader*: For writers, adhering to the revolution meant accepting in their own field the expectations of a political power that demands a "revolutionary" literature, and that also reads, critiques, and puts pressure on the writing. This process of quasi-co-authorship is the basic feature of the literatures of politics. Needless to say, there are antagonistic forms of this figure of power as reader and co-author, and revolution is one of its most atypical cases. At the opposite end is another case, the most common, which stimulates the production of "official" literature, written according to commandments (not always explicit) that are expressed more or less coercively. All censorship declines one of the modes of power as reader and co-author, in this case, not of a writing but of its silence.

It is not worth asking whether Cuban authors who embraced the revolution considered revolutionary power a co-author, at least in part, of their texts. What is important is the way in which their literary production takes into account that *power judged to be of excellence*. In this case, power and its cultural officials are a condition of the writing and of the reproduction and circulation of that writing. A literature like this that is compulsorily institutionalized includes a series of listening and attention strategies. Collaborative writing, but in which the two extremes of the agreement embody, through tradition and conjuncture, diverse logics.

2. *Overcoming tradition*: The literatures of politics face, among other things, the difficulties posed by the inert weight of a tradition, of the preexistence of a literary system, of aesthetic skills and acquired tastes, of a network of connections with international literature and art, and an intellectual field, all prior to the revolutionary process. This implies a greater heterogeneity of temporalities and traditions between

the aesthetic and the political, different residues that also address, in each block, the ideal of innovation. For Cuban literature, the revolution could not become stage zero of history. This requirement to adapt the heterogeneity of two historical series is another of the features of the literatures of politics.

3. *Programmatic uncertainty of aesthetic production*: The literatures of politics in Cuba had to interpret their insertion in a cultural policy that was never entirely explicit and was subjected, like all literature, to an aesthetic and ideological struggle for legitimacy among cultural producers. Despite the enthusiasm and fervor that artists demonstrated in their desire to collaborate with the revolution, from the very beginning there was a degree of uncertainty as to what their specific role in the revolution would be. There were also explicit differences about the type of culture to be practiced and promoted. But this gap was completely filled with the hypothesis that the time would come when the role of art would be fully reestablished, above the insufficient and partial point of view of the actors, immersed in history's present moment. When convening the First National Congress of Cuban Writers and Artists, Juan Marinello advised the revolutionary writer: "Keep your ear to the people and your mastery in the work; everything else will follow." The "everything else" is precisely the touchstone or philosopher's stone in which the alchemy of the revolution would offer its features to Cuban art and literature.

4. *Transience:* The definitive parameters of a revolutionary literature were, by definition, indefinable since, because the revolution was a living and ever-changing process and its writers, representatives of an "intermediate" historical moment, the final outcome depended on the future. The conviction that, once ideologically established, the new reality would produce new men and new sensibilities reinforced the transitory and instrumental character of the literary system in force.

5. *The need to emphasize a dual sense of belonging: to literature and to the revolution.* Cuban literature, after 1959, makes an effort to insert itself into the new social process without abandoning certain values associated with a modern literary tradition. This approach works literally in *Así en la paz como en la guerra* [In Peace as in War], where the book is the actual stage for the process: between each of his stories, Cabrera Infante "inserts" the vignettes in which he thematizes the violence of the struggle against Batista. Through this insertion, he

preserves his own place, midway between storyteller and reporter of the revolution. As if this splicing could only take place through juxtaposition and as if, even then, the project were doomed to failure, the last words of the book refer to the walls of a prison on which those who fought against Batista left their combative messages of farewell before their inevitable death. The graffiti of the fighters condemned by the dictator, says Cabrera, is the true revolutionary literature.

6. *The interpretation of the current ideals of political correctness.* If the true revolution had already been achieved, and the true revolutionary literature had already been written, the literatures of politics basically posed a question: How can the revolution be interpreted correctly and literarily? And how can "this" revolution be interpreted correctly and literarily? The many forms of the political nature of these literatures include the processes of interpreting and putting into writing the prevailing ideals of political correctness. At the level of strictly ideological content, the values of collectivism, solidarity, class struggle, the appreciation of the people, anti-individualism, the value of sacrifice for revolutionary morality, etc. come into play here. Of more interest than the thematic tracing of these ideals are their literary staging, that is, the way in which the ideals of political correctness *in the literature*—ideals that without being explicitly formulated constitute a characteristic tension of these literatures—are interpreted. In reality, this sort of precaution, anticipated reading, interpretation-prognosis, rather than being associated with the public that receives a new and revolutionary literature, is tied to the power of the reader, a co-author insofar as they constitute the implicit reader and, in many cases, coincide with the real. The need to correctly interpret what was expected can be said to be the main feature of the literature of politics. As a result, one of the strongest assessments of this literature is the affirmation of intellectuals as bearers of the misery of ideas and the misery of action. In anti-intellectualism, the literatures of politics confronted one of their truths.

Given that power does not provide aesthetic parameters, the ideals of political correctness in literature undergo a displacement similar to that observed in the oscillation between work and life in the case of commitment. Thus, the ambiguity perceived at each juncture with respect to the aesthetic ideals of the revolution means that the most easily interpretable ideals are transferred to the field of experience of the writers themselves in terms of political activism. For this reason, the literatures of politics tend to deploy an ideological critique of the figure of the writer in particular and of the intellectual in general, as if that figure were analyzed by power itself.

The panegyric of the ruler is a genre as old as the West. The ancient Greek name *basilixos logos* (which emphasizes the ruler as the origin of the sacralized word and does not involve the literary servant) expresses the situation of Cuban writers better than its translation: it is the words of the leader/revolution (insofar as in Cuba revolution and leader were associated, uniting in both name and person two concepts that were henceforth inseparable) that one seeks to translate. The literatures of politics took on a complex relationship with sincerity, even that of fiction. Of course, the insincere components are not entirely discardable, but they are not the object of this communication; the border between irony and enunciative seriousness is, in all cases, a matter of interpretable pragmatics, and even more so in the literatures of politics. In other words, if politics has a zone of Realpolitik, then its equivalent in the literatures of politics would be something like a "*Realliteratur.*"

In *Los niños se despiden*, winner of the 1968 edition of the Casa de las Américas Prize, there is a narrative of social foundation ab nihilo that operates as a parable of the revolution, written in a language of mystical rapture and loaded with secular religiosity. In this foundational description, the leader-creator prescribes tasks and trades to men. I quote: "'And what am I?'" (asked the narrator). "The angry leader retorted: 'What were you doing while everyone around me welcomed the distribution of work and tools?' And the man replied: 'I was contemplating your work and marveling at your judgment and fairness.' The leader, moved, answered him: 'You, sit on my right, for you are the poet.'"

Pablo Armando Fernández leads us directly to the quasi-collective response that, as an ideal of the political correctness of literature, the literatures of politics gave themselves: basically, the acceptance that the writer is subordinated to the directives of the state. Moreover, this question is one of the recurrences of these texts, that is, the fictional approach to the problems that the revolution poses to the writer or the artist. Zone of condensation, aleph, bridge between historical experience and historical imagination, the situation itself became literary material out of which the requirements of the revolution became productive for the writers. Bound by their respect for two logics that until then had operated in separate lanes (that of art, with autonomous pretensions, and that of politics, embodied in a perfect power), the writers made their position one of their main topics, both in countless declarations and in their texts. To that end, they appropriated one of the reproaches Ernesto Guevara had made of them when he declared that the original sin of those intellectuals was that they were not sufficiently revolutionary.

It was through self-abasement and anti-intellectualism that this revolutionary deficit was translated into writing, revealing that revolutionary subordination and discipline are manifested mainly through meticulous self-observation, which does not exclude the principle of self-suspicion. Hence the reiteration of texts that narrate conflicts of conscience—splitting—that afflict the intellectual alter egos. For example, *No hay problema* [There Is No Problem] (1961), by Edmundo Desnoes, or *La situación* [*The Situation*] (1963), by Lisandro Otero, in which this question is tackled in a surprisingly similar way.

Memorias del subdesarrollo [*Memories of Underdevelopment*] by Desnoes (1968) is a passionate literary translation of the problem. Taking advantage of the various narrative opportunities offered by fiction, Desnoes works ideologically and produces a complex text that lends itself to irony and, therefore, to a double reading: for and against the revolution. The reader's threshold of credulity is called into question when faced with these statements. Do we believe them wholesale? Which of all the statements? At the same time, the fact that the *author* is cited as a character full of negative traits (an accommodating, selfish, and ambitious writer) increases the irony as a procedure that does not necessarily overlook the narrator's stark vision of the Cuban present. *Memories of Underdevelopment* may have been published and celebrated in Havana, but it was also read as a vehicle for "sincere" statements. The review devoted to it in *Time* ("Punto de vista gusano," 1967) expresses astonishment that the book was published in Cuba, concluding that this demonstrates "that Cuban censorship is relatively tolerant of self-criticism."

The ironic duplicity achieved by Desnoes is thus another service rendered to Cuba by a writer. This procedure, in which the irony is practically physical, the daughter of duplication, reveals everything that in this problematic of the revolutionary intellectual is, in its own way, also ironic. The predictable frontier and difference between the public and private discourses of the writers, the negotiation of pacts with Truth for the benefit of the propaganda of Realpolitik, the desire to contribute to the revolutionary process and the need not to be excluded from the system, the paths by which one name accuses another of being a counterrevolutionary to end up, a short or long time later, in the position of the accused, reveal the farcical and at the same time tragic dimension of the question.

"Could you describe the size of the people with your tongue?" Heberto Padilla had asked himself in a poem, long before he became so scandalous. Calling that poem "Ahora que estás de vuelta" [Now That You Are Back] is a significant allusion to the return of many writers in the diaspora to revolutionary Cuba, including Padilla himself, as well as Calvert Casey, Edmundo Desnoes, Pablo Armando Fernández, and Fayad Jamís, among others. To be able to describe the size of the people (enormous) with the tongue of a poet (limited) is a literary program in itself. And if one must judge based on the need for self-defense that many writers seemed to experience at the time, such a task proved impossible.

As with any failure, part of the reason for it lies in the excessive ambitiousness of the program. A revolutionary literature required the accumulation of virtues that are hard to achieve; renewal with legibility, massive impact, generation of political awareness, excellence in line with the excellence that political power takes as a model, etc. This emulation of a Power that presents itself as the *pinnacle* of perfection obscured both the possibilities of the literary (because it expresses at its core an unequal competition) and the pretensions of the writers to exercise them in a context in which the situation of the latter was regulated by mechanisms of unprecedented control and self-control.

5. New Forms of Knowledge and Cultural Critique

Toward the end of the epoch, the incorporation of new forms of knowledge was one of the foundations of the aspiration to scientificity that characterized a new profile of intellectual practice in a specific area. The theoretical bias adopted by *Casa de las Américas* in the seventies (which marks a change in the publication's profile) is a good example of this valorization of theory. For example, issue 71 made reference to the fact that

> the fundamental task of this magazine is, of course, to disseminate the creations and study the problems of our America: it would be enough to recall the last three issues to keep in mind how we aspire to fulfill this task. *But it is also our responsibility to disseminate Marxist judgments of recent trends or scientific disciplines among Latin American countries. . . .* A relatively new discipline (semiotics), which is undergoing extensive development in socialist countries such as the USSR, is addressed for the first time in our journal ("Editorial" 1972; emphasis added)

The search for ideological legitimacy prompted the meticulous study of Marxist theory. The importance attributed in the seventies to the permanent rereading of Marxist classics cannot be underestimated; reading and rereading that frequently led to polemics among peers, who (in the name of Marxism-Leninism, Trotskyism, Guevarism, Gramscism, and others) debated each other over the right to determine what "true" socialism entailed. In short, the ideological justification was then elaborated within an eminently theoretical terrain.

The seventies also saw the birth of a theoretically innovative elaboration of the legitimacy of aesthetic and critical practice: the revolution of the signifier allowed its cultivators to gain a future position in the academies that would once again separate, in the following years, public commitment and professionalization.

Theory provided another possible justification for the intellectual task conceived not only as a denunciation but also as the specific domain of intellectuals. Theoretical practice was justified, in many cases, in the Althusserian positions that posited the essential identity of theory and practice. The amphibious character of Marxism (as theory and as practice) can serve to explain both the rupture of the Latin American intellectual left—and the formation of splinter groups—and the ways in which the contending factions claimed to be "Marxist" in all cases; some through theory, others through practice.

The figure of the intellectual as critic found a means of survival by finding a disciplinary object—*the cultural industry*—to which to apply a theoretical framework of analysis, as reflected in the number of works devoted to its analysis. The culture industry was thus read through the perspective of dependency theory. An entire issue of *Casa de las Américas* in 1972 was devoted exclusively to this question. But the translation into cultural terms of the slogan "liberation or dependence," a task also undertaken by literary criticism in the seventies, tended to reinforce the dominant role of the *structure* and weaken any transforming specificity of culture, which was also neutralized by the effects of cultural penetration, even in its most lucid segments. As Gustavo Luis Carrera says: "It may be surprising that so much is said here about dependence and liberation, when cultural matters could be discussed at other conceptual levels; but Latin America's reality, as well as the question of its fate, is posed in these terms" (1975). Two qualitatively different chronological moments of cultural penetration are thus distinguished, the latter being the hardest to identify and, therefore, to combat: "The current historical period is different; values are more relative. With subtlety, it is easy to make the *apparent* look *real*, just as it is easy to reduce the significant to the simple condition of detail" (Carrera 1975). Thus, although the theoretical foundations for critical action are achieved, its effectiveness is weakened. To a certain extent, this is the path taken by Althusser, who explains culture as a function of power, broadening the classical Marxist concept of social reproduction by assuming that culture is something more than the expressive medium of extracultural social structures, but theoretically limiting culture's capacity for contestation.

Theory also invaded literary criticism: a phenomenon that was simultaneous to its professionalization. Culture, as a *field of research*, enabled the founding of a literary science and the circulation of new forms of knowledge (considered as such for the first time), which found their way into the political and cultural publications of the time. Many of the publications that emerged at that time were theoretical and professional in nature and circulated strictly among intellectuals, who thus generated their own organs, without any pedagogical intent, since knowledge of almost everything was taken for granted. Through theory, an attempt was also made to revive the popular. The persistence of certain clichés and structures in popular culture was appreciated in that, unlike "high" culture, popular culture lacked the idea of novelty as a value, something condemned by anti-intellectualism. Starting with Bakhtin's reading, critics analyzed popular culture as parodic and carnivalesque, seeing in it signs of transgression and combat against the dominant culture. But analyzing part of the period's output, it is clear that one of the main interests of the critics was to determine, within an overly rigid framework, which ideological or class positions were expressed in literature. In order to identify this object, recourse was frequently made to the authors, leaving open, once again, the possibility of their ideological discrediting.

If politicians possessed a kind of know-how that the literati aspired to share, the frustration of this expectation had a lot to do with this spirit of literary scientism that, although it circulated among limited audiences, claimed to contemplate a politics of theory and a theory of politics. In these cases, the anti-intellectualism was nuanced, but the illusion that direct action (through literature) was possible was also weakened.

It is paradoxical that the need to theoretically politicize culture led to the antithesis of what Terry Eagleton (following the Habermasian scheme of transformations in the public sphere) characterizes as the ideal moment of criticism, the moment in which the critic addresses society as a whole. In this case, the theorization of the political nature of culture led to a marked specialization, in which the critic took an ever-greater distance from the role of the provider of collective meaning.

Another of the paradoxes of criticism was that, even when it set out to defend the interests of the less favored classes (logically, the majority), it was more comfortable representing the cause of society's marginalized minorities. While indigenism had nearly been swept away by the modernizing avalanche of the sixties, its theoretical-political recovery was one of the main resources of the professionalized critics of the seventies, who went in search of "Indians" and cultural minorities whose endangered cultural *authenticity* amazed them and which they deemed necessary to protect. Some of those who then represented this new critique were able, years later, to engage in a politics of resistance in those cases in which this knowledge, considered "pseudo-Marxist" by certain totalitarian governments in Latin America, circulated clandestinely. In many cases, some of these critics were sheltered by North American universities in Hispanic literature departments. Latin American intellectuals were also able to demonstrate their combativeness by challenging, with their works and declarations, the dictatorships that were in power in many of the continent's countries. The censorship, persecution, imprisonment, and torture many writers were targeted with led intellectuals to again believe that their word had value, at least in view of those who considered it an enemy.

The philosophy of action and the concept of autonomy, both implicit in the ethical-aesthetic imperatives that intellectuals legislated for themselves, could not be systematically combined, because the philosophy of action demanded that literature be *practical*, while the concept of autonomy—or specificity, one of its characteristics—hindered the transfer of literature to praxis, since it sharply distinguished art from reality. In the attempt to formulate the bases of a thought and practice capable of opposing the forms of existing domination, intellectuals theorized about mass media when they became aware of its role as a unifying force at the service of power, but that was a lost battle. What had appeared to be a crisis of the ideological legitimacy of the bourgeoisie was resolved fairly quickly in most of the continent's countries through a process of violent repression with the indispensable support of the mass media and the activity of a market that was completely regulated by publishing corporations. These, in turn, relied on the help of criticism disseminated through mainstream newspapers, that was always willing to endorse the works that triumphed in the market as good. When this happened, the epoch remained trapped in a past that was definitively closed off.

Closing Words: An Incomplete Project?

Politics, like the Word, came first. The idea that radical change was about to take place swept the world in the sixties and seventies. This sense of (desired) imminence in the discourses of the left-wing intelligentsia was also experienced by those who strongly opposed the prospect of transformation. Thus, Senator Robert Kennedy confirmed the widespread perception that the world revolution had been set in motion when he announced, in a 1966 speech, that revolution was *inevitable.* The simultaneity of this perception among absolutely antagonistic ideological camps suggests that the period under study constituted a true *epoch* on an international scale: a single map of the *times* covered all geographies.

History was changing location: the push toward the future appeared to come from a group of countries that had hitherto been in the shadows and suddenly became visible to such an extent that their historical protagonism seemed obvious to many observers at the time. The countries in which historical time seemed to be moving at a different, faster, and more decisive speed were called the Third World. In these regions, populated by remnants of the colonizing metropolises of yesteryear, revolutionary impulses were stirring and bubbling with hatred against the oppressors and with the resolve to decide their own future in opposition to amendments, interventions, delegates, and economies dictated by the metropolitan centers.

The Cuban Revolution provided the most obvious proof not only of the existence of revolutionary ferment but also of the possibility of triumph and the reconstruction of society on entirely new foundations. It signaled a path for the Latin American continent and was followed by other regions with considerable attention, a blend of admiration and perplexity.

The desire for transformation constituted, for intellectuals, an invitation to act in order to accelerate the path of history, which, it was thought at the time, would culminate with the exhaustion of the capitalist system. The Latin American intelligentsia, like that of the rest of the world, wished to play a leading role in new historical developments; writers, in particular, felt called to participate in the "liberation of their people." This manifested as the need to group together in collective identities and practices. "Intellectuals" is a word that was, and is, declined in *plural.* To form part of their epoch involved the creation of instruments to get to know and recognize each other, and cultural magazines were therefore the means and support for this need and also for another essential function: to *communicate* with a broader public.

The organization that the intelligentsia gave itself or attempted to give itself through successive encounters, which I have described in detail, was intended to create a true *Latin American community of writers* that would give a particular status to this new modality of intervention. The web of personal relationships generated at the time along with the strong associative ideal that characterized the behavior of the intellectuals in fact created a sort of intellectual "family," fundamentally aligned in terms of political agreements.

Initially, the writers of the epoch attempted to combine a specific practice—literature—with a work of enlightenment and propaganda that sought to convince society (or whoever their real or imagined audience might be) of the need for revolution. This mechanism transformed them into intellectuals, inasmuch as they situated their discourses and interventions in the public sphere.

Revolutionary Cuba was considered the model of the *new society* imagined for the rest of Latin America. Critics and writers became the "ambassadors" of that revolution. And the island, in turn, was the main host of countless encounters that cemented the unity of the Latin American intellectual field. Attempts to change the course of these alliances were the subject of fierce disputes, which initially resulted in the strengthening of the *Latin American Intellectual Party.* This was clearly reflected in the history of the magazine *Mundo Nuevo*, which was founded in 1966 and marked by the ideological weakness inherent in being financed with US funds. Its first director, Emir Rodríguez

Monegal, abandoned the project in 1968 after acknowledging that the campaign against him had left him without support.

However, most writers, while resolutely committed to the revolution, were simultaneously committed to the production of a new literature, as new as the new world and new man that would emerge from the revolutions. The impulse toward the new was not limited to the struggle for a new society; just as important as the change in the balance of power in the political arena was the aesthetic change: it was no coincidence that at that time there was talk of "new Latin American literature."

The possibility of reconciling a cultural agenda with a political and "revolutionary" one at a time when armed struggle was seen as the only path to revolution nevertheless problematized the notion of *commitment*, which had operated as an ambiguous slogan that reflected the dual nature of the politicization of writers: on the one hand "to work through their work" and on the other "to work through society." Between 1966 and 1968, the question of the identity of the revolutionary intellectual was raised repeatedly and insistently by the actors themselves. But more than this question, which was somewhat rhetorical, what guided this inquiry was a more categorical definition of the revolutionary's duty: formulated more strictly as the "duty to make the revolution." Writers therefore found themselves challenged by the concrete demands for immediate political effectiveness that came from sectors of political activists—as well as from intellectuals—who were beginning to feel that cultural intervention was not an appropriate mode of intervention on a continent mostly populated by illiterate masses with no access to cultural goods. According to many of these arguments, there was no alternative to the transformation that was limited to the small "enlightened" public. The Latin American masses whose enlightenment was sought were in fact passive recipients of the increasingly influential culture industry, the products of which came from the United States (or imitated them) and were therefore defenseless against "imperialist cultural penetration."

This context gave rise to the anti-intellectualist positions that I analyzed in the chapter "The Intellectual as a Problem." The dissemination of these positions was linked to aspects of Cuban cultural policy and to the diverse and complex problems facing the Cuban economy and the struggle for legitimacy in that country's cultural field. For this reason, I feel it is crucial to go beyond the generalized hypothesis that posits the influence of the Cuban Revolution on Latin American intellectuals in order to account not only for how the revolution influenced writers but also for how they, in turn, influenced the revolution. The community of Latin American writers intervened in many different ways to ensure that Cuba stood out from the rest of the socialist world in terms of its cultural policy. Various meetings with Fidel Castro, the leader of the revolution who welcomed hundreds of Latin American writers and discussed with them more or less as equals, led the writers to believe that their opinions and views were well received by Cuba's political leadership. In fact, for a time, this was the case.

But the Cuban Revolution went through different stages in relation to the aesthetic debate, which, as always, took place in a field of more or less public but always heated discussions. Around 1968, the dominant sectors in the cultural sphere imposed criteria that ran counter to the aspirations of many Latin American artists who had joined in defending the model established by Cuba. The emergence of significant dissent regarding the type of works that should be written and the criteria of authority for judging them gradually undermined the cohesion of the intellectual front. With the outbreak of the Padilla affair, a significant rift occurred, which I analyzed in terms of the breaking of "family ties," accounting for how questions such as the freedom of creation and the place of writers in the revolutionary process were discussed.

The literary market that consolidated the success of the new Latin American novel had a significant impact on the ideological assessment of works, both by those who had been fortunate enough to experience commercial success and those who had not had that opportunity. The influence that the existence of the publishing market had on intellectual debates was remarkable. On the one hand, it further divided those who had rallied in defense of Heberto Padilla from those who had defended the Cuban Revolution. On the other hand, the market had particular relevance in the arguments against the novel, the genre that had emblematically expressed the expectations and possibilities of writing a literature that was both Latin American and at the same time "universal." In this sense, since my methodological interest was "to follow the course of the words," I defined the meanings of what, in literature, was conceptualized and practiced in the name of "novelty." The word realism was re-semanticized in a way that served as a general slogan to describe much of the literature produced at the time: the uses of the term added a series of adjectives to the word realism, with "new" (realism) as the most frequently used. In reality, "realism" was above all a verbal artifact that did not refer to the traditional meaning of the concept and also included the experimental aspects of the new literature.

The novel occupied a prominent place in the reflections of authors and critics during the early years of the epoch. The political "neutralization" of the genre, once institutionalized by the market and recognized by critics and readers everywhere, as argued by the anti-intellectual faction of the literary field, led to the imagination of new formats conceived as more suitable for conveying whatever might be "revolutionary" in cultural practice. These new formats and genres were poetry, testimony, protest songs, and, most especially, political cinema, which, toward the end of the epoch, garnered awards at festivals and as much international prestige as novels had years earlier.

What I consider important to highlight is that I have worked with the hypothesis that in the period representing the object of study of this work, intellectual history and literary history were strongly interpenetrated to the point that each moment of intellectual history corresponds to a particular moment of literary history. The writer's transformation into an intellectual and the explicit search for an audience, the novel and the formation of the intellectual family, new formats and the breaking of family ties are some examples of how the elements of one series were permanently tied to the other.

Jean Genet declared to *Libre*: "I am against any government." That statement synthesizes a gesture of the modern artist, a characteristic gymnastics, from Baudelaire to the present, the preferred flexion of which is dissidence. This tradition not only creates an age-old image of the artist and bohemian, and their preference for marginality; it also provides a framework for conceptualizing their "politicization." From isolation to criticism and opposition, a whole varied repertoire of attitudes embodies negativity as a pretension of the genuine art of modernity.

It is not strange then that revolutions pose a rare challenge to writers (qua writers) when they support them: the requirements of positivity and affirmation that are implicit in a different relationship with political power undermine a foundational legacy. Something of this sort took place in Latin America with the centenary ideal that established that intellectuals could aspire to regard themselves as the "critical conscience of society."

The history of Latin American intellectuals of the epoch, in the words of one of its protagonists, moved from euphoria to depression. Not only because many of the expectations that guided the intellectuals' interventions dissipated. It was also because the future imagined for society as a whole came up against a scenario that most intellectuals had certainly not imagined even in their worst nightmares. Nor did many of its victims foresee it; in many Latin American countries, the promising future that became a horror remains a trauma that is not easy to overcome.

Paraphrasing Habermas and his vision of modernity as an incomplete project (27–31), perhaps we can speak of the incomplete project of the sixties/seventies. In fact, this period constituted a turning point between two epochs and, although it not only affected the possibilities of conceiving the intellectual category in terms of its long tradition, it was also crucial for the identity of the intellectual.

According to Zygmunt Bauman (1997), the vision of a world as an essentially ordered totality was replaced by another, which conceives it as an unlimited number of models of order, each of which is generated by a relatively autonomous set of practices, which cannot claim an external gauge of their legitimacy or validity.

This transition between two worldviews involves complex processes of closure and opening that can be traced back to the beginnings of the most important debates on the immediate past and attempts to characterize the present. This debate has only found its terminology retrospectively, with the emergence of the problematic concepts of postmodernity and postmodernism and the translation into these terms of discussions initiated long before that, which were later establishing consensual descriptions of the present.

The conditions of intellectual practice changed radically. Régis Debray refers explicitly to the transformations between that recent past—now closed off—and the present. For Debray, this frontier between past and present is marked by the shift from a lettered culture, which recognizes the written word as its fundamental means of communication, to an electronic, audiovisual culture whose forms of symbolic representation are anchored in the new mass media, already fully hegemonic in the second half of the twentieth century. In Debray's terms (1996), these transformations take place between a cultural period he has called the graphosphere and the more recent videosphere.

This shift occurs precisely during this epoch and constitutes one more aspect of its closure. The sixties/seventies were the last avatar of book culture (as George Steiner explains in "After the Book?"). Although Debray does not fully elaborate on all the consequences of the phenomenon he describes, the transformation he diagnoses is crucial from the point of view of the possibilities of intellectual intervention.

The videosphere, the transformations in the public sphere, and the role of the mass media have displaced the traditional (written) modes of intellectual intervention and, more especially, their possibilities of circulation and dissemination on a mass level. Beyond Debray's own reflections, the transition from lettered culture to the current electronic audiovisual culture has been a subject of reflection for many other authors (such as, for example, Walter Ong 1982). What is important here, however, is not so much the characterization of this new audiovisual culture as the sense of closure with respect to the previous period that most authors tend to emphasize. It is curious that those who, in recent years, have been criticizing the "betrayal" of intellectuals do not consider these transformations. What is interesting in this case is that many attribute to the intellectuals themselves the responsibility for the catastrophe due to their radicalization in the sixties. Norman Podhoretz (1979) goes so far as to suggest that the ambition of intellectuals to change the world was a kind of hubris that received the punishment it deserved: "not even 'the production of literary masterpieces' was good enough: one had to change the world" (362). Paul Hollander (1981) expresses a similar sentiment: "The persistence of Marxist belief in the West can most readily be ascribed to the institutionalization of the values of the protest movements of the 1960s giving rise to the adversary culture" (x).

Within this framework and in relation to the evaluation in terms of the intellectual history of the consequences of the political radicalization that characterized the sixties/seventies, the question (and consequent debate) emerges regarding the triumph or failure of the intellectual movements in favor of revolution. This discussion has taken place both in Latin America and in the developed world. There have been notable conversions, such as that of Uruguayan Danubio Torres Fierro and Frenchman Bernard Hénri-Levy, considered in France to be the intellectual with the most media presence. In articles published in *El País*, Torres Fierro (1989; 1990), a former contributor to *Marcha*, accuses the left of almost all the evils that have befallen the world, even refusing to grant his fellow workers at the time the critical impulse that led them to question many of the dogmatic nuances of some areas of the political culture of the left. The relationship between "rebels" and "academics" (a view similar to that of the apocalyptic and the integrated) constitutes a central point in the arguments of the polemicists.[56] What is being debated is whether this institutional foundation distorts the ethical and political aspirations of intellectuals or, in other words, what degree of "objectivity" can be granted to this insertion. The question is whether the success of left-wing intellectuals in inserting themselves into educational and cultural institutions is a betrayal, an abdication, or a failure compared to their prior ideals.

The privatization of existence that followed the evidence that the world revolution was not underway and that capitalism was surviving the diagnoses that foretold its imminent death turned many intellectuals into academics. Many of those mentioned in these works now hold important positions in university institutions. In many cases, the warning that the complexity of social antagonisms was greater than imagined meant replacing the defense of the exploited majorities with that of the rights of the dominated minorities. "Today the left intellectual is a feminist, an ecologist" argues Stanley Aronowitz (1990), defending the legitimacy of the academic institutional base of intellectuals (the caricature of this statement can be found in *Small World: An Academic Romance* and *Nice Work*, by literary theory professor David Lodge).

Rather than engaging in abstract analyses of an identity defined by some ontological-essential attribute, Bauman (especially in "Morality and Politics") sets out to analyze the conditions of possibility of the

56 See, for instance, Robbins and Aronowitz. Russel Jacoby condemns academic Marxism as the absorption of the left through academization, which removes intellectuals from their public roles. The entrenchment of progressivism in universities is clear.

practice of the intellectual category, comparing one way of being an intellectual linked to the modern and another linked to the postmodern. However, even if we fully agree with Bauman on the importance of contextual analysis to determine the conditioning factors of intellectual intervention and, above all, the identity models that these conditioning factors define, the persistence of the critical ideal in the self-definition of intellectuals is still surprising.

Added to this difficulty are the determinations in which the notion of intellectual field can be operative, given that it must first be applied within a national framework and always refers to a political field, the configuration of which must be present in the analyses that make use of this conceptual tool. Otherwise, as happens most of the time, "intellectual field" or "lettered city" become readily available metaphors, like "republic of letters" in the past or "literary milieu." In these terms, the hierarchy of the components remains in question; this is not the case with André Breton's palace, where he decides who enters and who is expelled, as a brief history of Surrealism would show.

Pierre Bourdieu's own trajectory, alongside the strikers in 1995, rejects the idea that an "autonomy" exists or should be emphasized, like that which seeks to stipulate the idea of a corporatism of the universal. The collective intellectual, he will later argue, must be in a position to commit his knowledge and not to brandish a supposedly committed knowledge. For this to happen, this knowledge must exist and must reach the collective intellectual. Keeping silent or reserving one's revelations only for the erudite (*savant*) world would be, in more than one case, a form of capitulation or desertion, the abandonment of someone in danger.

In his "post-scriptum" to *The Rules of Art*, Bourdieu pretended to wield, and to make others wield, autonomy as a guarantee of the critical power of intellectuals. His own subsequent trajectory reveals how much more he amplified his message by becoming a celebrity than he did when he sought to establish an autonomy that appeared to have no locus or inscription in the social world. It is to these refutations of Bourdieu's own theory that this book refers.

Postface to This Edition: A Wake-up Call on Ideas Received

> Isn't it a sign, all these intellectuals, coming from all corners of the globe, who rally around an idea and stand firm in their convictions?
>
> Georges Clemenceau (1898)

In what follows, I will summarize a few of the historical and functional hypotheses that have been used to identify intellectuals, those individuals "brought together by an idea." As those who have made it this far will have noticed that these are hypotheses that have proven fruitful in this book but have also obscured other observations made at a later date: people with intellectual dispositions have undoubtedly existed in all societies; even illiterate cultures have harbored individuals capable of tackling collective problems. Human groups develop if they find suitable institutional settings for eidetic exchanges and have at least one circle of people to address. It is often suggested that the conditions for the emergence of the intellectual stratum were favored by the collapse of medieval society and the movements that fragmented the unified authority of the Church. Religious groups, secular powers, and political systems sought to attract the loyalty of individuals who were no longer bound by their traditional ties: these "men of ideas" found favorable ground for constituting a conscious stratum of intellectuals with a specific *ethos* and a sense of vocation. The spread of typographic culture was crucial in the emergence of a group of conscious intellectuals capable of contributing to the formation of public opinion. In this process, certain phenomena converged, such as the increase in the number and specific influence of the middle class and expectations concerning the value of education. The formation of a mass culture, which is inscribed in the development of democratic characteristics established in free debate, is another factor contributing to the emergence of this microsociety and will be a constitutive and intrinsic characteristic of its functioning in associative networks.

In theory, intellectual association requires a cause so as to give meaning to efforts capable of wrenching individuals from their habitual state of general indifference to human affairs other than their own. Various institutional settings favored the formation of associations and groups: the salon, the café, the scientific society, magazines, the political party, and bohemia. Equally important was the emergence of an extensive book market in the eighteenth century and the concomitant appearance of booksellers and publishers as intermediaries between the author and the growing reading public, for whom reading became a favorite pastime as the middle class took shape. Direct contact was not always necessary because the printed page facilitated exchanges quite well, especially at a time in which the readership of serious intellectual productions had become extensive and was no longer a small subset.

All the hypotheses that address intellectual identity place this figure in a slightly separate position from the rest of society, which allows it to act according to "its own" supposedly "rational" standards of validity. This kind of collective participation in a type of culture brings together the members who share it. And this culture develops through debate and exchange. The very nature of the latter makes association—a place of convergence, mutual support, and political extrapolation—necessary and structurally creates between minds in proximity new and different ties than those of scholarly or professional solidarity. In this sense, there is a double reproduction of the sociability of the intellectual network: inward, in terms of peer relations, and outward, in terms of its intrusion into culture and society.

All the above hypotheses take for granted that intellectuals always gather together, invent networks, and take advantage of existing ones, and also create the spaces for their development, as a natural feature of their existence. Networks are themselves based on elements that are hard to discern. Sympathy and friendship, for example, and, conversely, rivalry and hostility, resentment and envy, rupture and disagreement, all play an occasionally decisive role, as in any microsociety. This sociability can be understood in another way because "networks" generate specific microclimates, and the word acquires, from this perspective, a double meaning of "networks" that structure and, at the same time, produce those microclimates that characterize a given intellectual milieu.

***

> I became convinced that a revolution that has all the intellectuals on its side is a just and necessary revolution. It cannot be any other way. It cannot be that hundreds of writers, poets, painters, and musicians are wrong.
>
> Julio Cortázar (1963)

This is how Julio Cortázar describes and justifies his complete support for the Cuban Revolution. What is most striking is that he can believe that a revolution that has all the intellectuals on its side is, for that reason, just and necessary. And yet, this act of true faith is based on a tradition that claims that artists and intellectuals are guarantors of objectivity, ethics, and justice precisely because they are artists and intellectuals. In other words, they embody a morality and an ethics of truth and justice that must be considered authentic, sincere, and "true." This act of faith in their "peers" evokes the dogmatic and ecclesiastical substratum from which "secularization" is a progression. The belief in peers is more convincing than the belief in the masses, toward whom Cortázar's position and that of his peers is well-known. The phenomenon of Peronism has also united Argentine intellectuals. Not only them: these assessments of "populisms" are shared by the "universal" intelligentsia. The leadership in Cuba launches lettered rereadings of these phenomena. So as not to be unfair or cynical with the events of recent history, many intellectuals actively fought for the advent and triumph of the Latin American, Third World, socialist, or nationalist revolution in a disinterested manner. For there to be intellectuals like those who came together in the "epoch of the sixties and seventies," there had to be certain material conditions. (Just as executives, in the words of María Elena Walsh's song, could go from the armchair to the airplane, intellectuals also had at their disposal frequent flights, making it easier for them to go from the airplane to the revolution). And, naturally, they also had to experience the desire and the duty to act as a community.

For its part, the Cuban Revolution benefited many of the soon-to-be famous novelists. These writers began to promote each other, recommend agents, and discuss contracts and, most importantly, translations into other languages. All this with the endorsement of the new critics who were emerging, just like the new writers, in a feedback loop that, as always, benefited the authors more than the commentators. Supporting the Cuban Revolution also meant traveling to Cuba and elsewhere to spread the word and meeting to reflect, sign manifestos, and engage in political activism in order to ensure future revolutions, on alert for the dangers that had beset the Russian and Chinese revolutions. These authors were not simply ideologues or chancellors without the blessing of the Cuban leadership: they believed in their autonomy and responsibility to legislate. They were treated as statesmen; they were listened to; and their opinions were given due consideration. Did they imagine themselves, perhaps, as members of a republic similar to the one Plato dreamed of? Parades, public events, and banquets, circulated in images and texts, depicted them side by side with the heroes of the moment. The conditions for reputation and fame still depended on literary competition.

1. Family or Brotherhood?

> The woman who studies does not regain her true intelligence until she is offered the opportunity to forget what she has learned or to apply it to life.
>
> Gina Lombroso (1945)

> *Pro patria mori* is nothing but the boundary of all the more or less noble and recognized ways of dying or living for causes or ends that are universally recognized as noble, that is to say, universal.
>
> PIERRE BOURDIEU (2000)

The study of the dynamics established between Latin American cultural magazines and the personal encounters of the critics and writers who contributed to them revealed the existence of an intellectual community that operated on the basis "of the imagination," but also on the basis of hard and pure sociability that generated a very effective community for producing "legitimate" discourses. There was talk of cronyism and mafia, in some cases, to criticize the power of the most visible "sprouts" when they began to publish works that were part of the sought-after "new Latin American literature." In many cases the logic of affiliation or belonging to the most visible group of writers, those who went from the airplane to the revolution, was explicitly "parentalized." "Another relative for the family" was the title used by the weekly *Primera Plana* to comment on the string of Seix Barral prizes awarded to Latin American novelists, in that case to the Venezuelan González León.

I used the term "family" to refer to a deliberate, empirical association of close ties in decidedly domestic settings, as the "boom" authors and the members of magazines such as *Libre* present themselves. In reality, I should have called it a brotherhood or fraternity, since the universal was mostly applied to heterosexual male writers.

We tend to forget that Aristotle's rational animal is still in effect and reappears intact in the category of "*men* of ideas." In the first case, women are explicitly excluded since they are not rational. They are not *politikós*, just as animals are not. The power of language veils the absence of women in this book. Men of ideas do not include women of ideas, contrary to what happens with the notion of humanity, which extends to both sexes. While there were many women writers and intellectuals, the great names of the top ranks kept their women within their patriarchal families, and, if the names of some of them became known, it was as solicitous wives. It is an absence that should have been anticipated when founding the intellectual category in the process of secularization. Historically, materially, empirically, secularization is basically the initial process by which a man of the Church abandons his habits, ceases to be regular, and becomes secular.

Another of the "revolutions" predicted at the time was the sexual revolution: conditions were emerging that gave women more control over their own bodies and their reproductive choices, influence in terms of public opinion, and the possibility of openly engaging in political activism. The future was heralding the birth of a new man in a present in which a new woman had already emerged and was available. She was not called upon.

Undoubtedly, the current advocacy for minority rights is rooted in the struggles of the sixties; although, beyond the conquests that have been achieved, it must be said that, instead of becoming more lax, sexual controls were redefined, marriage remained an option for the majority, stable unions continued to "ensure" the ideal framework for procreation, and even homosexual couples defended the stability of their ties and their right to form a legitimate family. The sex trade reinforced the domination and marginalization of women, who continued to bear the burden of domestic chores. The expectations harbored by the activists of sexual liberation in the sixties became limited. The power relations in capitalism were not drastically modified, nor did a society reshaped by new political principles, derived from a new sexual morality, emerge, as the optimism of Wilhelm Reich or Herbert Marcuse proposed. Nor did inequality in domestic relationships or discrimination against women disappear. The liberal and progressive wave of the sixties and seventies was followed by a period of reaction and conservatism (Cosse 2010).

Female sociability was not as effective as male sociability: the intellectual "family" I describe could really be called a "fraternity" or "brotherhood." It is, without a doubt, a patriarchal family. The defeats suffered, it can be supposed, are momentary, since predictions are only a possibility and closures can be a mirage, as the "end of ideologies" was at the time.

I believe that the cult of courage and heroism dominated the era; and honor is a law of equality between men: only the recognition given to a man (as opposed to a woman) is worthy of honor, and only a man is a worthy rival in the struggle for honor (Bourdieu 2000). Virtue and strength (*vis* and *vir*) are attributes that man does not share in the generalization of "humanity." In the absence of words, it is hard to include what is excluded and to remedy what is omitted.

2. Two for the Boom: Made in Uruguay

> Until now, each literature had its own unique history. Of course, they did not develop in isolation, but influences were usually slow, delayed, partial, and irregular. Furthermore, they occurred between the literatures of neighboring countries, or at least between languages with the same structure and related cultures. Today, thanks to the multiplicity of translations, the shrinking of distances, and the rapid pace of growth in human relations of all kinds (including the spread of science and technology, ideas, and lifestyles), influences, even in literature, at least through the amplifying and simplifying medium of the press, cinema, radio, and television, are felt immediately, massively, and constantly, defying antipodes and any contrast in climate or customs, tradition or situation.
>
> Roger Caillois (1961)

Due to their ongoing public feud, Guillermo Cabrera Infante went so far as to say that Ángel Rama and Emir Rodríguez Monegal were like Settembrini and Naptha "but in Spanish." Moreover, this antagonism was practically a spectacle. Vargas Llosa declared that "every organizer of symposia, roundtables, congresses, conferences, and literary conspiracies, from Rio Grande to Magallanes, knew that to secure the attendance of Ángel and Emir was to ensure the success of a meeting."

In a letter sent by post, dated May 9, 2000, Tulio Halperin Donghi generously comments on the manuscript of my doctoral thesis and adds, to my surprise, that the reading helped him understand why "although Ángel Rama said he did not understand why Emir was still so angry with him, he had plenty of reasons." For a long time, I assumed (and this is what my works have stated) that the rivalry was due to their political and ideological dispute (Gilman, 1993, 1995, 1996, 1999, 2001, 2003, 2009, and 2010).

But the truth is, before they hated each other for that, they hated each other for almost everything that can come between two people. The passionate and systematic rivalry between the two influenced their critical judgment to the point that they held antagonistic positions on any issue they addressed. Summoned to participate in a radio broadcast to debate their opinions on the subject "Escape and Rootedness" in Borges and Neruda, Rodríguez Monegal had stated that he and Rama were separated by "something irreconcilable, like the famous dispute about whether winter was better than summer," to which Rama confirmed that the disagreement between them was, indeed, "irreconcilable."

The violence with which Rama and Monegal confront each other reveals the intimate dependence that links both critics to the teachings of Carlos Quijano. It becomes imperative to define, therefore, the positions that the director of *Marcha* would never abandon. Beyond any "positive" conviction, Quijano, perhaps to a greater degree than the other intellectuals of his time, directed his compass at the entirety of the world. His writings continually reveal the experience of someone who has been touched by war and the awareness that the process that began in 1914, with the war that was misnamed the first, and continued with the one that was misnamed the second, and then with the poorly named postwar and the Cold War, is the horizon his lucidity cannot abandon. Both Rama and Monegal remain faithful disciples of Quijano. Claiming readers and a literature of their own in Uruguay, they turned to the rest of the continent, and their recommendations and choices also defined (simultaneously with the activities of reciprocal diffusion to which the most conspicuous members of the brotherhood devoted themselves) the onomatopoeia known as the boom. Rodríguez Monegal uses the expression, but it is Rama who, throughout 1967, which he defines as the year of the boom, employs it in flyers, titles, epigraphs, and notes celebrating the splendors of prizes and sold-out print runs in the literary pages of the weekly tabloid *Marcha*. The distance he later takes with respect to the boom implies, more than oblivion, a break with that past enthusiasm only refuted by Carlos Real de Azúa (1968).

The boom, with very little time separating its peak from its fall, although the onomatopoeia had and still has a longer and more enigmatic life, benefited only the authors blessed by both critics in critical opinions and market triumphs. On this point they contradicted the old acquired habit of never agreeing on anything, however much it might weigh on them.

It is true that volumes could be filled to account for the endless disputes between Ángel Rama and Emir Rodríguez Monegal and show that they were not always ideologically or politically motivated. But what would be the point of writing such books? Speaking of the crisis in the social sciences, Fernand Braudel expresses impatience with a recent study, posing a similar question: "And what interest can we, scholars of the human sciences, have in the comings and goings of a young lady between her home, her music teacher, and the Faculty of Political Science, the subject of a recent investigation on the comings and goings of which a vast and meticulous survey of the Parisian region informs us?" (Braudel 1958). Is the epistemological interest of the quarrels between Rama and Monegal more important than the interest generated by the reports on the intimate life of the celebrity of the hour? Will these conjectural and painful Balzacian anecdotes serve to break the usual recitative of the situation, the cycle, and even the inter-cycle and scratch at least the surface of long-held secrets? Why not?

3. Toward the Present

The intellectuals of the sixties and seventies did not have to compete with television or with growing masses of colleagues who, year after year, graduated from universities with degrees in the humanities and reinterpreted the topic of critical consciousness in disciplinary terms that later founded the field known as "criticism" and that, in many cases, is presented as a way of contesting the existing reality, even if the existing reality does not seem to notice or cease to be what it is. Declarative egalitarianism became the foundation for the production of theories and the contestations of other theories. And every practice, even the least concerned with political or ideological questions, was judged or absolved according to its authoritarianism.

However, in an apparent paradox and as a second indication, the system of scientific organization became bureaucratized. Although this may seem like a normal requirement, it was only after the second postwar period that peer review became institutionalized to the point of becoming the legitimizing element of a publication, precisely when—with the exception of *Casa de las Américas*—the cultural and political-cultural journals of massive scope—which animated intellectual life in the sixties and the community aspect of that life—were discontinued and began to decline, along with the teaching of typing, and were replaced by others of very restricted dissemination, where the never more famous "supposed knowledge" circulated, guarded by "evaluators."

The most ironic (even painful) fact is that there is a technology that has made networks a common reality: social networks are the phenomenon that today enables groupings of almost any kind and that renders unnecessary the human effort to create associations and new ties, so painstakingly sought and achieved by the literati in their interest in establishing an essential dialogue for the creation of shared knowledge and community and the communitarian as an epistemological foundation (Zanetti 1994, 2002). It was that foundation on which Karl Mannheim (1958) had placed so much confidence when he perceived, in the thirties, how difficult it was to establish any form of objectivity and, therefore, of knowledge. For Mannheim, as also for Julien Benda (1945), it was understood that the mission of intellectuals implied a vocation to maintain the cause of the universal in a state of openness, renouncing the naturally human egoism that he perceived at work in other strata or groups, whose interests competed (and continue to do so) with those of others whom, in the name of those antagonistic interests, were forced to harm in order to impose their own, in various battles in which, as usual, they wished to defeat the opposing interests without losing energy in ethical considerations that always weaken their own cause. In the seventies, Marshall McLuhan (1974) observed the generalized disinterest of people in understanding the world and the preoccupation with defining whether something is good or bad in order to judge it. The network of Facebook automatically satisfies this desire to judge by promoting the system of "like" or "dislike" options: forty years after the identification of the syndrome of giving a thumbs up or thumbs down to anything, it has expanded colossally in support of the "written."

Between that time and the present, the technologies initially based on writing have evolved and developed the conditions of association and, paradoxically, have hindered sociability among intellectuals who study these networks but do not use them as in the past. The "mass crystals" of the present are formed thanks to the existence of mechanical channels available to the majority of individuals who have access to social networks and who, through them, without the mediation of any consciousness, have the mercurial capacity to organize themselves and also, eventually, to overthrow a dictator. Does the process of the formation of public opinion, which was in the hands of the literati until very recently, no longer require these voices? Or does it no longer allow them?

Kant could question the meaning of current events because he wrote about them when they were taking place. Where, today, can an intellectual-academic think about current events when they have to wait years for the peer review process to publish their writings, which are bound to be outdated since the writer is aware of the protocols of waiting and cannot count on their words having an impact on the present? The idea that novelty is an absolute value has even led to mass-market products being promoted on the basis of their novelty, even when no one explains why they are said to be new. Or when their supposed novelty is an obvious hoax: it is argued, in public, without anyone objecting, that this or that laundry detergent is superior to others, which become "traditional" because they contain "extra cleaning molecules." No such molecules exist, and it is extremely strange that no one is interested in preventing the spread of false arguments to sell laundry detergent. It is surprising that the worlds of science, marketing, and common sense—which is not always the worst of the senses—are so far apart.

In his "rational and historical theory of beauty" (1964 [1863]), Charles Baudelaire, an indisputable defender of the new, in order to defend it must establish that "the current" is half of art. The other half, eternal and immutable, if we do the calculations from Baudelaire's time to the present, has grown larger and is no longer merely one-half. We must look to the past: we must seek there the arcana of novelty.

Alain Badiou calls the victory of globalized capitalism that took place in the mid-seventies the "second Restoration" (Badiou 2009). Experience suggests, however, that reality is sufficiently opaque to disprove our diagnoses and that the future—if there is one—is even more opaque as to tolerate our prognoses. The geographical spaces that Badiou identifies with "territories of the world" and the events that deserve his attention are geographically limited. The centrality of Cuba is impossible to overlook unless one buries the significance of the 1962 missile crisis, those tense days during which the world feared a generalized conflagration with nuclear weapons while in China "millions of demonstrators with portraits of Fidel Castro paraded through Shanghai, Beijing, Nankin, Canton, Wuhan" and "Cuban marches were sung, often in Spanish" (Kordon 1968, 12).

The perspicacious, disenchanted, and precise panorama that allows Badiou to describe the short twentieth century as a bloody, warlike, voluntarist, criminal historical distillate obsessed with engendering, through violence and at any cost, a new man, leaves out the figure that best encapsulates all the predicates that Badiou attributes to the century. It is surprising, from a Latin American perspective, to note that Ernesto Che Guevara, the ultimate figure of Badiou's "century object," does not appear, in his nomadic and international fame, on any page of a discourse that so vividly depicts him. The disquieting absence of that specter that seems inevitable to us nourishes a curiosity analogous to the one raised among specialists in Shakespeare regarding the correct interpretation (in all senses) of the scenic and symbolic nature of the ghost of the father in *Hamlet.* Is Badiou's becoming Hamlet a Eurocentric effect? Does it affect, perhaps, all the arguments he develops in *The Century*?

Only the future will bring an answer: in the short term, blindness is innate, and the stolen letter is sometimes not even the object of a search. It is difficult to bury Che Guevara once and for all and not mention him as an inseparable part of the century or of our recent past. It is important to mention him because in order to change the world we must know where he is situated. And that place goes beyond our locations, particularly if we situate ourselves in the comfortable world from where we can see very little of the planet's extension. Perhaps we are witnessing a long but consistent historical orbit around the geography that gave rise to the main monotheistic religions.

On the other hand, of all the transformations of the last forty years, the technologizing of the word has literally revolutionized the world. Vast majorities not only know how to read and write but also read and write, or rather, write. The distance between intellectuals and non-intellectuals was inherent to the very notion of intellectual. Now that this distance has been abolished, it is hard to conceive of strictly intellectual tasks, like those recorded at other times in the past.

The political-cultural magazines that functioned as contact networks for the intellectual brotherhood ceased to exist, and the existing ones, withdrawn, do not act as a network. However, the passions of rivalry and hatred that confronted Rama and Monegal remain because they cannot be made to disappear by decree or by ignoring the fact that these passions have existed and still exist and inspire all men and women, including, naturally, intellectuals.

The devaluation of academic careers and undergraduate degrees caused by the increase in graduating students and university enrollments led to a proliferation of disciplines and objects of study, which have become so irrelevant that they can be claimed as their own by all members of the community. The gaffe of the journal *Social Text* that, following routine peer review, published "Transgressing the Boundaries: Toward a Transformative Hermeneutics of Quantum Gravity," Alan Sokal's fictional physics and psychoanalysis paper, is emblematic of the capitulation of thought before everything that thought neither understands nor sets out to understand. The widespread conviction that science has nothing to do with truth was expressed and continues to be expressed in the immense production of works devoted to explaining why it is important to be relativistic, to such an extent that the postulate that proposes that even if we do not know whether a theory or hypothesis is true, we can at least know whether it is false, has lost its validity.

Along with the increasingly cryptic criticisms that benefit from the receding demands of truthfulness, objections to thought based on "boogeymen" such as binarism, biologism, and other academic reductionisms have become generalized, and the causes become declarations of principles that impede a practice based on these principles, which are not always irreconcilable. It is hard to make the rights of a whale coincide with those of the inhabitants of Rwanda. It is not as hard to advocate for a more radical rationality, for the abandonment of gloss and commentary, for the absurdity of certain fashionable authorities, prohibitions that are merely formal, theoretical phobias, external fears.

Actual human actions do not always inspire confidence in the rationality of *Homo sapiens*; rather an effort such as a "leap" is required to counter the force of gravity since the "human case" pulls strongly toward animality. Unlike the Pompeians who suffered the first eruption of Vesuvius and would never again build their homes next to the volcano, today's sages locate nuclear power plants in areas regularly and systematically affected by earthquakes and tsunamis, as scientists along with people who have minimal information are aware. So it is nothing extraordinary if what we knew could happen happens and has already happened. What is extraordinary is that that knowledge has not been of any use. Humans may be rational animals, but they are not obliged to be so. It is hard to imagine such irrationality in deliberate, conscious human actions with predictably fatal consequences. Neither ignorance, idealism, nor ideology can be considered explanations for such foolishness. One need only consult Wikipedia to learn that the geography of "Japan" is located in the middle of the highly seismic Pacific Ring of Fire. It has recorded earthquakes since the early eighteenth century and has experienced more than five in the last few years. Where is *Homo sapiens*?

The world, for Mallarmé, could well be something that was made to end in a Book. It is reasonable that one of the most eminent poets of a generation that became massively literate in a world so dominated by the exclusive presence of the written word should think that way. In a market regulated by rules that—we know—will not favor the production or collective circulation of new, better, and more knowledge, the rallying call has become a curfew.

Will we be up to the challenges posed today by the presumably simple creation of networks? Will we take advantage of the channels available to us, as those of the nineteenth and twentieth centuries did when they overcame obstacles that no longer exist and brought into play energy, resources, and determination to create communities in which they sought to think, dialogue, appreciate commonalities, integrate, meet, exchange, and collaborate? Let us hope so.

The past ironically warns us how inaccurate predictions are. Post-history? No. Nothing has ended. It is we who put an end to things and to our periodizations, not history. The word "end" does not mark an end, nor does the end limit itself to being a word. As Braudel (1958) reminds us and as we know from experience, humankind remains, as in the beginning, a prisoner of geography and a captive of the climate. For the time being.

Buenos Aires, March 2012

About the Author

Claudia Gilman holds a PhD in literature from the University of Buenos Aires. She also completed postgraduate studies in France at the École des Hautes Études en Sciences Sociales. She has held research fellowships at both the University of Buenos Aires and CONICET. Gilman has taught a variety of undergraduate and graduate courses at the Faculty of Philosophy and Letters, including on Argentine literature, twentieth-century literature, Latin American literature, and Cuban literature, as well as seminars on intellectual history at FLACSO (Latin American Faculty of Social Sciences). She has published numerous articles on topics related to her field of expertise. Her book *Entre la pluma y el fusil: Debates y dilemas del escritor revolucionario en América Latina* (*Between the Pen and the Rifle: Dilemmas of the Revolutionary Intellectual in Latin America*), published in 2003, has become a key reference in the field.

Bibliography

Primary Sources (Political-Cultural Magazines)

Amaru: Revista de Artes y Ciencias de la Universidad Nacional de Ingeniería, Lima

Anales de la Universidad de Chile, Santiago de Chile

Árbol de letras, Santiago de Chile, Editorial Universitaria

Arguments, Paris

Atenea, Concepción

Bohemia, Havana

Casa de las Américas, Havana

Confirmado, Buenos Aires

Cromos, Colombia

Cuadernos por la Libertad de la Cultura, Paris

Cuadernos Americanos, Mexico

El Escarabajo de Oro, Buenos Aires

El Grillo de Papel, Buenos Aires

El Corno Emplumado/The Plumed Horn, bilingual magazine, Mexico

El Caimán Barbudo, cultural monthly of the Juventud Rebelde, organ of the armed forces, Havana

Ercilla, Santiago de Chile

Hispamérica, College Park, Maryland

Hoy en la Cultura, Buenos Aires

L'Arc, Aix en Provence

La Bufanda del Sol, Quito

La Nouvelle Critique, Paris

La Palabra y el Hombre, Mexico

La Penseé, Paris

La Rosa Blindada, Buenos Aires

Latinoamericana, Buenos Aires

Libre, Paris
Los Libros, Buenos Aires
Lunes de Revolución, Havana
Macedonio "Literatura-Teatro-Cine-Artes," Buenos Aires
Marcha, Montevideo
Margen, Revista de Literatura en Lengua Castellana, Paris
Mensaje, Santiago de Chile
Mundo Nuevo, Paris and Buenos Aires
Nuevos Aires, Buenos Aires
Oiga, Lima
Papeles, Revista del Ateneo de Caracas, Caracas
Pasado y Presente, Córdoba
Plamen, Prague
Primera Plana, Buenos Aires
Problemas del Tercer Mundo, Buenos Aires
Revista de la Universidad de México, Mexico
Revista Mexicana de Literatura, Mexico
Siempre!, Mexico
Tiempos Modernos, Buenos Aires
Unión, Havana
Zona Franca, Caracas

References

Adorno, Theodor W., and Max Horkheimer. 1987 [1944]. *Dialéctica del iluminismo*. Buenos Aires: Sudamericana.

Adorno, Theodor W., and Max Horkheimer. 1971 [1970]. *Teoría estética*. Madrid: Taurus.

Adorno, Theodor W., and Max Horkheimer. 1984. *Notes sur la littérature*. Paris: Flammarion.

Aguirre, Mirta. 1963. "Apuntes sobre la literatura y el arte." *Cuba socialista* 3.

Agustín, José. 1996. *Tragicomedia mexicana. La vida en México de 1940 a 1970*. Mexico: Planeta.

Amaru. 1967. "Una revista de artes y ciencias." Editorial note, no. 1, January: 1.

Anderson, Benedict. 1993 [1983]. *Comunidades imaginadas. Reflexiones sobre el origen y la difusión del nacionalismo*. Mexico: FCE.

Anderson, Perry. 1978. *Las antinomias de Antonio Gramsci*. Barcelona: Fontanara.

Andrade, Joaquín. 1971. "Premio Casa de las Américas 1970. María Esther Gilio: La comunicación casi instantánea." *Casa de las Américas*, no. 64, January–February: 172–73.

Anhalt, Nedda G. 1989. "Heberto Padilla dentro del juego." *Vuelta*, no. 155: 54–58.

Aragon, Louis. 1964. "Prólogo a Roger Garaudy, *Hacia un realismo sin fronteras*." *Unión*, no. 1, January–March: 27.

Arenas, Reinaldo. 1968. "Benítez entra en el juego." *Unión*, no. 2: 146–52.

Arguedas, José María. 1968. *El zorro de arriba y el zorro de abajo*. In *Amaru*, 6, April–June and dated in Santiago de Chile, May 10: 42–49.

Arias, Salvador. 1982. "Literatura cubana (1959–1978)." In *La cultura en Cuba socialista*. Havana: Edición Letras Cubanas.

Aricó, José. 1964. "Examen de conciencia." *Pasado y Presente*, no. 4, January–March: 241–65.

Aricó, José. 1988. *La cola del diablo. Itinerario de Gramsci en América Latina*. Buenos Aires: Puntosur.

Arismendi, Rodney. 1976 [1974]. *Lenin, la revolución y América Latina*. Mexico: Grijalbo.

Aron, Raymond. 1955. *L'opium des intellectuels*. Paris: Calman-Lévy.

Aronowitz, Stanley. 1990. "On Intellectuals." In *Intellectuals, Aesthetics, Politics, Academics*. Bruce Robbins, ed. Minneapolis: University of Minnesota Press.

Aronowitz, Stanley. 1992. *The Politics of Identity: Class, Culture, Social Movements*. New York: Routledge.

Arrufat, Antón. 1963. "Función de la crítica literaria." *Casa de las Américas*, no. 17–18, March–June: 78–80.

"Artemio Cruz conquistó Dinamarca." 1966. *Siempre!*, no. 661, February 23: XIII- XI.

Asturias, Miguel Ángel. 1968. *Latinoamérica y otros ensayos*. Madrid: Guardiana de Publicaciones.

Ávila, Leopoldo (pseud.). 1968a. "Las respuestas de Caín." *Verde Olivo*, no. 44, November 3: 17–18.

Ávila, Leopoldo (pseud.). 1968b. "Las provocaciones de Padilla." *Verde Olivo*, no. 45, November 10: 17–18.

Ávila, Leopoldo (pseud.). 1968c. "Antón se va a la guerra." *Verde Olivo*, no. 46, November 17: 16–18.

Ávila, Leopoldo (pseud.). 1968d. "Sobre algunas corrientes de la crítica y la literatura en Cuba." *Verde Olivo*, no. 47, November 24: 14–18; *Unión*, VI, no. 3, September: 19–198.

Avilés Fabila, René. 1967a."Nueva encuesta sobre el congreso de escritores." *Siempre!*, no. 717, March 22: VIII- IX.

Ávila, Leopoldo (pseud.). 1967b. "La crítica literaria en México" (survey). *Siempre!*, no. 723, May 3.

Badiou, Alain. 2009 [1995]. *El siglo*. Buenos Aires: Manantial.

Baran, Paul. 1961. "El compromiso del intelectual" (speech delivered to the American Association for the Advancement of Science in New York in 1960). *Marcha*, no. 1089; *Casa de las Américas*, no. 71, July–August; *Monthly Review*, May; *Partisans*, no. 22: 41–46.

Baran, Paul. 1965. *Paul A. Baran (1910–1964): A Collective Portrait*. Edited by Paul Sweezy and Leo Huberman. New York: Monthly Review Press.

Barnet, Miguel. 1969. "La novela testimonio: socioliteratura." *Unión*, no. 4: 99–122.

Barthes, Roland. 1972. *Critical Essays*. Translated by Richard Howard. Evanston: Northwestern University Press.

Barthes, Roland. 1993. "A l'avant-garde de quel théâtre?" In *Essais critiques*, Œuvres complètes. Vol. 1. Paris: Seuil.

Batís, Huberto. 1967. "*Cien años de soledad*. La gran novela de América, ya inesperada, todavía oportuna." *Siempre!*, August 23.

Baudelaire, Charles. 1863. "Le peintre de la vie moderne." *Le Figaro*, November 26 and 29, December 3.

Baudelaire, Charles. 1964. "The Painter of Modern Life." In *The Painter of Modern Life and Other Essays*. Translated by Jonathan Mayne. London: Phaidon Press.

Bauman, Zygmunt. 1987. *Legislators and Interpreters: On Modernity, Post-Modernity, and Intellectuals*. Oxford: Polity Press.

Bauman, Zygmunt. 1995. "Morality and Politics." In *Life in Fragments: Essays in Postmodern Morality*. Oxford: Blackwell.

Bauman, Zygmunt. 1997 [1987]. *Legisladores e intérpretes*. Buenos Aires: Universidad Nacional de Quilmes.

Beauvoir, Simone de. 1984. *The Mandarins*. Translated by Leonard M. Friedman. London: Flamingo.

Bell, Daniel. 1978. *The Cultural Contradictions of Capitalism*. New York: Basic Books.

Bell, Daniel. 1988 [1976]. *Las contradicciones culturales del capitalismo*. Buenos Aires: Alianza.

Benda, Julien. 1975 [1927, expanded in 1945]. *La trahison des clercs*. Paris: Grasset & Fasquelle.

Benedetti, Mario. 1965. "Habanera." *La Rosa Blindada*, II, no. 8, April–May; *Casa de las Américas*, 38, September–October 1966; *Revista Civilizaçao Brasileira*, no. 16, November 1967 (translated by Octavio Mora under the title "Havaneira").

Benedetti, Mario. 1967a. "Las dentelladas del prójimo." *Marcha*, no. 1376, October 27; under the title "Vargas Llosa y su fértil escándalo." *Siempre!*, no. 777, May 15, 1968.

Benedetti, Mario. 1967b. "Ideas y actitudes en circulación." *Casa de las Américas*, no. 43, July–August: 102–3.

Benedetti, Mario. 1967c. *Letras del continente mestizo*. Montevideo: Arca.

Benedetti, Mario. 1967d. "Roberto Fernández Retamar. Poesía desde el cráter." *Marcha*, no. 1382, December 7; and in 1967c.

Benedetti, Mario. 1967e. "Situación del escritor en América Latina." *Letras del continente mestizo*: 13–21; and *Casa de las Américas*, no. 45, November–December: 31–36.

Benedetti, Mario. 1968a. "Gabriel García Márquez o la vigilia dentro del sueño." *Siempre!*, no. 762, January 31.

Benedetti, Mario. 1968b. "Situación actual de la cultura cubana." *Marcha*, no. 1431, December 27.

Benedetti, Mario. 1968c. "Sobre las relaciones entre el hombre de acción y el intelectual." *Casa de las Américas*, no. 47, March–April: 116–20.

Benedetti, Mario. 1968d. "Diálogo con Norberto Fuentes." *Marcha*, no. 1417, September 20.

Benedetti, Mario. 1969a. "El *boom* entre dos libertades" (I). *Marcha*, no. 1434, January 24: 30–31, and "El *boom* entre dos libertades" (II). *Marcha*, no. 1435, January 31: 30–31.

Benedetti, Mario. 1969b. "Conversación con Roque Dalton." *Marcha*, no. 1438, February 21; *Marcha*, no. 1439, February 28, and *Casa de las Américas*, 54, May–June.

Benedetti, Mario. 1970a. "Ernesto Cardenal: evangelio y revolución." *Marcha*, no. 1506, August 14; *Marcha*, 1507, August 21, and *Casa de las Américas*, no. 63, November–December: 174–83.

Benedetti, Mario. 1970b. "Gutiérrez, el poeta que vino del periodismo." *Marcha*, no. 1503, July 24: 29–31.

Benedetti, Mario. 1971a. "Las prioridades del escritor." *Cuba. Nueva política cultural. El caso Padilla, Cuadernos de Marcha*, no. 49: 35–45; *Casa de las Américas*, no. 68, September–October: 70–79.

Benedetti, Mario. 1971b. "Fernández Retamar, o las preocupaciones de un optimista" (interview). *Marcha*, no. 1562, September 24: 12–15.

Benedetti, Mario. 1971c: "Del testimonio a la metáfora." *Casa de las Américas*, no. 64, January–February: 177–79.

Benedetti, Mario. 1972. "Los resultados de un premio." *Marcha*, no. 1598, June 25.

Benítez, Fernando. 1967. "En defensa de Carlos Fuentes." *Siempre!*, no. 715, March 8: X.

Benítez Rojo, Antonio. 1968. "Condenados de Condado." *Casa de las Américas*, no. 49, July–August: 159.

Bianchi, Soledad. 1995. *La memoria, modelo para armar.* Santiago de Chile: Ediciones de la Dirección de Bibliotecas, Archivos y Museos.

Bianco, José. 1967. "Función social del escritor." *Casa de las Américas*, no. 43, July–August, and *Zona Franca*, II, no. 44, April.

Bignami, Ariel. 1969. *Notas para la polémica sobre el realismo.* Buenos Aires: Galerna.

Bignami, Ariel. 1973a. "Teoría y poética realista en la Argentina." In *Arte, ideología, sociedad.* Buenos Aires: Sílaba.

Bignami, Ariel. 1973b. "Realismo, verdad artística y vanguardia." In *Arte, ideología, sociedad.* Buenos Aires: Sílaba.

Blanco, Hugo. 1969. "Carta." *Oiga*, Lima, October 24.

Bobbio, Norberto. 1998 [1993]. *La duda y la elección. Intelectuales y poder en la sociedad contemporánea.* Barcelona: Paidós.

"Boletín con los del premio." 1974. *Casa de las Américas*, no. 87, November–December. In "Al pie de la letra": 156.

Boschetti, Anna. 1990 [1985]. *Sartre y Les Temps Modernes*. Buenos Aires: Nueva Visión.

Bourdieu, Pierre. 1966. "*Champ intellectuel et projet créateur.*" *Les Temps Modernes*, no. 246: 865–906.

Bourdieu, Pierre. 1971. "Champ de pouvoir, champ intellectuel et habitus de classe." *Scolies*, no. 1.

Bourdieu, Pierre. 1984. "Les intellectuels sont-ils hors jeu?." In *Questions de Sociologie*. Paris: Minuit.

Bourdieu, Pierre. 1992. *Les règles de l'art*. Paris: Seuil.

Bourdieu, Pierre. 2000. *La dominación masculina*. Barcelona: Anagrama.

Branly, Roberto. 1972. "Reseña deportiva," cited in Cardenal, Ernesto. *En Cuba*. Buenos Aires: Carlos Lohlé.

Braudel, Fernand. 1958. "Historia y ciencias sociales: la larga duración." *Cuadernos Americanos*, XVII, CI, no. 6, November–December.

Breton, André. 1992. *Manifiestos del surrealismo*. Buenos Aires: Argonauta.

Buck-Morss, Susan. 1977. *The Origin of Negative Dialectics: Theodor W. Adorno, Walter Benjamin, and the Frankfurt Institute*. New York: The Free Press.

Buck-Morss, Susan. 1981 [1977]. *Origen de la dialéctica negativa*. Mexico: Siglo XXI.

Bulletin of Latin American Research. 1984. III, no. 2 (monographic issue dedicated to culture in the sixties).

Bürger, Peter. 1983. "Literary Institution and Modernization." *Poetics*, no. 122, North-Holland: 419–33.

Bürger, Peter. 1985. "On Literary History." *Poetics*, no. 14, North-Holland: 199–207.

Bürger, Peter. 1987 [1974]. *Teoría de la vanguardia*. Barcelona: Península.

Bürger, Peter. 1990. "*The Problem of Aesthetic Value.*" In *Literary Theory Today*. Peter Collier and Helga Geyer-Ryan, eds. Ithaca, New York: Cornell University Press.

Bürger, Peter. 1992. *The Decline of Modernism*. Pennsylvania: Pennsylvania State University Press.

Cabrera Infante, Guillermo. 1960. *Así en la paz como en la guerra*. Havana: Ediciones R.

Cabrera Infante, Guillermo. 1968. "Las respuestas de Cabrera Infante." *Primera Plana*, no. 292, July 30.

Cabrera Infante, Guillermo. 1969. "La confundida lengua del poeta." *Primera Plana*, no. 316, January 14: 64–65.

Cabrera Infante, Guillermo. 1984 [1974]. *Vista del amanecer en el trópico*. Barcelona: Plaza & Janés.

Cabrera Infante, Guillermo. 1989. "Días callados en cliché." *Vuelta*, XIII, no. 154, September.

Cabrera Infante, Guillermo. 1992a [1982]. "Mordidas del caimán barbudo." In *Mea Cuba*. Barcelona: Plaza & Janés.

Cabrera Infante, Guillermo. 1992b [1982]. "La peliculita culpable." In *Mea Cuba*. Barcelona: Plaza & Janés.

Caillois, Roger. 1961. "Preface." In *Les littératures contemporaines à travers le monde*. Paris: Hachette.

Campbell, Federico. 1971. "Perplejidades, apoyos y condenas." *Siempre!*, no. 934, May 19: VII–X.

Campuzano, Luisa. 1992. "La revista *Casa de las Américas* en la década de los sesenta." *Cahiers du CRICCAL l*, Presses de la Sorbonne Nouvelle, on *Le discours culturel dans les revues latino-américaines (1940–1970)*, no. 9–10, Paris.

Carballo, Emmanuel. 1963. "Del costumbrismo al realismo crítico." *Casa de las Américas*, no. 19, July–August: 3–19.

Carballo, Emmanuel. 1966a. "Cuba: por decreto no se puede crear una literatura socialista." *Siempre!*, no. 664, March 16: XIII.

Carballo, Emmanuel. 1966b. "Novela y cuento 1965. La prosa mexicana, sin perder sus cualidades nativas, comienza a ser universal." *Siempre!*, no. 654, January 5.

Carballo, Emmanuel. 1967. "Sobre el Congreso." *Excelsior, Diorama de la Cultura*, March 12.

Cardenal, Ernesto. 1972. *En Cuba*. Buenos Aires: Carlos Lohlé.

Cardoso, Fernando Enrique, and Enzo Faletto. 1969. *Dependencia y desarrollo en América Latina*. Mexico: Siglo XXI.

Carpentier, Alejo. 1967 [1964]. "Literatura y conciencia política en América Latina" (dated August 1961, Havana). In *Tientos, diferencias y otros ensayos*. Montevideo: Arca.

Carpentier, Alejo. 1969. "Papel social del novelista." *Casa de las Américas*, no. 53, March–April: 8–18.

Carpentier, Alejo. 1970. "Intellectuels à Cuba." *Castro, le romantisme révolutionnaire, Planète Action*, Paris, July.

Carrera, Gustavo Luis. 1975. "Pénétration culturelle; signe essentiel à la littérature en Amérique Latine?" In *Ideologies, littérature et societé en Amerique Latine.* Brigitte Navalet, et al. Proceedings of the colloquium organized by the Institut de Sociologie of the Université Libre de Bruxelles and l'Ecole Practique des Hautes Études de Paris. Ediciones de la Université de Bruxelles.

Casa de las Américas. 1966. "Carta abierta a Pablo Neruda," no. 38, September–October: 131–55; *Granma*, July 31.

Casa de las Américas. 1967a. "Declaración," no. 43, July–August.

Casa de las Américas. 1967b. "Declaración de los 20," no. 43, July–August: 100–101.

Casa de las Américas. 1967c. "Editorial," no. 40, January–February: 2–3.

Casa de las Américas. 1967d. "Editorial," no. 42, May–June.

Casa de las Américas. 1967e. "En estos días." Editorial note, no. 44, September–October.

Casa de las Américas. 1967f. "Encuentro sobre Darío." Editorial note, no. 42, May–June.

Casa de las Américas. 1967g. "Primera declaración del Comité de Colaboración de Casa de las Américas," no. 41, March–April; "Los escritores asumen su responsabilidad." *Marcha*, no. 1337 February; *Siempre!*, no. 710, February 1; *Margen*, no. 2 to no. 3–4, Paris, Autumn.

Casa de las Américas. 1967h. "Una vez más," no. 45, November–December. In "Al pie de la letra."

Casa de las Américas. 1968–1969a. "Editorial," no. 51–52, November–February.

Casa de las Américas. 1968–1969b. "Literatura y revolución" (survey), no. 51–52, November–February.

Casa de las Américas. 1969a. "La Casa por fuera," no. 56, September–October: 159–61.

Casa de las Américas. 1969b. "El documental cubano," no. 53, March–April. In "Al pie de la letra."

Casa de las Américas. 1969c. "Por una nueva vanguardia latinoamericana," no. 53, March–April 1970: 161–64, and *Marcha*, 1434, January 24.

Casa de las Américas. 1969d. "Segunda declaración del Comité de Colaboración de *Casa de las Américas.*" no. 53, March–April: 3–6.

Casa de las Américas. 1969e. "Últimas actividades de la Casa de las Américas," no. 53, March–April: 167.

Casa de las Américas. 1969f. "Unión de libros," no. 53, March–April. In "Al pie de la letra": 165.

Casa de las Américas. 1970a. "¿El único encuentro del encuentro?," no. 58, January–February. In "Al pie de la letra": 160–61.

Casa de las Américas. 1970b. "Sin penas ni glorias," no. 63. In "Al pie de la letra," November–December.

Casa de las Américas. 1971a. "Con Vargas Llosa," no. 64, January–February. In "Al pie de la letra": 193–94.

Casa de las Américas. 1971b. "Declaración de intelectuales chilenos," no. 67, July–August.

Casa de las Américas. 1971c. "Declaración del Primer Congreso Nacional de Educación y Cultura de Cuba," no. 65–66, March–June; *Cuba. Nueva política cultural. El caso Padilla, Cuadernos de Marcha*, no. 49, May; *Libre*, 1, September–October–November.

Casa de las Américas. 1971d. "Editorial," no. 67, July–August.

*Casa de las Américas.*1971e. "Ellos escogieron la libertad," no. 69, November–December. In "Al pie de la letra."

Casa de las Américas. 1971f. "Final de Sur," no. 65–66, March–June. In "Al pie de la letra."

Casa de las Américas. 1971. "Suplemento. El caso Padilla," no. 67, July–August: 191.

Casa de las Américas. 1972. "Editorial," no. 71, March–April.

Casal, Lourdes, ed. 1971. *El caso Padilla: literatura y revolución en Cuba. Documentos.* New York: Nueva Atlántida.

Casaus, Víctor. 1967. "La poesía más joven: seis comentarios y un prólogo." *Unión*, VI, no. 3, July–September: 5–13.

Casaus, Víctor, and Raúl Rivero. 1972. "Prólogo a *Joven poesía cubana* (antología)," *Latinoamericana*, no. 1, December.

Casey, Calvert. 1962. "Comentario de Luis Agüero, 'De aquí para allá.'" *Casa de las Américas*, no. 13–14, July–October.

Caso, Elena. 1968. "¿Arte de vanguardia, arte de retaguardia? Encuesta sobre las posibilidades de expresión artística." *Siempre!*, no. 769, March 20.

Castillo, Abelardo. 1964. *Discusión crítica a la "crisis" del marxismo.* Buenos Aires: Biblioteca El Escarabajo de Oro.

Castro, Fidel. 1970a. "Discurso sobre la zafra." *Granma*, no. 20 and May 31; under the title "El pueblo merece la victoria," *Marcha*, no. 1504, July 21: 16–21.

Castro, Fidel. 1970b. "El pueblo merece la verdad." *Marcha*, no. 1504, July 21: 16–21.

Castro, Fidel. 1971. "Discurso de clausura del Primer Congreso Nacional de Educación y Cultura." *Casa de las Américas*, no. 65–66, March–June; *Libre*, 1, September, October, November; *Cuadernos de Marcha*, no. 49: 92.

Castro, Fidel. 1980 [1961]. "Palabras a los intelectuales." In *Revolución, Letras, Arte.* López, Virgilio, ed. Havana: Letras Cubanas.

Castro, Fidel. 1983a [1956]. "La historia me absolverá." In *José Martí. El autor intelectual.* Havana: Editora Pública.

Castro, Fidel. 1983b. "Es el Apóstol el guía de mi vida." In *José Martí. El autor intelectual.* Havana: Editora Pública.

Castro, Fidel. 1983c. "Como dijera nuestro Apóstol." In *José Martí. El autor intelectual.* Havana: Editora Pública.

Castro, Fidel. 1983d [1962]. "Segunda declaración de La Habana." *José Martí. El autor intelectual.* Havana: Editora Pública.

Castro, Fidel. 2008. *The Declarations of Havana.* London: Verso.

Certeau, Michel de. 1997. *The Capture of Speech and Other Political Writings.* Translated by Tom Conley. Minneapolis: University of Minnesota Press.

Charle, Christophe. 1990. *Naissance des intellectuels 1880–1900.* Paris: Minuit.

Chifflet, Guillermo. 1967. "Cultura y revolución en Cuba." *Siempre!*, no. 748, October 25.

Chifflet, Guillermo. 1971. "Cuba. Nueva política cultural. El caso Padilla." *Cuadernos de Marcha*, no. 49, May 1971.

Chifflet, Guillermo. 1972. "Entrevista con Homero Fariña." *Marcha*, no. 1585, March 17.

Cisneros, Antonio. 1967. "Siete Fideles en Londres." *Amaru*, no. 4, October–December.

Claudín, Fernando. 1971–72. "Respuesta al debate sobre libertad y socialismo." *Libre*, no. 2, December, January, February: 6.

Cofiño López, Manuel. 1975 [1971]. *La última mujer y el próximo combate.* Havana: Arte y Literatura.

Cohn-Bendit, Daniel. 1987. *La revolución y nosotros, que la quisimos tanto.* Barcelona: Anagrama.

Coleman, Peter. 1989. *The Liberal Conspiracy: The Congress for Cultural Freedom and the Struggle for the Mind of Postwar Europe.* New York: The Free Press.

Collazos, Oscar. 1969. "La encrucijada del lenguaje (I)." *Marcha*, no. 1460, August 29: 30–31.

Collazos, Oscar. 1969. "La encrucijada del lenguaje (II)." *Marcha*, no. 1461, September 5: 30–31.

Collazos, Oscar. 1970. "Contrarrespuesta para armar (I)." *Marcha*, no. 1485, March 13: 30–31.

Collazos, Oscar. 1970. "Contrarrespuesta para armar (II)." *Marcha*, no. 1485, March 20: 30–31.

Collazos, Oscar. 1971. "Escritores, revolución y cultura en América Latina." *Casa de las Américas*, no. 68, September–October: 110–19.

Conteris, Híber. 1977. "El escritor latinoamericano." *Marcha*, no. 1353, May 20.

Conti, Haroldo. 1971. Interview published in *El Tiempo*, Bogotá, November 28.

Cortázar, Julio. 1962–63. "Algunos aspectos del cuento." *Casa de las Américas*, no. 15–16, November–February: 3–14; *El Escarabajo de Oro*, IV, no. 26–27, February 1965.

Cortázar, Julio. 1963. *Rayuela.* Buenos Aires: Sudamericana.

Cortázar, Julio. 1965. "Reunión." *Revista de la Universidad Autónoma de México*; *El Escarabajo de Oro*, VI, no. 26–27, February; 1966. *Todos los fuegos el fuego.* Buenos Aires: Sudamericana.

Cortázar, Julio. 1967. "Carta." *Casa de las Américas*, no. 45, November–December: 4–12.

Cortázar, Julio. 1968. *62 modelo para armar.* Buenos Aires: Sudamericana.

Cortázar, Julio. 1969. "Un escritor y su soledad." *Life en Español*, New York, April 7.

Cortázar, Julio. 1970a. "Viaje alrededor de una mesa." *Marcha*, no. 1501, July 10: 29–31.

Cortázar, Julio. 1970b. "Revolución en la literatura y literatura en la revolución (I)." *Marcha*, no. 1477, January 9: 30–31, and "Revolución en la literatura y literatura en la revolución (II)." *Marcha*, no. 1478, January 16: 30–31.

Cortázar, Julio. 1971. "Policrítica a la hora de los chacales." *Cuadernos de Marcha*, no. 49, May: 33–36.

Cortázar, Julio. 1972. "Cortázar" (response to David Viñas). *Hispamérica*, no. 2, December: 55–58.

Cortázar, Julio. 1975. *Ideologies, littérature et societé en Amérique Latine*. Proceedings of the colloquium organized by the Institut de Sociologie of the Université Libre de Bruxelles and the École Pratique des Hautes Études de Paris. Bruselas: Ediciones de la Université de Bruxelles.

Cortázar, Julio. 1984. "Correspondencia." *Casa de las Américas*, no. 145–46, July–October: 17–21, 25–26, 31–33, 39–41, 44–46, 72–73, 102, 104, 116–17, 146–50.

Cortázar, Julio. 2000 [1963]. "Carta a Paul Blackburn." Vienna, April 1. In *Julio Cortázar. Cartas 1937-1963*. Vol. 1. Compiled by Aurora Bernárdez. Buenos Aires: Alfaguara.

Cosse, Isabella. 2010. *Pareja, sexualidad y familia. Una revolución discreta en Buenos Aires*. Buenos Aires: Siglo XXI.

Cuadernos de Marcha. 1971. "Introducción," no. 49, May: 4.

Cuba. Nueva política cultural. El caso Padilla, *Cuadernos de Marcha*. 1971. "Declaración de intelectuales y artistas uruguayos: No hemos apostado a la inocencia de Padilla sino a la revolución latinoamericana," no. 49: 24–26; *Libre*, no. 1, September–October–November: 136–37.

Dalton, Roque. 1963. "Poesía y militancia en América Latina." *Casa de las Américas*, no. 20–21, September–December: 13–20.

Dalton, Roque. 1969. "Literatura e intelectualidad: dos concepciones." *Casa de las Américas*, no. 57, November–December: 95–101.

Dalton, Roque, René Depestre, Edmundo Desnoes, Roberto Fernández Retamar, Ambrosio Fornet, and Carlos María Gutiérrez. 1969. *El intelectual y la sociedad*. Mexico: Siglo XXI (originally published in *Casa de las Américas*, no. 56, September–October: 7–52).

De Beauvoir, Simone. 1954. *Les mandarins*. Vol. II. Paris: Folio.

Debray, Régis. 1967a. "Le castrisme: la longue marche de l'Amérique Latine." In *Révolution dans la révolution et autres essais*. Paris: Petite Collection Maspero.

Debray, Régis. 1967b. "Le rôle de l'intellectuel." In *Révolution dans la revolution et autres essais.* Paris: Petite Collection Maspero.

Debray, Régis. 1970. "The Role of the Intellectual." In *Strategy for Revolution.* New York: Monthly Review Press.

Debray, Régis. 1996. *Loués soient nos seigneurs. Une education politique.* Paris: Gallimard.

De Campos, Haroldo. 1972. "Superación de los lenguajes exclusivos." In *América Latina en su literatura.* Fernández Moreno, César, ed. Mexico: Siglo XXI.

De Certeau, Michel. 1995a [1968]. "Tomar la palabra." In *La toma de la palabra y otros escritos políticos.* Mexico: Universidad Iberoamericana, Biblioteca Francisco Xavier Clavígero.

De Certeau, Michel. 1995b [1968]. "El poder de hablar." In *La toma de la palabra y otros escritos políticos.* Mexico: Universidad Iberoamericana, Biblioteca Francisco Xavier Clavígero.

"Declaración de la UNEAC." 1969. In *Fuera del juego.* Padilla, Heberto. Buenos Aires: Aditor.

1967. "Declaración de los 20." *Casa de las Américas,* 43, July- August: 100–101.

De Freitas, Gonzalo. 1959. "No vive nadie en el paraíso." *Marcha,* no. 990.

De la Torre, Gerardo. 1971. "Dos respuestas a las opiniones sobre el caso Padilla." *Siempre!,* no. 936, June 2.

Depestre, René. 1967. "Carta." *Casa de las Américas,* no. 45, November–December: 38–41.

Desnoes, Edumundo. 1961a. "Ocho pintores y escultores," *Casa de las Américas,* no. 9, November–December: 131–36.

Desnoes, Edumundo. 1961b. *No hay problema.* Havana: Revolución.

Desnoes, Edumundo. 1968. *Memorias del subdesarrollo.* Buenos Aires: Galerna.

Desnoes, Edmundo. 1984. "A falta de otras palabras." In *Más allá del* boom*: literatura y mercado.* Ángel Rama, ed. Buenos Aires: Folios.

Desnoes, Edmundo; Fernández Retamar, Roberto; Fornet, Ambrosio; Otero, Lisandro. 1966. "Sobre la penetración intelectual del imperialismo yanqui en América Latina." *Casa de las Américas,* no. 39, November–December: 133–38.

Díaz, Jesús. 1992. *Las palabras perdidas.* Barcelona: Destino.

Diazlastra, Alberto. 1967. "La definición literaria, política y moral de Carlos Fuentes." *Siempre!*, no. 719, April 5.

"Dictamen del jurado." 1969. In *Fuera del juego*. Padilla, Heberto. Buenos Aires: Aditor.

"Discurso de inauguración del Primer Encuentro de Escritores Americanos." 1960. *Atenea*, no. 387, January–March.

Donoso, José. 1981. *El jardín de al lado*. Barcelona: Biblioteca Seix-Barral, Sudamericana-Planeta.

Donoso, José. 1989 [1983]. *Historia personal del* boom. Appendixes by the author and María Pilar Serrano. Buenos Aires: Sudamericana-Planeta.

Donoso, Pilar. 1983. "El *boom* doméstico." In *Historia personal del boom*. Appendixes by the author and María Pilar Serrano. Donoso, José. Buenos Aires: Sudamericana-Planeta.

Dorfman, Ariel. 1965. "América, problema para escritores." *Anales de la Universidad de Chile*, no. 135, July–September: 201–5.

Droguett, Carlos. 1971. "El escritor y su pasión necesaria." *Casa de las Américas*, no. 68, September–October: 60–68.

Droguett, Carlos. 1971. Interview in *Prensa Latina*, reprinted in *Casa de las Américas*, no. 69, November–December.

Droguett, Carlos. 1971–1972. "Respuesta de Salvador Garmendia." *Libre*, no. 2, December, January, February: 11–12.

Dumont, René. 1970. *Cuba est-il socialiste?*. Paris: Seuil.

Eagleton, Terry. 1984. *The Function of Criticism*. London: Verso.

Echegoyen, Maruja. 1969. "Triunfo del cine latinoamericano en Venecia." *Marcha*, no. 1465, October 3.

Edwards, Jorge. 1982. *Persona non grata* (complete edition). Barcelona: Seix-Barral.

Edwards, Jorge. 1989. "Enredos cubanos (dieciocho años después del 'caso Padilla')." *Vuelta*, XIII, no. 154, September: 35–38.

Ehrman, Juan. 1969. "Entre la definición y el caos." *Ercilla*, no. 1784, August 27–September 2: 87–90.

El Caimán Barbudo (cultural monthly of the Juventud Rebelde). 1966. "Nos pronunciamos," no. 1, March.

El Corno Emplumado. 1963. "Nota de los editores," no. 7, July.

Enzensberger, Magnus. 1969. "Lugares comunes de la nueva literatura." *Unión*, no. 3: 149–61.

Enzensberger, Magnus. 1973. *El interrogatorio de La Habana: Autorretrato de la contrarevolución*. Barcelona: Anagrama.

Enzensberger, Magnus. 1974 [1962]. "The Aporias of the Avant-Garde." In *The Consciousness Industry*. New York: Seabury Press.

Ercilla. 1969. "Los escritores frente al compromiso." September 24–30.

Fanon, Frantz. 1969. *Sociología de la liberación*. Buenos Aires: Presente.

Fanon, Frantz. 1974 [1961]. *Los condenados de la tierra*. Sixth reprint. Buenos Aires: Fondo de Cultura Económica.

Fejtö, François. 1966. "Notas sobre Cuba." *Mundo Nuevo*, no. 1, July: 51–59.

Fell, Claude. 1990. "La revue *Mundo Nuevo*, catalyseur du *boom* latino-américain." *Cahiers de l'UFR d'Études Ibériques et Latino-Américaines*. Paris: Publications de la Sorbonne Nouvelle.

Fernández, Pablo Armando. 1968. *Los chicos se despiden*. Havana: Casa de las Américas, Colección Premio.

Fernández, Pablo Armando. 1989. *El vientre del pez*. Havana: Unión.

Fernández Moreno, César. 1959. "Reportaje literario en Buenos Aires. Situación actual de la novela." *Marcha*, no. 959, May 8: 29–30.

Fernández Moreno, César, ed. 1980. *Latin America in Its Literature*. Translated by Mary G. Berg. New York: Holmes and Meier.

Fernández Retamar, Roberto. 1962. "Carta a Cortázar," "Carta a Roque Dalton," "Carta a Juan Gelman," "Carta a Fayad Jamís." *Casa de las Américas,* no. 13–14, July–October: 27–30.

Fernández Retamar, Roberto. 1966. "El arte y lo histórico-fundamental. Notas sobre la esencia de lo artístico." *Casa de las Américas*, no. 38, September–October: 30–56.

Fernández Retamar, Roberto. 1967a. "Alrededores del congreso." *Casa de las Américas*, no. 43, July–August: 97–98.

Fernández Retamar, Roberto. 1967b. "Hacia una intelectualidad revolucionaria en Cuba." *Casa de las Américas*, no. 40, January–February: 4–17.

Fernández Retamar, Roberto. 1967c [1965]. "Tenía Ud. razón, Tallet, somos hombres de transición." *Marcha*, no. 1265, July 30; *Siempre!*, 734, July 19; *Revista de la Universidad de México*, XXI, no. 8, April; *Nuevos Aires*, no. 2, September–October–November 1970.

Fernández Retamar, Roberto, and Jorge Lafforgue. 1967d. "Contra la penetración cultural yanqui." *Marcha*, no. 1375, October 20.

Fernández Retamar, Roberto. 1968. "Responsabilidad de los intelectuales de los países subdesarrollantes." *Casa de las Américas*, no. 47, March–April: 121–23.

Fernández Retamar, Roberto. 1969. "Antipoesía y poesía conversacional en América Latina." In *Panorama de la actual literatura latinoamericana*. Roberto Fernández Retamar et al. Havana: Centro de Investigaciones Literarias de la Casa de las Américas.

Fernández Retamar, Roberto et al. 1969. *Panorama de la actual literatura latinoamericana*. Havana: Centro de Investigaciones Literarias.

Fernández Retamar, Roberto. 1971. "Calibán." *Casa de las Américas*, no. 68, September–October: 124–51; and in 1980. *Revolución, Letras, Arte*. Virgilio López Lemus et al. Havana: Letras Cubanas.

Fernández Retamar, Roberto. 1972. "Explico al lector por qué al cabo no concluí aquel poema sobre la Comuna." *Unión*, no. 1, and *Marcha*, no. 1581, February 11: 31.

Fernández Retamar, Roberto. 1974. "Sobre la vanguardia en la literatura latinoamericana." *Casa de las Américas*, no. 82, January–February.

Fernández Retamar, Roberto. 1981. *Para el perfil definitivo del hombre*. Havana: Letras Cubanas.

Fernández Retamar, Roberto. 2016. "You Were Right, Tallet: We Are Men of Transition" In *Nothing Out of This World: Cuban Poetry 1952-2000*. Translated by Katherine M. Hedeen. Grewelthorpe, UK: Smokestack Books.

Flores, Antonio. 1963. "Carta." *El Corno Emplumado*, no. 7, July.

Flores Olea, Víctor. 1962. "La crisis del stalinismo." *Cuadernos Americanos*, XXI, May–June: 80–108.

Fogel, J. F., and B. Rosenthal. 1992. *Fin de siècle à La Havane*. Paris: Seuil.

Fornet, Ambrosio. 1967. "New World en español." *Casa de las Américas*, no. 40, January–February.

Fornet, Ambrosio. 1971. "A propósito de *Sacchario*." *Casa de las Américas*, no. 64, January–February: 183–86.

Fornet, Ambrosio. 1980. "El intelectual en la revolución." In *Revolución, Letras, Arte*. Havana: Letras Cubanas.

Fornet, Ambrosio. 1987. "A propósito de *Las iniciales de la tierra*." *Casa de las Américas*, no. 164, September–October: 148–49.

Foucault, Michel. 1972. *The Archeology of Knowledge*. Translated by A. M. Sheridan Smith. New York: Pantheon Books.

Foucault, Michel. 1981. "Un diálogo sobre el poder." In *Un diálogo sobre el poder y otras conversaciones*. Madrid: Alianza. Originally published in *L'Arc*, issue dedicated to Gilles Deleuze, no. 7–19.

Foucault, Michel. 1984 [1969]. *La arqueología del saber.* Tenth edition. Mexico: Siglo XXI.

Foucault, Michel, and Gilles Deleuze. 1977. "Intellectuals and Power." In *Language, Counter-Memory, Practice: Selected Essays and Interviews.* D. F. Bouchard, ed. Ithaca: Cornell University Press.

Fourier, Charles. 1975 [1808]. *Théorie de quatre mouvements et des destinées générales.* Vol. 1. Paris: Grasset & Fasquelle.

Fraire, Isabel. 1971. *Siempre!,* 934, May 19; *Libre,* no. 1, September, October, November.

Franco, Jean. 1977. "Modernización, resistencia y revolución: la producción literaria de los años sesenta." *Escritura*, II, no. 3, January–June: 3–19.

Franco, Jean. 1984. "Memoria, narración y repetición: la narrativa hispanoamericana en la época de la cultura de masas." In *Más allá del* boom*: literatura y mercado.* Ángel Rama, ed. Buenos Aires: Folios.

Fuentes, Carlos. 1958. *La región más transparente.* Mexico: Fondo de Cultura Económica.

Fuentes, Carlos. 1962. "Conferencia." In "Antología de las intervenciones. Imagen del hombre en América Latina en la VII Escuela Internacional de la Universidad de Concepción." *Alerce*, no. 4, June.

Fuentes, Carlos. 1966. "El PEN: entierro de la guerra fría en literatura." *Life en Español*, August 1.

Fuentes, Carlos. 1967a. "Nuestras sociedades no quieren testigos y todo acto de lenguaje verdadero es en sí revolucionario." *Siempre!*, no. 742, September 13: VII–IX; and Árbol de Letras, no. 5, April 1968.

Fuentes, Carlos. 1967b. "Cartas a la Casa." *Casa de las Américas*, no. 43, July–August.

Fuentes, Carlos. 1969. *La nueva novela hispanoamericana*. Mexico: Joaquín Mortiz.

Fuentes, Carlos. 1971 [1962]. *La muerte de Artemio Cruz.* Navarra: Salvat.

Fuentes, Carlos. 1971. "La verdadera solidaridad con Cuba." *Siempre!*, no. 934, May 19.

Fuentes, Carlos. 1994 [1967]. *Cambio de piel*. Mexico: Alfaguara.

Fuentes, Norberto. 1968. *Condenados de Condado*. Havana: Casa de las Américas.

Fuentes, Norberto. 1970. *Cazabandido*. Montevideo: Libros de la Pupila.

Galeano, Eduardo. 1983 [1971]. *Las venas abiertas de América Latina*. Revised and expanded edition. Buenos Aires: Siglo XXI.

Garaudy, Roger. 1964 [1963]. *Hacia un realismo sin fronteras*. Buenos Aires: Lautaro.

Garaudy, Roger. 1966. *Marxisme du XXe siécle*. Paris: La Palatine.

Garaudy, Roger. 1971 [1968]. *Un realismo del siglo XX, diálogo póstumo con Fernand Léger*. Madrid: Siglo XXI.

García Ascot, Jomi. 1967. "*Cien años de soledad*, una novela de García Márquez sólo comparable a *Moby Dick*." *Siempre!*, no. 732, July 5.

García Canclini, Néstor. 1989. *Hybrid Cultures: Strategies for Entering and Leaving Modernity*. Translated by Christopher L. Chiappari and Silvia L. López. Minneapolis: University of Minnesota Press.

García Canclini, Néstor. 1990. *Culturas híbridas*. Mexico: Grijalbo.

García Grau, J. 1972. "Castellet y Barral hablan para Marcha." *Marcha*, no. 1598, June 25.

García Márquez, Gabriel. 1967. *Cien años de soledad*. Buenos Aires: Sudamericana.

García Márquez, Gabriel. 1971. Interview in *Diario del Caribe* (Barranquilla). Reprinted in: *Cuadernos de Marcha*, no. 49; and *Libre*, no. 1, September, October, November: 26–28 and 135–36, respectively.

García Márquez, Gabriel. 1994. "Una *addenda* de García Márquez." "Primer Plano," cultural supplement of *Página 12*, Buenos Aires, October 16.

García Ponce, Juan. 1971. "Perplejidades, apoyos y condenas." *Siempre!*, no. 934, May 19.

Garmendia, Salvador. 1971. Telegram to Goytisolo transcribed in *Libre*, no. 1, September, October, November: 134–35.

Garrels, Elizabeth. 1984. "Resumen de la discusión." In *Más allá del* boom*: literatura y mercado. Ángel* Rama, ed. Buenos Aires: Folios.

G. B. 1966. "Hacia una comunidad cultural iberoamericana." *Mensaje*, no. 147, March–April.

Gelman, Juan. 1962. "Carta-poema" and "Habana *revisited*." *Casa de las Américas*, no. 13–14, July–October.

Gerassi, John. 1971. "Nueva entrevista con Jean-Paul Sartre. El compromiso es un acto, no una palabra." *Marcha*, no. 1554, July 30: 14–16.

Gide, André. 1936. *Regreso de la URSS*. Buenos Aires: Sur.

Gide, André. 1937. *Return from the USSR*. Translated by Dorothy Bussy. New York: Knopf.

Gilio, María Esther. 1970. *La guerrilla tupamara*. Havana: Casa de las Américas.

Gilman, Claudia. 1993a. "Política y cultura: *Marcha* a partir de los años 60." *Nuevo Texto Crítico*, VI, no. 11, first semester, Stanford University: 153–86.

Gilman, Claudia. 1993b. "*L'anti-intellectualisme: topique des intellectuels 'révolutionnaires' dans les années soixante-dix*." Master's thesis, Diplôme d'Études Approfondies (DEA), École des Hautes Études en Sciences Sociales.

Gilman, Claudia. 1996a. "El semanario *Marcha* (1939–1974)." In *Diccionario enciclopédico de las letras de América Latina* (DELAL). Caracas: Fundación Biblioteca Ayacucho.

Gilman, Claudia. 1996b. "Intelectuales 'libres' o intelectuales 'revolucionarios': el caso de la revista *Libre*. Política y cultura sobre un campo minado." *América, Cahiers du CRICCAL*, no. 15–16; *Le discours culturel dans les revues latino-américaines de 1970 à 1990*. Paris: Presses de la Sorbonne Nouvelle. 11–20.

Gilman, Claudia. 1996c. "Intelectuales 'estatizados' e intelectuales 'revolucionarios': el caso de la revista *Libre*," *América. Cahiers du CRICCAL*, no. 15–16: 13–20.

Gilman, Claudia. 1997. "Política y crítica literaria. El semanario *Marcha* en los años de la revolución mundial." *Culturas*, no. 17–18, Paris: 217–27.

Gilman, Claudia. 1999. "Las revistas y los límites de lo decible: cartografía de una época." In *La cultura de un siglo: América Latina en sus revistas*. Saúl Sosnowski, ed. Madrid-Buenos Aires: Alianza.

Gilman, Claudia. 2001. "Mercado y consagración: la revolución cubana y la reconsideración de la 'nueva narrativa latinoamericana'

(1961–1971)." In *Territorios intelectuales. Pensamiento y cultura en América Latina.* Coordinated by Javier Lasarte. Caracas: La Nave Va.

Gilman, Claudia. 2003. "Batallas de la pluma y la palabra." In *Marcha y América Latina.* Mabel Moraña and Horacio Machín, eds. Pittsburgh: Biblioteca de América.

Gilman, Claudia. 2009. "El factor humano y una rivalidad histórica: Ángel Rama y Emir Rodríguez Monegal." In *Episodios en la formación de redes culturales en América Latina.* Buenos Aires: Prometeo.

Gilman, Claudia. 2010. "Ángel Rama y Emir Rodríguez Monegal en la tormenta revolucionaria." In *Pensamento latinoamericano: ultrapassando o Estado-nação.* Claudia Wasserman and Eduardo Devés Valdés, eds. Porto Alegre: Editorial a Universidade Federal do Rio Grande do Sul.

Gilman Claudia. 2011–12. "Enredos y desenredos de Ángel Rama y Emir Rodríguez Monegal." *Nuevo Texto crítico*, Stanford, Vol. XXIV–XXV: 55–79.

Gisselbrecht, André. 1964. "Questions posées." *La Nouvelle Critique*, no. 156, June–July.

Giunta, Andrea. 1994. "Arte, represión: cultura crítica y prácticas conceptuales en Argentina." In *Arte, historia e identidad en América Latina.* Gustavo Curiel Méndez et al. Mexico: Instituto de Investigaciones Estéticas, UNAM.

Giunta, Andrea. 1995. "Hacia las nuevas fronteras: Bonino entre Buenos Aires, Río de Janeiro y Nueva York." In *El arte entre lo público y lo privado.* Andrea Giunta et al. Buenos Aires: CAIA.

Giunta, Andrea. 1997. "Bienales Americanas de Arte. Una alianza entre arte e industria." In *Patrocinio, colección y circulación de las artes.* Gustavo Curiel, ed. Mexico: UNAM-IIE.

Glantz, Margo. 1971. "Estudio preliminar." In *Onda y escritura en México: jóvenes de 20 a 33.* Mexico: Siglo XXI.

González, Manuel Pedro. 1967. "Reparos al premio Rómulo Gallegos." *Zona Franca*, IV, no. 51, November.

González Bermejo, Ernesto. 1970. "García Márquez: ahora doscientos años de soledad." *Casa de las Américas*, no. 63, November–December: 159–73 (also "Y ahora, doscientos años de soledad." *Marcha*, no. 1510, September 11: 30–31; "Nuevos libros, nuevos mitos," *Marcha*, no. 1511, September 18: 28–29; and "El otoño del patriarca," *Marcha*, no. 1512, September 25: 30–31).

González Bermejo, Ernesto. 1970. "Los hijos de la revolución son otros." In "Norberto Fuentes: un escritor en discordia." *Marcha*, no. 1521, November 27.

González Bermejo, Ernesto. 1971. "Entrevista a Mario Benedetti" dated in Havana, February. *Casa de las Américas*, no. 65–66, March–June: 149–55.

González Echevarría, Roberto. 1985a. "Meta-end by Guillermo Cabrera Infante, translated, with an introduction, commentary, and notes." In *The Voice of the Masters: Writing and Authority in Modern Latin American Literature*. Austin: University of Texas Press.

González Echevarría, Roberto. 1985b. *The Voice of the Masters: Writing and Authority in Modern Latin American Literature*. Austin: University of Texas Press.

González Pedrero, Enrique. 1962. *El gran viraje*. Mexico: Era.

Gouldner, Alvin. 1979. *The Future of Intellectuals and the Rise of the New Class*. New York: Seabury Press.

Gouldner, Alvin. 1980. *El futuro de los intelectuales y el ascenso de la nueva clase*. Barcelona: Alianza.

Goytisolo, Juan. 1964. "Buenas y malas relaciones entre literatura y política." *Marcha*, no. 1192, January 31; *Casa de las Américas*, no. 26, October–November: 148–52.

Goytisolo, Juan. 1983. "El gato negro que atravesó nuestras oficinas de la rue de Bièvre." *Quimera*, no. 29, March: 12–25.

Gramsci, Antonio. 1984. *Notas sobre Maquiavelo, sobre la política y sobre el Estado moderno*. Buenos Aires: Nueva Visión.

Granma. 1967. "Sesión final del encuentro con Rubén Darío." January 29.

Guevara, Alfredo. 1963. "¿Cuáles son las mejores películas?." *Hoy*, December 18.

Guevara, Ernesto. 1969. "Socialism and Man in Cuba." In *Che: Selected Works of Ernesto Guevara*. Cambridge, MA: MIT Press.

Guevara, Ernesto. 1970. "La teoría del foco." In *Obras 1957–1967*. Havana: Casa de las Américas.

Guevara, Ernesto. 1977. "Pasajes de la guerra revolucionaria." In *Escritos y discursos*. Vol. II. Havana: De Ciencias Sociales.

Guevara, Ernesto. 1987 [1965]. "El socialismo y el hombre en Cuba." In *Marcha*, Montevideo, March 12, 1965.

Guillén, Nicolás. 1971. "Sobre el congreso y algo más…." *Verde Olivo*, XVIII, no. 22, May 30: 8–9.

Guillory, John. 1993. *Cultural Capital: The Problem of Literary Canon Formation*. Chicago and London: University of Chicago Press.

Gutiérrez, Carlos María. 1966. "Conversación con Fidel." *Marcha*, no. 1366, August 18.

Gutiérrez, Carlos María. 1968. "Mala conciencia para intelectuales." *Marcha*, no. 1386, January 12.

Gutiérrez, Carlos María. 1970. "Informe sobre la guerrilla boliviana." *Marcha*, no. 1480, January 30: 18–20.

Habermas, Jürgen. 1984. "La modernidad: un proyecto incompleto." *Punto de Vista*, no. 21: 27–31.

Habermas, Jürgen. 1989. *The Structural Transformation of the Public Sphere: An Inquiry into a Category of Bourgeois Society*. Cambridge, MA: MIT Press.

"Hacia el Congreso Cultural de La Habana." 1967. *Casa de las Américas*, no. 44, September–October. In "Al pie de la letra": 167.

Halperin Donghi, Tulio. 1984. "Nueva narrativa y ciencias sociales hispanoamericanas en la década del sesenta." In *Más allá del* boom*: literatura y mercado*. Ángel Ángel, ed. Buenos Aires: Folios.

Halperin Donghi, Tulio. 1997 [1986]. *Historia contemporánea de América Latina*. 5th edition. Mexico: Alianza.

Haro, Blanca. 1967. "Rulfo, Pellicer, Novo, Mutis y Revueltas hablan del Congreso de Escritores." *Siempre!*, no. 716, March 15: VIII.

Haroche, Charles. 1963. "Guerre, paix et dogmatisme." *La Nouvelle Critique*, no. 142, January–February.

Harss, Luis. 1969 [1966]. *Los nuestros*. Buenos Aires: Sudamericana.

Hart, Armando. 1970. "Carta a Roberto Fernández Retamar." *Casa de las Américas*, no. 59, March–April: 161–64.

Hinostroza, Rodolfo (comp.). 1971–72. "Antología peruana: 3 más 3." *Libre*, no. 2, December, January, February: 116.

Hirschman, Albert O. 1986 [1982]. *Interés privado y acción pública*. Mexico: Fondo de Cultura Económica.

Hobsbawm, Eric. 1960. "Para el estudio de las clases subalternas." *Societá*, XVI, no. 3, May–June.

Hobsbawm, Eric. 1995. *Historia del siglo XX*. Barcelona: Grijalbo-Mondadori.

Hohendahl, Pete Uwe. 1982. "The End of an Institution? The Debate over the Function of Literary Criticism in the 1960s." In *The Institution of Criticism*. Ithaca and London: Cornell University Press.

Hohendahl, Pete Uwe. 1989 [1985]. *Building a National Literature. The Case of Germany, 1830–1870*. Ithaca and London: Cornell University Press.

Hollander, Paul. 1981. *Political Pilgrims: Travels of Western Intellectuals to the Soviet Union, China and Cuba, 1928–1978*. Oxford: Oxford University Press.

Horowitz, Irving Louis, ed. 1963. *Wright Mills, Power, Politics, and People: The Collected Essays of C. Wright Mills*. New York.

Huyssen, Andreas. 1986. *After the Great Divide*. Bloomington and Indianapolis: Indiana University Press.

Jacoby, Russel. 1996. *The Last Intellectuals: American Culture in the Age of Academe*. New York: The Noonday Press.

Jameson, Frederic. 1997 [1984]. *Periodizar los 60*. Córdoba: Alción.

Jauss, Hans Robert. 1996. *Las transformaciones de lo moderno*. Madrid: Visor.

Jitrik, Noé. 1959. "Seis narradores argentinos." *Marcha*, no. 992, December 28.

Jitrik, Noé. 1960. "Un precursor argentino del nuevo realismo." *Marcha*, no. 1026, September.

Jitrik, Noé. 1966. "Situación actual del escritor argentino." *Marcha*, no. 1300, April 22.

Jitrik, Noé. 1967. "Literatura argentina: sobre el peligroso y ambiguo camino de su trascendencia." *Amaru*, no. 3, July–September: 81–83.

Jitrik, Noé. 1969. "Peligrosidad del escritor." *Macedonio*, II, no. 4–5, summer: 108–111.

Jitrik, Noé. 1984. *Las armas y las razones. Ensayo sobre el peronismo, el exilio, la literatura*. Buenos Aires: Sudamericana.

Julião, Francisco. 1970. "Carta abierta a los jóvenes revolucionarios brasileños." *Marcha*, no. 1502, July 17: 16–17.

Karol, K. S. 1972 [1970]. *Los guerrilleros en el poder*. Barcelona: Seix-Barral.

Kat, P. J. 1970. "Joris Ivens vuelve a Holanda." *Marcha*, no. 1510, September 11: 25.

Kermode, Frank. 1983. *El sentido de un final. Estudios sobre la teoría de la ficción*. Barcelona: Gedisa.

King, John. 1989. Sur. *Estudio de la revista argentina y de su papel en el desarrollo de una cultura 1931–1970*. Mexico: Fondo de Cultura Económica.

Konrád, George, and Ivan Szelényi. 1979. *The Intellectuals on the Road to Class Power*. Translated by Andrew Arato and Richard E. Allen. Sussex: The Harvester Press.

Konrád, George, and Ivan Szelényi. 1981 [1978]. *Los intelectuales y el poder*. Barcelona: Península.

Kordon, Bernardo. 1968. "Mi entrevista con Mao Tse-Tung." In *Testigos de China*. Bernardo Kordon et al., eds. Buenos Aires: Carlos Pérez.

Kowaleski, Martín. 1973. "El papel de la guerra revolucionaria en el desarrollo de la cultura." *Nuevos Aires*, no. 11, August–September–October: 69–90.

L'Express. 1968. "Pas de feuilles de vigne pour Fidel Castro." Paris, November 18–24.

La Bufanda del Sol. 1966. "Editorial," no. 3–4, March–July.

La Nouvelle Critique. 1964. "Entretien à Prague sur la notion de 'décadence,'" no. 165, June–July: 71–85.

La Nouvelle Critique. 1967. "Tel Quel nous répond," no. 8 (189), November: 50–54.

La Rosa Blindada. 1966. "Correspondencia Retamar-Monegal" 11, no. 8, April–May: 57–58.

Lafforgue, Jorge. 1967a. "La muerte de Buen día." *Primera Plana* V, no. 230, May 23–29.

Lafforgue, Jorge. 1967b. "La muerte de Buen día." *Primera Plana* V, no. 230, May 23–29.

Lafforgue, Jorge. 1972. "Consideraciones al margen de la nueva narrativa latinoamericana." *Latinoamericana*, no. 1, December: 26

Landazuri Ricketts, Juan. 1969 [1968]. "Discurso inaugural" (Segunda Conferencia General del Episcopado Latinoamericano). In *La iglesia en la actual transformación de América Latina a la luz del Concilio* (official text). Buenos Aires: Bonum.

Larco, Juan. 1966a. "La casa verde." *Casa de las Américas*, no. 38, September–October: 115.

Larco, Juan. 1966b. "Las buenas intenciones." *Mundo Nuevo* no. 2, August: 65.

Larco, Juan. 1966c. "Las malas traducciones de Marta Lynch" (1970–71). *Nuevos Aires,* no. 3, December, January, February: 73–74.

Lavín Cerda, Hernán. 1969. "Entrevista a Benedetti." *Punto Final.* Santiago de Chile, October 28.

Libre. 1971a. "Declaración de escritores cubanos," no. 1, September, October, November: 141.

Libre. 1971b. "Editorial," no. 1, September, October, November.

Libre. 1971c. "Llamamiento de intelectuales peruanos," no. 1: 135, and *Casa de las Américas*, no. 67, July–August.

Libre. 1971d. "Primera Carta al Comandante Fidel Castro," no. 1, September, October, November.

Libre. 1971e. "Segunda carta al Comandante Fidel Castro," no. 1.

Liehm, Antonin. 1964. "Entrevista a Lukács." *La Nouvelle Critique*, no. 156, June–July. (Reprinted in *Unión*, III, 4, October–December. Taken from the Czech weekly *Litearny Noviny*).

Lihn, Enrique, and Germán Marín. 1970. "Benedetti en Cormorán." *Cormorán*, no. 5, January.

Lihn, Enrique, and Germán Marín. 1971. "Carta abierta a Heberto Padilla." *Cuba. Nueva política cultural. El caso Padilla, Cuadernos de Marcha*, no. 49, May: 6.

Link, Daniel. 1994. "Los setenta, Walsh, y la novela en crisis." In *La chancha con cadenas*. Buenos Aires: Ediciones del Eclipse.

Liscano, Juan. 1967a. "Dos aclaraciones." *Siempre!*, no. 732, July 5: X.

Liscano, Juan. 1967b. "El segundo congreso latinoamericano de escritores o el imposible equilibrio." *Zona Franca*, II, no. 44, April: 2–9.

Liscano, Juan. 1967c. "Tercer año." *Zona Franca*, III, no. 48, August: 2–3.

List Arzturbide, Germán. 1971. "La conciencia revolucionaria y el caso Padilla." *Siempre!*, no. 936, May.

Lizalde, Eduardo. 1971. "Revolución, represión, falsos apóstatas." *Siempre!*, no. 934, May 19.

Llopis, Rogelio. 1963. "Las dos mitades del Vizconde." *Casa de las Américas,* no. 17–18, March–June.

Lombroso, Gina. 1945. *El alma de la mujer.* Buenos Aires: Emecé.

Longoni, Ana. 1995. "Sobre una antirrevista en el año del Cordobazo." *Causas y Azares*, no. 2, Autumn: 136–143.

Longoni, Ana. 1997. "Tucumán arde: encuentros y desencuentros entre vanguardia artística y política." In *Cultura y política en los años 60.* Enrique Oteiza et al. Buenos Aires: Instituto de Investigación Gino Germani, Facultad de Ciencias Sociales, Universidad de Buenos Aires.

López, César. 1989. "Persistance dans l'ombre." *Autrement.* Série Monde, no. 35 ; *Cuba, 30 ans de révolution.* Paris.

López Valdizón, J. M. 1962. "Daura Olema, maestra voluntaria." *Casa de las Américas*, no. 13–14, July–October: 55–56.

Loveluck, Juan. 1966. "Una revisión de la novela hispanoamericana." *Zona Franca*, II, no. 37, September.

Lukács, Georg, T. W. Adorno, Roman Jakobson, Ernst Fischer, and Roland Barthes. 1969. *Polémica sobre realismo.* Buenos Aires: Tiempo Contemporáneo.

Lukács, Georg. 1971 [1920]. *Teoría de la novela.* Barcelona: Edhasa.

Lunes de Revolución. 1961. "Un congreso de escritores y artistas," no. 109, June 11.

Lunes de Revolución. 1961. "Conversatorio con el poeta turco Nazim Hikmet," no. 109, June 11.

Lynch, Marta. 1969. "El cruce del río," *Casa de las Américas*, no. 53, March–April.

Macadam, Alfred, and Charles Ruas. 1996 [1995]. *Confesiones de escritores. Escritores latinoamericanos. Los reportajes del* Paris Review. Buenos Aires: El Ateneo.

Manet, Eduardo. 1961. "Cine cubano 1961." *Casa de las Américas*, no. 9, November–December.

Mangone, Carlos. 1997. "Revolución cubana y compromiso político en las revistas culturales." In *Cultura y política en los años 60.* Enrique Oteiza et al. Buenos Aires: Instituto de Investigación Gino Germani, Facultad de Ciencias Sociales, Universidad de Buenos Aires.

Mannheim, Karl. 1958 [1936]. *Ideología y utopía. Introducción a la sociología del conocimiento.* Madrid: Aguilar.

Marcha. 1959. "Reportaje literario en Buenos Aires. Situación actual de la novela," no. 959, May 8: 29–30.

Marcha. 1964. "Juicio a un joven poeta," no. 1224, September 25.

Marcha. 1967. "Los escritores asumen su responsabilidad," no. 1337, February; *Casa de las Américas*, no. 41, March–April; *Siempre!*, no. 710, February 1.

Marcha. 1968. "Respuesta a la carta del correo de lectores," no. 1421.

Marcha. 1969a. "Incidentes y perspectivas," no. 1466, October 10.

Marcha. 1969b. "Rehenes y atentados," no. 1466, October 10.

Marcha. 1969. "Sobre la penetración imperialista," no. 1462, September 12.

Marcuse, Herbert. 1968a [1964]. *El hombre unidimensional. Ensayo sobre la ideología de la sociedad industrial avanzada*. Mexico: Joaquín Mortiz.

Marcuse, Herbert. 1968b. *El fin de la utopía*. Mexico: Siglo XXI.

Marinello, Juan. 1971. "Literatura y revolución." *Casa de las Américas*, no. 68, September–October: 214–51.

Mario, José. 1973. "Prólogo." In *Provocaciones*. Heberto Padilla. Madrid: La Gota de Agua.

Marletti, Carlo. 1995. "Intelectuales." In *Diccionario de política*, Ninth edition. Bobbio, Norberto; Nicola Mateucci and Gianfranco Pasquino, eds. Mexico: Siglo XXI.

Martí Gómez, José. 1970. "Un premio que no fue. Diálogo con José Donoso." *Marcha*, no. 1496, June 5.

Martínez, Tomás Eloy. 1968. "América, los novelistas exilados." *Primera Plana*, VI, no. 292, July 30–August 6: 40–49.

Martínez Moreno, Carlos. 1960. "Escritores de América en Concepción." *Marcha*, no. 996, February 11.

Martini, Juan Carlos. 1969. "Defensa de la novela y el actual fenómeno narrativo latinoamericano." *Macedonio*, I, no. 2, Autumn: 29.

Martini, Juan Carlos. 1972. "Gabriel García Márquez o las fabulaciones peligrosas." *Latinoamericana*, no. 1, December: 140–43.

Masotta, Oscar. 1959. "Adolfo Prieto: un tímido aporte al mito de la indiferencia argentina." *Marcha*, no. 992, December 28.

Masotta, Oscar. 1967. *El "pop-art."* Buenos Aires: Columba.

Maspero, François. 1989. "Cahier d'un retour." *Cuba, 30 ans de révolution, Autrement*, no. 35, January.

Mazía, Floreal, James F. Petras, Maurice Zeitlin et al. 1970. *América Latina: ¿reforma o revolución?*. Buenos Aires: Tiempo Contemporáneo.

Mc Luhan, Marshall. 1974. *La cultura es nuestro negocio.* Mexico: Diana.

McQuade, Frank. 1992. "Mundo Nuevo: la nueva novela y la guerra fría cutural." *América,* no. 9–10: 17–26.

Memmi, Albert. 1969. "Retrato del colonizador." In *Retrato del colonizado, precedido por el Retrato del colonizador.* Buenos Aires: De la Flor.

Memmi, Albert. 2003. *The Colonizer and the Colonized.* Translated by Howard Greenfeld. London: Earthscan Publications.

Mensaje. 1962. "Revolución en América Latina." December.

Mercier, Lucien. 1964. "Ser Mallarmé o Lenin." *Marcha*, no. 1218, August 14.

Mestman, Mariano. 1995. "Notas para una historia de un cine de contrainformación y lucha política." *Causas y Azares*, no. 2, Autumn: 144–161.

Mestman, Mariano. 1997. "Consideraciones sobre la confluencia de núcleos intelectuales y sectores del movimiento obrero, 1968–1969." In *Cultura y política en los años 60.* Enrique Oteiza et al. Buenos Aires: Instituto de Investigación Gino Germani, Facultad de Ciencias Sociales, Universidad de Buenos Aires.

Minh, Ho Chi. 1972. *Prison Diary.* Translated by Dang The Binh. Hanoi: Foreign Languages Publishing House.

Miranda, Julio. 1991. "Carta de Venezuela. *TTT* sin censura en la Biblioteca Ayacucho." *Cuadernos Hispanoamericanos*, no. 495, September: 132–34.

Moncada, Julio. 1959. "Sobre la poesía peruana." *Marcha*, no. 976.

Monteforte Toledo, Mario. 1967. "Los intelectuales en la Cuba de Hoy." *Siempre!*, no. 718, March 29: 37 and 70.

Morandi, Julio. 1970. "El teatro argentino visto por tres autores." *Marcha*, no. 1496, June 5.

Morin, Edgar. 1959. "*Que faire?.*" *Arguments*, no. 16, 4th trimester: 1–10.

Morin, Edgar. 1960. "*Intellectuels: critique du mythe et mythe de la critique.*" *Arguments*, no. 20, 4th trimester.

Mudrovcic, María Eugenia. 1997. *Mundo Nuevo. Cultura y guerra fría en la década del 60.* Rosario: Beatriz Viterbo.

Mundo Nuevo. 1966a. "Comunidad cultural." "Sextante" section, no. 1, July.

Mundo Nuevo. 1966b. "Las buenas intenciones," no. 2, August: 65.

Mundo Nuevo. 1967a. "Lo que se lee en Colombia," no. 12, June.

Mundo Nuevo. 1967b. "México, Congreso de Escritores," no. 13, July: 76–79.

Nadeau, Maurice. 1970. "Ils aiment la sieste, le soleil, les couleurs, la danse. . . ." *Castro, le romantisme révolutionnaire*. Paris: Planète Action.

Navalet, Brigitte et al. 1975. *Idéologies, littérature et société en Amérique Latine*. Brussels: Editions de l'Université de Bruxelles.

Neruda, Pablo. 1966. "La barcarola" (fragments). *Mundo Nuevo*, no. 4, October: 19–22.

Noé, Luis Felipe. 1988 [1965]. *Antiestética*. Buenos Aires: De la Flor.

Nono, Luigi. 1971. "Autocrítica y telegrama dirigido a Juan Goytisolo por Luigi Nono." *Libre*, no. 1, September, October, November: 142–143.

Nuevos Aires. 1970–71. "Las malas traducciones de Marta Lynch," no. 3, December, January, February: 73–74.

Nuevos Aires. 1973. "XX aniversario del asalto al Moncada," no. 11, August, September, October: 50–51.

Núñez, Carlos. 1966. "El papel de los intelectuales en la liberación nacional." *Marcha*, no. 1292, January and subsequent, and *Casa de las Américas*, no. 35, March–April.

Núñez, Carlos. 1967. "Por Debray, por la revolución, por nosotros." *Marcha*, no. 1353, May 18.

Ollier, María Matilde. 1986. *El fenómeno insurreccional y la cultura política*. Buenos Aires: CEAL.

Ong, Walter. 1982. *Orality and Literacy*. London-New York: Methuen.

Oquendo, Abelardo. 1967. "Mundo Nuevo." *Amaru*, no. 1, January.

Orgambide, Pedro. 1965. "Libertad y compromiso." *Marcha*, no. 1266, August 7.

Ortega, Julio. 1971-1972. Review of *Condenados de Condado. Revista Libre* no. 147.

Norberto Fuentes, 1970. *Cazabandido*. Montevideo: Libros de la Pupila.

Otero, Lisandro. 1966. "El escritor en la revolución cubana." *Casa de las Américas*, no. 36–37, May–August: 203–209.

Otero, Lisandro. 1967. *Pasión de Urbino*. Havana: Instituto del Libro.

Otero, Lisandro. 1971. "Notas sobre la funcionalidad de la cultura." *Casa de las Américas*, no. 68, September–October.

Otero, Lisandro, and Francisco Martínez Hinojosa. 1972. *Cultural policy in Cuba*. Paris: Unesco.

Oviedo, José Miguel. 1967. "García Márquez, la infinita violencia colombiana." *Amaru*, no. 1, January: 87–89.

Oviedo, José Miguel. 1972. "Una discusión permanente." In *América Latina en su literatura*. Fernández Moreno, César (comp.). Mexico: Siglo XXI.

Padilla, Heberto. 1962. "Pancarta para 1960." In *El justo tiempo humano*. Havana: Contemporáneos.

Padilla, Heberto. 1968. "Respuesta a Cabrera Infante." *Primera Plana*, no. 313, December 24: 88–89.

Padilla, Heberto. 1969a. *Fuera del juego*. Buenos Aires: Aditor.

Padilla, Heberto. 1969b. "En la muerte de Ho-Chi-Minh." *Unión*, no. 4–69.

Padilla, Heberto. 1971. "Autocrítica" (transcription). *Casa de las Américas*, no. 65–66, March–June.

Padilla, Heberto. 1971. "Documentos. El caso Padilla. Intervención de Heberto Padilla en la UNEAC" (abridged version released by Prensa Latina). *Libre*, no. 1, September, October, November: 101–102.

Padilla, Heberto. 1973. *Provocaciones*. Madrid: La Gota de Agua.

Padilla, Heberto. 1983. *En mi jardín pastan los héroes*. Barcelona: Argos Vergara.

Padilla, Heberto. 1991. *La mala memoria*. Barcelona: Plaza & Janés.

Panorama. 1971. "Intelectuales versus Fidel: cartas de un joven poeta," no. 211.

Papeles. 1967–68. "Los novelistas y sus críticos (en el XIII Congreso Interamericano de Literatura)," no. 5, November–December–January.

Parmelin, Hélène. 1968. "Art et révolution à La Havane." *Les Temps Modernes*, XXIII, no. 263, March: 1662–70.

Pasado y Presente. 1963a. "Editorial," 1, no. 1, April–June.

Pasado y Presente. 1963b. "Nota Editorial," 1, no. 1, April–June.

Paz, Octavio. 1971. "La autohumillación de los incrédulos." *Siempre!*, no. 934, May 19.

Peri Rossi, Cristina. 1970. "Comentario a *Salmos* de Ernesto Cardenal." *Marcha*, no. 1496, June 5, section 2.

Piazza, Luis Guillermo. 1967. Interview conducted by Rosa Castro. *Siempre!*, no. 741, September 6: VI–VIII.

Piglia, Ricardo. 1964. Introduction to *Discusión crítica a la "crisis" del marxismo*. Abelardo Castillo. Buenos Aires: Biblioteca El Escarabajo de Oro.

Piglia, Ricardo. 1968. Prologue to *Las crónicas de Latinoamérica*. Buenos Aires: Jorge Álvarez.

Piglia, Ricardo, Ismael Viñas, and Andrés Rivera. 1968. "Repeticiones sobre los deberes del intelectual." *Revista de Problemas del Tercer Mundo*, no. 1, April: 45–51.

Platier, Jacqueline. 1964. "Entrevista a Sartre." *Le Monde*, April 18.

Podhoretz, Norman. 1979. *Breaking Rank: A Political Memoir*. New York: Harper & Row.

Portantiero, Juan Carlos. 1961. In *Realismo y realidad en la narrativa argentina*. Buenos Aires: Procyon.

Portocarrero, Ronald. 1970. *Oiga*. Lima, June 19.

Portuondo, José Antonio. 1971. "Una novela revolucionaria." *Casa de las Américas*, no. 71, March–April: 105–106.

Portuondo, José Antonio. 1972. "Crítica marxista de la estética burguesa contemporánea." *Casa de las Américas*, no. 71, March–April: 5–13.

Portuondo, José Antonio. 1980. "Itinerario estético de la revolución." In *Revolución, Letras, Arte*. Havana: Letras Cubanas.

Prada Oropeza, Renato. 1969. *Los fundadores del alba*. Havana: Casa de las Américas.

Prieto, Adolfo. 1956. *Sociología del público argentino*. Buenos Aires: Leviatán.

Prieto, Adolfo. 1983. "Los años sesenta." *Revista Iberoamericana*, no. 125, October–December: 889–901.

Primera Plana. 1965. "¿Puede el PEN Club rejuvenecer?," no. 143, August 3.

Primera Plana. 1967a. "Esperando a Godot," no. 254, November 7: 66.

Primera Plana. 1967b. "La muerte de Buendía," V, no. 230, May 23–29.

Primera Plana. 1968a. "Editores: la danza de los millones," no. 306, November 5.

Primera Plana. 1968b. "Otro pariente para la familia," no. 272, March 12.

Prochasson, Cristophe. 1993. *Les intellectuels, le socialisme et la guerre. 1900–1938*. Paris: Seuil.

Proceso a los escritores. El Estado soviético contra Siniavski y Daniel. 1967. Buenos Aires: Americana.

Quijano, Carlos. 1939. "Editorial." *Marcha*, no. 1, June 23.

Rama, Ángel. 1959. "Bertrand Russell ejercita el sentido común." *Marcha*, no. 973, August 21.

Rama, Ángel. 1960. "La construcción de una literatura." *Marcha*, no. 1040, December 26.

Rama, Ángel. 1960. "Panorama latinoamericano." *Marcha*, no. 1090.

Rama, Ángel. 1962. "La vanguardia diez años después." *El Escarabajo de Oro*, 3, no. 6, April: 16–19.

Rama, Ángel. 1964a. "Coloquio latinoamericano del Columbianum. El necesario diálogo intelectual." *Marcha*, no. 1238, December 31.

Rama, Ángel. 1964b. "García Márquez, gran americano." *Marcha*, no. 1193, February 7.

Rama, Ángel. 1964c. "García Márquez: la violencia americana." *Marcha*, no. 1201, April 17.

Rama, Ángel. 1964d. "En Cuba se polemiza: ¿arte burgués o arte socialista?." *Marcha*, no. 1196, March 6.

Rama, Ángel. 1964e. "Vanguardia en rosa sostenido." *Marcha*, no. 1234, December 4.

Rama, Ángel. 1964f. "De cómo sobreviene lo humano." *Marcha*, no. 1194, February 21.

Rama, Ángel. 1964g. "El duro ejercicio de la realidad." *Marcha*, no. 1230, November 6.

Rama, Ángel. 1964h. "Ya somos vanguardistas." *Marcha*, no. 1235, December 11.

Rama, Ángel. 1965a. "Coloquio de Génova: dos tareas que valen un viaje." *Marcha*, no. 1245, February 26.

Rama, Ángel. 1965b. "Del provincianismo cultural." *Marcha*, no. 1261, July 2.

Rama, Ángel. 1966. "Un fénix demasiado frecuente." *Marcha*, no. 1293, February 25.

Rama, Ángel. 1967a. "El *boom* editorial." *Marcha*, no. 1385, December 29.

Rama, Ángel. 1967b. "Introducción a *Cien años de soledad*." *Marcha*, no. 1368, September 2.

Rama, Ángel. 1967c. "Los desacuerdos de una comunidad." *Marcha*, no. 1348, April 13, and *Casa de las Américas*, 43, July–August: 114–15.

Rama, Ángel. 1968. "El *boom* editorial." *Marcha*, no. 1385, January 5, second section.

Rama, Ángel. 1970. "El 40, formalistas y la vida en Puerto Rico." *Marcha*, no. 1484, March 6: 30–31.

Rama, Ángel. 1971a. "Una nueva política cultural en Cuba." In "Cuba. Nueva política cultural. El caso Padilla." *Cuadernos de Marcha*, no. 49, May.

Rama, Ángel. 1971b. "Revueltas y el caso Padilla." *Marcha*, no. 1550, July.

Rama, Ángel. 1981. "La tecnificación narrativa." *Hispamérica*, no. 30: 29–82.

Rama, Ángel. 1983. "Norberto Fuentes: El narrador en la tormenta revolucionaria." In *Literatura y clase social.* Buenos Aires: Folios.

Rama, Ángel, ed. 1984. "El *boom* en perspectiva." In *Más allá del* boom*: literatura y mercado.* Buenos Aires: Folios.

Rama, Ángel. 1987. Prologue to *Antología de* El Techo de la Ballena. Caracas: Fundarte.

Rama, Ángel. 1995. "La imaginación de las formas." In *La riesgosa navegación del escritor exiliado.* Montevideo: Arca.

Ramos, Jorge Abelardo. 1973 [1959]. "Marxismo para latinoamericanos." In *El marxismo de Indias.* Barcelona: Planeta. Real de Azúa, Carlos. 1960. "La novela hispanoamericana." *Marcha*, no. 1040, December 26.

Ramos, Jorge Abelardo. 1968. "Opinión de un crítico." *Marcha*, no. 1385, January 5, second section.

Rest, Jaime. 1964. "El retorno del realismo." *Marcha*, no. 1233, November 27: 29–31.

Revueltas, José. 1971a. "La carta de Padilla y las palabras de Fidel." *Siempre!*, 934, May 19.

Revueltas, José. 1971b. "A favor y en contra," in "Cuba. Nueva política cultural. El caso Padilla." *Cuadernos de Marcha*, no. 49, May.

Revueltas, José. 1971c. "Opiniones de escritores latinoamericanos y europeos en relación con el caso," "Documentos. El caso Padilla." *Libre*, no. 1: 133.

Revueltas, José. 1971c. *Cuadernos de Marcha*, no. 49, May, and *Libre*, no. 1, September, October–November.

Rincón, Carlos. 1971. "Para un plano de batalla de un combate por una nueva crítica latinoamericana." *Casa de las Américas*, no. 67, July–August: 39–59.

Roa Bastos, Augusto. 1967. "Cartas a la Casa," *Casa de las Américas*, no. 43, July–August: 135–140.

Roa Bastos, Augusto. 1969–70. "América Latina: continente novelesco." *Macedonio*, no. 4–5, Summer: 44–54.

Robbins, Bruce, ed. 1990. "Introduction." *Intellectuals, Aesthetics, Politics, Academics*. Minneapolis: University of Minnesota Press.

Roca, Blas. 1963. "Preguntas sobre películas." *Hoy*, December 12.

Rocca, Pablo. 1993. "35 años en *Marcha*." *Nuevo Texto Crítico*, VI, no. 11, first semester.

Rocha, Glauber. 1967. "Una estética de la violencia: Nuestra originalidad es el hambre." *Marcha*, no. 1374, October 13.

Rocha, Glauber. 1983. "The Aesthetics of Hunger." Translated by Hollyman Burnes and Johnson Randal. In *Twenty-five Years of the New Latin American Cinema*. Edited by Michael Chanan. London: British Film Institute Books.

Rodaballo. 1996–97. "Un contrapunto entre Régis Debray y Daniel Bensaid," III, no. 5, Summer.

Rodríguez, Silvio. 1972. "Playa Girón." Transcription by Ernesto Cardenal. In *En Cuba*. Buenos Aires: Carlos Lohlé.

Rodríguez Elizondo, José. 1967. "Cine bajo el napalm." *Marcha*, no. 1367, August 25.

Rodríguez Feo, José, ed. 1967. *Aquí once cubanos cuentan*. Montevideo: Arca.

Rodríguez Feo, José. 1990. "Prólogo." In *El caserón*. Soler Puig. Havana: Unión.

Rodríguez Monegal, Emir. 1966a. "Diario del PEN Club." *Mundo Nuevo*, no. 4, October: 41–47.

Rodríguez Monegal, Emir. 1966b. "El memorial de Isla Negra." *Mundo Nuevo*, no. 1, July.

Rodríguez Monegal, Emir. 1966c. "Situación del escritor en América Latina" (interview with Carlos Fuentes). *Mundo Nuevo*, no. 1, July: 20.

Rodríguez Monegal, Emir. 1967a. "Diario de Caracas." *Mundo Nuevo*, no. 17, November: 4–24.

Rodríguez Monegal, Emir. 1967b. "Los nuevos novelistas." *Mundo Nuevo*, no. 17, November: 19–20.

Rodríguez Monegal, Emir. 1969. "La nueva novela latinoamericana." *Narradores de esta América*. Vol. 1. Montevideo: Alfa.

Rodríguez Monegal, Emir. 1976. *Narradores de esta América*. Alfargentina.

Rodríguez Monegal, Emir. 1969. "Un encuentro y varios desencuentros." *Marcha*, no. 1461, September 5.

Rodríguez Monegal, Emir. 1970. "Un hijo de la revolución." *Marcha*, no. 1518, November 6.

Rodríguez Monegal, Emir. 1970. "Las exclusiones peligrosas." In "Norberto Fuentes, un escritor en discordia." *Marcha*, no. 1521, November 27: 31.

Rodríguez Monegal, Emir. 1971a. "Entrevista con Eduardo Galeano. El escritor en el proceso americano." *Marcha*, no. 1555, August 6: 30–31.

Rodríguez Monegal, Emir. 1971b. "Escritora a los 5 años. La poesía a la hora del rocío." *Marcha*, no. 1561, September 17: 13.

Rodríguez Monegal, Emir. 1980. "Cuentos de la revolución cubana." *Marcha*, no. 1419, October 4.

Romualdo, Alejandro. 1967. *Casa de las Américas*, no. 45, November-December: 75.

Rojas, Manuel. 1967. "Responsabilidad del escritor ante América Latina y el mundo entero." *Casa de las Américas*, no. 43, July–August: 106–9.

Rossanda, Rossana. 1971. "Debate." *Libre*, 4: 80-82.

Sabato, Ernesto. 1960. "Sobre un congreso." *Clarín*, February 14.

Said, Edward. 1996. *Representaciones del intelectual*. Barcelona: Paidós.

Sainz, Gustavo. 1967. "Panorama 1966: Novela y cuento." *Siempre!*, no. 706, January 4.

Sánchez Vázquez, Adolfo. 1962. "Ideas estéticas en los manuscritos económico-filosóficos de Marx." *Casa de las Américas*, no. 13–14, July–October: 3–24.

Sánchez Vázquez, Adolfo. 1964. "Estética y marxismo." *Unión*, III, no. 1, January–March: 8–23.

Sánchez Vázquez, Adolfo. 1968. "Vanguardia artística y vanguardia política." *Casa de las Américas*, no. 47, March–April: 112–115.

Sánchez Vázquez, Adolfo. 1972. "Notas sobre Lenin, el arte y la revolución" [text dated November 1970]. *Casa de las Américas*, no. 71, March–April: 14–19.

Santamaría, Haydeé. 1971. "Respuesta de Haydeé Santamaría a Mario Vargas Llosa." *Libre*, no. 1, September, October, November: 122–24.

Sarandy Cabrera, Mario. 1965. "Yo que vuelvo." *Marcha*, no. 1261, July.

Sarandy Cabrera, Mario. 1970. "Revolución y literatura, por su orden." *Marcha*, no. 1483, February 27.

Sarlo, Beatriz. 1985. "Intelectuales: ¿escisión o mímesis?." *Punto de Vista*, VII, no. 25.

Sarlo, Beatriz. 1992. "Intelectuales y revistas: razones de una práctica." *Le discours culturel dans les revues latinoaméricaines de 1940 à 1970*, *América, Cahiers du CRICCAL*, no. 9–10. Paris: Presses de la Sorbonne Nouvelle: 9–16.

Sarlo, Beatriz. 1993. "Una sociología corrosiva." *Clarín*. "Cultura y Nación" supplement, Buenos Aires, May 27.

Sarlo, Beatriz. 1994. "La voz universal que toma partido." *Punto de Vista*, XVII, no. 50.

Sarlo, Beatriz. 2004. "Intellectuals: Scission or Mimesis?" In *The Latin American Cultural Studies Reader*. Edited by Ana del Sarto, Alicia Ríos, and Abril Trigo, 250–61. Durham: Duke University Press.

Sartre, Jean-Paul. 1949. "What is Writing?" In *What is Literature?* Translated by Bernard Frechtman. New York: Philosophical Library.

Sartre, Jean-Paul. 1964. *Las palabras*. Buenos Aires: Losada.

Sartre, Jean-Paul. 1970. *Plaidoyer pour les intellectuels*. Paris: Gallimard.

Sartre, Jean-Paul. 1972. "Entrevista con Jean-Paul Sartre." *Libre*, no. 4, Paris: 3-10.

Sartre, Jean-Paul. 1990 [1948]. ¿Qué es la literatura?. Buenos Aires: Losada.

Sarusky, Jaime. 1995. "Roberto Fernández Retamar: desde el 200, con amor, en un leopardo." *Casa de las Américas*, no. 200, July–September.

Segovia, Tomás. 1965. "365 días de novela mexicana." *Marcha*, no. 1241, January 29.

Selser, Gregorio. 1964. *Alianza para el Progreso. La mal nacida*. Second edition. Buenos Aires: Iguazú.

Schilling, Paulo. 1970. "El suicidio político de Julião." *Marcha*, no. 1503, July 24.

Schmucler, Héctor. 1963. "La cuestión del realismo y la novela testimonial argentina." *Pasado y Presente*, no. 1, April–June.

Schoó, Ernesto. 1967. "Los viajes de Simbad García Márquez." *Primera Plana*, no. 234, June 20: 52–54.

Shils, Edward. 1972. *The Intellectuals and the Powers and Other Essays.* Chicago and London: The University of Chicago Press.

Siempre!. 1966. "Cómo juzga el exigente Times de Londres la novela hispanoamericana": XIII.

Siempre!. 1967a. "La intervención de los Estados Unidos en la vida latinoamericana," no. 749, November 1, and Fernández Retamar, Roberto. "Contra la penetración cultural yanqui." *Marcha*, no. 1375, October 20.

Siempre!. 1967b. "Mexicanos en Sudamérica," no. 732, July 5.

Sigal, Silvia. 1991. *Intelectuales y poder en la década del sesenta.* Buenos Aires: Puntosur.

Skármeta, Antonio. 1971. *Ahora*, June 10.

Skármeta, Antonio. 1984. "Al fin y al cabo, es su propia vida la cosa más cercana que cada escritor tiene para echar mano." In *Más allá del* boom*: literatura y mercado.* Ángel Rama, ed. Buenos Aires: Folios.

Sokal, Alan D. 1996. "Transgressing the Boundaries: Towards a Transformative Hermeneutics of Quantum Gravity." *Social Text*, no. 46–47, Spring–Summer: 217–52.

Sontag, Susan. 1996 [1965]. "Una cultura y la nueva sensibilidad." In *Contra la interpretación.* Buenos Aires: Alfaguara.

Sontag, Susan. 1972. "Debate." *Libre*, no. 4: 83–101.

Steiner, George. 1978. "*After the Book.*" *On Difficulty and Other Essays.* Oxford: Oxford University Press.

Steiner, George. 1990. "¿Toca a su fin la cultura del libro?." *Vuelta*, no. 18.

Suárez, Luis. 1969. "Raimón: una canción puede substituir a un libro." *Siempre!*, no. 750, November 8.

Szichman, Mario. 1972. "Entrevista a David Viñas." *Hispamérica*, no. 1, July: 61–69.

Terán, Oscar. 1991. *Nuestros años sesentas.* Buenos Aires: Puntosur.

Thomas, Hugh. 1973. *Cuba, la lucha por la libertad, 1958–1970.* Barcelona: Grijalbo.

Time. 1967. "Punto de vista gusano." July 4.

Torres, Juan Manuel. 1971. "Dos respuestas a las opiniones sobre el caso Padilla." *Siempre!*, no. 936, June 2.

Torres Fierro, Danubio. 1989. "Una cultura confiscada." *El País*, December 24.

Torres Fierro, Danubio. 1990. "El luto intelectual." *El País*, January 7.

Torres Fierro, Danubio. 1990. "Los intelectuales de aquí y los de allá." *El País*, January 15.

Torres Fierro, Danubio. 1990. "Los fracasos de los ochenta." *El País*, January 21.

Torres Fierro, Danubio. 1990. "Anímense, o Lenin nuestro que estás en los cielos." *El País*, February 4.

Torres Fierro, Danubio. 1990. "Socialismo, una historia enterrada." *El País*, March 22.

Traba, Marta. 1971. "Sobre el caso Padilla." *El Tiempo*, reprinted in *Libre*, no. 1, September, October, November: 140.

Tuttino, Saverio. 1968a. *L'ottobre cubano*. Torno: Piccola Biblioteca Einaudi.

Tuttino, Saverio. 1968b. "Nouvelle attaque du journal des forces armées contre un auteur dramatique." *Le Monde*, November 17–18.

Tuttino, Saverio. 1968c. "L'hebdomadaire des forces armées renouvelle ses critiques contre les intellectuels hésitants et présomptueux." *Le Monde*, November 27: 11.

Unión. 1964. "Rinascità, entrevista a Sartre," no. 1, January-March.

Unión. 1967. "Vargas Llosa, aguafiestas en Caracas," no. 4.

Uriarte, Fernando. 1966. "Aspectos de la novela hispanoamericana actual." *Mapocho* 15, no. 4: 147–61.

Vanasco, Alberto. 1972. "Acerca del denominado *boom*." *Latinoamericana*, 1, December.

Varela, Blanca. 1967. "Las colinas de Iossip Brodski." *Amaru*, no. 13, July–September.

Vargas Llosa, Mario. 1966. "La patria de los cohetes que viajan a la Luna no está en peligro por dos relatos fantásticos." *Siempre!*, no. 664, March 16: 1.

Vargas Llosa, Mario. 1967a. "La literatura es fuego." *Marcha*, no. 1367, August 25; *Siempre!*, no. 290, September 6, under the title "El escritor como aguafiestas"; *Mundo Nuevo*, no. 17, November: 93–95.

Vargas Llosa, Mario. 1967b. "Sebastián Salazar Bondy y la vocación del escritor en Perú." *Casa de las Américas*, no. 45, November–December.

Vargas Llosa, Mario. 1967. "*Cien años de soledad*, el Amadís en América." *Amaru*, no. 3, July–September: 71–74.

Vargas Llosa, Mario. 1969. *Conversación en la catedral*. Barcelona: Seix-Barral.

Vargas Llosa, Mario. 1971. "Carta a Haydeé Santamaría." In "Documentos. El caso Padilla." *Libre*, no. 1, September, October, November: 122–124.

Vargas Llosa, Mario. 1971. *Gabriel García Márquez: Historia de un deicidio*. Barcelona: Seix-Barral.

Vargas Llosa, Mario. 1981. "Los otros contra Sartre." In *Entre Sartre y Camus*. Puerto Rico: Huracán, "La Nave y el Puerto" collection.

Vargas Llosa, Mario. 1981. *Entre Sartre y Camus*. Puerto Rico: Huracán, "La Nave y el Puerto" collection.

Vargas Llosa, Mario.1990. *Contra viento y marea*. Barcelona: Seix-Barral.

Vargas Llosa, Mario. 1993. *El pez en el agua*. Barcelona: Seix-Barral.

Vargas Llosa, Mario. 2001. Cited in Rosario Peyrou. "Prólogo." In *Diario 1974–1983. Ángel* Rama. Montevideo: Trilce.

Veloz Maggiolo, Marcio. 1967. "El escritor dominicano y las presiones sociales de su medio." *Casa de las Américas*, no. 43, July–August: 109–12.

Viglietti, Daniel. 1969. "30 preguntas a los Parra." *Marcha*, no. 1471, November 21.

Viñas, David. 1969. "Después de Cortázar: historia y privatización." *Cuadernos Hispanoamericanos*, no. 234, June: 734–39.

Viñas, David. 1971a. "Cortázar y la fundación mitológica de Paris." *Nuevos Aires*, no. 3, December, January, February: 27–34.

Viñas, David. 1971b. "Viñas o la otra alternativa en el debate acerca del caso Padilla." *La Opinión*, no. 11 from June: 23.

Viñas, David. 1971c. *De Sarmiento a Cortázar. Literatura argentina y realidad política*. Buenos Aires: Siglo Veinte.

Viñas, David. 1984. "Pareceres y digresiones en torno a la nueva narrativa latinoamericana." In *Más allá del* boom*: literatura y mercado*. Ángel Rama, ed. Buenos Aires: Folios.

Viñas, Ismael. 1968. "Aclaraciones sobre repeticiones: ¿Qué es el intelectual." *Revista de Problemas del Tercer Mundo*, no. 2, December: 61–69.

Walsh, Rodolfo. 1971. "Ofuscaciones, equívocos y fantasías en el mal llamado caso Padilla." *La Opinión*, no. 26 from May. Compiled in Daniel Link, ed. 1995. *Rodolfo Walsh. El violento oficio de escribir. Obra periodística, 1953–1977.* Buenos Aires: Planeta.

Weiss, Judith. 1977. *Casa de las Américas: An Intellectual Review in the Cuban Revolution*. Chapel Hill, NC: Castalia.

Williams, Raymond. 1979. *Politics and Letters: Interviews with New Left Review*. London.

Williams, Raymond. 1980 [1977]. *Marxismo y literatura*. Barcelona: Península.

Williams, Raymond. 1981. *Cultura*. Barcelona: Paidós.

Williams, Raymond. 1997. *La política del modernismo*. Buenos Aires: Manantial.

Wright Mills, C. 1960. "Izquierda, subdesarrollo y guerra fría. Un coloquio sobre cuestiones fundamentales." *Cuadernos Americanos*, no. 3, May–June: 53–69.

Wright Mills, C. 2008. "The Powerless People: The Role of the Intellectual in Society." In *The Politics of Truth: Selected Writings of C. Wright Mills*, 13–23. New York: Oxford University Press.

Yevtushenko, Yevgeny. 1963. *Autobiographie précoce*. Paris: Juilliard.

Yevtushenko, Yevgeny. 1969 [1963]. "Los herederos de Stalin." In *Autobiografía precoz*. Mexico: Era.

Yurkiévich, Saúl. 1972. "Cuba: política cultural. Reseña de una conferencia de prensa." *Libre*, no. 4.

Zanetti, Susana. 1994. "Modernidad y religación: una perspectiva continental (1880–1916)." In *América Latina. Palabra, literatura e cultura*. Vol. 2. Ana Pizarro, org. San Pablo: Unicamp.

Zanetti, Susana. 2002. *La dorada garra de la lectura. Lectoras y lectores de novela en América Latina*. Rosario: Beatriz Viterbo.

Zanetti, Susana. 2004. *Leer en América Latina*. Mérida: Ediciones El Otro, el Mismo.

Zedong, Mao. 1967. *Five Documents on Literature and Art*. Beijing: Foreign Languages Press.

Index

C

D

Q

R

S

T

About LASA Press

LASA Press is the open-access publishing house of the Latin American Studies Association (LASA), dedicated to academic research related to Latin America. It seeks to contribute to the dissemination of knowledge through the publication of new research and translations of fundamental works on Latin America from a variety of disciplinary perspectives. It gives priority to proposals that are relevant to the region as a whole, contribute to defining the public agenda, and serve as a bridge between cultures, languages, and academic traditions, thereby extending the impact of Latin American knowledge throughout the world.

www.ingramcontent.com/pod-product-compliance
Lightning Source LLC
LaVergne TN
LVHW041058080826
845145LV00007B/1620

* 9 7 8 1 9 5 1 6 3 4 5 8 2 *